# Sexual
# Salvation

# SEXUAL SALVATION

## Affirming Women's Sexual Rights and Pleasures

### NAOMI B. McCORMICK

*Forewords by Elizabeth Rice Allgeier and Albert Ellis*

Westport, Connecticut
London

**Library of Congress Cataloging-in-Publication Data**

McCormick, Naomi B.
   Sexual salvation : affirming women's sexual rights and pleasures /
Naomi B. McCormick ; Forewords by Elizabeth Rice Allgeier and Albert Ellis.
     p.  cm.
   Includes bibliographical references and index.
   ISBN 0–275–94359–3 (alk. paper)
    1. Women—Sexual behavior.    2. Sexual ethics.    I. Title.
HQ29.M46  1994
306.7′082—dc20       94–6378

British Library Cataloguing in Publication Data is available.

Library of Congress Catalog Card Number: 94–6378
ISBN: 0–275–94359–3

First published in 1994

Praeger Publishers, 88 Post Road West, Westport, CT 06881
An imprint of Greenwood Publishing Group, Inc.

Printed in the United States of America

The paper used in this book complies with the
Permanent Paper Standard issued by the National
Information Standards Organization (Z39.48–1984).

10 9 8 7 6 5 4 3 2 1

To John, my husband,
and Marcelle, my mother,
with all my love.

# Contents

# Foreword

Recently, a liberal and well-read academic colleague of mine stated that with all the issues swirling around, including the women's movement, the men's movement, pornography, prostitution, date rape, child sex abuse, false memory syndrome, issues of power use and abuse within relationships, and the like, he no longer knew where he was or what he thought. I was in the midst of reviewing Naomi McCormick's *Sexual Salvation*, and I told him that I was reading a book that I thought would help him to sort his ideas.

When Dr. McCormick asked me to read her book and provide a foreword, I reluctantly agreed to do so because of my workload. However, I *did* agree because of my long-standing admiration for her work and, more importantly, because I thought that I would be able to skim the book quickly. I was wrong. Her book is full of thought-provoking ideas. In her usual fashion, McCormick has provided thorough reviews of the relevant literature. However, her greater contribution is her refreshing and unusual *balance* in considering the topics she has included in her book. It is not just that she is a skilled writer; having chosen to venture into the contemporary sexual topics that are most filled with intellectually, ethically, and politically explosive land mines, she has deftly walked that land with care and insight.

Here are just a few of her important contributions in this book: She avoided the simplistic division of people into feminists and traditionalists. She squarely faced the fact that, depending on the issue, there are very different groups of people who might be lumped by the uninformed into the category *feminist*, but who hold very divergent points of view about, for instance, sexually explicit materials or "acceptable" personal relationships, or sex workers. One example of the balance that dominates her book involves her treatment of prostitution. Among the community of sexuality scholars, there are very strong feelings about the phenomenon of the exchange of sex for money or other desired resources. Unlike many of her colleagues, McCormick did not appear to feel the need to employ right and wrong thinking in her consideration of these (or other) issues. While writing pointedly about the economic factors that leave some people with very few options available to them as remunerative as prostitution, she simultaneously acknowledges that "the trade" is perceived and experienced as attractive and exciting for other people employed as sex workers.

McCormick's book is not value-free; it is value-aware. She is able to express her own viewpoints, and, with a rare skill, she is also able to give what I perceive to be fair descriptions of points of view that are discrepant from her own. In a period during which some of us become tongue-tied in our attempts to adhere to politically correct statements, McCormick has not written a politically correct book. She has provided a much more important service. She has written a book that displays sensitivity to the diversity of viewpoints surrounding the issues that she has tackled. While reading her book, I kept notes of sections that I thought were particularly valuable. My list is too long to present here. However, to get a feeling for her ability to handle complex issues in a coherent fashion, see her consideration of multiculturalism, social class, and sexual orientation in chapter 4. Although I was already impressed with McCormick's empirical research, I think that her integration of the literature and the diverse perspectives on volatile sexual topics that she has accomplished is truly breathtaking. I will assign this book to advanced undergraduate students in my sex research seminar. I will assign it to my graduate students. I will also purchase this book as gifts for my nonacademic, but interested, family members and friends who are mystified by the varieties of contemporary sexual expression. In summary, I think that McCormick has managed to accomplish an extraordinarily difficult task. This is a book that will be useful for academics and research-oriented scholars that is simultaneously accessible to intelligent, if not academically trained, citizens. Although there are other books that I have read and admired, I have never before had the experience of saying to myself, "Wow, I wish that I'd written that!" What a piece of work! Congratulations Naomi!

ELIZABETH RICE ALLGEIER

# Foreword

Naomi McCormick is unusually well qualified to write this excellent book, *Sexual Salvation: Affirming Women's Sexual Rights and Pleasures*. She is multiply endowed in the area of sexuality, being a fine sex educator, an outstanding researcher, and an effective sex and rational-emotive behavior therapist. I say this as one who has been in close touch with her work in the field of sex for the last decade and who has had the privilege of personally supervising her as a psychotherapist and workshop leader.

Naomi's book, despite much competition from other women's books on human sexuality, is indeed a landmark and will, I predict, become as authoritative a work as Bernie Zilbergeld's counterpart, *The New Male Sexuality*. It certainly deserves this status because it thoroughly covers virtually all the important areas of women's sexuality and does so in a highly readable, outspoken, and scholarly manner.

I could easily say so many good things about this book that I could go on almost endlessly. Let me briefly state a few. It is comprehensive and open-minded, covering, for example, relevant details of both the Radical Feminist and Liberal Feminist positions. It truly celebrates cultural and sexual diversity. It is remarkably up-to-date in covering an immense sex literature and research. It includes love and sociality and puts sex within a general human personality framework. It is as "sexy" as a book can be, but it is not at all hung up on or prone to sacredize orgasm and intercourse. It is unusually "objective," yet courageously critical of much sex research and therapy.

I must admit my own biases as I praise this book. I published my first article on sex, "The Sexual Psychology of Human Hermaphrodites," in *Psychosomatic Medicine* in 1945; and since that time have been a leading sex liberal. In reading this book, I was naturally curious to see whether Naomi, for all of her two-sidedness, endorsed some of my still-liberal sex views, such as the ones I espoused in *The American Sexual Tragedy* and *Sex Without Guilt* in the 1950s. Well, she does. While open-mindedly reviewing some views on pornography, prostitution, and abortion that I would describe as reactionary, she tends to end up with distinctly enlightened humanistic views on these and other "hot" subjects. Fine! But Naomi is always a scientist and a scholar. A great combination—and an outstanding book!

ALBERT ELLIS

# Acknowledgments

*Sexual Salvation* could never have been written without the support and capable assistance of many people. First, I want to thank my undergraduate students at the State University of New York, Plattsburgh, for encouraging me to write this book, suggesting articles to read, and providing constructive criticism on earlier drafts. I am grateful to Paul Macirowski of Praeger and Anne Smith of the Plattsburgh *Press-Republican* for their insightful suggestions on writing style and to the following distinguished colleagues for their careful, scholarly critiques of previous drafts of this book: Vern Bullough, Ph.D., State University of New York Distinguished Professor Emeritus; Sandra Byers, Ph.D., University of New Brunswick at Fredericton, and her graduate students; William Fisher, Ph.D., University of Western Ontario; Anne Peplau, Ph.D., University of California at Los Angeles; Esther Rothblum, Ph.D., University of Vermont; and Beverly Whipple, Ph.D., Rutgers University.

I am doubly indebted to Drs. Byers, Peplau, Rothblum, and Whipple for allowing me to interview them for this book. A special thank you goes out to these other distinguished feminist sexologists who provided me with many of their fine articles and were also interviewed for this book: Ellen Cole, Ph.D., Prescott College in Arizona; Irene Frieze, Ph.D., University of Pittsburgh; Janet Hyde, Ph.D., University of Wisconsin at Madison; Clint Jesser, Ph.D., Northern Illinois University; Charlene Muehlenhard, Ph.D., University of Kansas; Gina Ogden, Ph.D., Cambridge MA; Michael Stevenson, Ph.D., Ball State University; Leonore Tiefer, Ph.D., Montefiore Medical Center in Bronx, NY; and Wendy Stock, Ph.D., Pacific Graduate School of Psychology in Palo Alto, CA.

It is all too easy for Americans to have the illusion that the rest of the world is just like the United States and for heterosexuals to ignore the special concerns of lesbians, gay men, and bisexual persons. I wish to thank Professors Byers and Fisher, along with Dr. Ed Herold of Guelph University, for teaching me about sex research and sexual politics in Canada. I am beholden to Dr. Rothblum for her invaluable suggestions on what I should read to better understand lesbians and bisexual women.

I am most grateful to my two friends and mentors who have graciously agreed to write forewords to *Sexual Salvation:* Elizabeth Rice Allgeier, Ph.D., editor of *The Journal of Sex Research*, professor of psychology at Bowling Green University, and the sixteenth president of The Society for the Scientific Study of Sex; and Albert Ellis, Ph.D., president of the Institute for Rational-Emotive Therapy in New York City and a founding member and the first president of The Society for the Scientific Study of Sex. I would be remiss if I forgot to thank the capable librarians at Feinberg Library and Carla List in particular for helping me master electronic literature searches and providing me with access to books and articles from numerous university and public libraries.

I am especially grateful to my wonderful literary agent, Bertha Klausner, for her constant support and many wise recommendations throughout the four years I have labored on this book. I also want to thank Deborah Partington for her skillful copy-editing of the manuscript and both Publisher James R. Dunton and Production Editor Katie Chase of Greenwood Publishing Group, for their competent management of this project. Finally, a special debt of gratitude goes out to my husband and best friend, John W. McCormick, Ph.D., who is a professor of computer science at the State University of New York, Plattsburgh, and was busily writing two books of his own when he wasn't obliged to solve my nearly daily hassles with the computer and laser printer.

*Disclaimer:* Unless the true source of a personal narrative has been documented by an endnote, the anonymity and confidentiality of the women and men who are described in *Sexual Salvation* have been protected by changing their names, altering identifying information, and creating characters that are composites of more than one individual.

# Sexual
# Salvation

# ❧ 1 ❧

# The Search for Sexual Salvation

I'll be the first to admit it; I spend most of my free time reading about sex. I browse through popular psychology and health books, read the sex advice columns in newspapers, and devour every magazine article on women's sexuality I can lay my hands on. I really don't know what keeps me doing this because inevitably, I get disappointed. If I'm not reading Masters and Johnson reheated, I'm looking at the results of an unscientific survey that would have flunked its creator out of graduate school. It's difficult to say what bothers me the most: the advice columns promising me that the way to a man's heart is through his penis or feature articles in women's magazines explaining how I too can be sexy and fulfilled if only I would lose weight, exercise more regularly, do something with my hair, and buy the right clothes. And let's not forget books and articles by celebrity psychotherapists, epic sermons on sexual well-being based on a single therapist's experiences with a handful of clients.

Indulge me in my tirade. Here are other things that disturb me. Almost all the popular literature on sex I've seen is directed at young, able-bodied, middle-class, heterosexual, white women. Now I have nothing against these women. Before becoming forty-something and developing two chronic illnesses, I was young and perfectly healthy. The last time I looked, I was still middle-class, white, and happily married. Here's what I object to then. Is it fair to assume that the sexual experiences and attitudes of one group represents that of all women? What about women of color? What about poor women? What about middle-aged and older women? What about disabled and chronically ill women? What about lesbian and bisexual women? There

2 · Sexual Salvation

is no such thing as the average woman.[1] Isn't it time to recognize the diverse experiences women have had with sexuality and intimacy?

Here's something else that bothers me. The contemporary pop sex literature is almost completely devoid of a sense of history. You would think that sex had the same meaning for our ancestors as it does for us. We can't even be sure that sex has the same meaning for our parents or children, much less our grandparents and grandchildren, as it does for us. Here we go talking about sex as if it were something that never changes when realistically speaking, sex—just like diet, families, politics, economies, religion, art, work, and leisure—is continually shaped by historical and cultural forces.[2]

While I'm at it, here's another complaint. There really is an extensive and nourishing literature on sex out there—some written by sexologists, social and health scientists who specialize in sex research, some written by feminists, women and men who support women's rights, and some written by individuals falling into both groups. How do I know this? I am a sexologist, a feminist sexologist to be precise. When I'm not ranting and raving about flaws in the popular sex literature, I spend my time gainfully employed as a sex researcher, sex educator, and psychotherapist. Recently, I was elected the twenty-fifth president of The Society for the Scientific Study of Sex. A distinguished teaching professor of psychology at the State University of New York, Plattsburgh, I have been named a Fellow of both The Society for the Scientific Study of Sex and the Institute for Rational-Emotive Therapy.

It really bothers me that so little serious scientific and feminist work on sex has been available to the general public. I think readers deserve more! There was nothing else to do; I had to write a book that addressed my many concerns. *Sexual Salvation* is this book. In *Sexual Salvation*, I translate technical and theoretical information on women's sexuality into everyday English. Throughout the book, I talk about sexual salvation, the affirmation of women's sexuality. No, this is not a book that ignores men; men play a central role in women's sexual experience. But since one small book cannot do justice to every aspect of sexuality, I decided to focus on women more than men. Salvation is nothing more or less than self-preservation, deliverance from evil, and the search for fulfillment. Studying intimacy, sexual ecstasy and difficulties, commercial sex, and the pain of sexual abuse and exploitation in a woman-affirming way, *Sexual Salvation* explores the sexualities of diverse women. Throughout this book, I advocate greater sexual rights and pleasure for all women, something I firmly believe will improve the lives of men and women alike. As my friend and mentor, Anne Peplau, says,

Feminism has a lot to do with social change and trying to improve life for women and for men, trying to help people lead lives that are less constrained by arbitrary and other kinds of traditions. . . . Feminism is about increasing peoples' . . . choices. . . . If we really value sexual freedom, . . . we have to . . . tolerate diversity. That is, not everybody is going to make the same choices that you or I do.[3]

It is time for me to tell you more about *Sexual Salvation*. Later in this chapter, I describe important recent changes in sexual attitudes and behavior and introduce contrasting feminist ideologies about sex. In the subsequent six chapters, these historical and feminist ideas are put to work interpreting much of the best scientific and clinical literature on women's sexuality. Chapter 2 examines why women want sex, how they flirt, and how and why they seduce and reject potential partners. Love, intimacy, and jealousy are discussed in chapter 3. Chapter 4 discusses lesbians and bisexual women, comparing their political and sexual concerns with those of heterosexual women and gay men. Lesbian and bisexual women are not described there alone; *Sexual Salvation* includes information on women who love women in every chapter.

Chapter 5 discusses prostitution and other forms of sex work in terms of two contrasting feminist positions: one which views sex work as inevitably dehumanizing, coercive, and exploitative and the polar opposite view that sex work can be the ultimate expression of female sexual autonomy. Feminists today disagree whether pornography contributes to sexual violence against girls and women. Chapter 6 moves beyond the rhetoric into a close examination of the latest scientific and clinical work on pornography, rape, sexual harassment, and childhood sexual abuse. Sexual salvation isn't just about protecting women from sexual coercion, exploitation, and violence; it is also about fulfillment and joy. Chapter 7 presents woman-affirming information on sexual pleasure and difficulties for both physically disabled and able-bodied women of all ages, racial and ethnic groups, social classes, and sexual orientations. As the twentieth century draws to a close, chapter 8, the final chapter, takes a glimpse at changing sex roles and sexual options for women through the eyes of thirteen prominent feminist sexologists.

## SEXUAL REVOLUTIONS

We did not invent sexual freedom during the 1960s and 1970s only to give it up in the next two decades because of the acquired immune deficiency syndrome (AIDS) pandemic and arguments about sexual morality and abortion. Shifting sexual standards and behavior are hardly recent phenomena. AIDS is not the first sexually transmitted disease to threaten us. Major conflicts about sexual values and erotic behavior have erupted in North America and Western Europe at least since the first half of the nineteenth century.[4] Like us, our nineteenth-century ancestors were embroiled in controversies about prostitution, homosexuality, obscenity, women's reproductive rights, free love, and the extent to which the institution of marriage helps or harms women.

Scientific interest in sex and modern sex education began in the late nineteenth and early twentieth centuries and were not inspired by Masters and Johnson or even Kinsey, as some believe.[5] Political uproar about sex is not only long-standing, it has taken many forms. We continue to be influenced by as many as five separate but interdependent sexual revolutions, each having had a major impact on women's sexuality.[6] These five sexual revolutions are (1) the sexualization of the marketplace, (2) the development of unique youth subcultures, (3) the growth of sexual science and the rise of sex therapy, (4) the lesbian and gay rights movement, and (5) feminism.

### Sexualization of the Marketplace

In the dawn of mass consumption in the nineteenth and early twentieth centuries, printed advertisements depicting a pretty woman's face, hands, and stylish but amply clothed figure were considered titillating. Now, the cleavage of the woman on the cover of *Cosmopolitan* or *Glamour* rivals that of models gracing the fronts of *Playboy* or *Penthouse*. There is an amazing amount of female nudity in ads, including those found in women's magazines. Yesterday's films hinted at sexual interest. Nowadays, little is left to our imagination. In the romance novels of my youth, a book was half read before readers were rewarded by the big kiss; today's romances are a lot hotter. Sexual paraphernalia and specialized clothing can be purchased easily retail or through catalogues. Everywhere, there are products that are supposed to arouse us, make us more attractive, or improve our sexual performance. Films, television, and even music are often sexually explicit. Both hard-core and soft-core pornography are readily available through newsstands, video stores, and mail-order businesses. On the positive side, this sexual revolution has increased women's access to sexual materials and information. On the negative side, the sexual revolution of the marketplace has influenced women to equate female sexuality with being sexually attractive to men, resulting in large numbers of women becoming obsessed with their inability to be perfectly thin, young, firm, blemish-free, and fashionable.

The sexualized marketplace has sold women more products and services, but for the most part, it has not affirmed our sexual rights or pleasures.

## Youth Subcultures

In most industrialized countries, each new generation has embraced its own youth subculture. In youth subcultures, young adults, adolescents, and sometimes even older children establish a separate group identity from that of older generations. To some extent, the development of youth cultures is a marketplace phenomenon. That is, a great deal of money has been made targeting the young for special products and services—clothing, films, TV programming, music, computer games, cosmetics, food, telephones, automobiles, hairstyles, magazines, and books. Class and cultural distinctions aside, youth subcultures create age consciousness. How do young people prove their solidarity with peers? To demonstrate membership in a youth subculture, there is supposed to be at least one mild act of rebellion against adult authority or the status quo. The rite of passage may include unconventional dress or hair style, a preference for slang words adults don't understand, and for the boldest—some form of outrageous behavior, preferably one that gets noticed.

In the twentieth century, almost all youth subcultures have encouraged sexual experimentation, eventually making premarital sexual experience and early intercourse the norm for females and males alike. Having sex symbolizes peer acceptance. On my campus for example, students have had a standing joke about the eagle atop a local monument. According to legend, "If a virgin ever graduated from this school, the eagle would fly." This story might seem amusing because it is about young adults, college students. But, the reality is that high-school, junior high-school, and even some elementary school students today feel increasing social pressure to prove they belong by having sexual intercourse.

Youth subcultures have transformed what is considered socially acceptable. Today, residing with a sexual partner outside of marriage is no longer considered living in sin. Pregnant high-school students and single mothers are encouraged to stay in school; they are no longer secretly whisked away to a home for unwed mothers. There is every reason to believe that youth cultures will thrive in the twenty-first century, continually shaping sexual values and behavior. Previous youth cultures have been dominated by boys and young men. Only time will tell whether those of the future will be equally influenced by girls and young women.

## Sexual Science and Sex Therapy

Although Kinsey and Masters and Johnson did not invent modern sexology, they popularized it. The late twentieth century witnessed growth in the numbers of people engaged in sex research and education. Unfortunately, sexology remains a low-status specialization in academia and most sexual scientists have had to build their careers by publishing papers and getting grants to investigate supposedly more respectable topics.[7] Similarly, there are relatively few openings for full-time sex educators. Most individuals who provide sex education to children, teens, and adults are expected to teach other subjects too. Nonetheless, if current social trends prevail, sex educators and researchers are likely to become increasingly influential and numerous. AIDS, sexual coercion, and unplanned pregnancies are grave problems that cannot be managed without effective sex research and education; sexology is necessary to our very survival.

Sex therapy, with its roots in medicine, nursing, and psychotherapy, first became a unique profession in the final third of the twentieth century. During the past few years, however, sex therapy itself has become increasingly specialized. Some clinicians treat only survivors of childhood sexual abuse and rape, others treat only sexual offenders, others limit themselves to clients who think they have an excessive interest in sex, and still others devote their professional attention exclusively to individuals and couples who feel anxious about sex, disinterested in sexual activity, or sexually unfulfilled. Concomitant with an expansion of roles for sexual scientists, educators, and therapists, there has been a modest increase in the general and student memberships of sexological organizations in the United States, Canada, and abroad.

Politically liberal as they generally are, sexologists have not been especially quick to recognize women's needs or contributions. Although they acknowledge nurse and birth control activist Margaret Sanger (1879–1966) for founding Planned Parenthood, most contemporary sexologists seem to have forgotten the significant contributions of other late nineteenth- and early twentieth-century women.[8] For example, little homage is given to physician Clelia Duel Mosher (1863–1940) and suffragette and sociologist Katharine Bement Davis (1860–1935) for their pioneering feminist research on women's sexuality and early contributions to sex education. Until the mid-1980s, women and feminists were underrepresented as authors in sexual science journals, members of editorial boards, and in leadership positions of organizations devoted to sexual scholarship, education, and treatment.[9] Fortunately, this situation has begun to change dramatically in some sexological organizations and editorial boards, thanks to the efforts of groups like the Feminist Perspectives Special Interest Group of The Society for the Scientific Study of Sex. Nonetheless, as I point out in later chapters, too many sexologists, male and female alike, remain ignorant of the feminist perspective. Too many continue to define, study, and teach about sexuality in exclusively sexist and heterosexist terms. Too often, sex therapists ignore information that suggests that women experience sexuality differently than men or that socialization plays at least as big a role in sexuality as does biology.[10]

## Lesbian and Gay Rights Movement

Until recently, the persecution of lesbians and gay men was not only acceptable, it was expected. In the late nineteenth and early twentieth centuries, physicians and scientists acquired greater social influence and prestige than religious authorities. As morality became medicalized, characteristics once thought to be sinful were labeled as signs of mental illness or perversion with no loss of stigma in the process. So, it came to be that loving someone of the same sex changed from being a sin to being a sickness, and the sickness was supposedly curable through psychotherapy. Countless women and men lived in hiding, believing with good reason that if others guessed their true sexual orientation, they might be intimidated or arrested by the police and would also risk losing the love and respect of family and friends, a job or business, property, and their place of residence. Before the Lesbian and Gay Rights movement came into being, millions of dollars were spent on ineffective psychotherapy "cures" for homosexuality, which in many cases damaged the self-esteem of those able to afford such "help."[11] Then came the revolutionary struggle for gay and lesbian equal rights, a struggle which is far from over. Did this revolution begin in the United States on June 28, 1969, when gay men at New York City's Stonewall Inn rioted in response to police harassment? Not according to Eric Marcus who interviewed lesbian and gay rights activists who had made contributions as early as the 1940s.[12] Regardless of when we date the movement, however, we must recognize that the lesbian and gay movement, along with feminism, has undermined what Janice Irvine has called "the 'naturalness' and inevitability of traditional gender stereotypes and the monolithic nuclear family. . . . threat[ening] . . . the most fundamental underpinnings of the culture."[13]

As this book goes to press, lesbians and gay men face continuing oppression. "The only adult sexual behavior that is legal in every state of the Union is the placement of the penis in the vagina in wedlock."[14] The new "don't ask, don't tell" policy in the U. S. military implies that gay men and women can continue to serve their country only if they remain celibate and closeted. With the exception of a few employers, domestic partners of gay and lesbian workers lack health insurance and pension benefits, which are taken for granted by married employees. In the event of a domestic part-ner's death, the law automatically recognizes the inheritance rights of a wife or husband but not those of a widowed lesbian or gay man. Recently, a number of communities have considered legislation that would deny certain legal rights to individuals on the basis of their professed sexual orientation. It remains difficult for an openly homosexual person to find highly paid employment. Because they are women, lesbians, especially lesbians of color, face additional occupational discrimination. Lesbians, gay men, and bisexual persons are increasingly likely to become the victims of violent hate crimes.[15]

### Feminism

For over one-and-a-half centuries, feminists have advocated greater eco-nomic and political power for women. Sexuality has also been a major issue. Divided as to whether sex was dangerous for women or liberating, women's rights advocates influenced sexual attitudes and behaviors in diverse ways during both the first wave of feminism in the nineteenth and early twentieth centuries and the second wave of feminism which began in the second half of the twentieth century. Those who sought to protect women from sexual dangers organized against prostitution and husbands' expectations that their wives have sex on demand during the first wave of feminism and against rape, domestic violence, the sexual abuse of children, and pornography dur-ing the second wave.[16] Those who sought to increase women's sexual free-dom organized on behalf of birth control and free love outside of marriage during the first wave of feminism and on behalf of freer access to erotic materials, birth control, abortion, and a variety of sexual lifestyles for women during the second wave.

Defining "sexual relations as but one aspect of the power relations be-tween men and women," contemporary feminists continue to question tra-ditional definitions of women's sexuality.[17] But, there is no feminist party line on how to interpret the impact of various sexual revolutions on wom-en's lives. According to one point of view, women are beneficiaries of the sexual revolutions because men have learned the importance of clitoral stimulation, are more accepting of women who take the sexual initiative, and have gained skills in inducing orgasms in their partners.[18] At the same time, this optimistic group of feminists also believes that we have made progress in affirming the lives of lesbian and bisexual women. Contradicting these ideas, other feminists argue that women's subordination to men has been eroticized by sexual revolutionaries, no woman being truly free to refuse sex with a member of the dominant group.[19] This more pessimistic group of feminists points out that heterosexual women continue to enjoy social privileges denied to lesbians and bisexual women.

An alternative feminist opinion has been voiced by those seeking to increase women's opportunities to enjoy self-love, new sexual experiences, and contact with a variety of sexual partners.[20] According to feminists advocating sexual experimentation, the five sexual revolutions of our times have touched us only superficially; we continue to live in a restrictive culture which denies women sexual pleasures. Feminists who favor fewer sexual restrictions challenge the sexual morality of both the dominant culture and those feminists who view sexuality as dangerous to women.[21] Promoting increased erotic freedom, these feminists believe that

> most of the discourses on sex, be they religious, psychiatric, popular, or political, delimit a very small portion of human sexual capacity as sanctifiable, safe, healthy, mature, or politically correct.[22]

## TWO FEMINIST POSITIONS ON SEXUALITY

Feminists agree that male-dominant culture has had a negative impact on women's sexuality. Other than that, there may be as many feminist positions on sexuality as there are feminists. Despite their ideological diversity, however, it is fair to say that there are two major feminist positions on sexuality: the Radical Feminist position which emphasizes girls' and women's right to live free of sexual violence and exploitation and the Liberal Feminist position which advocates greater sexual freedom and pleasure for women. Simply put, Radical Feminists emphasize the extent to which girls and women are sexual victims who must be protected from manipulative and coercive men, whereas Liberal Feminists seek to remove any restrictions interfering with women's sexual autonomy and gratification, those imposed by men and those imposed by other women.[23]

I wish all feminists were reasonable, willing to listen to each other with respect despite their differences. Unfortunately, a few vocal extremists in both the Radical and Liberal Feminist camps have added a divisive note to the sexuality debates. I have read a great many books and articles by and about Radical and Liberal Feminists, often finding what I read quite disturbing.[24] Why? The extremists on both sides have dominated the debate about sexual politics although most supporters of the women's movement are likely to hold moderate views. For example, Catharine MacKinnon, one of the most outstanding feminist lawyers of all times, really does most of us a great disservice with this stinging attack on male sexuality.

> What is sexual is what gives a man an erection. Fear does; hostility does; hatred does; the helplessness of a child or a student or an infantilized or restrained or vulnerable woman does; revulsion does; death does. Whatever it takes to make a penis shudder and stiffen with the experience of its potency is what sexuality means culturally. Violation, conventionally through penetration and intercourse, defines the paradigmatic sexual encounter. Transgression . . . is necessary for penetration to experience itself. . . . what is called sexuality is . . . male dominance.[25]

There has been too much harsh rhetoric, too much name calling, and too little willingness to listen to reasonable arguments from the other side. Some Radical Feminists have called the opposition sex liberals, an insult, I imagine, to anyone who agrees with the quote from MacKinnon I just cited. A few Radical Feminists have even implied that Liberal Feminists are not feminists at all, working from the premise that anybody who disagreed with them couldn't possibly be feminist. On the other hand, the ultraextremists from the Liberal Feminist movement have also contributed to the fracas, suggesting that any woman who wasn't comfortable with bondage and discipline and all forms of pornography had limited herself to vanilla sex. I mean, what's wrong with vanilla sex or vanilla ice cream or vanilla anything else? Isn't the women's movement a big enough place for people who have a variety of sexual tastes?

Calling themselves sex radicals, still other Liberal Feminists have poured gasoline on the fire by suggesting that antipornography feminists were cultural feminists, not Radical Feminists at all. According to these self-proclaimed sex radicals, cultural feminism is a diluted, apolitical form of feminism that is more concerned with promoting the idea that women are inherently good and men are inherently bad than making meaningful political and economic changes. And, let's not forget Liberal Feminists who have called their opponents right-wing feminists, always a major insult in left-wing circles. Not surprisingly, there have even been Liberal Feminists who have insinuated that Radical Feminists and everybody else who disliked pornography must be antisex prudes. Ironically, this insult has backfired since many Radical Feminists don't mind being called prudes for criticizing men who engage in child sexual abuse, rape, and sexual harassment.

Some women have taken the sexuality debates so seriously that they have been unwilling to address any academic or political meeting that featured speakers from the other side. Although I consider myself to be a relative nobody in the Liberal-Radical Feminist debates, even I have had two experiences with political intolerance. Years ago, I appeared with a number of other speakers at a women's studies forum on pornography held on my campus. After a few women presented poetry and logical arguments describing their opposition to pornography, I came on stage to discuss psychological research which suggested that women are often just as aroused as men by nonviolent pornography and that some sexually explicit materials can actually help couples better enjoy their sexual relationship. My students in the audience told me that if looks could kill, the expressions on the faces of some of the speakers who preceded me would surely have given me a heart attack.

A second vexing experience with intolerance occurred more recently. I was invited to be a speaker at a scientific meeting, discussing some of the ideas from this book. I told the conference organizers that I wanted to do a feminist analysis of prostitution, a topic covered in some depth in chapter 5. Specifically, I said that I planned to present the Liberal Feminist idea that we should respect women's right to exchange sexual services for money and support women employed as prostitutes as they campaigned throughout the world for decriminalization and better working conditions. Again, although I am a relative nobody in the feminist sexuality debates, I learned that another academic, a major figure in feminist circles, declined to appear on the same stage with me because she firmly believed that all prostitution involved the coercion and exploitation of women by men. Apparently, her conscience would not permit her to speak at a program that included someone as wrong-headed as me. "Whatever happened to the open exchange of ideas?" you might ask. I certainly did.

There are all too many books, chapters, articles, and speeches that argue that there is only one feminist truth. It bothers me that extremists from both sides of the Radical-Liberal Feminist debates have jumped to the conclusion that those who disagree are in bed with the enemy. Where is the evidence that by opposing censorship and advocating fewer sexual restrictions on women, Liberal Feminists are sleeping with rapists, pimps, and the worst sort of male pornographers? Yes, Radical Feminists emphasize that large numbers of women have been sexually abused or exploited, and yes, they call our attention to the ways in which male sexual aggression has been romanticized in pornography and even mainstream films, TV programs, and advertising. But, how does this prove that Radical Feminists are all in cahoots with the right-wing, patriarchal moralists who oppose, not only pornography, but also birth control, abortion, sex education, and any sexual alternatives for women other than procreative, marital sex with the man on top?

Personally, I think that the feminist sexuality debates have been a tremendous waste of time and energy. They have distracted women from working together and working with men on our really important shared goals: greater educational and economic opportunities for women, better health and child care, reproductive choice, legal rights, and greater political power. The debaters have ignored the moderate feminist majority, women and men who see wisdom in both the Radical and Liberal Feminist positions. After all, wanting to protect girls and women from sexual abuse and exploitation is not incompatible with wanting to empower women to have greater sexual freedom and pleasure! This is what *Sexual Salvation* is all about. Throughout this book, I look at Radical and Liberal Feminist ideas, not dogmatically, but as contrasting theories about the nature of women's sexual experience which are worth testing. In every chapter, I compare Liberal and Radical Feminist ideas about women's sexuality with scientific findings and clinical insights from feminist therapists. I guess that makes me an Empirical Feminist, someone who thinks feminist ideas about sexuality can and should be verified.

If we really want to make this a better world for women, we don't want to alienate potential sympathizers. If we really want women's sexual rights and pleasures to be affirmed, women and men will have to work together. In my heart, I think most feminists are not extremists. I think most of us respect our differences, even honor them. Feminism should be inclusive, embracing democracy and rejecting dogma. Anne Peplau explains why.

> I think that most feminists are or should be skeptical inquirers who go around challenging traditional wisdom. But, if they are intellectually honest, they will also challenge and be skeptical of their own ideas or the ideas of other feminists.[26]

*Sexual Salvation* is a special type of feminist book. I have not written this book to promote one feminist sexual ideology over another. Instead, I have written *Sexual Salvation* to examine and affirm the best contributions of both Liberal and Radical Feminist thinkers.

## NOTES

1. See Yoder and Kahn, Inclusive Psychology of Women, pp. 846–50.
2. See Foucault, *History of Sexuality;* Tiefer, Social Constructionism, pp. 70–94.

3. Peplau, Telephone Interview.

4. See D'Emilio and Freedman, *Intimate Matters*, pp. 139–360; DuBois and Gordan, Seeking Ecstasy on the Battlefield, pp. 31–49; Rubin, Thinking Sex, pp. 267–319; and Vance, Pleasure and Danger, pp. 1–27.

5. See Haeberle, Destruction of Sexology, pp. 270–87; Robinson, *Modernization of Sex*, pp. 1–41; and Swan, Sex Education in the Home, pp. 3–10.

6. See D'Emilio and Freedman, *Intimate Matters*, pp. 301–25; Ehrenreich, Hess, & Jacobs, *Re-making Love*, pp. 65–102; and Irvine, *Disorders of Desire*.

7. See Abramson, Sexual Science, pp. 147–65.

8. See Bullough, letter to Author; Sternberg, In *Human Sexuality: An Encyclopedia*, pp. 167, 403, 528–29.

9. See Pollis, Impacts of Feminism, pp. 85–105.

10. See Irvine, *Disorders of Desire*.

11. See Duberman, *Cures*.

12. See Marcus, *Making History*.

13. Irvine, *Disorders of Desire*, pp. 139–40.

14. Rubin, Thinking Sex, p. 291.

15. See Herek, Hate Crimes, pp. 948–55.

16. See DuBois and Gordan, Seeking Ecstasy on the Battlefield, pp. 31–49; Rubin, Thinking Sex, pp. 267–319; and Vance, Pleasure and Danger, pp. 1–27.

17. Shulman, Sex and Power, p. 28.

18. See Ehrenreich, Hess, and Jacobs, *Re-making Love*, pp. 74–102.

19. See Jeffreys, Eroticizing Women's Subordination, pp. 132–35.

20. See Rubin, Thinking Sex, pp. 267–319; Vance, Pleasure and Danger, pp. 1–27.

21. See Rubin, Thinking Sex, pp. 267–319.

22. Ibid., p. 282.

23. See Ferguson et al., Forum, pp. 106–35.

24. See Diamond, Pornography and Repression, pp. 129–44; Dworkin and MacKinnon, *Pornography and Civil Rights*; Leidholdt and Raymond, *Sexual Liberals and the Attack on Feminism*; MacKinnon, Pleasure Under the Patriarchy, pp. 65–90; Rich, Compulsory Heterosexuality, pp. 62–91; Tavris, *Mismeasure of Woman*; Valverde, Theory and Ethics in the Sex Debates, pp. 237–53; Vance, *Pleasure and Danger*; Williams, *Hard Core*.

25. MacKinnon, Pleasure Under Patriarchy, p. 75.

26. Peplau, Telephone Interview.

# 2

# Lessons in Seduction

I was sixteen years old and so was he. We were parked, looking into each other's eyes, talking about nothing in particular. It was a long time ago. I can't vouch for his feelings, but I do remember mine. I was distracted by new emotions, strange and tingling sensations that seemed to pulse forth from the very center of my body. I wanted to touch him, kiss him like I saw in the movies, get closer than I ever had been with anybody. I didn't know the rules so I made them up as I went along. I made the first move and possibly the second and who knows, maybe the third as well. He was flushed and sweaty; he seemed to be in shock; he didn't know what to do. He fell across the steering wheel. Our intimacy evaporated.

No, this is not how I met my husband. Neither is it a description of the precipitating event for an adolescent depression requiring years of psychotherapy. This incident actually marked the beginning of my career as a sex researcher. My mother must have given me the right messages about self-acceptance because I didn't feel foolish and rejected. Instead, I felt downright curious. That night, I began to wonder about things I still wonder about. Why wasn't I supposed to make the first move? Why was this adolescent boy so startled and anxious? What rules had I broken; what script for proper female behavior had I failed to follow? This chapter describes my scientific journey, seeking answers to these questions and many others.

When I was sixteen, I was just curious. Now, I am more than that. My life-long interest in sexual influence may have political as well as scientific value. Flirtation and seduction are key issues for Liberal Feminists who do battle with the traditional patriarchal expectation that good women neither want nor seek sex. I believe that consensual flirtation and seduction should be of central concern to Radical Feminists too. Why? Because as long as we live in a society in which women are supposed to be sex objects and not sexual actors in their own right, then women cannot be sexually empowered. For women, being able to say Yes to sexual feelings and having permission to initiate and orchestrate sexual intimacy are deeply connected with the equally important right to say No. Female sexual autonomy is all about the best kind of power: the power to make and reject sexual advances, to have control over one's own body.

Women do not have a weaker, paler sexuality than men. Women flirt with and seduce men and each other; they are not just sex objects. But, most women have not yet achieved the sexual empowerment advocated by many Liberal Feminists. We do not yet feel free to be in the sexual driver's seat. Traditional sex roles, culturally learned scripts for who does what to whom in a sexual relationship, often hold us back.[1]

## SEXUAL SCRIPTS

Sexual identity plays a major role in the development of sexual scripts or expected patterns of behavior during sexual encounters. Before we learn to be sexual, we learn how to be masculine or feminine. As children, we are taught that boys and men initiate, control, and dominate situations whereas girls and women should do as they are told. By adolescence, sex-role stereotypes generalize to erotic interactions, reinforced by a culture in which it is assumed that males are inherently more sexual than females. As a result, adolescent boys masturbate earlier, more frequently, and more often with the goal of achieving orgasm than adolescent girls. Masturbation provides training for partnered sex.[2] Therefore, when young heterosexuals begin to interact with partners, boys and men have more developed sexual scripts than girls and women. Orchestrated to follow the male masturbation experience, heterosexual intercourse often produces orgasm and emotional satisfaction more efficiently in men than in women.

If men learn about sex mostly from masturbation, women learn about sex mostly from partners.[3] Thus, heterosexual women learn to become aroused from breast fondling, not as a result of biology, but because this activity excites men. The typical sequence of heterosexual sexual activities, from kissing to sexual intercourse, is neither natural nor inevitable. The expectation that the man should remove the woman's clothing before his own are removed is not biologically determined. Even arousal (when to be aroused,

why to be aroused, who is arousing) is produced by years of sex-role socialization and sexual scripting.

The culture provides sexual scripts which enable us to know what to do
and what to expect from sex. The prevailing script for sexual morality is the
double standard which restricts women's sexual behavior more than men's.[4]
The boy or man who has multiple sexual partners and strong sexual interest
is a "stud"; a similar girl or woman is a "slut." Males are encouraged to
adopt a recreational sexual script; it is okay to have sex with casual partners
or for physical release. Females are urged to adopt a relational sexual script;
sexual interactions should be limited to one loving partner. It is not surprising then, that women describe the genitals and sex with sanitized medical
terms like "vagina," cute little euphemisms like "penie" and "ding-a-ling,"
and vague romantic concepts like "sleeping together," "doing it," and "going all the way."[5] Men, in contrast, talk about sex aggressively. Masculine
sexual slang equates the penis with a weapon (e.g., "womp," "rod," "pistol,"
and "stick") and sexual intercourse with battle (e.g., "poking," "stroking a
hole," and "hosing").

The double standard is nurtured by cultures such as our own in which
men dominate politics and the economy. Sexual access to women is part of
the property system; men assert their high status by having sex with as
many partners and as often as possible, whereas women keep themselves
precious (and worthy of marriage) by saving themselves for the right man.
In the absence of the double standard, personality differences would exert
more influence than gender on sexually scripted behavior. Women and men
who are especially dominant, independent, active, and self-confident report
being more relaxed about sex and having had greater numbers of sexual
partners and experiences than their gentler, emotionally expressive, and
more modest counterparts.[6] The greater women's power, the more sexual
rights they are free to enjoy.

Accommodating to a culture that both rejects homosexuals and programs
women to be romantic and asexual, it is difficult for lesbians and bisexual
women to show affection publicly.[7] Not free to hold hands in public, the
path of least resistance is to continue denying sexual feelings in private.
Because both partners were socialized as women, neither is likely to feel
comfortable initiating sex. Therefore, genital activity may decrease substantially when the novelty of their relationship wears off.

## SEXUAL MOTIVATION

As a result of the double standard, women learn to want sex for different
reasons than men.[8] Most men say that they have sex to relieve tension and

experience physical pleasure. In contrast, the majority of women say that they have sex to strengthen emotional ties with a partner. Not only do women want sex for different reasons than men, they also have different expectations for lovers' behavior.[9] Women want their partners to talk "lovingly"; men want their partners to talk "dirty." Women are hoping for a sensitive and tender man; men think about a sexually adventurous woman who takes the initiative, is ready for sex on the spur of the moment, and is willing to fulfill their wildest fantasies. Simply put, women don't value sexual fireworks nearly as much as men, and men are more inclined than women to separate sexual feelings from those of affection. Fortunately, although women are scripted to make love and men are scripted to have sex, male-female differences in sexual motivation diminish over time. Mature, single men and women generally have similar sexual expectations.[10] By midlife, more men are willing to admit that they have sex primarily to express love and more women are willing to say that physical pleasure is their major reason for having sex.[11]

## ATTRACTING A PARTNER

Whatever reasons they have for wanting sex and in direct contradiction with sexual scripts promoting female sexual passivity, research suggests that women work harder at attracting partners and starting new relationships than men.[12] How do women pull this off without causing a man to go into shock like the unfortunate sixteen-year-old boy described at the beginning of this chapter? The trick is to be so subtle that the man never guesses what happened. Men are generally unaware of the subtle maneuvering that often goes on behind the scenes, moves which give women the ability to start a relationship without seeming to break the unwritten law that permits men, but not women, to be sexual actors. For example, take this couple's responses to a friend's question: "How did you meet?"

> *Steve:* "Let's see, we met about five years ago at a cocktail party. Kathy was standing next to the bar with Meg, the woman who threw the party. I couldn't help but notice her. She had on a spectacular black dress. And her hair, it was curly and styled just perfectly. What a conversationalist too. The first thing she did was ask me about my work. It turns out she is an attorney too; we even had some of the same friends."

> *Kathy:* "Steve is telling it just like it happened except there are a few details he may not be aware of. I had finally gotten over the

breakup with Brian a few weeks before; I was ready to circulate again. So, I asked my good friend, Meg, if she had anybody in mind for me and if she would throw a party so I could get to meet the man without having to go on a blind date. While working on the guest list, Meg told me about Steve. I inquired about his job and his interests; it sounded like we had a lot in common. Meg even gave me some tips on his taste in women so I planned ahead before dressing for the party and styling my hair. At the party, I stood around talking to Meg when he entered the room, just close enough to get noticed and make it obvious that I wasn't there with another man. I smiled at him just so and did my famous flirtatious head tilt, leaned forward slightly, and looked at him in the friendliest possible way. The rest was easy."

Most of us think that it is more socially appropriate for a man to initiate a conversation or dinner invitation than a woman.[13] However, this has not stopped all women in their tracks, especially those in the younger generation. By now, most single heterosexual men have had at least one experience with being asked on a date by a woman.[14] Typically, men respond positively to female-initiated dates. And, women who are persistent often get their way. Many men say that they have been asked for more than one date by the same woman. Ironically, the double standard, which enjoins men to adopt recreational sexual scripts and women to adopt relational ones, may play into women's hands. Researchers have found that when young adults approach attractive strangers and invite them variously to go on a date, visit their apartments, or go to bed with them, women reject men but men greet women's sexual offers with enthusiasm.[15] Whether or not they are in touch with their sexual power, women who do the unexpected can and often do succeed in getting their way with an attractive new acquaintance.

Fortunately, sexual scripts are not as rigid as when I was sixteen. More men than ever before, especially young and feminist men, are pleased when women take the dating initiative.[16] The only thing holding women back today may be their own fear of breaking the rules. I would like to see more women take chances in initiating romantic relationships. After all, showing interest in a man is a far cry from forcing him into a relationship he doesn't want. Studies completed by my friend Charlene Muehlenhard and her colleagues provide some reassurance. It really doesn't matter if a woman drops hints, takes the initiative, or waits for the man to make the first move. If the man likes her, he will agree to go out with her; if he doesn't, he won't. In fact, many men are relieved, not horrified, when women show an interest in them. How can a woman tell if a man likes her? Again, Muehlenhard's research provides clues. First, the woman should pay close attention to how the man reacts when they're together. If he looks at her frequently, talks about both personal and impersonal topics, and seems relaxed, chances are good that he will respond positively should she initiate a date. Second, the woman needs to compare her interactions with the man with those he has with other men. If he treats her like "one of the guys," he may not be as interested in a romantic relationship as she is. However, if their friendly relationship includes a hint of flirtation, then the man is likely to welcome the woman's romantic interest.

I wish I could share extensive scientific research on the courtship of women who love women. Unfortunately, this is a topic which has been largely ignored by sexologists. The little we know is based on studies of a very small number of lesbians and anecdotal information that women have shared with friends and therapists. According to these sources, lesbian courtship is quite similar to the way that heterosexual women make friends with other women. Lesbian and bisexual women do not as a rule cruise bars and other public places in search of sexual adventure.[17] Placing a premium on sexual fidelity and long-term relationships, they meet new romantic partners primarily at private gatherings, rarely initiating sexual intimacy until they know one another fairly well. Most women believe that it is important to be good friends with a prospective partner before allowing sexual passion to intervene.[18] Typically, talking about feelings and mutual self-disclosures precede any genital activity. As such, lesbian courtship is a romantic and sexually charged extension of women's friendship. Lengthy conversations, numerous nonsexual, social interactions, dates, and the exchange of flowers, notes, and gifts are often seen as necessary preliminaries to physical intimacy. Once two women become lovers, however, they customarily move towards a committed relationship more rapidly than would male or heterosexual couples. My friend Esther Rothblum uses this humorous story to portray lesbians' relationship scripts: "You know, there are all sorts of jokes about what does a lesbian bring to her second date and the answer is a U-Haul meaning that you move in immediately."[19]

Although we know little about the courtship of lesbians and bisexual women, there is a great deal of research on heterosexual courtship. How do heterosexuals attract potential partners? The most obvious way is to begin a conversation, something men are more willing to do than women.[20] How effective are opening lines? As far as women are concerned, the best lines are innocuous remarks such as "Are you having a good time?" or "I've seen you before."[21] In contrast, the cute, flippant lines that many men favor like "Your place or mine?" or "I've got an offer you can't refuse" leave most women cold.[22] Men don't just like using cute flippant lines, they wish women would use them too.[23] Generally, men make greater use of opening lines than women. However, increasing numbers of single women initiate conversations with men they want to meet, a few even employing some rather aggressive and raunchy lines. Recording conversations taking place in urban dating bars, a communications researcher overheard women telling men the following things: "I like your ass." "What skillful-looking hands." "Can I sharpen your point?" "I love lollipops." and "Wanna fuck?"[24] So much for our stereotypes of female sexual passivity! Still, relatively few women are comfortable talking about sex so explicitly with strangers. Does this mean that the majority are sexually passive? Hardly. Women are probably more active than men in nonverbal flirtation.

What happens when people flirt? Fortunately, Tim Perper and other researchers have been able to answer this question objectively by making unobtrusive observations in public places like bars. Over half the time, women initiate flirtation.[25] Typically, the process occurs in four stages: (1) approaching an attractive stranger, (2) turning to look at him (or her), (3) touching, and (4) synchronizing body movements and facial expressions. For example, this is how Estelle met Juan at a wedding reception:

It was crowded but Juan immediately caught Estelle's eye. She *approached* him, *turning* until their eyes met. Just as she turned, she found him smiling at her. He introduced himself and asked her name. The conversation intensified. She began to like Juan a great deal and was relieved to learn that he was also single. Estelle wanted to get closer to him. She brushed against him ever so quickly with her right hip, half accidentally and half not; it was a fleeting *touch* but one which Juan reciprocated immediately. He took her hand, now quite warm, and held it tenderly; Estelle was enchanted. Soon, the friends and relatives around them seemed to disappear into the distance. There was only Estelle and Juan; their bodies fully *synchronized*, two to three inches apart, mirroring one another's animated facial expressions and body postures as they spoke. As far as they were concerned, they were completely alone, immersed in one another so completely that they appeared to have joined as one.

As this example demonstrates, flirtation is not unilateral. It is a delicate process that progresses only when partners reciprocate one another's advances. In actuality, I would be hard pressed to think of any sexual interaction that is more egalitarian than flirtation. Flirtation research provides some validation for Liberal Feminist theory; women exert a powerful influence over the course of flirtation. In a study of couples in rural bars, for example, Andrew Jones and I noticed that women were more active than men in flirtatious interactions.[26] Specifically, the women we observed were more likely than men to use nonverbal signals to communicate sexual interest and disinterest. If they were disinterested in a partner, women were more likely than men to display closed body posture, crossing their arms and tightening their bodies, as if to signal "please go away." They were even more active nonverbally when they seemed attracted to a man. Compared to the men, the women we observed were more likely to flash loving gazes, smile, and attempt to improve their appearance by doing things like smoothing their hair or tightening stomach muscles. Like the example of Estelle above, we found that the first fleeting touch in a flirtatious interaction was often the woman's. In fact, the women we observed were much more likely than men to engage in brief touching. Was there anything men did more than women in flirtation? Yes. Men were more likely than women to signal sexual interest by engaging in intimate touching. Only when touching becomes obvious and clearly erotic did men take the lead in flirtation. So much for traditional sexual scripts!

Far from being sexually passive, women may orchestrate flirtation. The more nonverbal and verbal signals a woman sends and the richer the variety of her flirtatious behaviors, the more likely she will be approached by one or more men.[27] There are so many things women do to attract men. A woman may glance around the room, fixing her gaze on the one man she finds most attractive. She may toss her hair, raise her eyebrows, tilt her head coyly, pout, purse her lips for a kiss, and move her face next to a partner coyly. The woman could tap her fingers to get a man's attention, primp her clothing, or hike her skirt to expose more leg. Later, she might move her hands sensuously, caressing objects or the man while she moves. The woman may be an expert at seductive postures—leaning forward, hanging against the man, positioning herself so that her knees or shoulders touch his ever so slightly. Perhaps, she sways her hips while walking past a man she likes; maybe, she dances by herself invitingly. Playfully, she may pull up a chair next to the man, pinch, or tickle him. Through nonverbal eloquence, women can and do affirm their power in courtship.

## INITIATING SEX

No matter how much women might control flirtation, they exercise considerably less influence over other sexual interactions. Female sex-role socialization inhibits lesbians and bisexual women from making sexual advances.[28] As Radical Feminists might predict, the culture scripts men, not women, to push for sex.[29] In heterosexual relationships, it is common for the man to initiate any and all sexual behaviors, from kissing through inter-course.[30] Until now, most studies suggested that men are more likely than women to begin both conventional and novel sexual practices, and women are more likely than men to restrict sexual activities.[31] Encouraging to Lib-eral Feminists, however, the latest Canadian studies suggest that young adults are beginning to challenge patriarchical sexual scripts.[32] At least once during the previous year, Lucia O'Sullivan and Sandra Byers note, most young heterosexual singles recollect that the woman sought greater sexual intimacy than the man. In other recent Canadian studies, women were no more likely than men to reject a regular partner's sexual advances.

Of interest to Liberal Feminists and sex therapists, research has identified those women who are most likely to break free of traditionally restrictive sexual scripts.[33] Unconventional, assertive, sexually liberal women are more willing to initiate sex than their conservative counterparts. Which women are best able to be sexual actors in their own right? The answer is women who are willing to masturbate, those who show lovers how to arouse them, and women whose partners share their own sexual desires openly. Women initiate sex most often when they are young and/or have a highly satisfying sexual relationship.[34] Even shy, conservative women are able to describe preferred seductive strategies.[35] When asked how they might influence a man to go to bed with them, young single women mention a multitude of strategies—some to get a man interested in sex and others to follow through should their initial attempts fail. Exquisitely aware of the impor-tance of their physical attractiveness, young lesbians are highly attuned to how physical rapport is developing with a date and the best timing for a touch or kiss. Imagination aside, most people live out culturally approved sexual scripts. Even highly romantic lesbians use their experiences on a first date to evaluate whether or not they should pursue a long-term relationship with another woman. When my colleagues and I asked single men and women about their actual experiences with sexual influence, most everyone agreed that strategies for having sex were largely used by men and strategies for avoiding sex were largely used by women.[36] Among cohabiting and mar-ried couples, women generally agree to have sex with a partner but are rarely given the opportunity to initiate sex themselves.[37] Men think about initiating sex and actually make the first move in a sexual encounter signifi-cantly more than women. Their scripted eagerness may preempt women from becoming sexual actors in their own right.

Research on seduction and rejection has political implications. As Liberal Feminists would hope, women are generally successful when they attempt to initiate sex with a man.[38] But, Radical Feminists are also correct; women tend to treat sexual partners far better than they are treated in return. Far more frequently than women, men admit that they pressured or manipulated their last partner to have sex by doing things like playing on the woman's mood, trying to get her drunk or high, persistently demanding to have sex, telling lies, ignoring a woman's objections, and threatening to break off the relationship.[39] Still, there is no evidence for concluding that heterosexual women are always sexual victims whereas heterosexual men are always sexual aggressors. Research indicates that antisocial tactics for influencing someone to have sex are more strongly associated with motivation than gender. Inconsistent with Radical Feminist theory, both women and men who view themselves as desperate for sexual contact admit that they have threatened, ridiculed, sulked, cried, acted ill, pleaded, or even used force to try to get their way sexually.[40] As Liberal Feminists are likely to conclude, men are not necessarily sexual beasts nor are women necessarily sexual saints; some women readily assume aggressive, recreational, supposedly male sexual scripts.[41] When women want to increase physical intimacy more than men, most use sexually enticing strategies like touching or stroking the man, self-disclosing, and taking off their clothing. But some women use coercive strategies as well—pouting, sulking, refusing to talk, trying to make the man feel guilty, attempting to get the man drunk, and even telling him that the woman was too aroused to stop or ignoring his refusal. Sexual scripts aside, men perceive women as more sexually aggressive than women see themselves.

Fortunately, the most socially sensitive strategies are also the most effective ones for increasing physical intimacy.[42] Women and men who emphasize emotional and physical closeness are generally successful in increasing their partners' sexual involvement. Most lesbians employ a mutual decision-making process to initiate sexual intimacy. In my own research, women were just as likely as men to prefer three socially sensitive strategies for having sex: body language, relationship conceptualizing, and seduction.[43] Women who employed body language used facial expression, posture, and physical closeness to signal sexual interest, for example, "I would test my limits by holding hands, sitting closer to this person . . . doing more listening and minimal talking."[44] Those who used relationship conceptualizing liked to get sex rolling by talking about the status of the couple's relationship, sharing feelings, and being especially considerate. Consistent with the opinions of Liberal Feminists, seduction, a step-by-step plan for having sex which emphasized sexual stimulation of a partner, appeared to be the single woman's (as well as the single man's) favorite strategy for influencing a partner to have sexual intercourse. Here is one woman's account of how she seduced her husband when the couple was still dating.

It was clear that Raymond was too shy to do anything but kiss me at the doorway. I was determined to go to bed with him. After our sixth date, I asked him in for a drink. I dimmed the lights and put on some romantic music. I got closer and closer to him on the couch, touching him a little at first and then slowly rotating my fingers on his shoulders, chest, back, face, and hair while we talked. When he started to kiss me, I made certain I returned his kisses passionately. I asked if he wanted a back rub. He said Yes. I suggested that he take off his shirt for a massage. Then, I let my fingers wander everywhere; Raymond got the message.

## REFUSING SEX

Sex is costly for women; women are more likely than men to be maligned for being sexually active outside of marriage. In addition to risking exposure to sexually transmitted diseases such as AIDS, sexually active heterosexual women continue to face the possibility of unwanted pregnancies. Even women in loving, committed relationships complain that sexual intercourse, which too many couples think is the only acceptable way to have sex, seems to be more fun for the man than for the woman. It is not surprising that women are scripted to say No to sex.[45] However, we should not stereotype them as using excuses, like headaches, to get out of having sex. Researcher Sandra Byers explains, "It turns out that men and women refuse [a partner's sexual advances] the same percentage of the time, and we've now found that in three studies, two studies with married couples and one study with dating couples."[46] Why do women appear to be rejecting their partners so often then? According to Byers, most heterosexual women like sex but end up saying No much of the time because the men in their lives are constantly trying to have sexual intercourse. When men's excess number of sexual invitations are controlled statistically, women and men do not differ in their likelihood of responding negatively to a regular partner's sexual initiative.[47]

In one out of ten dates in which sexual activity takes place, the man seeks more sexual intimacy than does the woman.[48] The more a couple has dated and had sex, the more predisposed they are to sexual disagreements. In most cases, partners had engaged in consensual sexual activities before the disagreement. Clearly, women are much more likely than men to risk being coerced into having sex. Worse still, we live in a culture in which women are blamed for any sexual victimization they had endured that was not the direct result of severe physical violence. No wonder women have developed numerous strategies for resolving sexual disagreements beginning with nonverbal rejections of a partner's sexual advances, moving on to attempts to divert the conversation or move to a less private setting, followed by a clear No, which may or may not be accompanied by an explanation, and ending up in threats or, if necessary, physical struggle.[49] If the man refuses to stop an unwanted sexual activity after all of this, the woman faces a very difficult predicament as few women are as physically powerful as the typical man. Chapter 6 goes into greater depth on the dynamics of sexual coercion than is possible here. However, I do want to share some empowering information for those who subscribe to the Liberal Feminist idea that women's sexual interactions are more likely to be pleasurable than dangerous. Yes, women have good reason to be afraid of men and sexual disagreements are commonplace. But, the majority of men are not rapists. In two different studies, Sandra Byers and her colleagues found that most men would respond swiftly and appropriately to a woman's unambiguous and repeated attempts to stop unwanted sexual activity.[50]

Unfortunately, sex-role socialization and inequality makes it difficult for women to frankly reject unwanted sexual advances. Some women are so tactful and exaggeratedly concerned about protecting a man's feelings that they sometimes don't say how they feel and comply with sexual activities they dislike. Many other women are forced to meet a man's sexual demands because they are justifiably afraid, afraid of losing economic support should they say No often enough and, worse still, afraid of bodily injury and even death for saying No at all.[51] Both Radical and Liberal Feminists have provided us with important insights into the politics of sexual rejection. Before sex can be truly pleasurable for women, women's right to stop unwanted sexual intimacy must be recognized, not only by partners, but by the culture as a whole.

## SEXUAL CHOREOGRAPHY

I wish it were otherwise but the conventional way of performing heterosexual intercourse typically requires a dominant man who is willing to adapt the script he learned for masturbation during adolescence to his sexual interactions with a woman.[52] That is, the man, not the woman, is supposed to intensify the physical activity from looking, cuddling, and (dare we think) talking, to "the real thing"—breast play and genital contact. He, not she, generally removes the partner's clothing. Her breasts, not his nipples, are fondled. He, not she, gets on top and does most of the thrusting. Most everyone expects heterosexual sexual interactions to follow the culturally prescribed sequence: (1) kissing and snuggling, (2) breast fondling, (3) genital caressing (first by the man and possibly later by the woman), (4) oral sex (optional), (5) sexual intercourse (required and probably with the man on top), and (6) climax. Sex is supposed to be masculine or goal-oriented with orgasm as the grand finale. Like classical music, sex is expected to start softly and build—increased muscle tension, increased blood engorgement, more rapid breathing, increased heartbeat, sweat, grimacing, and groaning, and finally—the crescendo of orgasm and sexual intercourse. And, what is the right way to dance, the "right" way to have sex? Penis-in-vagina sex is equated with normality, the highest form of sex. The right way to have orgasm is during sexual intercourse, preferably for both partners at once (although liberal couples will permit the woman's orgasm to occur first). Ideally both partners should "come" but it is still real sex if only the man does.

Just like we have rehearsed our first romantic kiss long before it takes place, we enter our first sexual encounter with a well-developed idea of what is supposed to take place, who is supposed to do what and when. Remarkably, sexual scripts are so well coordinated that most of us don't even need to talk during the process. We live in a heterosexist culture which erroneously holds that women are less sexual than men. Therefore, lesbians and bisexual women are less likely than heterosexual women to acquire clear messages about appropriate sexual scripts.[53] Expressions of physical affection and sensuality are commonplace among female couples, perhaps more so than among heterosexuals, but genital sex is rarer, especially in longer-term relationships. This is not necessarily a bad thing. There is nothing wrong with regarding cuddling, touching, hugging, sensual massage, and intimate conversation as prized goals in themselves, rather than as mere "foreplay" that inevitably should lead to genital sex or orgasm. In fact, many heterosexual couples might enjoy sex more if they were more sensual- and less goal-oriented. Too many of us have very constricted scripts for the doing of sex. For many women and men, sexual activity is remarkably brief and goal-oriented, rarely departing from the expected routine of a few minutes of foreplay followed by a few minutes of sexual intercourse.[54]

Heterosexual sexual scripts have changed in the latter part of the twentieth century, shifting from procreative scripts, which limited a sexual encounter to coitus, to pleasure scripts, which encouraged experimentation with oral sex and greater attention to the woman's pleasure.[55] Does this mean that Liberal Feminists have had their way, that sex has become more "natural" or less culturally restricted? Not quite. As John Gagnon argues, "oral sex is a sexual technique which is characteristic of better washed and more experimental social groups in which the erotic serves as an affirmation of interpersonal relationships."[56] So, more of us do oral sex than before, but we still subscribe to rigid rules. Because genital discharges are viewed as unsanitary, oral sex typically precedes rather than follows coitus.[57]

Sexual scripts specify everything, not just the correct sequence of sexual acts but the socially approved way of performing these acts. It may surprise Liberal Feminists to learn that women have more conservative opinions about coital positions than men.[58] Young men evaluate all positions for sexual intercourse as equally good; young women prefer the woman-below position, judging women who do this more favorably than those who get on top. According to women, the woman who gets on top of her man during sex is "dirtier, less respectable, less moral, less good, less desirable as a wife, and less desirable as a mother . . . than when she was beneath the man during intercourse."[59] And, how do women look at men who (shudder) allow their partners to mount them during sex? Very harshly. Consistent with rigid sex roles, the man who is beneath the woman during sexual intercourse is viewed as less masculine than one who gets on top. Sexual conservatism on this issue is disappointing to those, like Liberal Feminists, who hope to enhance women's sexual pleasure. Female orgasm during intercourse is more likely when the woman is able to control the rate and position of thrusting. Furthermore, the male-superior coital position is not practical for many older persons and couples in which one or both partners has chronic illness or a physical disability.

Liberal Feminists advise women to experiment sexually. Some women thrive as "the top," the individual who takes major responsibility for choreographing the sexual interaction; others prefer to be "the bottom," the one "who responds, acts out, makes visible or interprets the sexual initiatives and language of the top."[60] Erotic preferences transcend an individual's sex, sex roles, and sexual orientation. Bottoms may be more physically active and verbally expressive than tops. Straight men and "masculine" lesbians and gay men are not necessarily tops. Both Radical and Liberal Feminists are right in criticizing the patriarchal assumption that only men should be the top and only women should be the bottom in sex and the rest of life. But, it is just as misguided for Radical Feminist extremists to draw their own conclusions about politically correct sex, insisting upon "egalitarian sexuality, . . . sexual partnering involving the functional (if not literal) interchangeability of partners and acts" for everybody.[61]

Sexual interactions need not be bland or predictable. The use of power or influence by one or both partners during sex is inevitable. Sex is, by definition, a process of mutual influence. Employing power strategies to attract and influence a partner does not necessarily victimize. Total equality during the sexual influence process should not be a prerequisite for status as a feminist and does not guarantee the experience of sexual pleasure. It is okay for women to want sex. It is okay for lovers to influence each other sexually, providing they remain sensitive to the possibility that their sexual advances are not always welcome. Knowledge is power. We are free to change sexual scripts at any time, fostering intimacy and pleasure in the process.

## NOTES

1. See Gagnon, Scripts, pp. 27–59; Gagnon, Scripting Perspective in Sex Research, pp. 1–43; Simon and Gagnon, Sexual Scripts, pp. 97–120.

2. Ibid.

3. Ibid.

4. See DeLamater, Sexual Scenarios, pp. 127–39; McCormick, Sexual Scripts, pp. 3–27.

5. See McCormick, Sexual Scripts, pp. 12–27; McCormick & Jesser, Courtship Game, pp. 81–86.

6. See Leary and Snell, Instrumentality and Expressiveness, pp. 509–22.

7. See Loulan, Sex Practices of 1566 Lesbians, pp. 221–34.

8. See Carroll, Volk, and Hyde, Motives for Engaging in Sexual Intercourse, pp. 131–39; Leigh, Reasons for Having and Avoiding Sex, pp. 199–209.

9. See Hatfield et al., Gender Differences in What Is Desired, pp. 39–52.

10. See Murstein, Dating, pp. 13–28.

11. See Sprague and Quadagno, Sexual Motivation, pp. 57–76.

12. See Remoff, *Sexual Choice*.

13. See Green and Sandos, Perceptions of Male and Female Initiators, pp. 849–52.

14. See Kelley, Pilchowicz, and Byrne, Female-Initiated Dates, pp. 195–96.

15. See Clark and Hatfield, Sexual Offers, pp. 39–55.

16. See Muehlenhard and McFall, Dating Initiation, pp. 682–91; Muehlenhard and Scardino, What Will He Think?, pp. 560–69.

17. See Allgeier and Allgeier, *Sexual Interactions*, p. 533.

18. See Johnson, *Staying Power*; Meichenbaum et al., *Exploring Choices*, pp. 297–301; Rose, Zand, and Cini, Lesbian Courtship Scripts, pp. 70–85.

19. Rothblum, Telephone Interview; see Rose, Zand, and Cini, Lesbian Courtship Scripts, p. 70.

20. See McCormick & Jesser, Courtship Game, pp. 64–86; Meichenbaum et al., *Exploring Choices*, pp. 302–06.

21. Kleinke, Meeker, and Staneski, Opening Lines, pp. 588; 596.

22. Ibid., p. 588.

23. See ibid., pp. 585–600.

24. Murray, Language of Singles Bars, pp. 21–26.

25. See Perper, *Sex Signals*.

26. See McCormick and Jones, Nonverbal Flirtation, pp. 271–82.

27. See Moore, Nonverbal Courtship, pp. 237–47; Moore and Butler, Courtship Behavior in Women, pp. 205–15; Muehlenhard et al., Cues that Convey Interest, pp. 404–19.

28. See Johnson, *Staying Power*, p. 160; Loulan, Sex Practices of 1566 Lesbians, p. 225; Rose, Zand, and Cini, Lesbian Courtship Scripts, pp. 70–85.

29. See McCormick and Jesser, Courtship Game, pp. 64–86.

30. See DeLamater, Sexual Scenarios, pp. 134–36.

31. See Ibid.; LaPlante, McCormick, and Brannigan, Living the Sexual Script, pp. 338–55; McCormick, Come-ons and Put-offs, pp. 194–211; McCormick, Brannigan, and LaPlante, Social Desirability, pp. 303–14.

32. Byers, Telephone Interview; see O'Sullivan and Byers, Eroding Stereotypes, pp. 270–82.

33. See Grauerholz and Serpe, Initiation and Response, pp. 1041–59; Jesser, Male Responses, pp. 118–28.

34. See Byers and Heinlein, Predicting Initiations and Refusals, pp. 210–31.

35. See Perper and Weis, Proceptive and Rejective Strategies, pp. 462–64; Rose, Zand, and Cini, Lesbian Courtship Scripts, pp. 70–85.

36. See LaPlante, McCormick, and Brannigan, Living the Sexual Script, pp. 338–55; McCormick, Come-ons and Put-offs, pp. 194–211; McCormick, Brannigan, and LaPlante, Social Desirability, pp. 303–14.

37. See Byers and Heinlein, Predicting Initiations and Refusals, pp. 210–31.

38. See Jesser, Male Responses, pp. 118–28.

39. See Christopher and Frandsen, Influence in Sex and Dating, pp. 89–105.

40. Ibid.

41. See O'Sullivan and Byers, Women's Strategies, pp. 30–34; O'Sullivan and Byers, Female Use of Sexual Influence; O'Sullivan and Byers, Eroding Stereotypes, pp. 270–82.

42. See Christopher and Frandsen, Influence in Sex and Dating, pp. 89–105; Rose, Zand, and Cini, Lesbian Courtship Scripts, pp. 70–85.

43. See La Plante, McCormick, and Brannigan, Living the Sexual Script, pp. 338–55; McCormick, Come-ons and Put-offs, pp. 194–211.

44. McCormick, Come-ons and Put-offs, p. 199.

45. See LaPlante, McCormick, and Brannigan, Living the Sexual Script, pp. 338–55; McCormick, Come-ons and Put-offs, pp. 194–211; McCormick, Brannigan, and LaPlante, Social Desirability, pp. 303–14; McCormick and Jesser, Courtship Game, pp. 81–86.

46. Byers, Telephone Interview; see Byers and Heinlein, Predicting Initiations and Refusals, pp. 210–31.

47. Ibid.

48. See Byers and Lewis, Dating Couples' Disagreements, pp. 15–29.

49. See Byers, Sexual Disagreement Situations, pp. 235–54; Christopher and Frandsen, Influence in Sex and Dating, pp. 89–105; McCormick, Come-ons and Put-offs, pp. 194–211; Perper and Weis, Proceptive and Rejective Strategies, pp. 469–71.

50. See Byers, Sexual Disagreement Situations, pp. 235–54; Byers and Lewis, Dating Couples' Disagreements, pp. 15–29.

51. Frieze, Telephone Interview; Tiefer, Telephone Interview.

52. See Gagnon, Scripts, pp. 27–59; Gagnon, Scripting Perspective in Sex Research, pp. 1–43; Jemail and Geer, Sexual Scripts, pp. 513–22; McCormick, Sexual Scripts, pp. 3–27.

53. See Blumstein and Schwartz, *American Couples;* Johnson, *Staying Power;* Loulan, Sex Practices of 1566 Lesbians, pp. 221–34; Rothblum and Brehony, *Boston Marriages.*

54. See Gagnon, Scripts, pp. 27–59; Gagnon, Scripting Perspective in Sex Research, pp. 1–43; Jemail and Geer, Sexual Scripts, pp. 513–22; McCormick, Sexual Scripts, pp. 3–27.

55. See Gagnon, Scripting Perspective in Sex Research, pp. 1–43.

56. Ibid., p. 20.

57. See Jemail and Geer, Sexual Scripts, pp. 513–22.

58. See Allgeier and Fogel, Coital Position, pp. 588–89.

59. Ibid., p. 589.

60. Newton and Walton, More Precise Sexual Vocabulary, p. 246.

61. Ibid., p. 247.

# ❧ 3 ❧

# Love and Intimacy

A few years ago, I submitted a paper on love to the organizers of a major sexology conference. The paper was rejected, not on scientific grounds, but because the reviewers believed that love was irrelevant to sex research. Last semester, a young man informed other college students that my human sexuality class had been a major disappointment because I had wasted class time on several topics that had nothing to do with sex such as love, intimacy, jealousy, lesbians, and feminist thinking on sexual inequality. When asked why he had signed up for the class in the first place, the young man replied confidently, "I thought that she would teach us about sex, you know, different positions for doing it; what turns women on; things like that."

What does love have to do with sex? Both Liberal and Radical Feminists think that love, destructive love relationships, and the inability to love have a great deal to do with sex, and I agree wholeheartedly. Unfortunately, a number of men and the majority of sexologists seem to disagree. Most scientific and popular writers define sex as what people do with their genitals. In our patriarchal culture, sexual behavior is equated with the insertion of tab A into slot B, a phenomenon sexual scientists are expected to measure and improve. As we move into the twenty-first century, it is time to make sexology holistic and woman-affirming. Too many years have been devoted to sexual bookkeeping, recording the frequency and variety of peoples' genital experiences. This distracts us from more important aspects of sexuality, how we think and feel about intimacy.[1] Reducing sex to a juxtaposition of genitals and orifices denies the magic and breadth of sexual experiences. Opening our hearts to a partner is just as sexual as opening our legs. Regardless of how sex is defined, we should not ignore how people feel about one another. With the exception of the most casual sexual encounters, with the exception of abusive or exploitative sex, most people who join bodies have at least some warm feelings for one another. So, love is relevant to sex!

For a long time, scientists ignored a topic that they considered mushy, subjective, and ephemeral, leaving the contemplation of love to poets, philosophers, and theologians. By the middle of the twentieth century, however, love became an acceptable topic for scientific investigation, respectable even compared with the more controversial topic of sexuality. Not surprisingly, relatively few scientific studies of love have considered erotic or explicitly sexual features of close relationships. Whether or not love scientists are simultaneously sexual scientists, however, their work is crucial for those who are concerned with women's sexual salvation.

Feminists, especially Radical Feminists, define sex as spiritual, not just physical.[2] For feminists, thinking about and doing sex is closely aligned with the management of intimacy in general. No treatise on women's sexual salvation would be complete without a thorough analysis of love. This chapter relies on the burgeoning scholarly work on close relationships to define love, explore different types of love, and consider how sex, sexual orientation, and personality shape love relationships.

## INTIMACY

Intimacy is the human ability to connect with somebody else, emotionally, intellectually, and physically.[3] Whether they are friends, lovers, or both, intimate partners have a shared sense of destiny, interact in diverse ways, freely exchange ideas and feelings, and devote considerable time, effort, and personal resources to the relationship. Frequent, honest, and intense communication is necessary for a relationship to thrive. In loving relationships, partners feel especially close, are committed to the relationship even in the face of adversity, and ideally, remain passionately involved as the years go by.[4]

Who is more capable of intimacy, women or men? It all depends on the way that intimacy is defined. On the whole, women are much more likely than men to think that friends and lovers should exchange self-disclosures or sensitive, personal information about themselves regularly. Women for the most part value emotional intensity in their close relationships more highly than do men. Women often like to show how much they love somebody by being affectionate and sentimental; men typically prefer to demonstrate caring by performing helpful services. Consistent with Radical Feminist theory, most studies of friendships and love relationships suggest that women have greater intimacy skills than men.[5] However, these conclusions generally define intimacy in feminine, not masculine ways.[6] Miscommunication and frustration are inevitable when heterosexual partners, like the couple described below, fail to realize that they follow completely different scripts for intimacy.

> *Susan:* Mark hardly ever says he loves me. Whenever I want to work on our relationship, he would rather read or watch television. I feel like we have grown apart. Oh yeah, we see eye to eye about raising the kids and our sex is still great, but why won't Mark talk to me?
>
> *Mark:* I'm not the type of person who can say "I love you; I love you" every minute. How can Susan question my feelings? I've done everything I could to help her. I work two jobs so she can go back to school and [I] do a lot around the house. What else does she want? This business about talking about our relationship— What is there to talk about? I love her; I don't want to get into a fight.

Susan and Mark are a fairly typical couple. As a group, women evaluate their intimate heterosexual relationships more negatively than men.[7] Women describe themselves as devoting more time to their relationships than do men. Men perceive their relationships as more affectionate than do women. Do men deny problems in their heterosexual love relationships or are women too critical? Research does not provide a clear-cut answer. Although women disclose more personal information to same sex friends than men throughout their lives, sex differences in self-disclosure are few and small in loving heterosexual relationships.[8] With the exception of working-class couples where women say more about themselves than their husbands do, mutual self-disclosures are common among loving heterosexuals, especially when both partners are highly educated, middle class, and share feminist values. Does this mean that feminist criticism of male difficulties with intimacy is unfounded? Hardly. Several studies suggest that lesbians and heterosexual women place more positive value on emotional expressiveness, sharing feelings, and on having an egalitarian relationship with a lover than do either gay or heterosexual men.[9]

How do people describe their ideal partner or lover? There are surprisingly few differences between descriptions gathered from women and men or, for that matter, between those provided by homosexuals, bisexuals, and heterosexuals.[10] Most people want partners who are understanding, personable, physically attractive, intelligent, honest, affectionate, and dependable. Most struggle to reconcile the need for intimacy with an equally powerful desire for self-realization. Women and men, lesbians, gay men, bisexuals, and heterosexuals, say much the same things when asked to describe the best and worst aspects of their love relationships. All groups agree that lovers should feel the same level of affection for one another, share similar interests, agree on important values, and be similar in age, educational background, and socioeconomic class. Consistent with these goals, the majority of loving couples have a great deal in common, socially and psychologically.[11] But, no one is more closely matched than loving female couples. Because they stress equality in relationships more than either heterosexuals or gay men, lesbian partners are especially similar in age, income, and educational background. Thanks to the ease with which two women can achieve empathy for one another and bond emotionally, lesbian couples agree about the strengths and problems of their relationship more than any other type of couple. As some Radical Feminists have theorized, research points to many positive features of lesbian and female bisexual relationships.

Feminist analysis is appropriate even when women and men agree about what they want. Numerous studies indicate that heterosexuals believe that the ideal match includes a physically attractive woman and a financially prosperous man.[12] No doubt, these ideals are part and parcel of a patriarchal society that gives men economic advantages over women. Encouraging for Liberal Feminists, however, women are becoming decreasingly likely to trade youth and beauty for economic security. Fewer women than ever before contemplate marriage for practical reasons alone.[13] Financially secure, professional women have much higher standards for heterosexual relationships than their less affluent counterparts.

## TYPES OF LOVE

When I was nineteen, I fell in love for the first time. I couldn't resist telling the young man so. He responded in his characteristically philosophical manner. "What kind of love do you feel?" he asked, proceeding to list several books he had read on the subject and various theories about the nature of love. I was infuriated! Why wasn't he saying that he loved me too? What was the matter with him?

Years after this conversation, I stopped remembering my first love as an intellectualizer who was afraid of his feelings and realized instead that there was some merit in what he had said. There is now a considerable body of scientific evidence which indicates that love can be experienced in many ways. Women and men do not differ in the overall amount of love they have for partners.[14] However, there are reliable sex differences in attitudes toward love and the types of love people feel. As both Radical and Liberal Feminists would anticipate, sex differences in heterosexual love reflect women's economic dependency on men.[15] Because many women are obliged to look for providers and not just partners, they often take a man's occupation, education, and family background into account before allowing themselves to get emotionally involved. Men, in contrast, are free to fall head over heels in love for no good reason or merely because they are attracted to a woman. Extensive study has been made of North Americans' experiences with six different types of love: romantic love, self-centered love, companionate love, practical love, dependent love, and altruistic love.[16] Each type of love can be experienced alone or in combination by one or both partners.

*Romantic love* is an intense, passionate sense of connection with a partner. Often associated with high levels of sexual arousal, romantic love tends to be most intense early in the relationship, while fantasies about a partner outweigh realistic appraisals. Romantic lovers have a strong identification with each other. *Self-centered love* is love in name only. The self-centered lover has a detached, exploitative attitude towards partners. Frequently, commitment is shunned and multiple relationships are juggled; the goal is to enhance status by conquering someone's heart, not necessarily to be intimate. Based on caring, similar values, and shared experiences, *companionate love* is the love of two best friends. More than romantic love, companionate love increases over time. Trust and acceptance of a partner's foibles are characteristic; the cozy warmth of companionate love contrasts with the thrilling heat of romantic lovers' passion. Companionate love is a necessary ingredient in happy, successful, long-term relationships. "While intimate relationships may be built on [romantic love], they need liking [companionate love] to thrive from day to day."[17] *Practical love* is generated by socio-economic considerations and the desire to please others, especially the extended family. Wherever marriages are still arranged by parents, practical love is the only culturally acceptable reason for matrimony.[18] Practical love is by no means obsolete in our own culture. Before falling in love, today's practical lovers complete a cost-benefit analysis of the partner's religious and political convictions, economic prospects, social status, and compatibility with friends and family members. Often confused with romantic love, *dependent love* is obsessive and irrational.[19] Dependent lovers are unable to act independently; their love relationships are emotional roller coasters during which they experience the extremes of joy, hope, anxiety, jealousy, anger, and depression, sometimes in rapid succession. Embedded too much in their partners' lives, dependent lovers isolate themselves from other interests and worse yet, other people or alternative sources of social support. Rarest of all, *altruistic love* is based on empathy, a lover's willingness to place a partner's welfare before his or her own interests.

Both women and men can experience various combinations of the six types of love. However, numerous studies indicate reliable and sometimes unexpected sex differences in love styles.[20] Inconsistent with popular opinion, men are more likely than women to be romantic lovers. Men, more than women, are in love with love, fall in love at first sight, and believe that true love overcomes all obstacles. Surprisingly, although men hold more romantic beliefs than women, women describe greater numbers of emotional symptoms associated with being in love. Women more than men in love say that they feel like they are floating on air, have trouble concentrating, and can think of nobody else but the beloved. Do women's symptoms mean that they are the more romantic lovers? Probably not. Women are simply more likely than men to admit to emotional responses of any kind. In fact, men have less at stake economically than women when they lose their heads romantically.

Self-centered love is by no means an exclusively male phenomenon. Nonetheless, men are more predisposed than women to admit that they have played games with someone else's feelings, took advantage of a partner, or have had numerous, simultaneous affairs. Sex differences in the reported experience of self-centered love are closely associated with exaggerated masculinity and casual, callous attitudes towards sex. As they stand, research findings on self-centered love support the Radical Feminist idea that men are sexually exploitative. Radical Feminists would also predict that women are more affectionate and loving than are men. There is limited empirical support for this point of view as well. Women like the men in their lives more than they are liked in return. Sex-role socialization encourages women but not men to regard love as an intense friendship. Until late in life, women report having more companionate love for men than men report feeling for them. Historical and contemporary studies suggest that friendships between women have frequently been emotionally rich love affairs, regardless of whether or not partners had genital sex or labeled themselves as lesbians.[21] Current research suggests that lesbians trust their lovers more than gay men and remain more satisfied with the relationship as the years go by.[22] Some of the frustration women experience within heterosexual relationships could occur because their same-sex friends might treat them better than do their male lovers or husbands.

Women experience more practical love for heterosexual partners than do men.[23] As explained earlier, women are more likely than men to see lovers as potential economic providers. Furthermore, women are more likely than men to be socialized to please others. As long as there is sexual inequality, women will have to consider their financial self-interest when contemplating love matches. The pragmatic pull of practical love also contributes to women's lesser susceptibility to romantic love. What about dependent love? Most studies suggest that women are more likely to be dependent or needy lovers than men.[24] These findings are compatible with both Radical and Liberal Feminist descriptions of an oppressive, sex-role ideology which smashes female autonomy and teaches women that they are worthwhile only insofar as they have a successful, intimate relationship with a man. Yet, this appealing feminist argument is simplistic. Why would any individual remain with a needy partner unless he or she also experienced some pathological neediness? In my clinical experience, after the women I have treated for dependent love problems rediscovered self-worth and autonomy, their supposedly independent male partners fell apart. Are women more dependent lovers than men or do they simply have more permission to appear needy? Some Radical Feminists have described men as emotionally detached and incapable of having tender, vulnerable feelings. In glaring contrast, research indicates that men are much more likely than women to become depressed, lonely, and suicidal when their relationships have failed.

Clearly, men and women are inclined to approach love differently. But, the meaning of this is not obvious. Sex differences in love styles should be viewed contextually. Women and men are not members of two different species; individual variation can and often does overpower gender differences. Sex-role socialization is not the only force that shapes behavior. Personality traits also contribute to love attitudes and experiences.[25] No matter what kind of genitals they have, some people have "feminine" personality traits and others have a more "masculine" disposition. Feminine individuals are especially affectionate, trusting, tender, and yielding; masculine persons are highly task-oriented, dominant, and competitive. Feminine men and women are highly romantic; they expect sexual activity to culminate in sexual communion, the mystical merging of two souls. In contrast, masculine women and men view sex as purely utilitarian; the feminine idea that sex should be spiritual would strike them as fanciful and ridiculous. For masculine persons, sex has one and only one purpose, physical satisfaction. Masculine women and men are likely to be self-centered lovers but are unlikely to be dependent lovers. Feminine men and women, in comparison, are predisposed to love partners romantically, companionately, practically, and altruistically. Androgynous individuals, women and men whose personalities are equally masculine and feminine, are especially likely to be in touch with their feelings, affectionate, sensitive, emotionally supportive, and tolerant of a partner's flaws.

A few Radical Feminists have argued that women are better at love than men. Specifically, they have suggested that women love men more than they are loved in return and that lesbian relationships are more loving than heterosexual and gay relationships. With the exception of the findings cited above which indicate that women feel more liking and companionate love for lovers than do men, most empirical data refutes these theories.[26] As explained earlier, women and men report similar overall levels of love for their heterosexual partners. There are no consistent, systematic differences in the closeness of lesbian, gay, and heterosexual relationships. Instead of lamenting men's alleged flaws or the impossibility of heterosexual relationships, feminists should advocate the flowering of love-positive, personality traits in all types of couples.

## ATTACHMENT VERSUS AUTONOMY

Maurice and Theresa, a young married couple, struck up a friendship with their lesbian neighbors Laura and Victoria. All four were amazed by one thing; both couples had the same conflict. In each relationship, one partner was very independent and the other thought the couple didn't spend enough time together. Maurice and Laura were very successful professionally and devoted many long hours to their respective jobs. This was deeply resented by Theresa and Victoria who saw their partners as "workaholics." Exacerbating the conflict, Maurice and Laura liked to go out with their own friends just as much as they were willing to socialize as couples. Furthermore, both Maurice and Laura had hobbies and athletic interests that neither Theresa nor Victoria cared to pursue. When Theresa and Victoria complained about their partners' independence, which they did frequently, Maurice and Laura felt like they were being "suffocated" by their partners' "neediness" and demands for attention.

Each love relationship challenges partners to strike a balance between intimacy and independence. Every couple negotiates the extent to which they emphasize dyadic attachment, participating in joint activities and emotional sharing, or personal autonomy, being free to act and think independently. Conflicts over attachment and autonomy are at the heart of our culture's mythology about male-female relationships. According to prevailing sex-role stereotypes, women push for dyadic attachment (commitment and togetherness) whereas men struggle to retain personal autonomy (or independence). Buying into these stereotypes, Radical Feminists sometimes argue that heterosexual relationships are doomed because few men are capable of meeting women's desires for intimacy. Rebelling against the same stereotypes, Liberal Feminists argue quite the opposite. According to some Liberal Feminists, too much "togetherness" or dyadic attachment oppresses both women and men. Interestingly enough, the scientific literature contradicts both points of view.[27] Men and women who are well educated and middle class place equal value upon attachment and autonomy. For lesbians, gay men, and heterosexuals alike, the two goals, dyadic attachment and personal autonomy, are not viewed as incompatible. All types of loving couples want ample measures of both.

A number of writers have suggested that dyadic attachment and autonomy issues are especially keen for lesbian couples.[28] Lesbians are more likely than gay men to live with their primary partners and currently be involved in a steady relationship. Lesbians value sexual exclusivity and emotional sharing more than do gay men. Lesbians agree with their partner's assessment of qualitative aspects of their loving relationship more than either heterosexuals or gay men.[29] Compared to other types of loving couples, lesbians report fewer differences in attraction to partners and the importance partners place on being together. Women are socialized to be interpersonally sensitive. Heterosexual women and lesbians pride themselves on their understanding of a partner's feelings and point of view. In this context, it is not surprising that lesbian couples emphasize emotional closeness and bonding. What is more interesting is the fact that psychotherapists, including a number of feminist clinicians, have interpreted this emphasis as evidence of psychopathology. Assuming that loving female couples sacrifice personal autonomy for dyadic attachment more than either male or heterosexual couples, psychotherapists who specialize in lesbian issues speak about the risks of too much emotional closeness.[30] Painstakingly, they describe therapeutic interventions with lesbians who have muted all self-expression for fear of losing a relationship, with female couples who present themselves for treatment with almost identical values, interests, and ideas, with women who are afraid to spend time alone or with other friends. Labeling extreme dyadic attachment as "fusion," "merger," or "co-dependency," such therapists worry aloud that too many lesbians have neglected self-interest, personal development, and support systems to become clones of their partners.

Are lesbian relationships riddled with co-dependency problems? Do lesbian couples merge or fuse more than gay or heterosexual couples? Can women have too much empathy and sensitivity? The little empirical evidence that is available suggests that psychotherapists have exaggerated the extent to which female partners are too dependent upon one another. Among nonclinical couples, lesbians have diverse opinions about the extent to which their loving relationships are or should be characterized by dyadic attachment or personal autonomy.[31] Generally, younger and less religious individuals, highly educated women, feminist activists, and lesbians who belong to a women's community which promotes group loyalty emphasize personal autonomy in their loving relationships more than dyadic attachment. Apparently, merging or fusion may be a major issue for lesbians entering psychotherapy but is not necessarily characteristic of lesbian and female bisexual couples in the larger population.

Rather than being inclined to sacrifice their autonomy for the sake of a relationship, young women may be more concerned than young men about their ability to remain individuals despite being involved in a loving relationship.[32] Research with heterosexuals suggests that most men and women place equal value on dyadic attachment (having a close, secure, long-term relationship with a partner) and personal autonomy (partner independence). However, women and feminists are slightly more likely than men and sex-role traditionalists to think that personal autonomy is more important than dyadic attachment. In general, feminist men and women advocate more mature attitudes about loving relationships than their counterparts who advocate traditional sex roles.[33] For men and women both, traditional sex-role ideology contributes to romantic dependency, the belief that personal happiness is determined entirely by the current status of the primary love relationship. Likewise, sex-role traditional individuals subscribe to more unrealistic notions about romantic compatibility than feminists. Traditional women and men, but not feminists, expect lovers to share identical moods, think it is possible to live in total harmony with a partner, and imagine that just being with a loving partner will guarantee happiness.

All loving couples have to strike a balance between intimacy and autonomy. In contrast with our culture's mythology, women do not seem to have greater difficulty with this process than men. Instead, it appears that irrespective of sex and sexual orientation, people who uphold traditional sex roles are more likely to sacrifice their individuality to strengthen the relationship than are those who adhere to feminist values.

## POWER AND EQUALITY

Radical and Liberal Feminists alike subscribe to the idea that the personal is political. Therefore, an analysis of power relationships, including power in the home, is central for a feminist understanding of intimate relationships. As Radical Feminists have taught, the home can be a very dangerous place for women. Unquestionably, women are more likely than men to be the victims of domestic violence, an abomination perpetuated largely, but not exclusively, by male partners. Equally compatible with Radical Feminist thinking, few would disagree that men as a group have greater economic resources than women. Men's superior financial security gives them an edge in negotiations and interactions with a lover or wife. What are the implications? Many women remain in psychologically and/or physically abusive heterosexual relationships because they don't think they could support themselves if they left. Let me give you an example from my clinical practice.

Ursula was referred for therapy by her family doctor who indicated that she was suffering from depression. During our first session, it became clear that Ursula's husband was an abuser. He drank heavily, called her hostile names in front of their four children, and slapped her around regularly. The husband had raped Ursula vaginally, anally, and orally on several occasions; she had made many visits to the emergency room for injuries suffered during beatings. Ursula was a full-time homemaker who had completed neither high school nor any job-training program. She had very limited employment experience prior to her marriage at age nineteen. Ursula's husband had a high-paying job with good benefits, but he would not provide her an allowance for household expenses and refused to allow her to have her own car. Ursula liked me and was enthusiastic about therapy. Unfortunately, she never returned after the first visit because her husband wouldn't let her.

As I point out throughout chapter 6, there is a great deal of merit to what Radical Feminist activists have been saying and doing about domestic and sexual violence directed against women. However, as commonplace as abuse is, Liberal Feminists are also correct in pointing out that most homes and most heterosexual relationships are not dangerous. When social scientists examine how ordinary couples influence their partners, women are more powerful in their homes than Radical Feminist rhetoric suggests. Large-scale studies of heterosexual and homosexual couples indicate that the use of power, including a preference for coercive strategies, is not entirely determined by an individual's sex or economic resources.[34] Female homemakers, for example, are more likely than employed women to admit that they have threatened and ridiculed the men in their lives to get their way.

If sex doesn't completely determine power strategies in intimate relationships, what does? Again, personality disposition and the level of emotional involvement in the relationship are important. Research indicates that low masculinity, being a sensitive and submissive person, is associated with pleading, crying, and acting ill and helpless to influence a partner for men and women alike. The extent to which a person feels involved with a partner or dependent on a relationship for personal well-being is also important. When involvement is low, men and women feel free to be domineering and direct in their use of power; when involvement is high, they try to get what they want indirectly, doing their best not to call attention to their attempts at influence. The association between involvement and the exercise of power within intimate relationships holds true for individuals of both genders and all sexual orientations.

The majority of young heterosexuals think that both partners should have equal power in a loving relationship.[35] Unfortunately, true equality exists for only half these couples. Who has greater power when a heterosexual relationship is unequal? As Radical Feminists would predict, the man usually dominates in such cases. Several factors increase the likelihood of a woman having power within heterosexual relationships: feeling less invested in the relationship than a partner, access to desirable alternatives to the intimate relationship, education, and high career goals and achievements. Research refutes sexist and racist mythology about African-American and Hispanic couples. African-American women do not generally dominate African-American men; Hispanic women are not necessarily the subordinates of Hispanic men. Regardless of social class or income, African-American and Hispanic marriages are no less egalitarian than Anglo marriages.

Lesbians endorse equal power in relationships nearly unanimously and are more likely than either heterosexuals or gay men to be involved in relationships in which both partners have equal say.[36] Keeping in mind the importance placed on equality in love relationships for women of all sexual orientations, there is strong empirical support for the Radical Feminist assumption that lesbian and bisexual relationships affirm women's lives. However, it would be wrong to describe the relationships of women who love women in an overly positive way. Despite their strongly egalitarian ideals, a sizeable minority of lesbian relationships are dominated by one partner. Inequality is most likely when the emotional involvement of partners is asymmetrical and when the two women's educational accomplishments and economic resources are not well matched. Be that as it may, it is still fair to say that lesbian relationships are characterized by greater levels of trust and more frequent instances in which both partners assume equal responsibility for important decisions than either gay or heterosexual relationships.

For women, equality and happiness are interrelated. Relationship satisfaction is strongly associated with sharing decisions and feeling equal to a partner, whether the partner is female or male.[37]

## EMOTIONAL SHARING AND COMMUNICATION

If Radical Feminists are right, good verbal and nonverbal communication is more precious to women than is good genital sex. Unfortunately, the properly socialized man is supposed to be strong but inexpressive. Most published studies report reliable differences in the extent to which gay and heterosexual women and men share feelings, provide others with emotional support, and are willing to make risky self-disclosures.[38] The stereotype of the strong, silent man is so widely accepted that some feminist scientists have designated it as a veritable social disease, male inexpressiveness.[39] Men, they point out, have difficulty talking about feelings, showing feelings, and understanding other peoples' feelings. Advised not to get close to other men lest they appear weak or homosexual, rigid sex-role socialization ironically makes heterosexual men excessively dependent upon women. For some men, a wife or lover may be the only person they can trust. Unlike extremist Radical Feminists who regard the problem as an inherited, antisocial, male personality trait, Liberal Feminists believe that male inexpressiveness is socially constructed, the inevitable result of a patriarchal power structure. If manhood is equated with wielding power, a man is allowed to show only two emotions, anger and sexual desire. Genital sex may assume exaggerated importance for inexpressive men because it is their only socially approved outlet for displaying tender emotions. Sadly enough, however, such men often expect to be in control even during sex; they are allowed to make love physically but they are silenced from talking about feelings.

Evidence for male inexpressiveness in love relationships is oddly inconsistent with studies documenting men's susceptibility to romantic love. As explained earlier, men are more likely than women to be romantic lovers who fall in love at first sight. In fact, men generally say "I love you" long before the women they date do.[40] As one young man explained, "I'd known I was falling in love with her . . . but I never thought I'd tell her . . . 'I love you' before I knew what I was doing! . . . it was like I was someone else or like a dog foaming at the mouth out of control."[41] Why do men blurt out budding feelings of love even though they have been socialized to be emotionally inexpressive? Two factors seem to account for this inconsistency. First, impulsive statements of attraction may help men control relationships by influencing women to commit their hearts to the men who seem to be so taken with them. Second, a number of men lack women's sophisticated emotional vocabulary. Unable to discriminate between a variety of warm emotions such as lust, liking, friendship, and at least six types of love, some men say "I love you" simply because these are the only words they know for expressing positive feelings.

Cultural rules for manliness may make it difficult for men to display emotions freely. However, research contradicts the stereotype that women are more emotional than men.[42] As Liberal Feminists have suggested, sex differences in emotional communication are neither inborn nor inevitable. As men mature and learn from their interactions with women, they become more comfortable and skillful in sharing their innermost thoughts and feelings with those they love.[43] In addition, personality disposition and values may determine how people manage intimate relationships more than sex. Inconsistent with sex-role stereotypes, lesbian and heterosexual women fail to work harder at saving troubled relationships than gay and heterosexual men.[44] Instead, feminine, that is, nurturing and accommodating, heterosexual and homosexual men and women are more likely to assume constructive roles in intimate relationships than their masculine or independent, dominant counterparts. When a love relationship is troubled, feminine persons are more likely than masculine persons to discuss problems openly with a partner, engage in appropriate confrontation, compromise, seek professional or religious help, and remain loyal and emotionally supportive despite the couple's current problems. In glaring contrast, masculine women and men often try to improve things for themselves at the expense of the relationship. More than their feminine counterparts, masculine persons threaten to leave, withdraw or spend less time with partners, behave abusively, and complain while failing to offer constructive criticism as soon as problems surface in a relationship. Complementing the positive aspects of feminine personality traits, feminist values also improve love relationships. Compared to their sex-role traditional counterparts, feminist lovers respect and understand each other more, feeling freer to exchange feelings.[45]

## SEXUAL EXPRESSION

Numerous studies of loving couples document the power of the patriarchy in shaping heterosexuals' sexual attitudes and experiences.[46] Compared to men, women are more sexually restrictive. Women are less likely than men to desire casual sex or multiple sexual partners; women are also stronger advocates of sexual exclusivity or monogamy in their long-term relationships. Sex even appears to have different meanings for heterosexual men and women. Men more than women view sex as primarily instrumental, a physical release which decreases tension and brings about pleasure.

In contrast, women more than men emphasize the possibilities of sexual communion; the best part of sex is partners' emotional and spiritual connection. Not surprisingly, sex differences in heterosexual sexual expression are duplicated among lesbians and gay men.[47] Lovers' expression of physical affection and their intimate verbal communication are more valued or just as highly valued by lesbians as is genital sex. This is not true for gay men. Like their heterosexual counterparts, lesbians prize and practice monogamy more than gay or heterosexual men. Up until the AIDS epidemic dampened a sexual freedom movement within the gay community, gay men had sex more often and with many more partners than any other group. Promiscuity, however, has never been characteristic of loving female couples. Lesbians restrict their number of sexual partners and avoid the temptation of affairs outside their primary relationship less than heterosexual women but more than gay and heterosexual men.

There is no such thing as a typical lesbian couple. Current research indicates that lesbians' sexual experiences closely resemble those of heterosexual women. Like their heterosexual counterparts, most lesbians dated men in the past. The majority experienced one or more romantic, sexual relationships with men before coming to terms with a preference for female partners. Gay men, in contrast, have had less heterosexual experience as a group. Heterosexual experiences are likely to generalize to homosexual relationships. Given their extensive past experience with male lovers, lesbians may be more influenced by heterosexual sexual scripts than gay men. Many lesbian couples enjoy sex, making love to their partners as often as the typical heterosexual couple their age. Others appreciate the freedom to refrain from genital sex, an alternative that is far less available to heterosexual women. Lesbians, as a group, have sex with primary partners less often than heterosexual women although their probability of achieving orgasm and sexual satisfaction may be higher. Lesbian couples continue to define themselves as lovers even when they are no longer sexually active. With heterosexual men programmed to push for sex, even if the women in their lives seem reluctant, romantic celibacy is not an option for most coupled heterosexual women.

Empirical findings support Radical Feminist assumptions about what sex means to women. Women for the most part reject casual sex, viewing sex instead as the expression of love for a special partner, even the merging of two souls. The extremist Liberal Feminist assumption that women feel oppressed by the expectation that they restrict sexual activities to a single partner is not yet substantiated by research. Both patriarchal restrictions on female sexual activity and appreciation for emotional intimacy have shaped women's sexual values and behavior within love relationships. In sharp contrast with heterosexual men, heterosexual women support sexual values and interests which are markedly similar to those held by bisexual women and lesbians.

## MANAGING JEALOUSY

Jealousy is how people feel, think, and act when they believe that a rival has threatened their love relationship.[48] For both women and men, jealousy is greatest when a potential rival is perceived as extremely sexy and attractive. There are striking cross-cultural similarities in the kinds of situations that make people jealous.[49] As a rule, a partner's explicit erotic behavior with a rival, activities like flirting and having sex, is more disturbing than simply friendly behavior. Romantic or sexual jealousy varies from normal levels, where the individual is upset but is highly capable of exercising self-control, to morbid jealousy, where the individual has paranoid ideation, obsesses continuously about the threatened relationship, stalks the rival and partner aggressively, and may even engage in physical assault or murder.[50] No comparison of women and men in love would be complete without a feminist analysis of jealousy.

There are tremendous individual differences in susceptibility to jealousy.[51] Emotionally dependent persons experience higher levels of jealousy than those who are confident that they could cope well, even if a love relationship failed. Jealousy is strongly related to past or anticipated experiences with sex outside of the primary relationship. Women and men who have had or anticipate having affairs describe themselves as less jealous than those who are strong advocates of monogamy. Highly jealous people believe that jealous rages prove their love; less jealous people would draw the opposite conclusion. Sex-role oppression, translated into emotional dependency, encourages some heterosexual women to try to make their partners jealous.[52] Tragically, manipulating jealousy is like playing with fire. As discussed in detail later, men are more susceptible to morbid jealousy than women. Throughout the ages, morbidly jealous men have physically abused and murdered the women they claimed to have loved.[53] Both Radical and Liberal Feminists would agree that morbid jealousy is promoted by a patriarchal value system which regards women as men's possessions and not as separate individuals with equal rights.

Although women and men experience equal levels of normal jealousy, their jealousy is stimulated by different cognitions, values, and situations.[54] More than men, women feel threatened by the possible loss of an emotionally intimate relationship. More than women, men feel threatened by the potential sexual relationship between their partner and a rival. Heterosexual women are more likely than heterosexual men to feel threatened by a part-love relationship was volatile. Although he maintained a separate apartment and was often away on business, Alvin insisted on keeping constant tabs on Janine's whereabouts. He called her at work and home several times a day, talking for hours about his worries that Janine might be seeing someone else. Each time they talked or got together, Alvin insisted on Janine giving him a complete account of all her activities that day, which he would cross reference with mutual acquaintances. Obsessed with the idea that Janine needed multiple lovers to be satisfied, he engaged in odd rituals after returning from a business trip. After checking to see if the toilet seat was up, assuming that this was a sign that another man had been in the house, Alvin carefully inspected the sheets for evidence of another man's pubic hairs. Frequently and almost unpredictably, Alvin flew into jealous rages.

Consistent with Radical Feminist theory, domestic violence experts in all professions acknowledge the strong connection between men's jealous rages and female victimization. However, it is important to remember that jealousy is not always sexual in nature. Many abusive husbands become violent because they object to their wives having an independent social life with women friends and their extended family, not just because they imagine there is another man. Fear of jealousy-provoked male violence constrains the behavior of countless women around the world. Male jealousy is a leading motive for homicide as well as most cases of spousal abuse. The prevailing cultural myth in many societies is that a jealous man's murder of a lover and/or his rival is a crime of passion.[57] As a result, such murders are considered manslaughter in many jurisdictions, rather than being given the charge with more severe penalties, murder. The psychological and social realities of such crimes contradict the myth in powerful ways. Typically, so-called crimes of passion are preceded by years of psychological and physical abuse. Homicide is usually the last of many violent acts, not an anomaly in an otherwise warm and peaceful relationship.

Radical Feminist analysis of the patriarchal legal tradition sheds light on the terrifying dynamic of male jealous rage. Adultery laws have only recently moved toward viewing women and men as having equal rights.[58] Cross-culturally and historically, women were viewed as the property of men. Therefore, when a wife had sex with someone other than her husband, the husband was seen as a victim who was entitled to damages. Typically, the law allowed the husband to punish both the woman and her lover severely. Male marital infidelity, in contrast, was not criminalized until the nineteenth century and then, only in limited ways. Historically, the wom-

ner's devotion to a hobby, male friends, or his family. Jealous
women worry about different things. Women worry that their pa
find a rival who has a more captivating personality, is superior in
attractiveness, and is easier to talk to. Men worry that their partner
out that the rival is a superior sexual partner. Heterosexual men a
that a partner's interest in a rival was precipitated by their perso
culties with intimacy, specifically their failure to commit themselv
relationship. Consistent with the sexual double standard and femin
sis, sexual issues push men while intimacy issues push women into
Feminist values, high self-esteem, and the preservation of person
omy in love relationships attenuate jealousy. Sex-role traditional, h
ual men are especially susceptible to jealousy because they subscri
double standard, believing that women should lead more restrict
lives than men. Dependent women are especially prone to jealousy
they have poor self-esteem, measure their worth in terms of how
treats them, and believe that survival outside the relationship is im

There are critical sex differences in the expression of normal je
Not surprisingly, these differences are consistent with expected s
More often than women, jealous men become angry, withdrawn
threatening, and willing to consider hasty sexual involvement wit
partner to get even. In predictable contrast, jealous women are r
than jealous men to experience anxiety, fear, depression, and se
Jealous women cry more than jealous men. They are more likely t
ous men to suffer silently or feign indifference. Far more than men
blame themselves for a partner's wandering eye. Unlike jealous men
women make desperate attempts to improve their physical app
through exercise, hair styling, and the purchase of new makeup an
ing. Jealous men, unlike jealous women, are likely to promise an a
lover that they will change for the better or be more cooperative. H
jealous women do more than make promises. Women generally att
make the jealousy-provoking experience a constructive stimulus for
ing the relationship. Characteristically, women are often prepare
most of the work to make these needed improvements.

Normal jealousy provokes hostility in men more than in women.
young, heterosexual men sometimes confront a rival verbally, pic
with him, or vandalize his property. Men's morbid jealousy has mo
ous implications for women than for male rivals. Men are much m
ceptible to morbid jealousy than women.[56] Here is an example of thi
lem from my own clinical practice.

Janine and Alvin met shortly after Alvin's divorce; their sexual life
   extremely passionate. They sought therapy, however, because t

an's marital status and not the man's determined whether an incident was punishable as adultery. The law permitted men to take violent revenge upon an adulterous wife and her lover in our own culture until the twentieth century. "Besides criminalizing adultery, legal traditions commonly acknowledged that when adultery is discovered, a jealous rage on the part of the victimized husband is only to be expected."[59] Even today in the most progressive nations, the criminal justice system often excuses violent male sexual jealousy. As pointed out earlier, men who kill their wives or lovers in a jealous rage sometimes succeed in having their charges lowered from murder to manslaughter.

Radical and Liberal Feminists are both right. Morbid jealousy is part and parcel of life in a patriarchal society. Until men no longer view women and children as personal property, until our culture no longer restrains women from exercising the right to be socially and sexually independent, women will fall prey to morbidly jealous men. The time for social change is now! Feminist analysis is critical for the understanding of normal jealousy too. Jealousy oppresses women by locking them into excessive dependency. By encouraging women to equate their self-worth with physical attractiveness and the status of their relationships with men, patriarchal values encourage women to feel jealous, depressed, and anxious. Jealousy oppresses men by locking them into aggressive behavior and fostering social withdrawal and substance abuse. Jealousy prevents men from developing skills to foster intimate relationships. It is doubtful that men are able to love women fully if they cannot forgive their partners for the possibility of violating monogamy rules. Feminist women and men are less susceptible to jealousy than those who uphold traditional sex-roles. Sexual salvation, the affirmation of women's sexuality, cannot occur until we tackle the problem of jealousy in a patriarchal society.

## SATISFACTION AND COMMITMENT

Consideration of problems such as jealousy notwithstanding, satisfaction and commitment are the quintessence of love relationships. What then, should feminists make of the lack of consistent sex differences in personal satisfaction within intimate heterosexual relationships?[60] There is little empirical evidence to support the belief, held by extremist Radical Feminists, that marriage or living with a man necessarily are bad for women. Some heterosexuals find it difficult to believe that homosexual relationships could be as fulfilling as their heterosexual equivalents.[61] Nonetheless, research shows that many lesbians and gay men enjoy successful long-term relationships. In fact, the majority of studies fail to find any differences between how lesbians, gay men, heterosexual women, and heterosexual men evaluate closeness to a partner or overall satisfaction with a relationship.[62] Homosexuals and heterosexuals, for the most part, are indistinguishable on measures of couple adjustment and sexual satisfaction. Inconsistent with both Liberal and Radical Feminist assumptions, closeted lesbians are no less happy with their partners than are women who are openly lesbian.[63] Instead, as explained earlier, equality between partners in emotional involvement and commitment are the key constituents of satisfaction within lesbian relationships.[64] The little research that exists that includes lesbians of color suggests that there is no link between relationship satisfaction, love, and closeness and being matched with a partner from the same or another ethnic group.[65]

Who makes a relationship work? Consistent with Radical Feminist theory, research suggests that lesbians and heterosexual women invest more of themselves into loving relationships than either gay or heterosexual men.[66] Sex differences aside, however, Liberal Feminists are also right. Relationship skills and commitment are by no means entirely determined by someone's genitalia. Here again, regardless of gender or sexual orientation, feminine and androgynous persons have been found to perform better in their intimate relationships than masculine persons.[67] Women and men want much the same things from a lover; heterosexual and lesbian relationships can be equally fulfilling. Even though patriarchal institutions remain powerful, it is possible for women to find happiness, sexual salvation if you will, with either male or female lovers.

## NOTES

1. See Schneider and Gould, Female Sexuality, pp. 120–53.

2. See Echols, Taming of the Id, pp. 50–72; Rich, Compulsory Heterosexuality, pp. 62–91; Rothblum and Brehony, Boston Marriages.

3. See Kelley et al., Analyzing Close Relationships, pp. 20–67.

4. See Sternberg, Triangular Theory, pp. 119–35; Sternberg, Triangle of Love; and Sternberg and Grajek, Love, pp. 312–29.

5. See Sternberg, Triangle of Love, especially pp. 13–16, 93, and 210–20.

6. See Tavris, The Mismeasure of Woman.

7. See Sternberg, Triangle of Love, especially pp. 13–16, 93, and 210–20.

8. See Peplau and Gordon, Women and Men in Love, pp. 257–91.

9. See Peplau, Homosexual Love Relationships; Peplau, What Homosexuals Want, pp. 28–38.

10. See ibid. and see Engel and Saracino, Love Preferences, pp. 241–50; Peplau and Gordon, Women and Men in Love, pp. 257–91.

11. See Kurdek and Schmitt, Partner Homogamy, pp. 212–32.

12. See Hirschman, People as Products, pp. 98–108; Nevid, Romantic Attraction, pp. 401–11; Sternberg, *Triangle of Love;* Tooke and Camire, Mating Strategies, pp. 345–64.

13. See Ambert, Separated Women and Remarriage, pp. 43–54; Simpson, Campbell, and Berscheid, Romantic Love and Marriage, pp. 363–72.

14. See Peplau and Gordon, Women and Men in Love, pp. 257–91.

15. See Foa et al., Sexual Attitudes, pp. 511–19; Hatfield, Love and Sex?, pp. 106–34; Hendrick et al., Do Men and Women Love Differently?, pp. 177–95; Hendrick and Hendrick, Theory and Method of Love, pp. 392–402.

16. See Hatfield, Love and Sex?, pp. 106–34; Lee, *Colors of Love.*

17. Sternberg, *Triangle of Love*, p. 20.

18. See Desai, McCormick, and Gaeddert, Beliefs About Love, pp. 93–116; Simmons, Vom Kolke, and Shimizu, Attitudes Toward Romantic Love, pp. 327–36; Simpson, Campbell, and Berscheid, Romantic Love and Marriage, pp. 363–72; Vandewiele and Philbrick, Attitudes of Senegalese Students, pp. 915–18.

19. See Hatfield, Love and Sex?, pp. 106–34; Lee, *Colors of Love.*

20. See Averill and Boothroyd, Romantic Ideal, pp. 235–47; Hatfield, Love and Sex?, pp. 106–34; Hatfield and Rapson, Love and Intimacy, pp. 15–26; Hatfield et al., Passionate Love, pp. 35–51; Hendrick et al., Do Men and Women Love Differently?, pp. 177–95; Hendrick and Hendrick, Theory and Method of Love, pp. 392–402; Hendrick and Hendrick, Rose Colored Glasses, pp. 161–83; Hendrick and Hendrick, Love and Sexual Attitudes; pp. 281–97; Hendrick, Hendrick, and Adler, Romantic Relationships, pp. 980–88; Hong, Romantic Love, p. 922; Lester, Romantic Attitudes, p. 622; Peplau, Roles and Gender, pp. 220–64; Peplau and Gordon, Women and Men in Love, pp. 257–91.

21. See Faderman, *Surpassing the Love of Men;* Rothblum and Brehony, *Boston Marriages.*

22. See Kurdek, Follow-Up Study, pp. 39–59.

23. See Hatfield, Love and Sex?, pp. 106–34; Hatfield and Rapson, Love and Intimacy, pp. 15–26; Hendrick et al., Do Men and Women Love Differently?, pp. 177–95; Hendrick and Hendrick, Theory and Method of Love, pp. 392–402; Peplau, Roles and Gender, pp. 220–64; Peplau and Gordon, Women and Men in Love, pp. 257–91.

24. Ibid.

25. See Baily, Hendrick, and Hendrick, Love, Sexual Attitudes, and Self-Esteem, pp. 637–48; Coleman and Ganong, Love and Sex-Role Stereotypes, pp. 170–76; Sprecher and Metts, Romantic Beliefs Scale, pp. 387–411.

26. See Peplau, What Homosexuals Want, pp. 28–38; Peplau and Gordon, Women and Men in Love, pp. 257–91.

27. See Cochran and Peplau, Heterosexual Relationships, pp. 477–88; Peplau, What Homosexuals Want, pp. 28–38.

28. See Peplau, Homosexual Couples, pp. 3–7; Peplau, Lesbian and Gay Relationships, pp. 177–96.

29. See Kurdek and Schmitt, Partner Homogamy, pp. 212–32.

30. See Browning, Lesbian Clients, pp. 45–52; Elise, Lesbian Couples, pp. 305–10; Smalley, Lesbian Relationships, pp. 125–35.

31. See Peplau and Amaro, Lesbian Relationships, pp. 233–47; Peplau et al., Loving Women, pp. 7–27.

32. See Margolin, Prerogatives of Dating and Marriage, pp. 91–102; Peplau and Gordon, Women and Men in Love, pp. 257–91.

33. See Critelli, Myers, and Loos, Components of Love, pp. 354–68.

34. See Howard, Blumstein, and Schwartz, Sex, Power, and Influence Tactics, pp. 102–09; Peplau, Lesbian and Gay Relationships, pp. 177–96; Peplau and Cochran, Relationship Perspective, pp. 321–49.

35. See Peplau and Campbell, Power in Dating and Marriage, pp. 121–37.

36. See Caldwell and Peplau, Power in Lesbian Relationships, pp. 587–99; Kurdek, Follow-Up Study, pp. 39–59; Peplau, Homosexual Couples, pp. 3–7; Peplau and Amaro, Lesbian Relationships, pp. 233–47; Peplau and Cochran, Relationship Perspective, pp. 321–49; Peplau, Padesky, and Hamilton, Satisfaction in Lesbian Relationships, pp. 23–35.

37. See Cochran and Peplau, Heterosexual Relationships, pp. 477–88; Kurdek, Gay and Lesbian Cohabiting Couples, pp. 93–118; Peplau, Homosexual Love Relationships; Peplau and Amaro, Lesbian Relationships, pp. 233–47; Peplau, Padesky, and Hamilton, Satisfaction in Lesbian Relationships, pp. 23–35.

38. See Buhrke and Fuqua, Supportive Relationships, pp. 339–52; Hatfield and Rapson, Love and Intimacy, pp. 15–26; Hendrick, Hendrick, and Adler, Romantic Relationships, pp. 980–88; McAdams et al., Sex and the TAT, pp. 397–409; Peplau, Homosexual Love Relationships; Peplau, What Homosexuals Want, pp. 28–38; Peplau, Roles and Gender, pp. 220–64; Peplau and Gordon, Women and Men in Love, pp. 257–91.

39. See Dosser, Balswick, and Halverson, Male Inexpressiveness, pp. 241–58.

40. See Owen, Verbal Expression of Love, pp. 15–24.

41. Ibid., p. 20.

42. See LaFrance, Emotional Intensity; Shields, Gender and Emotion.

43. See Mark and Alper, Intimacy Motivation, pp. 81–88.

44. See Rusbult, Zembrodt, and Iwaniszek, Dissatisfaction in Close Relationships, pp. 1–20.

45. See Critelli, Myers, and Loos, Components of Love, pp. 354–68.

46. See Hendrick and Hendrick, Rose Colored Glasses, pp. 161–83; Hendrick and Hendrick, Love and Sexual Attitudes, pp. 281–97; Hendrick and Hendrick, Sexual Attitudes, pp. 502–26; Hendrick, Hendrick, and Slapion-Foote, Sexual Attitudes, pp. 1630–42; Margolin, Prerogatives of Dating and Marriage, pp. 91–102; Roscoe, Kennedy, and Pope, Adolescents' Views, pp. 511–15; Sternberg, *Triangle of Love*.

47. See Blumstein and Schwartz, *American Couples*; Faderman, *Surpassing the Love of Men*; Kurdek, Gay and Lesbian Cohabiting Couples, pp. 93–118; Peplau, Homosexual Love Relationships; Peplau, What Homosexuals Want, pp. 28–38; Peplau, Lesbian and Gay Relationships, pp. 177–96; Peplau and Cochran, Relationship Perspective, pp. 321–49; Peplau, Cochran, and Mays, Black Lesbians.

48. See White, Jealousy and Partner's Perceived Motives, pp. 24–30.

49. See Buunk and Hupka, Cross-Cultural Differences, pp. 12–22.

50. See Daly, Wilson, and Weghorst, Male Sexual Jealousy, pp. 11–27.

51. See Buunk, Anticipated Sexual Jealousy, pp. 310–16; Greenberg and Pyszczynski, Proneness to Romantic Jealousy, pp. 468–79; Weiss and Slosnerick, Extramarital Involvements, pp. 349–58.

52. See Buss, Vigilance to Violence, pp. 291–317; Salovey and Rodin, Envy and Jealousy, pp. 221–46.

53. See Daly, Wilson, and Weghorst, Male Sexual Jealousy, pp. 11–27.

54. See Buunk and Hupka, Cross-Cultural Differences, pp. 12–22; Hansen, Dating Jealousy, pp. 713–21; Hansen, Marital Jealousy, pp. 262–68; White, Correlates of Romantic Jealousy, pp. 129–47; White, Jealousy and Partner's Perceived Motives, pp. 24–30; White, Jealousy Scales, pp. 115–30; White and Mullen, *Jealousy*.

55. Buss, Vigilance to Violence, pp. 291–317; Daly, Wilson, and Weghorst, Male Sexual Jealousy, pp. 11–27; McCormick and Solomon, Jealousy, pp. 25–29; White and Mullen, *Jealousy*.

56. See Daly, Wilson, and Weghorst, Male Sexual Jealousy, pp. 11–27.

57. See Salovey and Rodin, Envy and Jealousy, pp. 221–46.

58. See Daly, Wilson, and Weghorst, Male Sexual Jealousy, pp. 11–27.

59. Ibid., p. 13.

60. See Peplau and Gordon, Women and Men in Love, pp. 257–91.

61. See Testa, Kinder, and Ironson, Heterosexual Bias, pp. 163–72.

62. See Duffy and Rusbult, Homosexual and Heterosexual Relationships, pp. 1–23; Peplau, What Homosexuals Want, pp. 28–38; Peplau, Lesbian and Gay Relationships, pp. 177–96; Peplau and Amaro, Lesbian Relationships, pp. 233–47; Peplau and Cochran, Relationship Perspective, pp. 321–49.

63. See Peplau, Padesky, and Hamilton, Satisfaction in Lesbian Relationships, pp. 23–35.

64. See ibid. and Peplau and Amaro, Lesbian Relationships, pp. 233–47.

65. See Peplau, Cochran, and Mays, Black Lesbians.

66. See Duffy and Rusbult, Homosexual and Heterosexual Relationships, pp. 1–23; Hendrick and Hendrick, Rose Colored Glasses, pp. 161–83.

67. Kurdek and Schmitt, Relationship Quality and Relationship Beliefs, pp. 365–70.

# ❧ 4 ❧

# Lesbian and Bisexual Identities

Until the twentieth century women felt free to have romantic friendships with each other.[1] Nobody thought twice about two women who caressed in public, slept together, exchanged passionate letters, liked to spend all their time together, and vowed everlasting love. In previous centuries, life-long, female romantic friendships enabled wives to tolerate bad, arranged marriages. Survey research in the 1920s found high rates of affectional and sexual experience with other women common among the graduates of American women's colleges.[2] Until the 1920s, passionate female friendships occurred for many reasons. Women and men interacted little; women were viewed as too childish or intellectually limited to be suitable for friendships with men. Since "respectable" middle- and upper-class women used to be entirely dependent upon their husbands economically and were stereotyped as disinterested in sex, their romantic friendships did not threaten the patriarchy.

Because women's sexuality is socially constructed by men, contemporary sexologists are inclined to demand genital proof of sexual orientation. Before labeling her as bisexual or lesbian, most sex researchers expect a woman to have had genital relationships with other women. Feminists have pointed out some serious shortcomings with this assumption. Female bisexuality and lesbianism may be more a matter of loving other women than of achieving orgasm through genital contact. It is entirely possible that many passionate female friendships enjoyed by our foremothers excluded the mutual genital stimulation that people in our time expect before categorizing a relationship as sexual or erotic.[3] Even today, some contemporary lesbians have "Boston marriages," romantic partnerships which are no longer genitally active or which had never been consummated in the first place.[4] The absence of genital juxtaposition hardly drains a relationship of passion or importance.

Why are female romantic friendships no longer acceptable? Two circumstances of enormous historical importance should be considered: men's negative reactions to feminism and the contributions of early sexologists. During the first wave of feminism (1880–1914), spinsterhood was common among the early feminists who saw marriage as oppressive and were able to support themselves through outside employment. Men began to label women's romantic friendships as sexually perverse only after feminists challenged the institution of marriage and competed with men economically.[5] To protect patriarchal interests, men in the emerging discipline of sexology concluded that women were no longer oblivious to their genitals and labeled female romantic friendships as sick or sexually perverse. The "normal" sexual choice was supposed to be heterosexuality, a rejection of the feminist movement, and a return to the male dominance of hearth and home. By teaching men sexual techniques to increase female sexual pleasure, the early sexologists endeavored to preserve the institution of marriage and eliminate women's discontent. Lesbianism and feminism were equated with moral failure; women were taught to be afraid and ashamed of their attraction to other women.[6] Suspected lesbians and bisexual women were diagnosed as mentally ill, discriminated against, threatened with the loss of their children, verbally abused, and targeted for violent hate crimes.[7] Until late in the twentieth century, working-class lesbian bars and clubs were raided by police vice squads.

Lesbian and male homosexual sexual activity remains illegal in about half of the United States. Although these laws are rarely enforced, many states invoke severe criminal penalties for any sexual act other than the placement of the penis inside the vagina in wedlock.[8] The U.S. Civil Rights Act of 1964 forbids employment discrimination on the basis of sex and race but fails to protect the rights of lesbians and gay men to hold jobs. Unless they remain closeted and celibate, lesbians and bisexual women are still discharged from the United States military regardless of how well they have served their country. Antigay prejudice is so prevalent in the educational system that women are routinely fired from their jobs as teachers simply because they are suspected of being lesbians. Married couples enjoy many legal and economic benefits related to insurance, inheritance, and property rights that are denied categorically to cohabiting, loving, long-term lesbian couples. Although loving other women can be personally and politically fulfilling, it is often costly economically, socially, and legally.

## SOCIAL AND HISTORICAL CHANGES

Until 1973, homosexuality was considered a form of mental illness.[9] Lesbians and gay men who sought the services of mental health professionals were likely to be diagnosed as emotionally disturbed based only on their sexual orientation. Pointing out that research failed to find any evidence that homosexuals as a group were more poorly adjusted than heterosexuals, lesbian and gay activists succeeded in removing homosexuality from the list of mental disorders published by the American Psychiatric Association. Since the lesbian and gay rights movement gained momentum in the 1960s and 1970s, there have been other milestones. Increasing numbers of lesbians have won child-custody cases. A number of communities have enacted civil rights legislation to protect the housing, economic, and political rights of their lesbian and gay citizens. In 1990, Congress removed prohibitions against lesbians and gay men who immigrated to or visited the United States. That same year, the U.S. Congress passed an act that recognized that homosexuals, like members of ethnic minorities, require protection from hate-motivated crimes.

Meanwhile, lesbian and bisexual women have played a major role in the second wave of feminism, a social movement which originated in the middle of the twentieth century.[10] At first, heterosexual, bisexual, and lesbian feminists worked together to expand women's economic, political, and reproductive rights. Then, just as they had done in the nineteenth and early twentieth centuries, opponents of feminism attacked the movement for being lesbian. The attack worked. Openly lesbian and bisexual women were purged from more conservative feminist organizations and accused of being emotionally disturbed. During the 1970s, American feminists divided into two separate movements, some identifying with predominantly heterosexual, mainstream organizations and others organizing lesbian separatist groups.[11] A movement divided cannot be an effective force for social change. And so, there was an attempt to heal the wounds and get lesbian and heterosexual feminists to work together again. These efforts were largely successful. Today, mainstream feminist organizations like the National Organization for Women have added lesbian and gay rights to their political agenda.

As they attempted to hasten the reconciliation of various factions within the women's movement, some Radical Feminists desexualized lesbianism, making it less threatening to heterosexual women. Instead of being an erotic orientation, lesbianism became a political choice, the ultimate expression of the conviction that women should be independent of men and male-dominated institutions. Rhetorically, lesbianism was made more acceptable because it promoted "woman-bonding" and freed women from the patriarchal nuclear family. The debate as to the extent to which lesbianism is a sexual orientation or a political stance continues. Adding fuel to the fire, bisexual activists have formed their own social movement accusing both lesbian feminists and the heterosexual community of oppression.[12] Meanwhile, Radical Feminists have mixed reactions to "gay affirmative" sex research.[13] Since the 1970s, the scientific paradigm of sexology has shifted from viewing homosexuality as psychopathology to perceiving it as a legitimate, sexual lifestyle. This Liberal Feminist and humanistic model equates lesbianism with a mentally healthy alternative lifestyle, a way of loving, and a means for achieving sexual fulfillment. Some Radical Feminists distrust the new liberal sexology because it ignores the revolutionary nature of lesbian feminist politics. For these women, lesbianism is not just a private sexual choice; it is a political stand taken against compulsory heterosexuality and the patriarchal oppression of women.

## LESBIANS AND BISEXUAL WOMEN DEFINE THEMSELVES

Influenced by a patriarchal model of human sexuality that equates sex with genital juxtapositions, traditional sexologists argue that genital behavior is the key to sexual orientation.[14] According to these sex researchers and therapists, lesbians are women who experience genital relationships and orgasms largely or exclusively with other women. Consistent with this idea, traditional sexologists maintain that bisexual women have genital relationships and orgasms with equal numbers of women and men whereas heterosexual women limit their genital relationships and orgasms to predominantly male partners. Influenced by this point of view, some women define their relationships with other women as "platonic," regardless of duration or emotional intensity, when no genital sex takes place and "lesbian" when they and their partner bring one another to orgasm just once. Ironically, nobody expects genital proof of heterosexual romance. Heterosexual women frequently see themselves as romantically or sexually involved with men even if genital sex has not occurred. It is misleading to focus on genital sexual expression as the distinguishing feature of lesbian or bisexual identity. Other facets of a relationship, including love, communication, commitment, attitudes toward a partner, mutual activities, and shared ideology, may be equally or more important.

Most lesbians and bisexual women define themselves and their close relationships in terms of emotional bonds, not sexual behavior. Lesbian feminists and bisexual activists in particular argue that a life centered on loving and relating to other women is the crucial variable for determining sexual orientation. However, lesbians and bisexual women are not unique in their ability to feel passion for other women.[15] Many contemporary heterosexual women report instances in which they have been intensely preoccupied or emotionally involved with other women. In larger cities where the most visible women's community is dominated by lesbian feminists, bisexual and heterosexual feminists face a unique dilemma. How can they fit into a community of choice when their personal sexual orientation doesn't fit prevailing sexual politics?[16] Women defy easy categorization; they may feel and act "straight" but be woman-identified, emotionally and ideologically.

Women define themselves as lesbians in multiple ways and for many reasons.[17] The two clearest distinctions are based on the perception that lesbianism is inborn or the result of early socialization (in which case the woman identifies herself as a primary lesbian) or chosen in adulthood, often after considerable heterosexual experience (in which case the woman identifies herself as an elective lesbian). The *primary lesbian* describes herself as a born or life-long homosexual. Betty is just such a woman. When interviewed about her sexual orientation, Betty tells us,

I really can't understand these women who say that they chose to be lesbians. Lesbianism doesn't seem like a choice to me at all; I know I was born that way. To me, being a lesbian is about who you love and who you want to go to bed with, not feminist politics or personal preferences. I must say, I get a little nervous about these women who say they are political lesbians. I'd hate to make love to a woman who was doing it because lesbian sex is the politically correct thing to do!

Although many women, like Betty, view themselves as primary or life-long lesbians, almost all research linking homosexuality to heredity and brain structure has been done with gay men, not with women who love women.[18] In addition, scientific studies claiming to have found biological reasons for homosexuality are controversial.[19] Human sexuality is not entirely anchored in anatomy. To the best of our knowledge, sexual orientation is simultaneously influenced by biology, personal experience, culture, and historical forces, causal factors which are not separable. Many studies that conclude that sexual orientation is biologically determined are beset with methodological problems such as small and unrepresentative samples or unsystematic laboratory procedures; others don't distinguish between human and rat sexual behavior. In addition, gay and lesbian rights activists have criticized biologically essentialistic research for legitimizing the belief that there is something wrong with homosexuals, that being lesbian or gay is a genetic, anatomical, or hormonal deviation which medical science could and should prevent. Finally, critics have argued that even if a few people became more accepting of gay men and lesbians because sexual orientation appeared to be biologically caused and not a conscious choice to "sin," prejudice has little to do with the reasons for human differences.[20] For example, nobody would argue that genetics and family of origin largely determine whether or not a person will be African American, American Indian, Inuit, Hispanic, Jewish, or Asian. Nevertheless, racism and anti-Semitism are alive and well throughout the world. Attributing homosexuality to biology exclusively is unlikely to reduce antigay prejudice in any appreciable way.

In contrast with primary lesbians, *elective lesbians* believe that they have made a conscious choice in their sexual orientation.[21] Often, they have had histories of prior sexual involvement with both men and women. Feminist politics and humanistic ideals play a crucial role in lesbian identification. Anna is just such a woman. Here is what Anna has to say about her sexuality.

> When I started college, I continued going out with guys but something was missing. Sure, I could have orgasms with men, but I didn't like the way they tried to control me. Then I met Laura; I never had such a great relationship. After getting involved with Laura, I knew lesbianism was the right choice for me.

Why do women see themselves as lesbian or bisexual? Some see their sexual orientation as a rejection of male dominance, others as a personal decision or path to personal fulfillment. Other women regard sexual orientation as a manifestation of destiny or luck. Still others look at their sexual orientation as just one aspect of their multifaceted selves. Elise explains, "Certainly I'm a lesbian. But I am also a Republican, a stockbroker, an avid gardener, and a single mother. Don't pigeon-hole me!"

Celia Kitzinger's research suggests that five belief patterns account for most women's identification of themselves as lesbians or bisexuals.[22] Speaking in their own words, here is how women define themselves. Sylvia is a divorced mother of two. Before her early forties, she had sex only with men. After breaking up with her husband, she acknowledges,

> I was sick and tired of trying to please men. It was wonderful when I met Jan who was openly lesbian from the beginning of our friendship. We talked, we went out together, and she was great with my kids. Eventually, I fell in love and when we finally had sex, it was dynamite.

If I had known sex could be so good with a woman, I would never have spent so much time with men.

Sylvia elected to be a lesbian because she sees this lifestyle as more personally fulfilling and growthful than heterosexuality. Like many others, she believes that lesbianism has made her a more self-accepting woman. She cherishes her intimate connections with other women, both sexually and interpersonally. Although such women may have feminist convictions, personal fulfillment and not political convictions are central to their decision to become lesbians.

A second large group of women see themselves more as bisexuals than as lesbians. Because we live in a culture that dichotomizes people into two polarized groups, heterosexuals and homosexuals, both sexologists and ordinary citizens underestimate the number of bisexual persons in their midst.[23] Tina is just such a woman.

My parents think I'm a lesbian because I am involved with Karen. But, they forget that I have had some significant love relationships with men in the past. I'm neither lesbian nor heterosexual; I'm bisexual.

Remember Elise, the woman who described her lesbianism as just one aspect of her multifaceted personality? Elise is an excellent example of the large group of women who define their lesbianism as a personal sexual orientation and nothing more, just one part of their complete set of behaviors, aspirations, attitudes, and relationships. Where does this leave feminist politics? A number of women are elective lesbians because loving a woman is an expression of their feminist politics. As long as ours is a male-dominated culture, such women will probably refuse to have sexual relationships with men. Although many Radical Feminists are heterosexual and many others are lesbian and bisexual women who relate well to men, a few extremists are lesbian separatists like Katrina:

I don't sleep with men any more. How could I have sex with someone who sees me as a thing, not a person? Just look at how many women in our society have been sexually exploited or abused. I have some gay male acquaintances, but it is hard for me to relate to them. They aren't very different than straight men; they're less political and more interested in sex and material things than the lesbians I know. If my lover and I didn't have sex for over a month, it wouldn't be a big deal. You'd never find two gay men who felt that way!

Despite greater toleration of homosexuality, a few women who identify themselves as lesbians are far from self-accepting. Coming from unsupportive or even abusive families and communities, some lesbians have internalized antigay prejudice, feeling ashamed of their sexuality and inability to conform to the heterosexual norm. Thanks to feminism and the lesbian and gay rights movement, relatively few lesbians believe that their sexual orientation is demonstrative proof of personal shortcoming.

## BISEXUAL WOMEN SPEAK OUT

There is nothing rare about bisexuality.[24] Yet, very little is known about bisexual women and men. Anywhere from 15 to 35 percent of the female population may be bisexual. Nearly half the self-proclaimed lesbians studied by investigators at the Kinsey Institute have had sex with men recently. About one-third of adult white lesbians and nearly half of adult African-American lesbians have been married at some time in their lives, many bringing children from their heterosexual relationships into their new primary relationships with other women.[25] Three out of four typically lesbian women note that in one or more instances, they had been sexually aroused by a man, had erotic dreams about a man, or had sexual fantasies about men during masturbation. Even more remarkable, the majority of lesbians provide sexual histories which closely resemble those of heterosexual women.[26] Most describe themselves as heterosexual during childhood and adolescence. In their youth, most lesbians dated men and saw themselves as physically attractive to men. Although many lesbians had engaged in sexual experimentation with other girls when growing up, heterosexual experiments were even more customary.

A number of women who identified themselves as lesbians in adulthood had their first orgasm with a male partner. White lesbians were younger the first time that they had sexual intercourse with a man than their heterosexual peers. Women who eventually define themselves as lesbians have had more heterosexual experiences in their backgrounds than gay men.[27] The overwhelming majority of lesbians discover their sexual orientation in young or middle adulthood, in the context of a loving relationship with a devoted, same-sex friend after considerable heterosexual experience. Women's sexual orientation may be less biologically fixed (or more culturally influenced) than male sexual orientation. Among the descendents of Dutch slaves in Suriname, lesbianism is virtually unknown but many women practice "mati-ism," a West African form of bisexuality in which women are expected to bear children and have love affairs with both women and men.[28] In contrast, romantically involved North American black women, like their white counterparts, identify themselves exclusively as lesbians, not as bisexuals, even when one or both women used to be heterosexual.

For bisexuals, homosexuality and heterosexuality are not bipolar opposites.[29] Rather than being a dichotomy, sexual orientation may be a continuum, a broad set of possibilities for loving women and men. Bisexuals are oppressed first and foremost because they are an invisible minority. Told that they do not and cannot exist, they are ignored by sex researchers at the same time that they have been victims of ridicule and prejudice among heterosexuals and homosexuals alike. Many studies that purport to investigate homosexual persons in fact include sizeable numbers of bisexual individuals.[30] Homosexuality is believed to be so powerful that just having sex with a same-sex partner once is enough to convince some sexologists that an individual who is being studied must be a lesbian. Yet, mere participation in sexual activity with another woman is no proof that a woman sees herself as a lesbian or even as a bisexual.

Prejudiced heterosexuals falsely blame bisexuals for being members of a promiscuous group that is responsible for spreading the AIDS epidemic and other sexually transmitted diseases to the heterosexual population.[31] Prejudiced homosexuals describe bisexuals as immature persons, unable to decide whether to sleep with women or men. According to widely held but erroneous beliefs, bisexuals are destined to become unfaithful lovers who will destroy the hearts (and possibly the health) of their devoted lesbian, gay, or heterosexual partners. For obvious reasons, bisexual and even heterosexual women sometimes try to pass as lesbians when residing and interacting in the lesbian feminist community.[32] To avoid criticism for being a "fence-sitter," "cop out," or "closet case," they may keep their heterosexual relationships secret.

Bisexuals are individuals who refuse to allow the sex of a person determine whether or not they will fall in love or become sexually aroused.[33] As such, they threaten the monosexual orientation of both heterosexual-dominant society and homosexual subcultures alike. Like other disenfranchised groups such as African Americans, bisexual persons are the victims of several pejorative stereotypes. For example, bisexuals are accused of being oversexed, fickle, and unreliable. Although their sexual attractions may be fluid, this does not imply that bisexuals are unreliable and promiscuous! Some bisexual women have had multiple partners; many others are monogamous. In contrast with the cruel jokes made at their expense, the vast majority of bisexuals do not have the need to have male and female lovers concurrently to feel fulfilled. Bisexual women are not confused; they are not "unfinished" or "politically incorrect" lesbians. Plainly put, bisexual women exist in substantial numbers; many have become involved in the new bisexual rights movement. Bisexual women want nothing more or less than the rest of the population, the right to their sexuality and the right to be seen as whole persons who defy simple categorization.

## MULTICULTURAL AND SOCIAL CLASS ISSUES

If lesbians and bisexual women are invisible in our culture, those from ethnic minority, lower income, and rural groups are especially invisible. Disturbingly, many sexologists are not troubled by the fact that most research on lesbians has been conducted with samples limited to urban, white, Christian or nonreligious, middle-class, educated women. When cultural and regional background, religion, ethnicity, and social class are considered in studies of lesbians and gay men, there is the naive assumption that any and all group differences are worth reporting, regardless of why they might occur. It could safely be concluded that we know next to nothing about lesbians and bisexual women from nondominant groups. Feminists are well aware of the need to be sensitive to issues faced by women of different social classes, regional backgrounds, religious convictions, and ethnic groups. "Multiculturalism" and "women of color" have become the buzz words of our times. But, for all their liberal rhetoric, when feminists from privileged groups talk about lesbians from minority groups, they are more likely to promulgate myths than facts.

For the most part, majority-group feminists who tackle lesbian multiculturalism start off correctly by noting that ethnicity and social class are just as crucial to a woman's identity as is her sexual orientation.[34] Their next conclusion is equally sound. Because poor and minority lesbian and bisexual women belong to at least two, different, devalued groups, it is likely that they face more serious hardships and discrimination than their counterparts from the majority culture. So far so good. But then, feminist thinkers from the dominant group make their first mistake. Inasmuch as minority and low-income groups are held in contempt by the general public and oppressed economically and/or politically, it is assumed that heterosexuals from these same groups are particularly hostile to or resentful of lesbians and bisexual women in their ranks. Allegedly, antigay prejudice is especially pronounced in minority and low-income communities because such groups are believed to cherish traditional family roles and male supremacy more than the rest of us. But, this is not necessarily true. There is certainly no absence of patriarchal rigidity and discrimination against women in the majority culture.

There are two major problems with the belief that minority groups discriminate against lesbians and bisexual women more than the dominant group. First, there is little hard data to support this conclusion. Despite their supposed, extraordinary hostility to homosexuals, a number of studies suggest that Hispanics hold similar attitudes towards lesbians and gay men as does the general population and that blacks may be even more tolerant than whites.[35] A second fallacy is overgeneralization. There are substantial regional differences among minority populations. Native Americans are not one undifferentiated group but belong to numerous, distinct, Indian, and Inuit (Arctic peoples') tribal cultures. Asian Americans, Hispanics, and Jews come from multiple cultural and economic groups; they are far from homogeneous. African Americans are culturally dissimilar from black people whose families originated in the Caribbean. Many of the supposed differences between blacks and whites are more likely the result of poverty than ethnicity. Numerous so-called racial differences disappear when studies control for social class differences. Middle-class, African-American lesbians, for example, report many of the same sexual and relationship experiences that are described by middle-class, white lesbians.[36]

The obvious solution to cultural and social class bias is to listen to the voices of lesbians and bisexual women from ethnic and religious minority groups, to pay attention to the opinions of lesbians and bisexual women who grew up in lower- and working-class homes. This kind of enlightenment is beginning to take place in literary form. Recently, small presses have published several intriguing anthologies in which Latina, Caribbean, Asian, Pacific Rim, Native American, Jewish, and African-American lesbians speak out about their sexuality from their own experiences.[37] With eloquence, lesbian and bisexual women of color and from religious minority groups write about erotic experiences, political ideals, prejudice, hardships, and people who have touched their lives in their essays and poems. These books also contain insightful commentaries on discrimination against minority groups from inside the homosexual community. Like members of other minority groups, white and middle-class lesbian and bisexual women must contend with negative stereotypes, discrimination, and barriers to their full social participation. However, suffering does not always enhance empathy; prejudice against poor and minority lesbians exists in the lesbian and bisexual communities. Fortunately, women like Barbara Smith have broken through the chains of hatred and ethnocentricity.

> What I really feel is radical is trying to make coalitions with people who are different from you. I feel it is radical to be dealing with race and sex and class and sexual identity all at one time. . . . That is why Third World women are forming the leadership in the feminist movement because we are not one dimensional, one-issued in our po-

litical understanding. Just by virtue of our identities we certainly define race and usually define class as being fundamental issues. . . . The more wide-ranged your politics, the more potentially profound and transformative they are.[38]

## THE DEVELOPMENT OF LESBIAN AND BISEXUAL IDENTITY

As pointed out previously, most bisexual and lesbian women have had much the same early heterosexual dating and sexual experiences as "straight" women. Moreover, bisexual women and lesbians are no more likely to have been victims of male sexual aggression and exploitation than heterosexual women.[39] What, if anything, is unique about their life histories? Lesbians and bisexual women are more likely than heterosexual women to say that they had been dissatisfied with traditional sex roles while growing up and had experimented sexually with other girls.[40] Given that many heterosexual women engaged in sexual play with other girls while growing up, homosexual feelings appear to play a far more important role in predicting adult, lesbian, sexual orientation than does homosexual experience. Michael Storms has a developmental explanation for this.[41] Girls who develop sexual feelings early in life, before they and their friends are socializing with boys, will be more likely to eroticize and romanticize their relationships with girlfriends than later-maturing girls. Eventually, this early sexual maturation could contribute to a lesbian or bisexual identity. Jennifer's case is typical.

> I remember my first crush on another girl when I was about eleven. I wrote her a million love letters in my head but of course, I never sent them. I didn't want to be a "dyke" so I quietly passed as straight until the grand old age of 28 when I had my first, honest to goodness, lesbian sexual relationship.

Sexual activity with other women usually takes place for the first time months or years after women first suspect that they are lesbian or bisexual. However, most women gravitate towards the lesbian community, socializing largely with others who share their sexual orientation, soon after they first accept their lesbian feelings. There are no age limits on sexual identity formation. Living as heterosexuals for years, often maintaining traditional sex roles as wives, mothers, and even grandmothers, some women don't perceive themselves as lesbians or bisexuals until midlife or old age when they are widowed, divorced, or separated from their husbands.[42]

Other than the fact that they choose to focus their lives on women and not men, lesbians and bisexual women share many of the same life experiences as heterosexual women.[43] However, because they belong to two oppressed groups, women and homosexuals, their lives may be especially challenging. Adolescent lesbians are obliged to balance dual lives: their lives as young women in a male-dominated, adolescent subculture and their secret lives as lesbians.[44] They yearn to be accepted by adult lesbians at the same time their adolescent rebellion is directed at them and other adults. Carole's story provides us with insight into the lives of the youngest lesbians.

The first time I snuck into a lesbian bar, I was sixteen. My fake ID worked! But, once inside the bar, most of the women ignored me because they suspected I was underage; they called me a "baby dyke." Anyway, I really don't want to go out with older women. We don't like the same music, fashions, movies, or anything. I just want to meet other girls who feel like me. Why is it so hard to find lesbians my age?

As clarified in the last chapter, young women are taught to rely too much on romantic relationships to define themselves and experience personal happiness. Because of this, many depend completely on lovers for emotional support and validation. This is especially risky for the youngest lesbian and bisexual women. Unlikely to fully accept their sexual orientation, cut off from the larger lesbian community, lovers may be the only lesbians these women know. Therefore, when their romantic relationships fail, they may be left depressed and confused about their sexual orientation.[45] Early lesbian love relationships can provide the emotional security necessary for further development. Alternatively, such relationships can be constricting and may inhibit personal growth. Female love relationships of adolescence and early adulthood seem to be especially prone to the "fusion" or "merger" problems addressed in chapter 3.

Regardless of sexual orientation, adult development is enhanced by emotional maturity. Older lesbians and bisexual women often lead socially and personally rich lives.[46] They frequently report being in a satisfying, long-term relationship with another woman, having close and regular ties with family members, and participating in multiple social interactions with a supportive network of both homosexual and heterosexual friends. The respected elders in the lesbian community continue to be active in women's social, civic, and religious activities as long as health allows. Whether or not they have grandchildren or have survived their partners, they are likely to feel less lonely and isolated than older heterosexual women who interacted almost exclusively with immediate family members before their children left home and they were widowed or divorced.

## THE COMING OUT PROCESS

Lesbians and bisexuals may use any of three different strategies to manage their public image.[47] First, they can try to pass as heterosexual. Joan, for example, flirts with men everywhere and always brings a male "date" to corporate and family social events. Alternatively, they can confront heterosexuals with their lesbian identity. Ruth, who is openly lesbian at work, for instance, keeps a photograph of her female lover on her desk. A third coping strategy is lesbian separatism. Women may remain inside the lesbian community to feel protected from heterosexual and male hostility. Nancy, who manages a lesbian feminist bookstore and spends almost all her time interacting with other lesbian activists, exemplifies this coping strategy.

Because same-sex sexual relationships remain stigmatized, lesbianism or bisexuality are accepted only after someone has undertaken a long and sometimes painful, developmental process. Alternatively, homosexual feelings and behavior may never be integrated with identity. "Coming out is the process through which gay women and men recognize their sexual orientation and choose to integrate this knowledge into their personal and social lives."[48] The coming out process consists of five developmental stages, each of which is explained below.[49]

1. *Pre-Coming Out:* The individual is confused about her sexual identity. Although she suspects that she may be lesbian or bisexual, she is convinced that heterosexuality is superior. Suffering from internalized antigay prejudice, the woman is likely to be depressed or anxious. She does her best to "pass" as a heterosexual and is certain that others would despise her if she didn't.

2. *Coming Out:* No longer fighting her sexual orientation, the woman begins to tell other people that she is lesbian or bisexual. If loved ones reject her or she doesn't learn to be self-accepting, regardless of what others think, she risks returning to the "closet" of stage 1.

3. *Identity Acceptance and Exploration:* The woman explores affectionate and romantic relationships with other women more freely. Increasingly, she makes long-term, social contacts inside the lesbian community. Her identity as a lesbian or bisexual is now stable. A support system or chosen family of women friends may replace the role once assumed by a potentially less-accepting biological family.

4. *First Serious, Sexual Relationship:* Thanks to increased self-acceptance and support from other lesbian and bisexual women, the individual is ready for her first, serious, long-term sexual relationship with another woman. It is likely that she will choose to live with her lover.

5. *Integration:* The individual approaches self-actualization, taking pride in being a lesbian or bisexual woman. Increasingly less concerned about possible negative reactions from heterosexuals, her private and public identities are united. Viewing lesbianism or bisexuality as a sociopolitical stance, Radical Feminists maintain that women at this stage of development are likely to remain in touch with righteous anger at heterosexual and patriarchal oppression, possibly choosing the path of lesbian separatism in defiance.[50] Liberal Feminists, in contrast, believe that women who have integrated their lesbian and bisexual identities are able to give up anger and hurt, having the potential to relate just as well to heterosexuals and gay men as to other lesbians and bisexual women.[51]

Far from absolute, sequencing of the five stages of coming out can vary considerably. Stage 4, for instance, may precede stages 1 or 2 for those women who discover their lesbianism or bisexuality after (and not before) they fell in love with or had a significant sexual relationship with another woman. Married and cohabiting heterosexual women, for example, may not commence bisexual activity until they are in their thirties or forties, after first having genital relations with female partners while "swinging" with other "heterosexual" couples.[52] Encouraged by male partners, a number of former exclusively heterosexual women first taste the delights of making love to other women through the context of "swinging" or group recreational sex. Typically apolitical, typically with no prior history of bisexual fantasy or behavior, some of these women eventually define themselves as bisexuals, a number inspired further to join the women's movement. Although feminist ideology precedes sexual activity with other women for some individuals, the reverse may also occur. Sexual pleasure taken with multiple female partners precedes feminist identity for a substantial minority of former heterosexual swingers.

Fascinating as swingers are, they make up a very small subculture. The overwhelming majority of bisexual and lesbian women have sexual feelings for other women before they act upon them. Unlike a number of men who have their first male sexual contact before fully accepting their gay and bisexual orientation, most women have an intellectual understanding and emotional acceptance of lesbianism and bisexuality long before they first have genital sex with another woman.[53] Consistent with the traditional sexual scripts for women and men discussed in chapter 2, lesbian and bisexual women are more reluctant than their male counterparts to have genital relations before there is strong emotional attachment and commitment to the relationship.

## PSYCHOLOGICAL AND SOCIAL ADJUSTMENT

Since the 1970s, scientific and psychotherapeutic paradigms have shifted from attributing homosexuality to psychopathology to accepting the Liberal Feminist stance that lesbianism and bisexuality are mentally healthy, legitimate, alternative lifestyles.[54] Apart from their sexual orientations, lesbian and bisexual women fail to share any common characteristics and function just as well in their lives as heterosexual women.[55] Numerous studies refute the heterosexist assumption that homosexuality is caused by growing up in a dysfunctional family or that lesbians, gay men, and bisexuals suffer from emotional disturbance at higher rates than the rest of the population.[56] Lesbians, bisexuals, and gay men who have achieved an advanced stage of "coming out" may have higher self-esteem than most heterosexuals, exhibiting especially excellent psychological and social adjustment.

Since it is futile and oppressive to attempt to change sexual orientation, it makes sense for psychotherapists to help women function better as lesbians and bisexuals.[57] For instance, psychotherapy could address specific problems that women experience in loving relationships with other women such as becoming a stepparent to a partner's biological children or negotiating friendships with women outside the primary relationship. Some women seek therapy because they and their lover are mismatched in stages of coming out. This is why Morgan sought the services of a lesbian, feminist therapist.

> Tia seemed like the perfect partner at first. We could really talk about how we felt openly, and our sexual relationship was terrific. But then, it came time to integrate our relationship with the rest of our lives. She knows that my parents and brother accept my lesbianism. Yet, when I introduced her to them, she acted as if we were only casual friends. She refuses to allow me to meet her family. She has specifically forbid me to call her at work for any reason, and I am not allowed to socialize with her straight friends. I'm just not sure I can keep throwing myself into this relationship. I feel like Tia has placed a lead wall between us, separating me from the rest of her life.

Some Radical Feminists accuse psychotherapy of being a hopelessly, conservative, social institution with the less-than-laudable goal of helping lesbians adjust better to heterosexist hegemony and male dominance.[58] This is unfair. A truly effective feminist therapist can help women do more than make peace with a homohating culture. Through therapy, women can decide to become political activists, affirming their sense of self as women who love women by fighting against sexism, racism, and antigay prejudice.

## LESBIAN FEMINIST POLITICS

Lesbians and bisexual women overall are more politically liberal and more inclined to be active in the feminist and lesbian and gay rights movements than heterosexual women.[59] This does not prevent them from being sharply divided along political lines, however. The conflict between Radical and Liberal Feminists, discussed at length in chapter 1, is a significant source of contention in the lesbian community. Most lesbians prefer female over male partners for predominantly sexual and romantic reasons. In other words, they would rather sleep with women because women make them "hot" and men don't; they would rather share their lives with other women because women strike them as warmer, more empathic, more nurturing, and more lovable than men. "Political lesbians," in contrast, give ideological (not personal) reasons for loving women.[60] For them, being "a woman-identified woman" is more of a political statement than a sexual one. Political lesbians remove the eroticism from their sexual orientation.[61] By limiting intimate relationships to women only, they protest "compulsory heterosexuality" and male domination.

Frequently taking an extremist Radical Feminist position, political lesbians believe that they should devote their lives to the challenge of "heteroreality," the belief that women exist for men and in relationship to men only.[62] Highly critical of Liberal Feminist or "lifestyle" lesbians for placing too much emphasis on activities below the waist, political lesbians believe that the sexualization of women's bodies is dehumanizing, whether it is done by men or by other women. They complain that lesbian erotica and some lesbian sexual activities imitate the worst characteristics of heterosexual sex, the reduction of relationships to the dynamics of dominance and submission. In theory, political lesbians are more concerned with relating to women as whole human beings than making love, which they view as the moral equivalent of connecting only with another person's genitals. Political lesbians sometimes see Liberal Feminist lesbians as ideological enemies.[63] By stressing similarities between lesbians and heterosexual women, by focusing on lesbianism as little more than an alternative sexual lifestyle, liberal lesbians are charged with presenting an assimilationist, apolitical point of view. Political lesbians or extremist Radical Feminists, in comparison, think that lesbianism should be threatening to male heterosexuals because it challenges the patriarchy. In their counterattack, Liberal Feminists criticize Radical Feminists for extracting the sex out of lesbianism, speculating that their political justification of sexual orientation is simultaneously a reflection of their personal, sexual inhibitions and little more than a ruse to make lesbianism less sexually threatening to heterosexual feminists.[64] Liberal Feminists, unlike political lesbians, seek to expand female sexual turf.

## SEX ROLES AND EROTIC ROLES

Before the twentieth century, individual women cross-dressed to pass as men to improve their economic lot and status, to seek adventure, and to enjoy greater sexual freedom.[65] Mannish, tie-wearing lesbians had access to professional and personal opportunities that ordinary women were denied. Frankly presenting themselves as sexual actors, as women eager to take charge of sexual interactions with other women, mannish lesbians challenged the dominant culture's image of female, sexual passivity. By the beginning of the twentieth century, male sexologists convinced the general population that cross-dressing was symptomatic of emotional disturbance. To be well adjusted, they maintained, women should dress femininely, want sex only with men, and act like "ladies." This male sexological point of view was a direct attack on the sexual symbolism of the era's lesbian counterculture. Until the second wave of feminism in the 1960s and 1970s, two erotic roles prevailed in the lesbian community: the "butche" role (in which stereotypically masculine appearance and behavior conveyed a woman's interest and skill in making love to other women) versus the "femme" role (in which stereotypically feminine appearance and behavior communicated a woman's desire to be the sexually insatiable target of other lesbians' amorous moves).[66] Butche-femme roles were especially popular among working-class, urban lesbians, including lesbians of color, during the 1940s and 1950s.[67] Working-class butches and femmes were trailblazers. They dressed and acted as they pleased and built a women's community during a period in our history when most heterosexual women and middle-class lesbians led highly restricted lives. During the first half of the twentieth century, working-class butche lesbians supported themselves as skilled laborers when few women had the courage to seek work in the male-dominated, better paid occupations.

Probably nothing else about homosexuality disturbs heterosexuals more than the possibility of sexual role playing. One of our most cherished assumptions is that nobody plays a man better than a man and nobody takes on a feminine role better than a woman. But, the butche role is not a woman's vain attempt to act like a man. Butche and femme appearances do not necessarily convey economic or household roles.[68] A femme woman may earn a higher income than her butche lover, who in turn might be just as interested in creative sewing as in the more "masculine" chore of taking the car to the garage. Moreover, butche and femme roles have uniquely lesbian political and erotic significance. Butche lesbians, for instance, assume the duties of social critics in a heterosexual and male-dominant culture, rebelling against the limitations on dress, behavior, and power which confine most women's lives. They are the erotic actors who dare to be experts in the fine art of making love to another woman. Likewise, the femme role is not a cartoon-like imitation of the traditional female role in heterosexual relationships. Femme women are the ones who seduce butche lesbians; they are the women who take special delight in telling a partner how to arouse them more, in being made love to by another woman. There is nothing sexually passive about femme lesbians. Femme lesbians are younger than other types of lesbians the first time they have sex with another girl or woman; femme lesbians are more likely than butche lesbians to enter a partner's vagina during sex.

Because the patriarchy is hostile to lesbians, many contemporary women are ashamed of butche and femme roles. Since the second wave of feminism in the 1960s and 1970s, a number of women have come to believe that butche and femme roles are "politically incorrect." According to Liberal and Radical Feminists alike, intimate partners should have an egalitarian division of labor. No one partner should bear most of the responsibility for childcare, housework, errands, or outside earnings. Some Radical Feminists have applied these egalitarian standards to sex too. In politically correct sex, both partners should want sex just as much, initiate sex just as much, and have sex in such a manner that neither partner appears to dominate the interaction.

The cult of "androgyny" (a perfect mixture of the best of classically feminine and masculine traits) has taken hold among many lesbian, bisexual, and heterosexual feminists. The uniform is simple: an uncomplicated, short hair style, an athletic build, a T-shirt or flannel shirt, jeans or shorts, comfortable flat shoes or sandals, no makeup, no hose, no dresses, minimal jewelry, and no hair ornaments. The idealized behaviors of an androgynous woman are a bit more challenging to come up with. What is the androgynous woman supposed to be like? She should be warm but strong, independent but tremendously empathic and sensitive, and physically active but incredibly intellectual. Ideally, she is a sentimental soul with a no-nonsense practical side, a great mother and an equally great plumber and electrician. The androgynous woman is a feminist, of course. She is a skillful lover who is equally comfortable both in initiating sex and in being on the receiving end. She is someone who is just as competent in the world of paid employment as she is in assuming the responsibilities of a homemaker. As complete a person as anyone could be, the androgynous woman's personality includes all that is best of traditional male and female sex-role characteristics without any undesirable side effects (e.g., no male-typed aggression and competitiveness; no female-typed dependence and excitability).

No other type of intimate couple has taken androgyny and the new egalitarian norms for intimate relationships more seriously than lesbians. Although a few women are still willing to admit that they adhere to butche and femme roles in their personal lives, the overwhelming majority of today's lesbians embrace androgyny and egalitarianism wholeheartedly.[69] Who are the hold outs for butche and femme roles? The answer is lesbians who are outside of the dominant cultural group—poor and working-class women, women of color, older women, and the very youngest of lesbians (adolescents and young adults who use butche and femme roles to tell the world about their pride in so recently coming out as lesbians). Who conforms the most to the androgynous norm? The answer is white, middle- and upper-middle class, highly educated women. Since most sexologists obtain samples of convenience (read in people most like themselves in ethnicity, social class, and values), almost all studies since the 1970s find lesbians to be a highly androgynous population.

What does the future hold? Hopefully, women will give themselves the freedom to show their diversity, to express their individuality, their joy in loving women, in countless ways. In place of a dress code and rules for splitting housework, dividing economic responsibilities, and having sex, it would be desirable for women to see their intimate relationships with other women as safe places to explore all the consensual possibilities. Women need not limit relationships to the confines of androgyny or butche and femme roles. Preliminary research findings suggest that regardless of gender or sexual orientation, the best relationships include partners who are either highly feminine (very emotionally warm and responsive) or androgynous (skilled at solving both practical and interpersonal problems).[70] Since women and lesbians are more likely to have these characteristics than men, female couples may enjoy advantages over other types of couples. Irrespective of erotic roles, the happiest lesbians are those who feel empowered in their close relationships.[71]

## SEXUAL DESIRES, PLEASURES, AND PROBLEMS

No issue is the source of more controversy than that of lesbian sexuality. Sexologists and feminist theorists alike have suggested variously that compared to gay and/or heterosexual sexual interactions, lesbian genital sex is either more spiritual or more physical; unimportant or crucial; more monogamous or more adventurous; just as frequent or much less frequent; free of sexual coercion or susceptible to its own kind of coercion; and much better or much worse. Drawing conclusions from the contradictory findings and statements is a ticklish problem. On the one hand, political lesbians (typically orthodox Radical Feminists) maintain that genital sex gets in the way of true lesbianism. In addition to disputing the importance of genital juxtapositions, they speculate that lesbian sexuality is an ancient, spiritual aspect of all women's lives.[72] Some of these women conclude that their emotional and political comradery with other women plays a greater role in their experience of the erotic than does physical contact. Radical Feminist ideology is sometimes downright antipathetic with the ordinary person's conception of sexual behavior and feelings. In sharp contrast with this book, political lesbian Janice Raymond, argues,

> Can we so readily believe that sex is our salvation? Haven't we heard this line before—that what really counts is the quality of our sex lives, our orgasms? . . . What the libertarian position has succeeded in doing is re-sexualizing women, using feminist and lesbian liberation rhetoric to assert that sexuality is a radical impulse. But sexuality is no more radical than anything else. . . . It is ironic that the libertarians want to reassert the male-power forms of sexuality to empower women.[73]

Certainly, genital sex and orgasms are not the be-alls and end-alls of women's existence. But, Liberal Feminists have a point; sexual feelings and activity are significant in their own right. Traditional sex roles deny women their right to be sexual actors, ensuring that men get most or all of the sexual pleasure and that women are much more likely than men to be victims of sexual aggression. Sexuality itself has all too often been defined by and for men. It is possible to talk about women's sexuality, especially lesbian and bisexual sexuality, in an empowering way. Lesbians and bisexual women have a uniquely feminine, sexual vocabulary.[74] Their sexual argot (e.g., "clit" instead of "vagina" or "pussy"; "suck" instead of "blow job" and "eat"; "making love" instead of "fuck") demonstrates an awareness of what turns women on.

What straight women like best about sex is identical with what turns on lesbians and bisexual women, mainly oral sex followed in popularity by manual stimulation of the clitoris.[75] But, there is tremendous variation in the frequency with which the average female couple engages in and enjoys genital sex; sexual activity takes place anywhere from once a month or less to daily.[76] Several studies with predominantly young samples of lesbians and bisexuals in relatively new relationships suggest that they actively pursue genital interactions with primary and sometimes outside partners and are frequently orgasmic. On the other hand, several studies of more mature lesbians and bisexuals in long-term relationships suggest that the longer two women remain together, the more likely they will suffer from "bed death." Young bisexual and lesbian women report stronger and more frequent orgasms than do heterosexual women. In some studies, they describe themselves as having sex more times per week and with a greater number of partners than their female heterosexual counterparts. Research suggests that lesbian sexual activity is an especially dependable source of sexual pleasure.

Despite their lack of emphasis on genital relationships, lesbians do feel much better about their partners if they remain sexually active in a conventional, genital way. Lesbian, feminist therapists are sensitive to the sexual problems experienced by women who love women, some of which are shared with heterosexual women and others of which are unique to lesbian couples.[77] They point out that lesbian sexuality has been mythologized and ignored by too many sexologists. It is falsely assumed, for instance, that lesbians suffer from fewer sexual problems than do heterosexual women. One of the most destructive myths about lesbians is that women possess inborn or intuitive knowledge about how to please each other sexually. In fact, there are two major barriers to sexual pleasure for female couples: (1) being socialized as women and (2) internalized antigay prejudice. Like other women, bisexuals and lesbians have been taught to repress their sexual feelings at the same time that they learn that "nice" women don't initiate sex or tell partners how to please them. Even when they speak of lesbian pride, some women may still experience self-hatred. Internalized antigay prejudice can make lesbians ashamed of their sexual feelings and may also contribute to alcoholism and drug abuse. Substance abuse sometimes occurs among lesbians who medicate themselves for sexual anxiety. When these women join Alcoholics Anonymous or return to a drug-free existence, they may find that their sexual arousal has been impaired by sobriety. A third cause of sexual dysfunction among female couples is lesbian cultural mythology. The new women's erotica often presents lesbian sex as magical. Few women could live up to the "super dyke" standards propagated by lesbian romantic and erotic novels and magazines. No wonder so many women are anxious and depressed about sex!

Most lesbian and female bisexual couples who seek sexual therapy complain that one or both partners suffers from inhibited sexual desire. Once sexual relations have begun, however, the majority have little difficulty achieving orgasm. The problem is not so much a deficit in the physical ability to achieve pleasure as reluctance to have sex in the first place. Guilt, anxiety, and shame related to both female sex-role socialization and internalized antigay prejudice may play key roles in lesbians' arousal difficulties. A number of therapists believe that "merger" (or intense mutual dependence combined with a couple's refusal to voice anger or differences) causes "bed death" for some long-term couples. Feminist sex therapy for lesbians is addressed fully in chapter 7. For now, it is sufficient to conclude that women face both special problems and special advantages in their erotic and loving relationships with each other.

## NOTES

1. See Faderman, Love Between Women, pp. 23–42; Faderman, Romantic Friendship, pp. 26–31; Faderman, *Surpassing the Love of Men*.
2. See D'Emilio and Freedman, *Intimate Matters*.
3. See Faderman, Love Between Women, pp. 23–42; Faderman, Romantic Friendship, pp. 26–31; Faderman, *Surpassing the Love of Men*.
4. Rothblum, Telephone Interview; see Rothblum and Brehony, *Boston Marriages*.
5. See Faderman, Romantic Friendship, pp. 26–31; Kitzinger, *Lesbianism*.
6. See ibid. and D'Emilio and Freedman, *Intimate Matters*, pp. 948–55.
7. See Herek, Hate Crimes, pp. 948–55; Herek, Violence Against Lesbians and Gay Men; Kennedy and Davis, *Boots of Leather, Slippers of Gold*.
8. See Rivera, Homosexuality and the Law, pp. 323–36; Rubin, Thinking Sex, pp. 267–319.
9. See Falco, *Lesbian Clients*; Morin and Rothblum, Removing the Stigma, pp. 947–49.
10. See D'Emilio and Freedman, *Intimate Matters*; Echols, Taming of the Id, pp. 50–72; Kitzinger, *Lesbianism*.
11. See Blumfeld and Raymond, *Looking at Gay and Lesbian Life*, pp. 303–04.
12. See Hutchins and Kaahumanu, *Bisexual People*.
13. See Kitzinger, *Lesbianism*.
14. See Peplau and Cochran, Relationship Perspective, pp. 321–49.
15. See Loewenstein, Love Object Orientations, pp. 7–23.
16. See Silber, Negotiating Sexual Identity, pp. 131–40.

17. See Falco, *Lesbian Clients*; Kitzinger, *Lesbianism*; Unger and Crawford, *Women and Gender*.

18. See Paul, Resurgence of Biological Models, pp. 41–54.

19. See ibid. and De Cecco and Elia, Biological Essentialism and Social Constructionist Views, pp. 1–26; Rist, Are Homosexuals Born That Way?, pp. 424–29.

20. See Cooper, Queer Baiting, pp. 29–35; Rist, Are Homosexuals Born That Way?, pp. 424–29.

21. See Falco, *Lesbian Clients*; Kitzinger, *Lesbianism*; Unger and Crawford, *Women and Gender*.

22. See Kitzinger, *Lesbianism*.

23. See Hutchins and Kaahumanu, *Bisexual People*; Unger and Crawford, *Women and Gender*.

24. See Bressler and Lavender, Sexual Fulfillment, pp. 109–22; Dixon, Bisexual Activity, pp. 71–90; Hutchins and Kaahumanu, *Bisexual People*; MacDonald, Sexual Orientation, pp. 94–100.

25. See Bell and Weinberg, *Homosexualities*; Wyers, Lesbian and Gay Spouses, pp. 143–48.

26. See Bell, Weinberg, and Hammersmith, *Sexual Preference*.

27. See Dixon, Bisexual Activity, pp. 71–90; Henderson, Homosexuality, pp. 216–19.

28. See Wekker, Mati-ism and Black Lesbianism, pp. 145–58.

29. See Hutchins and Kaahumanu, *Bisexual People*.

30. See Bressler and Lavender, Sexual Fulfillment, pp. 109–22; Dixon, Bisexual Activity, pp. 71–90; Hutchins and Kaahumanu, *Bisexual People*; MacDonald, Sexual Orientation, pp. 94–100.

31. See Hutchins and Kaahumanu, *Bisexual People*.

32. See Silber, Negotiating Sexual Identity, pp. 131–40.

33. See Hutchins and Kaahumanu, *Bisexual People*.

34. See Falco, *Lesbian Clients*; Unger and Crawford, *Women and Gender*.

35. See Paul, Minority Status, pp. 351–69.

36. See Peplau, Cochran, and Mays, Black Lesbians.

37. See Kantrowitz, Radical Jew, pp. 264–87; Moraga and Anzaldua, *This Bridge Called My Back*; Smith, *Home Girls*.

38. Smith, *Home Girls*, pp. 126–27.

39. See Brannock and Chapman, Negative Sexual Experiences, pp. 105–09; Falco, *Lesbian Clients*.

40. See Bell, Weinberg, and Hammersmith, *Sexual Preference*.

41. See Storms, Erotic Orientation Development, pp. 340–53.

42. Berger, Gay and Lesbian Aging, pp. 57–62; Unger and Crawford, *Women and Gender*.

43. See Peplau, A Decade Review.

44. See Schneider, Growing Up Lesbian, pp. 111–30.

45. See Browning, Lesbian Clients, pp. 45–52.

46. See Berger, Gay and Lesbian Aging, pp. 57–62.

47. See Falco, *Lesbian Clients*.

48. Monteflores and Schultz, Coming Out, p. 60.

49. See Coleman, Coming Out, pp. 149–58; Falco, *Lesbian Clients;* Monteflores and Schultz, Coming Out, pp. 59–72.

50. See Kitzinger, *Lesbianism*.

51. See Falco, *Lesbian Clients*.

52. See Dixon, Bisexual Activity, pp. 71–90.

53. See Monteflores and Schultz, Coming Out, pp. 59–72.

54. See Garnets, Hancock, Cochran, Goodchilds, and Peplau, Psychotherapy with Lesbians and Gay Men, pp. 964–72; Kitzinger, *Lesbianism*.

55. See Gonsiorek, Testing on Homosexual Populations, pp. 71–79; Herek, Kimmel, Amaro, and Melton, Avoiding Heterosexist Bias, pp. 957–63.

56. See Coleman, Treatment of Homosexuality, pp. 81–85.

57. See Falco, *Lesbian Clients;* Ibid.

58. See Kitzinger, *Lesbianism*.

59. See Bell and Weinberg, *Homosexualities;* Caldwell and Peplau, Power in Lesbian Relationships, pp. 587–99.

60. See Falco, *Lesbian Clients*.

61. See Echols, Taming of the Id, pp. 50–72.

62. See Raymond, Putting the Politics Back, pp. 149–56.

63. See Kitzinger, *Lesbianism*.

64. See Echols, Taming of the Id, pp. 50–72.

65. See Bullough and Bullough, *Cross Dressing;* Newton, Mannish Lesbian, pp. 557–75.

66. See Loulan, *Lesbian Erotic Dance*.

67. See Kennedy and Davis, *Boots of Leather, Slippers of Gold*.

68. See Loulan, *Lesbian Erotic Dance*.

69. See Caldwell and Peplau, Power in Lesbian Relationships, pp. 587–99; Falco, *Lesbian Clients;* Hellwege, Perry, and Dobson, Gender Ideals, pp. 735–46; Kurdek, Schema and Psychological Adjustment, pp. 549–62; LaTorre and Wendenburg, Psychological Characteristics, pp. 87–97; Peplau, What Homosexuals Want, pp. 28–38; Peplau, Research on Homosexual Couples, pp. 3–7; Peplau, A Decade Review; Peplau, Lesbian and Gay Relationships, pp. 177–96; Peplau and Amaro, Lesbian Relationships, pp. 233–47; Schneider, Cohabiting Lesbian and Heterosexual Couples, pp. 234–39.

70. See Kurdek and Schmitt, Relationship Quality and Relationship Beliefs, pp. 365–70.

71. See Eldridge and Gilbert, Satisfaction in Lesbian Couples, pp. 43–62.

72. See Rich, Compulsory Heterosexuality, pp. 62–91.

73. Raymond, Putting the Politics Back, p. 152.

74. See Wells, Sexual Language Usage, pp. 127–43; Wells, Sexual Vocabularies, pp. 139–47.

75. See Bressler and Lavender, Sexual Fulfillment, pp. 109–22.

76. See ibid. and Bell and Weinberg, *Homosexualities;* Blumstein and Schwartz,

*American Couples;* Coleman, Hoon, and Hoon, Arousability and Sexual Satisfaction, pp. 58–73; Hall, Sex Therapy, pp. 137–56; Johnson, *Staying Power;* Kassoff, Nonmonogamy, pp. 167–82; Loulan, Sex Practices of 1566 Lesbians, pp. 221–34; Nichols, Inhibited Sexual Desire, pp. 49–66; Peplau, What Homosexuals Want, pp. 28–38; Peplau and Amaro, Lesbian Relationships, pp. 233–47; Peplau and Cochran, Relationship Perspective, pp. 321–49.

77. See Brown, Internalized Oppression, pp. 99–107; Falco, *Lesbian Clients;* Hall, Sex Therapy, pp. 137–56; Nichols, Inhibited Sexual Desire, pp. 49–66.

# ⊰ 5 ⊱

# Women Sex Trade Workers

Throughout history and in numerous cultures, women have been paid to be attractive or to provide men with sexual gratification. If prostitution is equated with providing men with sex in exchange for money, dinner, wine, gifts, or a lifetime job as a wife and mother, then many heterosexual women are prostitutes.[1] But, women are not so easily classified in the patriarchy. Those who limit sexual favors to one man only, husband or boyfriend, are classified as good women, respectable women, "Madonnas"; all others are bad. Lesbians are branded as unfeminine, hostile "dykes" because they refuse men's sexual advances. Heterosexual women who have multiple partners, promiscuous women according to their detractors, and female sex workers, women who exchange sexual services for money, are despised as "whores." The division of women into the categories, good and bad, is often hypocritical. An elite model who uses her seminude body to sell merchandise in magazine and television advertisements is admired and earns thousands of dollars daily.[2] Yet, if the same woman wore the same skimpy outfit in a pornographic film, she would not be as highly paid or respected.

Technically speaking, prostitution is the institutionalized marketplace for the sale of sex, and a prostitute is a person who engages in nonmarital sexual activity in exchange for money.[3] Prostitutes are distinguished from sexual slaves, a group also considered in this chapter, insofar as prostitutes, but not slaves, freely choose their vocation and prostitutes, unlike slaves, can keep a sizeable portion of their earnings. Since payment occurs immediately and services are scripted to be recreational, men who desire uncommitted, anonymous, sexual encounters find themselves especially attracted to prostitutes. However, many clients have long-term, regular relationships with prostitutes. Moreover, most prostitutes have a noncommercial lover, sometimes male and sometimes female, with whom they are deeply involved.

To the outsider, a prostitute is a *type* of person. But nobody else is defined by others solely in terms of vocation. The majority who are involved in prostitution view sex work as temporary. Often, women engage in prostitution part-time, supplementing income received from traditionally female, poorly paid employment to support themselves and their families.[4] Many former prostitutes marry, some meeting future husbands through contacts made as sex workers.[5] Despite the intentions of most sex workers to go "straight" or eventually leave "the life" of commercial sex, the stigma of the prostitute label remains oppressive. As Karen, a former prostitute now completing law school, explains:

> I met this wonderful man, Joe. Everything was great: sex, our communication, just being together. When I felt we were close enough, I explained that I had been a call girl and madam for a couple of years when I used to live in another city. I'm not ashamed of what I did. I earned a great deal of money, met interesting people, and felt like I was helping clients feel better about themselves, you know, sort of like a therapist. Well, anyway, Joe became vicious. He wouldn't allow me to meet his parents; he called me a "dirty whore" and cancelled our engagement. It hurt so much.

The prostitute/whore stigma does more than hurt women emotionally. It can also influence them to remain in sex work longer than they desire because once labeled as whores, women are denied alternative vocational opportunities.[6] Without resumes and references documenting involvement in "legitimate" employment during the period in which they had engaged in full time sex-work, for instance, women are unlikely to be hired for conventional jobs even when they exceed criteria for educational background and job-related experience. Vocational change is more difficult still for the great number of prostitute women who lack extensive formal education and conventional job histories. Historically speaking, vocational "rehabilitation" programs for sex workers have been the exception, rather than the rule. When prostitute women are offered vocational counseling, they are expected to assume poorly paid, traditionally female jobs. For example, when Japanese women gained the right to vote after World War II, many became activists in the antiprostitution movement.[7] Through their efforts, formerly legal brothels were closed and Japanese brothel workers gained access to social work and vocational services. But, women were not retrained for interesting, high-paying jobs. Instead, they were encouraged to either return to their rural villages or work as maids, shop workers, and factory hands. Predictably, many returned to sex work.

Prostitutes are typically women; their clients are typically men. Most prostitutes limit themselves to strictly conventional sexual behaviors such as sexual intercourse and manual or oral stimulation of a man's penis. Others help men act out cross-dressing, sadomasochistic, and other fantasies, charging a higher fee for sexual experiences that the men cannot or will not have with their wives and romantic partners.[8] Most men who rely on prostitutes are rather ordinary, middle-class, middle-aged, married men looking for sexual variety. However, it is also true that prostitutes service men, who as a result of physical deformity, emotional difficulties, or lack of attractiveness, would find it difficult to find a noncommercial sexual partner. Not all women who are labeled as whores provide orgasms in exchange for money. There are a variety of commercial sex careers including erotic modeling and entertainment that carry the stigma of prostitution. Moreover, a woman doesn't have to be a sex worker to be viewed as a whore. Historically and today, prejudiced men from dominant groups have despised poor women, women of color, immigrant women, and Jewish women as whores. How have feminists responded? Just as some lesbians and bisexual women have assumed ownership of the word "dyke," defining themselves joyously as women who love and respect women, Liberal Feminists have reclaimed the word "whore" for all women.[9] In the patriarchy, the stigma of the label "whore" has been used to divide women along race and class lines. Politicized and reclaimed by women, regardless of their vocation, the whore label affirms women's rights.

## THE HISTORY AND GEOPOLITICS OF PROSTITUTION AND SEXUAL SLAVERY

Prostitution and sexual slavery have been commonplace throughout history and around the world.[10] Both institutions thrive in rigidly patriarchal societies, especially during wars and difficult economic times. Women are most likely to be employed in sex work wherever female sexual expression is restricted and virginity is prized, wherever girls and women are considered property of their fathers or husbands, wherever poverty is extreme, and wherever there are few or only poorly paid, legitimate occupations open to women outside of marriage. There have always been many classes of prostitutes and considerable variation in the extent to which women exercised control over their working conditions and income. For women in prostitution, periods of relative tolerance have been offset by those of great repression. The lower women's overall social status has been in a given society, the more despised and mistreated prostitute women were, especially during epidemics of sexually transmitted disease. Throughout history, repressive regimes have forced prostitutes to dress in distinctive ways and confine themselves to specific, devalued districts of a town or rural community.[11] In medieval Paris, most prostitutes lived in the Clapier, a district so named for the slang term for gonorrhea. In Europe today, streetwalkers and brothel employees work on some of the same streets that prostitutes used centuries before. North American prostitution flourishes in the "tenderloin" or "combat zone" communities where sex workers first established themselves during the Industrial Revolution when a massive influx of impoverished women from rural areas and abroad came to major cities in search of work and found that only prostitution provided them with a living wage. Internationally, government policies and police activities force many prostitutes to live and work in specific communities. Almost always, the streets where visible prostitution is tolerated are located in the least desirable neighborhoods, slums and high-crime areas where working women are subjected to high rates of violence, robbery, and exploitation.

It is not prostitution itself but the appearance of prostitution that disturbs us.[12] Prestigious sex workers, courtesans in former times and call girls or escorts today, are tolerated in the most desirable communities if they service the rich and powerful with discretion. Lower socioeconomic status sex workers are seen as a social scourge, not so much for the work they do as for their public presence and clientele. Periodically, the public demands "street sweeps" during which women believed to be soliciting clients are arrested in ever-increasing numbers.

Instead of eradicating street prostitution as promised, frequent arrests result largely in the geographical displacement of sex workers. For example, French Canadian sexologist Robert Gemme studied the impact of Canadian Law C-49, which made it easier to arrest and fine women for solicitation and prohibited them from returning to traditional sectors frequented by streetwalkers following sentencing. Although Montreal police arrested 1,439 individuals for solicitation in 1992, prevalence of streetwalking remained the same as before passage of the law in 1985 when nobody was arrested. Since prostitutes were not allowed to return to their original strolls, they began to work in more residential communities, producing more problems for the city than before the law was passed. Predictably, crown prosecutors stopped restricting street prostitution in traditional sectors of Montreal but enforced solicitation laws more vigorously in the residential communities that had become the new sites of commercial sexual activity.

As Richard Symanski explains, the principal response of the patriarchy to prostitution is the geopolitical confinement of women to an "immoral landscape." Street prostitutes are harassed through arrests and incarceration. They are confined spatially and temporally, free to work in some areas but not others, able to engage in sex work only during hours when they will be least visible to the general public.

Prostitutes are especially likely to be marginalized if they come from poor and working-class, immigrant, and nonwhite families. There are historical precedents for this. In the late nineteenth and early twentieth centuries, European and North American middle-class leaders stereotyped the poor as hopelessly immoral, unintelligent, lustful, and animal-like.[13] They established "red light" districts in undesirable neighborhoods where prostitution, a major source of political graft, was concentrated and tolerated and outside of which it was punished. Without "sexual combat zones," the self-appointed protectors of middle-class morality reasoned that the lustful lower-class, immigrant, and nonwhite males would "ruin" their respectable daughters. Ironically, leaders of nineteenth and early twentieth-century middle-class society saw no contradiction in their horror of prostitution and female sexual promiscuity and their expectation that poor women, immigrant women, and women of color should engage in such despised activities. We have not outgrown class prejudices.[14] Streetwalkers are arrested when they work in "respectable" neighborhoods but are generally tolerated in aging, disorganized, minority communities.[15] By selectively enforcing laws prohibiting sexual solicitation, contemporary law enforcement officers reinforce the middle-class public's belief that poor women and women of color are inferior to white middle-class women and are responsible for prostitution and its associated social problems. Economic factors also drive street women to congregate in particular neighborhoods. Women work the streets where the "johns" expect to find them.

Legalization of prostitution, translated into state control, constricts the lives of sex workers to the breaking point.[16] Nevada is the only state in the United States that includes counties that permit legal prostitution. In legal brothels in Nevada, prostitutes are allowed outside for very limited hours. Police expect prior notice if a brothel is closed and information on the exact location of all women who typically work there. Frequently, women are not free to leave a brothel on Sunday and are excluded from bars, casinos, and residential communities. In some counties, prostitutes are not allowed to enjoy meals at local restaurants and are forbidden from starting even the most casual conversations with anyone on the street. The boyfriends and husbands of prostitutes, not just their pimps or business managers, are often restricted from living nearby. The number of women who may accompany a Nevada madam on an excursion to the nearby town may be strictly limited. Rules and regulations are frequently used to restrict a woman's proximity to her family, changes in her employment, and "out dates," temporary employment in another brothel. If a woman quits or is fired, she may be forced to leave her county within a fifteen-day to three-month period. Legal (registered) prostitutes are hardly better off in Germany and the Netherlands where they are obliged to pay taxes but are ineligible for unemployment compensation, national health insurance, and social security benefits. In countries like Germany, Ecuador, Austria, and Switzerland stigma discourages women from registering as legal prostitutes or organizing to improve working conditions.[17] And, registration and political organizing makes prostitutes increasingly susceptible to constant government surveillance. Where the state controls prostitution, rigid guidelines constrict how, where, and for whom sex workers can be employed. For example, women may be told that they are only free to work in government-supervised brothels. Given the fact that prison-like regulations are associated with legalized prostitution, it is no wonder that many women prefer to practice their profession on a free-lance basis, despite the risks of street crime, police harassment, arrest, and incarceration.

Prostitution is not a new issue for feminists. Over a century ago, women involved in the first wave of feminism made prostitution and sexual slavery a major issue in their political work. Today's feminists need to appreciate the historical basis for present-day movements to eliminate sexual slavery and give consensual sex workers greater control over their lives, economically and politically.

In eighteenth- and nineteenth-century Europe, military effectiveness was undermined by epidemics of syphilis and gonorrhea affecting large numbers of servicemen.[18] Then as now, prostitute women were blamed for the spread of sexually transmitted diseases to more highly valued citizens, soldiers, sailors, and "innocent" women and children. Military authorities inspired police departments to establish morals' divisions or vice squads which were given the authority to regulate and contain prostitution. In Great Britain, for example, Contagious Diseases Prevention Acts were passed in 1864, 1866, and 1869 which gave officials the right to inspect by force any woman believed to be a prostitute and detain her if she refused. If a woman was judged to be infected, she could be detained without benefit of a trial or hearing for six months. Typically, women accused of prostitution were picked up by male police officers and forced to endure brutal and unsanitary medical exams during which some women may have contracted infection from unsterilized instruments.

Officers forced those they detained to register as prostitutes after which the women were denied most civil rights. Registered prostitutes had to admit police officers to their dwellings for any reason (no search warrant was necessary) and were obliged to give police information about themselves and clients on demand. Once registered as prostitutes, it was difficult for women to remove their names from police lists and leave "the life." Hypocritically, some officers, working for morals' divisions, used their law enforcement powers to blackmail women into providing them with bribes or sexual services. The end result was the police harassment of any woman or girl who walked the streets at night. Needless to say, most of those who were detained were poor and working-class women who had to walk to jobs regardless of whether or not they engaged in commercial sex.

The male-dominated political establishment was unresponsive to the protests of poor and working-class women whom they devalued as whores or potential whores. This brought heroines from the first wave of feminism, typically married, economically privileged women, into the fray. The first confrontation between feminists and male officials who harassed women accused of prostitution in Great Britain took place under the leadership of Josephine Butler.[19] Butler, a "respectable" middle-class Victorian woman, organized the Ladies National Association to repeal the Contagious Diseases Prevention Acts. In her political work, Butler noted that any woman who ventured out of her home could be subjected to brutal vaginal exams at the whim of the police, that the acts were unfair to women, and that they discriminated against poor and working-class individuals. Thanks in large part to her efforts, the Contagious Diseases Prevention Acts were repealed. Butler went on to organize feminists concerned about prostitution and the sexual exploitation of women. Instrumental in curbing child prostitution in Victorian England, she also struggled against the international sex trade and other forms of sexual slavery.

Nineteenth-century feminists formed a coalition with politically reactionary and moralistic men to end the sexual trafficking in women and children. Unfortunately, coalition politics backfired; the initially feminist reform movement was co-opted. Eventually, leaders from the patriarchal Social Purity movement upstaged feminists, focusing their wrath not just on the institution of prostitution but on the women and girls who practiced it. To her credit, Butler left the antiprostitution movement in protest, but the damage was already done by the Purity crusaders. When the British Contagious Diseases Prevention Acts were finally repealed, prostitutes were treated worse than ever. Women became less free to enter prostitution casually or engage in part-time commercial sex. Female sex workers were forced to join a special, permanent class of prostitute outcasts subjected to police interference and demands for graft and "protection" money. Unfortunately, the dangers of forming a political coalition with moralistic, right-wing groups continued to be ignored by a number of early feminists. At the turn of the twentieth century, American feminist reformers united with religious zealots and political reactionaries against the alleged corruption of urban red light districts.[20] Hysteria about a wave of sexually transmitted diseases fueled their efforts. By the end of World War I, red light districts were destroyed and employees of the great majority of well-known American brothels were disbanded. Needless to say, prostitution was not abolished. Instead, women in prostitution were obliged to work underground. Sex work became more dangerous and, often, less profitable for women.

Thanks largely to the efforts of right-wing Purity crusaders, the sexual double standard was enforced on the bodies and minds of poor and working-class women.[21] Both the madonna/whore dichotomy and class distinctions were reinforced. In the late nineteenth and early twentieth centuries, sensationalistic stories in North American and European newspapers exaggerated the extent to which young, innocent girls from "good" white families were kidnapped, forced into sexual slavery, and sent abroad. In contrast, the mass media and officials of the day communicated nothing but contempt for the vast majority of prostitutes who lived and worked among them (immigrants and women of color, those who did not come from middle-class homes, and women who were not virgins before entering prostitution). Limited efforts to save these "fallen women" from themselves focused on prayer and hymn singing, not attractive vocational options. Although their coalition was well intended, early feminists who allied themselves with the male-dominated, right-wing Social Purity movement, contributed to the deteriorating life circumstances faced by women in prostitution.[22] Unfortunately, these early feminists (foremothers of some of today's Radical Feminists) never overcame their Victorian, religious, middle-class bias. "Fallen women" were seen, at best, as victims of male greed and brutality, never as individuals who might choose their vocation because it was the best economic alternative available to women in their social class. Because antiprostitution feminists saw good women as relatively asexual (or too pure to desire and enjoy sex), the virgin/whore dichotomy gained legitimacy. Then as now, some feminists ignored the possibility that sex work might be interesting and exciting (or at least not repulsive) for particular women.

Feminists who remained in the Social Purity movement lobbied to give police greater jurisdiction over poor, working-class women suspected of engaging in sex work. In their outrage against the evils of prostitution, Social

Purity feminists and religious zealots succeeded in ending politicians' toleration of prostitution by the end of World War I. Legal brothels were destroyed and prostitutes were dispersed from stabile homes in red light districts to the city at large where they were less likely to be self-employed or work for other women and more likely to be controlled by exploitative men including pimps, gangsters, slum landlords, unscrupulous club owners, and corrupt politicians.

## WHY WOMEN BECOME SEX WORKERS

Why do women engage in commercial sex? Experts' answers are deeply rooted in their political and academic biases. Conservative thinkers, clinicians, and criminologists generally think that women become prostitutes because something is wrong with them. According to many psychiatrists, psychologists, and social workers, girls and women enter or are unable to leave the sex trades as a result of having grown up in a dysfunctional family in which they were the likely childhood victim of mental, physical, and sexual abuse. Compared to peers who have never engaged in commercial sex, girls and women in prostitution are described as having had worse peer and family influences, greater individual psychopathology, and higher amounts of deviant or illegal behavior. Instead of viewing prostitution as symptomatic of mental illness or criminal deviance, both Radical and Liberal Feminists believe women enter sex work because they lack economic and political power. As long as most societies are dominated by men, they argue, female prostitution will flourish as the only or best way for unmarried women to survive economically.

From the 1920s through the 1950s, the male psychiatric establishment viewed prostitution as a form of sexual pathology that was unconsciously rooted in latent homosexual desire (prostitute women were seen as frustrated lesbians), hatred of men, and the desire women had to punish their mothers for emotional unavailability.[23] Typically, authoritarian psychiatrists saw no need to validate their theoretical speculations by sharing them with prostitute women who after all couldn't be conscious of their true motives. Unfortunately, many clinicians still base their understanding of prostitution solely on experiences with a small number of psychotherapy patients, a population unlikely to be high in either self-esteem or personal happiness regardless of vocational background. Even today, research purporting to prove that prostitutes suffer from more mental health problems than other women is often flawed by unexamined biases about the inherent sickness or deviance of sex work and questionable methodology. For example, studies that suggest that prostitutes are more likely than other women to be depressed, anxious, alienated, emotionally volatile, or engage in criminal activities and excessive use of alcohol and street drugs are often based on small and unrepresentative samples of girls and women (such as runaway juveniles, older women who remain in sex work long after it is profitable, institutionalized or incarcerated women, and women treated for sexually transmitted diseases at public clinics).[24] In fact, the psychological and social problems attributed to prostitutes are often faced by equally sexually active women who do not accept money for sex. At least one study found that the best paid prostitutes (call girls and middle-class brothel employees) were just as well adjusted as a control group matched for age and educational level who had never engaged in commercial sex. At least some symptoms attributed to prostitutes more than other women, for example, alienation and unusual experiences are probably the result of working in a stigmatized, illegal profession, not individual psychopathology.

Women who begin their careers in prostitution as young adults do not appear to be especially predisposed to emotional disturbance. However, a number of studies suggest that juvenile prostitutes enter "the life" in part because they grew up in dysfunctional, abusive families.[25] Many young prostitutes came from homes in which their parents were alcoholic, addicted to street drugs, neglectful, or cold, critical, and unloving. Very frequently, adolescent prostitutes were victims of verbal and physical child abuse. Although approximately 20 percent of the female population has experienced sexual abuse in childhood or adolescence, a much higher proportion of juvenile prostitutes (between 29 and 65 percent) are incest and child sexual abuse survivors. Nonetheless, juvenile prostitution cannot be explained by bad parenting and sexual abuse alone.[26] A large proportion of the general female population has been abused. Sexual and physical abuse seems to be related to prostitution, indirectly, not causally. Some young girls run away from home after being abused. They are taken advantage of by adult pimps because they are emotionally vulnerable and too young to get legitimate jobs, rent apartments, or apply for social services. In exchange for housing, food, clothing, what passes for affection, and in some cases drugs, the runaways and street girls become prostitutes. Economic survival, not psychopathology, may be the major factor in most decisions to enter prostitution. This is especially true in the developing world where many youngsters and women are left to fend for themselves or are sold as servants because their impoverished families can no longer support them.

In developed nations as in the rest of the world, the major reason for entering sex work is economic. Adolescent runaways could not survive on the streets without hustling for sex.[27] Poor women enter prostitution because it is the best paying or only job available.[28] Even women from privileged backgrounds can be attracted to sex work.[29] Temporary employment in prostitution or the pornography industry has enabled some middle-class women to recover from major debts incurred after family disruption or a dependent's serious illness. A woman I know was able to fulfill her dream of attending college full-time by supporting herself comfortably as a call girl. Typically, female-dominated professions like nursing, social work, and teaching command lower salaries and permit less autonomy than careers dominated by men.[30] One former nurse turned prostitute disclosed that she made more than ten times as much money and received much more gratitude when she digitally manipulated a man's penis than when in her former career, she completed a manual evacuation of a patient's stools.[31] Sex work, more than conventional work, enables women to earn a high income and control their working hours in order to spend more time with spouses, lovers, or children.

Radical Feminists have equated female prostitution with institutionalized misogyny and male aggression.[32] But, some prostitutes view their occupation positively. Many women say that the first time they felt powerful with men was when they "turned their first trick," demanded that the man pay for sex, or first went on stage or film as a sexual entertainer.[33] In contrast with the clinical interpretation that prostitutes are masochistic women who learned to devalue themselves as a result of prior sexual victimization, some prostitutes feel that accepting money for sex has been therapeutic. For women who were exploited or abused by men in the past, assuming a dominant role with a client and demanding to get paid for sexual services may feel affirming, not demeaning. Other women say that sex work is at times enjoyable, adventurous, and creative; they take pride in getting paid for what they do well. To their surprise, some women are physically aroused by commercial clients. Although sex with noncommercial lovers is described as more satisfying by most women, many sex workers say that they enjoy many aspects of sex on the job and achieve orgasms regularly with customers.[34] Finally, sex work may seem more interesting and less menial than conventional women's work, especially the types of jobs (such as cleaning or working in a sweatshop for less than minimum wage, low pay, and no benefits) which are available to women from oppressed groups.

To be sure, many women detest every minute they have been obliged to perform sexual services for money. But, other women, like Nell, feel affirmed by prostitution.

I figured out that by the time I was twenty, I had gone to bed with a hundred guys and never gotten paid for one of those tricks, right? Not one. I could have made a fortune when I was young, getting screwed by all those assholes. Now I think differently. . . . I don't sell myself short . . . I know my value, and I know my worth. I know what I can do with my body. . . . So it has been good for me to get that sense of possession, of worth about my body, being able to use it for something, knowing what I can do with it.[35]

## TYPES OF SEX WORK

Prostitutes specialize in the types of services they offer and vary greatly in status, income, and working conditions.[36] Women from dominant racial and ethnic groups, privileged social classes, and especially young, slender, and beautiful women command the highest fees and best working conditions. Because women of color, immigrants, older, and heavy-set women are discriminated against in North America and Europe, they are likely to receive lower pay for sex work and have limited employment opportunities. The streets are the great force of democracy in commercial sex; minimal job discrimination takes place where prostitution is most public.

Like the courtesans of historic times, call girls are the contemporary aristocrats of prostitution. Earning the highest fees, they typically see a small number of clients (who are often "regulars") through prior arrangement. Normally college-educated, white, well-mannered, tastefully dressed, and financially independent, call girls take pride in their technical skills. Brothel employees work in a wide variety of settings from clandestine bordellos situated in elegant, stately, private homes where clients are carefully screened prior to admittance, to giant government-owned and operated institutions in some countries, to the simple but tidy mobile-home encampments or "ranches" in Nevada where prostitution is legal, to the shabby, crowded, and unsanitary settings common in the developing world. Traditionally, women both lived and worked in the brothels. Today, the brothel may be no more than a place of business. Massage parlors operate wherever prostitution is illegal but nongenital sexual services are not. Male clients select the woman of their choice, pay for a standard massage, and move to a private room. What happens afterwards is up to management and the personal inclinations of the masseuse. In Japanese "soaplands," women wash and massage male clients, providing orgasms for an extra fee. Some prostitutes operate out of particular hotels or bars. To have the freedom to look for potential clients, they must bribe and make arrangements with a dizzying variety of middlemen from cab drivers who are a source of referrals to bartenders, bellhops, and hotel management staff. "Hospitality girls," women employed by night club owners to welcome male customers, are common in Asia and the Pacific Rim, especially near large U.S. military bases.[37] Earning a small commission for drinks purchased by men who find them attractive, hospitality girls have to put up with a great deal of sexual harassment. Because of low wages, debts to male managers, and high expenses, many hostesses resort to prostitution to survive economically.

No consideration of prostitution is complete without an analysis of military-sponsored rest and recreation (R & R) centers.[38] Throughout recorded history, invading armies had "camp followers." But, the modern military has actually invested heavily in the infrastructure of commercial sex. During World War II, the Japanese military captured, relocated, and forced many women from Korea and other conquered nations into sexual slavery. The tragic plight of these so-called comfort women has only recently received international attention. Although the modern U.S. military has not engaged in sexual slavery, it has played a major role in promoting institutionalized prostitution. Allegedly to control sexually transmitted disease and prevent the rape of civilians, the American military built, encouraged, and supervised massive R & R centers, employing Asian and Filipino women during and after World War II. At the height of the Vietnam War, there were approximately 400,000 prostitutes in Saigon alone. At one time, 30,000 women in the Philippines worked as prostitutes or "rented wives" for U.S. servicemen stationed at nearby bases. In Thailand, advertised by its government as the "Land of Smiles," sex tourism is a major business.

R & R centers continue to play a major role in the economies of Asian and Pacific island nations, employing thousands of poor women who are locked out of their country's male-dominated job market. In debt to club owners, these women find it difficult to leave sex work because local men expect to marry virgins. Called "little brown fucking machines powered with rice," by racist GIs, the women face many hardships and indignities.[39] Often, American fathers disown their mixed-race children, who ostracized by the "respectable," racially pure members of the local community, may have little choice but to follow their mothers into sex work. R & R centers perpetuate racism, sexism, and imperialism. In American military culture, sex with foreign prostitute women can be "the cap to the socialization process."[40] Supposedly, R & R centers are necessary for good GI morale. Through the male-bonding ritual of getting drunk and visiting prostitutes with military unit buddies, each man "becomes the 'fuckin-hey right' soldier ready to lay down his life for" unit and country.[41] Women are no longer humans but vessels to be filled in exchange for U.S. dollars. Purchase of a "three-holer," for example, enables a man to enter a woman orally, anally, and vaginally.[42] No wonder American military bases are unpopular in this region!

With the end of the cold war, large U.S. bases still exist, but there is a rollback in the number of servicemen stationed abroad. As economics and changing world politics lead to a major decrease in American military presence, communities housing old established R & R centers have tried to replace lost customers with new ones, male sex tourists from Europe, North America, and nearby Japan.[43] With the approval and encouragement of government officials in poor nations, men pay in advance for all travel, food, and entertainment costs. Sex partners, including women who are instructed to wash shirts and underwear for no extra charge, are part of the package. The commercial exploitation of Asian women would astonish most Western sex workers. For example, although a tourist may pay high fees for his sex tour, each woman providing sex might receive only a few dollars. Most profits go to male middlemen: club owners, tour operators, and guides.

The "mail-order bride" business is another loathsome variant of prostitution originating in developing nations. Capitalizing on racist stereotypes of the Asian woman as docile and obedient, male entrepreneurs market arranged marriages by mail to men from prosperous, industrialized nations. To buy a bride, all that is necessary is payment of a fee (almost all of which goes to the company), limited written correspondence exchanged with the woman, and reimbursement for her cost of passage. Given extreme poverty and lack of employment opportunities in their home countries, some women are willing to sell themselves to the highest bidder either as brides to men they have never met or as migratory sex workers who provide cut-rate services as visitors or illegal immigrants in affluent, industrialized nations. Japan, for example, is temporary home to numerous *Japayuki-san*, women from Latin America, the Philippines, Thailand, Taiwan, and South Korea, who work as hospitality girls and prostitutes at a much lower fee than Japanese women.[44] Recruited by unscrupulous male agents, the women are supplied with clothing, a plane ticket, a false passport, and a counterfeit work permit describing them as entertainers, the costs of which are eventually deducted from their pay.

Because the primary motivation for engaging in sex work is economic, poor and working-class women have always been tempted to become prostitutes, even though they had little access to the best and safest positions in the commercial sex trades. Throughout the world, at least since the days of ancient Rome, women with limited means have supported themselves as streetwalkers.[45] Streetwalkers solicit clients out of doors, typically doing a "stroll" by walking down a particular street with other women in a metropolitan neighborhood well known for the ready public availability of prostitutes.[46] In the United States, glamorous, sexy clothing, outrageous hair styles (or wigs), and extravagant makeup are characteristic of streetwalkers who must signal their availability for commercial sex efficiently to a quickly moving crowd of men. Although streetwalkers may provide a variety of sexual services, a number specialize in fellatio because "blow jobs" are quick, lucrative, and can be done nearly anywhere without removing clothing. Selling streamlined sex, streetwalkers rarely kiss or hug clients.[47] A relatively new variation of streetwalking occurs in truck stops and highway rest areas where "commercial beavers," who contact potential clients via CB radio, deliver services directly in drivers' cabs.[48]

All sex work, not just prostitution, carries the "whore stigma." The same culture that encourages women to be attractive and stimulate male sexual interest damns them for being paid to do just that. There are a variety of erotic entertainment jobs open to women, few of which pay as well as prostitution: erotic dancing, live pornography or peep shows, and acting roles in pornographic films.[49] To many women, these jobs appear to be more interesting and financially rewarding than the menial, traditional jobs they have held in the past. However, women in the sex industry realize and resent the fact that the male entrepreneurs they work for get the lion's share of profits. All too frequently, women are exploited by being sent into competition against each other. There is no job security and no fringe benefits.

Strippers, erotic dancers, and topless waitresses attract a large and diverse male clientele who are allowed to remain in an establishment as long as they purchase overpriced, alcoholic drinks. For economic reasons, burlesque queens, well-paid performers who turned the casting off of clothing into a woman's art form, have largely been replaced by poorly paid, amateur "table dancers" in Canada and the United States. Table dancers serve alcoholic drinks for commission and dance all night for tips which must be shared with management. Dancers and topless waitresses may be tightly regulated by club owners. In communities with especially active vice squads, women are fined or fired for dating or leaving the club with customers. In other cities, management looks the other way when women earn extra dollars for "dirty mixing," bringing men to orgasm in darkened corners of the house, if provided with a percentage of the women's profits. Reflecting the male dominance of the larger economy, most owners and managers of pornographic businesses and sex clubs are men.[50] The jobs available to women tend to be limited to that of clerk or sex worker. Women, many of whom are single mothers, must often work more than one part-time position to earn a living; health benefits, sick pay, and job security are virtually nonexistent. To correct inequities, some Liberal Feminists are attempting to organize unions for sex workers which push for better working conditions and higher pay. Feminist sex workers are also trying to raise capital to enable women to buy and manage their own businesses.

## SEXUAL SLAVERY AND JUVENILE PROSTITUTION

Sexual slavery has been around as long as prostitution, existing wherever and whenever a girl or woman is coerced into providing commercial sex.[51] The decision to sell sex simply because it is the best vocational alternative available should be distinguished from sexual slavery. In sexual slavery, but not prostitution, an individual is deceived into providing sexual services or is forced to do so as a result of threat and violence. The prostitute is a free agent in the sexual marketplace, the sexual slave is not. The prostitute profits from her vocation financially; the sexual slave cannot.

Until the end of the American Civil War in the nineteenth century, sexual slavery prevailed in the United States.[52] As soon as white men set foot on American soil, Native American women and white, female indentured servants were sexually exploited. No accounting of the evils of the African slave trade in the United States is complete without considering the repeated rape and sexual abuse of black women by white men. Some of the founding fathers purchased black women for their sexual use as did many other admired men of their day. Beautiful slave women who were genetically the product of white masters and enslaved black mothers were prized for their "white features" and sold as "fancy girls" for further sexual exploitation. Incest was commonplace in the Old South. According to historical records, one eighty-year-old white master succeeded in sexually abusing four generations of his female descendants: his daughter, granddaughter, great-granddaughter, and great-great-granddaughter. Feminist abolitionists who turned their attention to sexual slavery after the emancipation of slaves following the American Civil War focused their concern on young white girls who were tricked or coerced into commercial sex, sometimes shipped abroad for this purpose. Tragic as this situation was, the sexual slavery of women of Northern European descent was and continues to be far more unusual than the sexual slavery of women of color and women from developing nations.[53] North American railroads and Western expansion were built upon the flesh of Chinese women, sold by their impoverished parents as "brides." Although some of these young women were married off to Chinese-American laborers, many more were shipped to the United States as sexual slaves to satisfy the physical needs of exploited, male, Chinese railroad workers. Treated worse than beasts of burden, many Chinese women died in passage to the American West Coast. Once on shore, the survivors received no money for their sexual work and were whipped, branded, and tortured. Forced to have sex with multitudes of men in squalid conditions, the average Chinese brothel girl lived for only six years.

Today, sexual slavery is rare in developed countries but the horror story is far from over.[54] In impoverished nations, it is quite common for parents and other adults to sell girls into sexual slavery. Wherever massive poverty exists, wherever large numbers of women are illiterate, wherever refugees flee from shattered societies, wherever human rights are trampled, female sexual slavery thrives. Sold by parents or child labor brokers, picked up off the streets where millions of homeless, street children live without benefit of adult protection, large numbers of developing-world children are susceptible to commercial, sexual exploitation.[55] Disturbingly, the very core of national politics and the economy in some regions depends on sexual trafficking. Dictatorships and social upheaval are especially friendly to sexual slavery.[56] Where civilians are tortured routinely, girls and women are vulnerable to extensive sexual abuse from authorities. Moreover, authorities frequently have forced women, especially those from conquered groups, to provide sex to servicemen in times of war. In World War II, as I pointed out earlier, the Japanese military forced "comfort women" from Korea and other countries into brutal and involuntary sexual servitude. Throughout the world, refugee girls and women have been gang raped by soldiers and forced to use their bodies to purchase escape from repressive regimes. In the former Yugoslavia recently, Moslem girls and women have been repeatedly raped and impregnated by Christian Serb soldiers as part of military strategy.

Radical and Liberal Feminists generally disagree about voluntary prostitution but stand united in their opposition to sexual slavery. Together with activists in the prostitutes' rights movement, feminists—especially Radical Feminists have worked to abolish sexual slavery. Unfortunately, this problem is not taken seriously enough by the political and law enforcement establishment. Officials at INTERPOL, the International Criminal Police Organization, claim that relatively few women and girls have been forced into prostitution internationally through kidnapping, physical coercion, and trickery. However, Radical Feminist research suggests otherwise. Women and girls who flee political unrest, oppression, and violence are vulnerable to sexual exploitation and abuse at every step of their journey. Poor women from developing nations, including those who had never engaged in prostitution before, are recruited with the false promise of glamorous jobs abroad as models, secretaries, and cabaret stars. After the women leave their home countries, they are coerced or tricked into prostitution.[57] Marketplaces for women who may be shipped for commercial sexual exploitation elsewhere are believed to exist throughout the world.

Although the sexual slavery of adult women appears to be the exception rather than the rule in developed nations, juvenile prostitution remains widespread.[58] The child prostitution business is fed by runaways who could not otherwise survive economically. As clarified earlier, these girls may have been seasoned for further exploitation by the sexual abuse which took place in their own families. Since most girls are not coerced into sex work physically, juvenile prostitution in North America and Western Europe generally fails to satisfy the strictest definition of sexual slavery. However, the trafficking in young girls' bodies cannot be regarded as voluntary. The girls may believe that there is no other way to be free of their abusive, dysfunctional families. They have been recruited into prostitution by unscrupulous men, professional pimps, or members of motorcycle and street gangs they wished to join, who grab most of their profits. Along with "straight" Radical and Liberal Feminists, professional adult prostitutes are deeply opposed to juvenile prostitution. They recognize that hungry for affection and attention, juveniles are not free agents in the world of commercial sex. Unfortunately, the harsh realities of the juvenile justice system and teenage prostitutes' own histories of abuse in dysfunctional families create great barriers between the girls and those adults who would like to rescue them from sexual exploitation.

## SEX WORK AND LESBIANS

Clinicians have long stereotyped the majority of female sex workers as man-hating lesbians and bisexuals.[59] Why? Because psychiatrists, psychologists, and social workers reasoned either women involved in commercial sex were acting out their unconscious hatred of men or alternatively, the abuse they experienced from pimps and tricks as sex workers turned them off to men and on to women. Certainly, a number of women who work as strippers, erotic dancers, prostitutes, madams (managers of sex workers), and actresses in pornographic films are lesbians and bisexual women.[60] Unquestionably, some began sex work as women who preferred female lovers whereas others changed their sexual orientation afterwards. But, the reasons lesbians and bisexual women have for being involved in commercial sex are much the same as those of heterosexual women: good money, reasonable hours, and less tedium than traditional women's work. And, lesbian and bisexual women are no more likely than their heterosexual counterparts to hate having sex with male tricks. Nor are they less likely to take pride in their skills as sex workers. Anecdotal evidence suggests that the sexual orientation of sex trade workers resembles that of the larger population; most women are predominantly heterosexual, whereas a minority are bisexual or lesbian.

Lesbians and prostitutes share a common history.[61] Both groups have been stigmatized as outsiders and oppressed by male authorities. The successful prostitute, like the "mannish" lesbian, was a woman who had freed herself from the rigid controls placed upon most women's lives. During the early twentieth century, police officers from vice or morals' squads treated lesbians and prostitutes alike: both groups were harassed, arrested, and forced to undergo examinations for sexually transmitted diseases. The first lesbian bars were established in the "red light" districts that were home to most prostitutes. Because their rejection of stereotypically feminine dress and hairstyle prevented them from attaining many traditional female jobs, "butche" lesbians of the past were more inclined than their feminine-appearing counterparts to work as prostitutes, serving a largely male clientele. Prostitution, at least, was an occupation that allowed these women to act and dress as they pleased and have a measure of personal autonomy in their work. It is no accident that sex trade workers share the same street language as do lesbians and gay men. For all three groups, going "straight" means conforming to the sexual values of the conservative, heterosexual, dominant culture.

Although lesbian, feminist, political activists have been among the strongest supporters of prostitutes' rights, they have not always been well received by the predominantly heterosexual members of the commercial sex community. Homohatred is encouraged by male pimps who don't want "their ladies" to become independent or share profits with women they love.[62] Pimps manipulate streetwalkers who work for them into isolation by cultivating their jealousy and mistrust. Lesbian relationships worry pimps because most streetwalkers go through a period during which they reject all social and affectionate contact with men before leaving "the life" for good. Verbal abuse directed at lesbians serves the pimp's economic interests.

## RACE AND CLASS DIVISIONS

The best positions in the sex trades, along with the best pay and most favorable working conditions, have always gone to women from dominant groups.[63] White women, especially educated middle- and upper-middle-class women, are provided with the best opportunities to become call girls and escorts or to work indoors. In contrast, women of color, especially poor women, are expected to work outdoors and take on the most dangerous types of sex work. In the United States and Canada, for instance, white call girls enjoy a regular clientele and a relatively high degree of social acceptance. In contrast, black, Hispanic, Asian, and Native American women are relegated to the streets where they are most likely to encounter violent clients, be exploited by a male-dominated criminal element, and be on the receiving end of police harassment. Furthermore, streetwalkers more than other sex workers are seen as the "real hookers" who are detested by the passersby simply for appearing in public. Sex workers aren't immune from race and class prejudices. Call girls and women employed by escort services often see themselves as superior to streetwalkers, who unlike them, after all, didn't come from the "best" families.

When laws against prostitution are enforced, discrimination against poor women and women of color prevails.[64] Although only 10 to 20 percent of all prostitutes are streetwalkers, 90 percent of those arrested are street prostitutes. Women of color, especially black women, are much more likely than white women to get arrested or be sentenced to jail for soliciting. Poor women and minority women don't choose to be on the streets; they are obliged to be there because they are prevented from picking up clients in white-dominated establishments. In Las Vegas, Nevada, security staff at casinos and hotels make a practice of forcing black women "suspected" of being prostitutes to leave. Needless to say, many women they escort outside are probably guests, and there is no parallel effort to remove the white "showgirl" types who use these facilities to practice prostitution. In major U.S. cities, vice squad officers arrest women suspected of street prostitution, often black and Hispanic women, routinely and frequently.[65] In New York City, women arrested for this reason are strip searched for hidden contraband, a humiliating procedure which male prisoners do not undergo unless they are suspected of being violent felons. Held in crowded holding cells, the street women typically await arraignment for many hours. Their ordeal does not end in the courtroom where it is often "open season" on prostitutes. Courtroom personnel may make these women the subject of cruel jests; no group of prisoners is treated with less respect. Arrests or threatened arrests can take place at any place and time. Officers know the names and faces of professional streetwalkers well and do not always recognize whether or not the women are working.

## SEX WORKERS AS SCAPEGOATS

Wherever prostitution is against the law, female sex workers are much more likely to be arrested and jailed than male prostitutes, the men they work for (pimps), and their male clients.[66] Although men create the market for prostitution, women pay the price. Laws prohibiting solicitation and loitering force police officers and sex workers into a "cat and mouse" game. To satisfy quotas imposed by superiors, officers may be obliged to make frequent arrests of women accused of soliciting. In the United States, the "johns," are either asked to be witnesses against the prostitutes or are allowed to go free. In Canada, men are much more likely to be arrested for seeking the services of a female prostitute, but the law is still applied unequally. Women more than men become victims of the "victimless crime" of prostitution. Unfortunately, not all police officers behave in a professional and law-abiding manner. Some officers make illegal arrests, target prostitutes for extortion schemes, or abuse the women verbally, physically, or sexually. A few prostitutes are reluctant to carry an ample supply of condoms because in the past, police officers cut holes in their rubbers "as a joke" or confiscated them "for evidence."[67]

Although the vast majority of police officers do their best to treat those they investigate and arrest professionally, a misogynistic and sadistic minority present special dangers for women in prostitution.[68] Calling the women "bitches," some officers have been known to steal or dump streetwalkers' possessions into the gutter for their amusement. Others have forced women to participate in sadistic contests (such as having fifteen minutes or less to catch a "date" on the street to avoid arrest). Some officers have burned the hands of suspected prostitutes on the hoods of their car engines or piled so many women into a police car that they were obliged to sit on top of each other for a lengthy ride. Prostitutes have been raped or coerced into performing fellatio by officers who have a reputation for cruelty.

Even when a woman has been arrested fairly and legally, she is in a difficult situation.[69] Her cell is likely to be crowded and unsanitary. Typically, she is denied privacy and waits much longer than a male defendant to be seen by a judge. She is not likely to be granted an individual court appearance. Instead, she appears before the judge as part of a larger group of women, all charged with soliciting. Chances are, all women who appear before a particular judge will get the same sentence, regardless of circumstances. Judges' attitudes toward prostitutes, not the unique circumstances of a woman's arrest history, determine sentencing. Lenient judges release any and all prostitutes who stand before them for time served. Less tolerant ones sentence them to brief jail terms or fines that must be paid in one month's time. The hypocritical wheels of the system grind on; women are fined for being prostitutes by judges who realize full well that prostitution may be their only means for paying their fines.

The typical streetwalker who may be carrying a lot of cash is obliged to work in the poorest, most crime-ridden neighborhood, and lacks the sympathy of the general public. As a result, she is highly vulnerable to violence from street thugs and male "tricks."[70] An estimated 35 percent of streetwalkers have been physically abused on the job and between 30 and 70 percent have been raped repeatedly while prostituting.[71] In a study of 200 girls and women who had been involved in prostitution, one in four who had been raped on the job mentioned that their attacker used images from violent pornography as a script for conducting the rape.[72] While beating and raping the women, some men discussed pornographic images that they had seen. When victims told perpetrators that they were hookers and would turn a free trick if the aggression ceased, the men's brutality increased. Even in the case of violent rapes, prostitutes are reluctant to report the crime to authorities because they fear, quite understandably, that they will not be taken seriously.[73] Prostitutes, especially streetwalkers, are exceptionally vulnerable to murder, being the primary targets of misogynistic serial killers.[74] Tragically but predictably, their lives are regarded as having little value, especially when victims are poor or are women of color. As a result, police and reporters often fail to investigate suspected serial killings thoroughly until one or more of the murdered women is "innocent" or untainted, someone who was never known to engage in sex work.

Prostitutes are scapegoated in multiple ways. Encouraged by misinformation, the general public stereotypes most sex workers as either alcoholics or as heroin and crack abusers. Research, however, is inconclusive as to the proportion of prostitutes who are addicted to drugs or alcohol.[75] Many women in prostitution consider it unprofessional to get "high" when working and criticize those who do. In sharp contrast with the tabloid stereotype of a pimp who purposely gets his prostitutes hooked on drugs, many pimps refuse to work with women who have substance abuse problems for sensible economic reasons. Costly drug habits decrease profits; an alcoholic or drug-addicted woman will be unable to turn as many tricks as a drug-free woman and is more vulnerable to frequent arrests.

Throughout history, prostitutes have been held responsible for various epidemics of sexually transmitted diseases (STDs). Well into the twentieth century in Western nations and in the developing world today, prostitutes have been subjected to "sanitary policing" abuses, during which they were rounded up, jailed, and forcibly committed to prison hospitals whenever the public was alarmed about an ongoing epidemic.[76] There is anecdotal evidence that military or police death squads in some countries today murder prostitutes who are viewed as infected. Historically, prostitutes have been blamed for the spread of STDs, but syphilis rates were quite high among the general population in North America and Western Europe before penicillin.[77] Today, American soldiers and sailors are warned to stay away from foreign prostitutes to avoid AIDS (Acquired Immune Deficiency Syndrome). However, epidemiological data suggests that American military men first transmitted HIV infection (the virus that causes AIDS) to the prostitute women employed in Asian and Pacific R & R centers.[78] Whenever and wherever women in prostitution have been afflicted with diseases like syphilis, gonorrhea, and AIDS, there has been little sympathy for their suffering.[79] Rather, as "fallen women," they have been seen as deserving divine retribution. Nobody asks, "Who infected the prostitutes?" Instead, prostitutes have been held responsible for spreading STDs to men who in turn infect "innocent" women and children.

Today, North American prostitutes are blamed for transmitting the deadly AIDS virus to heterosexual men.[80] However, information collected by the Center for Disease Control (CDC) in the United States and Canadian health authorities suggests that only a small proportion of AIDS patients were infected with the virus through sexual contacts with prostitutes. Relatively few men with AIDS describe contacts with prostitutes as their only risk factor. Prostitution, in and of itself, does not contribute either to testing seropositive for HIV antibodies (being infected with the virus but free of symptoms) or to developing full-blown AIDS; IV (intravenous) drug use does. Studies of streetwalkers who are IV drug users show high rates of infection. In the United States, studies of call girls and other populations of prostitutes which rarely use IV drugs show low rates of infection. The rates of HIV infection among prostitutes varies wildly from nearly zero among groups where condom use and regular medical care is customary to above 80 percent among IV drug users in the developed world or impoverished women in Africa.[81] Research on the high rates of seropositivity among prostitutes in Africa does not necessarily generalize to sex workers in more affluent nations.[82] Regardless of occupation, many women in Africa have been infected with the virus for three reasons. First, extreme poverty, which contributes to inadequate health care and poor sanitation plays a major role in the African AIDS epidemic. Throughout Africa and other poverty-stricken regions, hypodermic needles for administering medication or blood transfusions have been used on multiple patients, often without being bleached or sterilized. Second, female circumcision (mutilation of the clitoris and labia) is a commonplace cultural practice in Africa, women's genital scars becoming a likely site for bleeding and future infection. Third, condoms are often unavailable, too expensive for poor couples, or rejected by local men as an affront to their masculinity.

Just because women exchange sex for money does not in itself transform them into a health risk. Several recent studies have found comparable or even lower rates of infection with sexually transmitted diseases among female prostitutes than in the general female population.[83] As Donna King explains,

> The targeting of women prostitutes as deadly vectors for AIDS, despite a dearth of data demonstrating this, can be traced to a long-standing myth of female pollution, where sexual women are feared

and despised by men as dangerous sources of contamination. Prostitutes, by virtue of their open sexuality and promiscuity, are in double-jeopardy for misogynist censure.[84]

In North America and Western Europe, professional prostitutes engage in safer sex practices and have a lower risk for acquiring and passing STDs than many teenagers.[85] In affluent, industrialized nations, professional prostitutes use condoms reliably and regularly in their work, even in communities where IV drug use is high.[86] Therefore, they are unlikely to be transmitting HIV to their clients even after they have been infected. In North America, most professional prostitutes insist that clients use condoms, not only to prevent disease and pregnancy, but also because the rubber signifies professional distance from a client. Unfortunately, not all prostitutes insist that their boyfriends use rubbers.[87] When unprotected sex symbolizes the love and intimacy women deny "tricks," they stand a much greater chance of being infected with HIV and other STDs when making love to boyfriends than when working as prostitutes. Infection from boyfriends is particularly likely if the men are "shooting partners," individuals with whom women share IV drugs and hypodermic needles.

## MALE PROFITEERS

Nowhere is male economic dominance more evident than in the sex trades. In prostitution and erotic entertainment alike, workers are predominantly female and managers and entrepreneurs are predominantly male.[88] Ironically, male domination of prostitution is in part the result of previous, misguided attempts at reform. Before the red light districts were shut down, most North American brothels were managed and owned by women.[89] In the past, women had an opportunity to work their way up the ranks, from brothel girl to madam to brothel owner. Today, upward mobility in the sex trades is more restricted. With the exception of call girl and brothel operations which cater to upper-class clientele, few contemporary sex businesses are owned and managed by women. Streetwalkers who live and work alone or support a lesbian lover instead of a man are regarded as "outlaws."[90] Whether they are engaged in streetwalking or other illegal activities, impoverished female hustlers are unable to function unless they work for a man.[91]

Street prostitutes are expected to turn over all their earnings to the pimp for safe keeping.[92] In exchange, he may pay bail or fines when they are arrested for soliciting, provide rent money, and furnish them with food, clothing, and expensive gifts. The professional pimp reveals neither his profits nor the percentage of women's earnings appropriated for his own gain. Legally, a pimp is anyone who lives off the earnings of a prostitute.[93] As such, the pimp could be a lover or husband working alongside his woman on the street. Alternatively, the pimp may have a strictly economic relationship with one or several women, even though the business aspects of the relationship are sometimes disguised as romantic love or friendship.[94] Law enforcement officers, social scientists, and journalists often stereotype pimps as lazy, violent men who trick and drug women into sex work.[95] Why? Because most pimps come from disenfranchised groups. In the United States today, a disproportionate number of pimps are black. In Europe, a great many are recent immigrants. Throughout the world, the majority of pimps come from lower socioeconomic status communities. Not all pimps are sociopaths, however. Despite living in the criminal underworld, some pimps are kind and charitable, some rescue young girls from juvenile prostitution, some distribute income fairly to employees, and some are devoted family men who are faithful to the prostitute they love.[96] Neither is the pimp-prostitute relationship necessarily violent.[97] Violent pimps are regarded with contempt by the more respected members of their profession. Moreover, given the high prevalence of domestic violence in general, it is questionable whether pimps are any more psychologically or physically abusive than the husbands and romantic partners of "straight" women.

There appears to be great variability among pimps from the "sweet mac" or " player" who manipulates women with sex and affection to the emotionally reserved "business manager" to the "gorilla pimp" who controls women through fear and force.[98] But, it is difficult for feminists to sympathize with any pimps. To stay in business, pimps customarily exploit women's romantic feelings and economic worries.[99] By encouraging prostitutes to be jealous of one another, pimps prevent women from comparing notes, airing dissatisfactions, and either gaining independence or working together to improve working conditions. Pimps are sometimes the ultimate male chauvinists, showing off to their friends by treating women who work for them in a domineering fashion. Judging one another in terms of how many prostitutes each man controls or how much conspicuous wealth women generate, pimps inform one another when a prostitute is seen resting or is unwilling to solicit every passing car. In exchange for their complete devotion and economic support, pimps offer women relatively little. Prostitutes on a stroll are more likely to look after each other than to have a pimp intervene when they face attack or arrest. Some pimps are extremely violent, punishing women for independence or disobedience through beatings, public humiliation, and in some cases, carefully coordinated gang rapes.[100]

In the underground culture of street hustling, prostitutes are free to leave a pimp whenever and for whatever reason they choose. But, the cost is great.[101] The only acceptable way to leave a man is for another; pimping is self-perpetuating. Since women don't control their own earnings, they rely on expensive gifts for income, gifts which they cannot take with them when they leave their pimp suddenly after a jail term, a beating, or a jealous rage. With a new man, women start on the bottom, with low status and no economic resources. The more women change men, the less wealth they accumulate. Radical and Liberal Feminists alike oppose the sexual exploitation of women by male pimps.

## FEMINISTS AND SEX WORKERS FACE TO FACE

Whether they label themselves as such, a number of sex workers are feminists insofar as they demand women's equality, sexually and economically.[102] But, most feminists have never met a sex worker, and most sex workers know little of feminism. This creates something of a dilemma. Unfamiliarity breeds fear and contempt. In one recent study, for example, feminism was associated with intolerance.[103] The more profeminist an undergraduate was, the less sympathy she had for decriminalizing or legalizing prostitution. Ironically, profeminist students were less inclined to recognize the economic reasons for prostitution than those who professed traditional sex-role attitudes. According to these young feminists, women involved in prostitution were to blame for their own supposed subordination and exploitation. Prostitution, as alluded earlier, has been a thorny issue for feminists since the nineteenth century.[104] On the one hand, feminists (especially Radical Feminists) are opposed to all sexual exploitation and objectification of women by men. On the other, nearly everyone recognizes the futility of outlawing prostitution. Rather than liberating women, antiprostitution laws and the stigmatization of sex workers have brought further oppression. Where prostitution is illegal, women live in fear of a justice system that defines them as criminals. Laws are enforced largely against women in the sex trades, not against the men who use or profit from their work. Little effort is made by authorities to train women for jobs that pay as well as prostitution or offer equally flexible hours.

Many Radical Feminists insist that prostitution and sexual slavery are identical. Kathleen Barry, for instance, argues that female sexual slavery takes place wherever and whenever a woman has no control over the immediate conditions of her existence.[105] According to this definition, a woman is a sexual slave (not a prostitute) if she becomes involved in commercial sex as a result of the lack of better economic alternatives, not just in response to force or trickery. Barry and other Radical Feminists do not distinguish between the international sex trade and prostitute-pimp relationships in affluent nations; both are viewed as colonizing women's bodies for the benefit of the patriarchy. And, a number of women who have worked in prostitution agree. Members of WHISPER (Women Hurt in Systems of Prostitution Engaged in Revolt), an American organization devoted to rescuing women and children from commercial sex work, believe that Liberal Feminists are wrong to represent prostitution as a voluntary and legitimate career, business, or sign of sexual freedom.[106] In the experience of these women at least, commercial sex is degrading, frequently violent, and not at all unlike the extreme sexual and physical abuse many prostitute women experienced as children.

Relying upon the same logic that they use to discredit pornography, Radical Feminists argue that prostitution harms both prostitutes and all women because it perpetuates beliefs that marginalize women politically and socially: that sex is a male drive which requires immediate satisfaction, that men should dominate women, and that repeated sexual contact pollutes or devalues women.[107] Like the college students who used feminist beliefs to distance themselves from prostitutes, some mature Radical Feminists liken prostitutes to "Uncle Toms" who make money by allowing men to exploit them, causing all women to suffer social degradation in the process. Although prostitution appears to exist in nearly every historic period and culture, more than a few Radical Feminists maintain the hope that the institution would disappear completely if and when true sexual equality is obtained.

For Radical Feminists, prostitution is the end result of patriarchal systems which lock women into limited economic and political roles.[108] Radical Feminists ask, How does pornography and prostitution shape the way that all women are perceived? This question is turned on its head by Liberal Feminists. Never questioning the right of women to engage in commercial sex, Liberal Feminists insist that the appropriate question to ask is instead, How do patriarchal perceptions of women in general influence the way we look at and treat women in the sex trades?[109] Liberal Feminists complain that in trying to "save" women from prostitution and erotic entertainment, Radical Feminists end up alienating sex workers and worsening their lives.[110] For example, by striving to eliminate businesses like adult bookstores, massage parlors, erotic night clubs, and pornographic movie theaters, the leadership of Women Against Pornography advocates the loss of the safest and most publicly scrutinized jobs in commercial sex. When fewer legal, inside jobs are available, increasing numbers of women in the sex trades are forced underground where they become even more susceptible to misogynistic abuses.

Many sex workers are angry at Radical Feminists for infantalizing them and sustaining the madonna/whore dichotomy. By insisting that commercial sex always degrades women and that all prostitutes and pornographic entertainers are oppressed by definition, extremist Radical Feminists deny women adult status. Regardless of what Radical Feminists think, these women believe that they have the right to engage in prostitution and erotic entertainment voluntarily and to experience sex work on their own terms. Liberal Feminists argue that the Radical Feminist position on prostitution buys into the sexual double standard; women are not permitted to separate sex and love.[111] The conflict between politically active sex workers and Radical Feminist leaders of the modern antiprostitution movement has been exacerbated by political rigidity. When researching her groundbreaking exposé of sexual slavery, the international trade in the bodies of girls and women, Radical Feminist Kathleen Barry obtained invaluable information from Margo St. James, the former prostitute who founded the prostitute's advocacy group COYOTE (Call Off Your Old Tired Ethics). However, Barry wouldn't share the stage with the ex-prostitute during a television interview and limited the role that Margo St. James could play in an important conference which had a goal that both women shared, the elimination of forced prostitution throughout the world.[112] Not all the criticism directed at Radical Feminists is justified, however. Although a few women in the movement have put too much social distance between themselves and sex workers, many more are highly sympathetic. Regardless of how personally distasteful they find commercial sex, most contemporary Radical Feminists believe that prostitution should be decriminalized.[113] Like their sisters in the Liberal Feminist camp, they believe that outlawing commercial sex does more harm than good. Radical and Liberal Feminists alike agree that the rights of women in prostitution should be protected whereas laws prohibiting involuntary sexual servitude and juvenile sexual exploitation must be enforced more rigorously.

Both Radical and Liberal Feminists have allies among current and retired sex workers. As pointed out earlier, the Radical Feminist position is supported by the membership of WHISPER (Women Hurt in Systems of Prostitution Engaged in Revolt) and various antislavery groups such as the European organization, the Foundation Against Traffic in Women.[114] Other prostitutes' advocacy groups, probably most, voice Liberal Feminist ideology. Since the 1970s, numerous Liberal Feminist organizations for sex workers came into being including American alliances like COYOTE and U.S. PROStitutes, De Rode Draad (The Red Thread) in the Netherlands, Comitato Per I Diritti Civili Delle Prostitute (Italian Committee for the Civil Rights of Prostitutes), the Zenia Society (a Swiss prostitutes' rights organization), CORP (Canadian Organization for the Rights of Prostitutes), Verbandes der Prostituierten Osterreichs (an Austrian group), Rede de Prostitutas (Brazil's Network of Prostitutes), PLAN (Prostitution Laws are Nonsense, a British group), and the Good Friend, a feminist organization for lesbian prostitutes in Indonesia.[115] Recently, Liberal Feminists, inside and outside of the sex industry, have coordinated their efforts by founding the International Committee for Prostitutes' Rights (ICPR) which sponsored two World Whores Congresses in the 1980s, the first in Amsterdam and the second in Brussels. Liberal Feminists support the right of sex workers to work without harassment or excessive regulation, establish their own professional standards, and organize labor unions in order to achieve fair pay, decent working conditions, and reasonable job benefits such as pensions and health insurance.[116]

At the first two World Whores Congresses of all time, sex workers and their Liberal Feminist allies from several countries came up with a simple platform.[117] Most delegates agreed that prostitution should be decriminalized (neither prohibited and punished by the State nor legalized). Prostitutes' rights advocates were wary of legalized prostitution (as in Nevada and certain European, Asian, and Latin American cities). When prostitution is legal, the State usually assumes control over the most minute details of prostitutes' lives and benefits from sex work far more than the women so employed. Most delegates agreed that the civil rights of sex workers should be respected by the State. That is, sex workers were seen as deserving the right to life, liberty, and security, just like other citizens in a free society. Only present and former sex workers were allowed to vote. The following positions were agreed upon by the majority:

1. Adult voluntary prostitution should be decriminalized (neither subject to criminal penalties nor controlled by and for the profit of the State). However, the State should assume a greater role in protecting women, particularly poor women, from sexual slavery.

2. Individuals who engage in commercial sex, like other citizens, should be protected by law enforcement agencies from fraud, extortion, robbery, coercion, violence, sexual abuse, and racism. Presently, no other group is robbed, raped, threatened, and murdered more than prostitutes. Police must make a greater effort to stop such crimes.

3. All laws that deny prostitutes the freedom to travel freely within and between countries or associate with friends and lovers of their choice privately should be eradicated. Rather than eliminating

sexual slavery as intended, these laws have been used to oppress immigrants and women of color.

4. Prostitutes are entitled to the same human rights and civil liberties enjoyed by other citizens: freedom of speech, the right to marry, the right to have and raise children, the right to decent housing, and the right to unemployment insurance. Employment in sex work alone does not prove that a woman is an unfit parent.

5. Working conditions for sex workers must be improved. No law should deny prostitutes the freedom to choose where they live and work.

6. Representatives of the State should encourage sex workers to have periodic medical examinations, including screening for sexually transmitted diseases. However, these examinations must be private, confidential, and consensual, never mandatory. The Health Care System should be available to help sex workers, not persecute them.

7. The State should provide social services, housing, and employment training for runaway children to prevent juvenile prostitution and promote child welfare.

8. Prostitutes should pay regular taxes but also should receive the same social benefits as other tax-paying citizens (e.g., social security, unemployment compensation, national health benefits, etc.).

9. The State should fund shelters and vocational retraining programs for sex workers who wish to leave prostitution and support educational programs directed at changing social attitudes that contribute to discrimination against prostitutes and ex-prostitutes.

10. Antipimping laws should be eliminated. They are often used to press criminal charges against the families and loved ones of prostitutes. This is wrong.

11. Prostitutes should have the right to organize and join trade unions. They are entitled to a fair share of their earnings and decent working conditions.

12. Prostitutes' testimony in courts of law should be held with the same respect as that of other citizens. Prostitutes have the right to create literary and artistic work about their lives. Their profits should not be forfeited to the State nor should their work be used against them as evidence of criminal activity.

Nobody has been a more articulate spokesperson for Liberal Feminists and prostitutes' rights than Margo St. James who said, "Prostitution laws are how women are controlled in this society."[118] Throughout the world, sex workers are silenced and regarded as a public nuisance, not as citizens. By reclaiming the word "whore" and redefining a prostitute as a woman who has the power to establish the financial aspects and other terms of a sexual exchange, activists for prostitutes' rights, including many current and retired sex workers, are in the forefront of feminism.[119] No longer is it possible for feminists to assume, without question, that sexual freedom and equality for women necessarily excludes involvement in commercial or impersonal sex.

Writing this chapter has been exciting. Learning about the struggles of women in prostitution has inspired me to think about my own life as a privileged academic who supports herself as a sex researcher, sex educator, and psychotherapist.

Each day I get paid for sex work, not always handsomely but regularly. I see private clients who pay me for friendship and warm advice. Often, we talk about sex: what it is and what to do. Generally, I give homework assignments including explicitly sexual ones. Throughout therapy, my clients and I exchange sensitive, personal information. Our close relationships are licensed by the State and reimbursed by major insurance companies. How fascinating! My form of commercial intimacy is seen as legitimate, even altruistic, whereas the physical equivalent (commercial sexual intimacy) would not be. As a sex educator and researcher, I am free to talk about sex, write about sex, and study sex. It is perfectly legal for me to collect sexual data from survey respondents and experimental subjects. True, my words and deeds are sometimes criticized, but my work is not prohibited. Often my sex work is rewarded. Papers are accepted at prestigious conferences; journal articles, chapters, and this book are published; rewards and honors are bestowed. Students look up to me and become my friends; colleagues praise my efforts. At no time are my activities considered illegitimate or criminal. Yet, if my business was to deliver the services I write about for money, I would no longer be viewed with respect, no longer be free to work as I saw fit. How odd! I get money and admiration for writing about what other women are stigmatized and arrested for doing. Maybe prostitution is the ultimate feminist issue, the ultimate test of a woman's right to control her own body.

## NOTES

1. See Albert Ellis cited in Benjamin and Masters, *Prostitution and Morality*, p. 24; Summers, Prostitution, pp. 113–18.

2. See Tetzelli, Recession-Proof Supermodels, pp. 12–13.

3. See Benjamin and Masters, *Prostitution and Morality;* Bullough and Bullough, *Women and Prostitution.*

4. See Potterat et al., Career Longevity of Prostitute Women, pp. 233–43.

5. See Benjamin and Masters, *Prostitution and Morality.*

6. See Pheterson, Category "Prostitute," pp. 397–407.

7. See Sachiko, Women of Kabukicho, pp. 84–89.

8. See Evans, *Harlots.*

9. See Pheterson, *Rights of Whores;* Pheterson, Unchastity, pp. 215–30.

10. See Bullough and Bullough, *Women and Prostitution;* Symanski, *Immoral Landscape.*

11. Ibid.

12. See Gemme, Prostitution, pp. 227–37; Symanski, *Immoral Landscape.*

13. See Shumsky, Tacit Acceptance, pp. 665–79.

14. See Faludi, *Backlash,* especially chapters 9–11.

15. See Symanski, *Immoral Landscape.*

16. Ibid.

17. See Pheterson, *Rights of Whores.*

18. See Bullough and Bullough, *Women and Prostitution.*

19. See ibid. and Barry, *Sexual Slavery;* Pheterson, *Rights of Whores.*

20. See Benjamin and Masters, *Prostitution and Morality;* Evans, *Harlots.*

21. See ibid. and Barry, *Sexual Slavery;* Pheterson, *Rights of Whores.*

22. See Bullough and Bullough, *Women and Prostitution;* DuBois, and Gordon, Seeking Ecstasy on the Battlefield, pp. 31–49; Musheno and Seeley, Prostitution Policy, pp. 237–55; Pheterson, *Rights of Whores;* Walkowitz, Politics of Prostitution, pp. 145–57.

23. See Newman et al., Female Prostitution, pp. 80–86.

24. See De Schampheleire, MMPI Characteristics, pp. 343–50; Gibson-Ainyette et al., Adolescent Female Prostitutes, pp. 431–38; James and Davis, Female Sexual Role Deviance, pp. 345–50; Miller, *Street Woman;* Potterat et al., Becoming a Prostitute, pp. 329–35, for examples and Pheterson, Category "Prostitute," pp. 397–407, for a critique.

25. See Bracey, Juvenile Prostitute, pp. 151–60; Campagna and Poffenberger, *Sexual Trafficking;* Giobbe, Liberal Lies About Prostitution, pp. 67–81; Seng, Sexual Abuse and Adolescent Prostitution, pp. 665–75; Sereny, *Invisible Children;* Silbert and Pines, Early Sexual Exploitation, pp. 285–89.

26. See Arrington, Under the Gun, pp. 173–78; Shaver, Critique of the Feminist Charges, pp. 82–89.

27. See Sereny, *Invisible Children;* Yates et al., Runaway and Non-Runaway Youth, pp. 820–21.

28. See Campagna and Poffenberger, *Sexual Trafficking;* Carmen and Moody, *Working Women;* Everts, Triple Treat, pp. 37–38; Giobbe, Liberal Lies About Prostitution, pp. 67–81; Lopez-Jones, English Collective of Prostitutes, pp. 271–78; Naoko, Japayuki-San, pp. 84–88; O'Campo, Prostitution in the Philippines, pp. 67–76; Romenesko and Miller, Female Street Hustlers, pp. 109–35.

29. See Carter, Tool, pp. 159–65; Sanders, She's a Whore, pp. 12–14.

30. See Faludi, *Backlash*.

31. See Sanders, She's a Whore, pp. 12–14.

32. See Barry, *Sexual Slavery*.

33. See Alexander, Prostitution, pp. 184–214; Alexander, Why This Book, pp. 14–18; Aline, Bad Girls, pp. 131–34; Hartley, Feminist Porno Star, pp. 142–44; Schaffer and DeBlassie, Adolescent Prostitution, pp. 689–96.

34. See Savitz and Rosen, Sexual Enjoyment Reported by "Streetwalkers," pp. 200–08.

35. Alexander, Interview with Nell, pp. 54–55.

36. See Alexander, Prostitution, pp. 184–214; Benjamin and Masters, *Prostitution and Morality*, Campagna and Poffenberger, *Sexual Trafficking*; Carmen and Moody, *Working Women*; Edelstein, Massage Parlor, pp. 62–69; Freund et al., Sexual Behavior of Resident Street Prostitutes, pp. 460–78; Sachiko, Women of Kabukicho, pp. 84–89; Symanski, *Immoral Landscape*.

37. See Naoko, Japayuki-San, pp. 84–88; O'Campo, Prostitution in the Philippines, 67–76; Sturdevant and Stoltzfus, *Let the Good Times Roll*.

38. See Barry, *Sexual Slavery*; Granik and Shields, Trafficking in Women, pp. 1–3; Louie, Third World Prostitutes, pp. 14–15; O'Campo, Prostitution in the Philippines, pp. 67–76; Sturdevant and Stoltzfus, *Let the Good Times Roll*.

39. Sturdevant and Stoltzfus, *Let the Good Times Roll*, p. 40.

40. Ibid., p. 326.

41. Ibid.

42. Ibid., p. 123.

43. See Barry, *Sexual Slavery*; Granik and Shields, Trafficking in Women, pp. 1–3; Louie, Third World Prostitutes, pp. 14–15; O'Campo, Prostitution in the Philippines, pp. 67–76; Sturdevant and Stoltzfus, *Let the Good Times Roll*.

44. See Naoko, Japayuki-San, pp. 84–88.

45. See Bullough and Bullough, *Women and Prostitution*.

46. See Alexander, Prostitution, pp. 184–214; Benjamin and Masters, *Prostitution and Morality*, Campagna and Poffenberger, *Sexual Trafficking*; Carmen and Moody, *Working Women*; Freund et al., Sexual Behavior of Resident Street Prostitutes, pp. 460–78; Gemme, Prostitution, pp. 227–37; Symanski, *Immoral Landscape*.

47. Freund et al., Sexual Behavior of Resident Street Prostitutes, pp. 460–78.

48. See Campagna and Poffenberger, *Sexual Trafficking*.

49. See Alexander, Prostitution, pp. 184–214; Aline, Bad Girls, pp. 131–34; Cooke, Stripping, pp. 92–99; Enck and Preston, Counterfeit Intimacy, pp. 369–81; Everts, Triple Treat, pp. 37–38; Hartley, Feminist Porno Star, pp. 142–44; Johnson, CABE and Strippers, pp. 109–13; Morgan, Living on the Edge, pp. 21–28; Potter, Retail Pornography Industry, pp. 233–51; Sundahl, Stripper, pp. 175–80.

50. See Potter, Retail Pornography Industry, pp. 233–51.

51. See Alexander, Prostitution, pp. 184–214; Benjamin and Masters, *Prostitution and Morality*.

52. See Benjamin and Masters, *Prostitution and Morality*; Hooks, *Ain't I a Woman*.

53. See ibid. and Bullough and Bullough, *Women and Prostitution*; Evans, *Harlots*.

54. See Alexander, Prostitution, pp. 184–214; Cole, Rothblum, and Espin, Refugee Women.

55. See Campagna and Poffenberger, *Sexual Trafficking.*

56. See Barry, *Sexual Slavery;* Cole, Rothblum, and Espin, Refugee Women.

57. See Barry, *Sexual Slavery;* Nagot, Tricked into Prostitution, pp. 10–11.

58. Alexander, Prostitution, pp. 184–214; Bracey, Juvenile Prostitute, pp. 151–60; Campagna and Poffenberger, *Sexual Trafficking;* Gibson-Ainyette et al., Adolescent Female Prostitutes, pp. 431–38; Linedecker, *Children in Chains;* Schaffer and De-Blassie, Adolescent Prostitution, pp. 689–96; Seng, Sexual Abuse and Adolescent Prostitution, pp. 665–75; Sereny, *Invisible Children.*

59. See Newman et al., Female Prostitution, pp. 80–86.

60. See Benjamin and Masters, *Prostitution and Morality;* Edelstein, Massage Parlor, pp. 62–69; Morgan, Living on the Edge, pp. 21–28; Nestle, Lesbians and Prostitutes, pp. 131–40; Wardlaw, Nightmare, pp. 108–12.

61. See Nestle, Lesbians and Prostitutes, pp. 131–40

62. See Carmen and Moody, *Working Women.*

63. See Alexander, Interview with Nell, pp. 53–55; Arrington, Under the Gun, pp. 173–78; Carmen and Moody, *Working Women;* Symanski, *Immoral Landscape.*

64. See Alexander, Prostitution, pp. 184–214; West, U.S. PROStitutes, pp. 279–89.

65. See Carmen and Moody, *Working Women.*

66. See ibid. and Arrington, Under the Gun, pp. 173–78; Carole, Interview with Barbara, pp. 166–74; Gemme, Prostitution, pp. 227–37.

67. See Lockett, Destroying Condoms, p. 158.

68. See Carmen and Moody, *Working Women;* Carole, Interview with Barbara, pp. 166–74; Lockett, Arrested, pp. 39–40.

69. See Carmen and Moody, *Working Women.*

70. See ibid. and Arrington, Under the Gun, pp. 173–78; Gemme, Prostitution, pp. 227–37; Symanski, *Immoral Landscape.*

71. See Alexander, Prostitution, pp. 184–214; Gemme, Prostitution, pp. 227–37.

72. See Silbert and Pines, Sexual Abuse, pp. 857–68.

73. See Karen, Protection from Rape, 145–46.

74. See Alexander, Prostitution, pp. 184–214; Arrington, Under the Gun, pp. 173–78; Summers, Prostitution, pp. 113–18; West, U.S. PROStitutes, pp. 279–89.

75. See Symanski, *Immoral Landscape.*

76. See Brock, Prostitutes as Scapegoats, pp. 13–17; Zalduondo, Prostitution Viewed Cross-Culturally, pp. 223–48.

77. See ibid. and Bullough and Bullough, *Women and Prostitution;* Sturdevant and Stoltzfus, *Let the Good Times Roll.*

78. See Sturdevant and Stoltzfus, *Let the Good Times Roll.*

79. See ibid. and Evans, *Harlots;* Zalduondo, Prostitution Viewed Cross-Culturally, pp. 223–48.

80. See Alexander, Scapegoated, pp. 248–63; Brock, Prostitutes as Scapegoats, pp. 13–17; King, "Prostitutes as Pariah," pp. 155–76.

81. See Brock, Prostitutes as Scapegoats, pp. 13–17; Pheterson, *Rights of Whores.*

82. See Alexander, Scapegoated, pp. 248–63; Brock, Prostitutes as Scapegoats, pp. 13–17; King, "Prostitutes as Pariah," pp. 155–76; Zalduondo, Prostitution Viewed Cross-Culturally, pp. 223–48.

83. See Brock, Prostitutes as Scapegoats, pp. 13–17; Symanski, *Immoral Landscape*.

84. King, "Prostitutes as Pariah," pp. 174–75.

85. See Brock, Prostitutes as Scapegoats, pp. 13–17; Pheterson, *Rights of Whores*; Symanski, *Immoral Landscape*.

86. See Freund et al., Sexual Behavior of Clients, pp. 579–91; Freund et al., Sexual Behavior of Resident Street Prostitutes, pp. 460–78; Gemme, Prostitution, pp. 227–37; Pheterson, *Rights of Whores*.

87. See Shayne and Kaplan, Poor Women and AIDS, pp. 21–37.

88. See Barry, *Sexual Slavery*; Campagna and Poffenberger, *Sexual Trafficking*; Carmen and Moody, *Working Women*; Miller, *Street Women*; Potter, Retail Pornography Industry, pp. 233–51; Romenesko and Miller, Female Street Hustlers, pp. 109–35; Sundahl, Stripper, pp. 175–80.

89. See Alexander, Prostitution, pp. 184–214.

90. See Carmen and Moody, *Working Women*.

91. See Miller, *Street Women*; Romenesko and Miller, Female Street Hustlers, pp. 109–35.

92. See Carmen and Moody, *Working Women*.

93. See Alexander, Prostitution, pp. 184–214.

94. See Miller, *Street Women*; Romenesko and Miller, Female Street Hustlers, pp. 109–35.

95. See Benjamin and Masters, *Prostitution and Morality*; Campagna and Poffenberger, *Sexual Trafficking*; Sereny, *Invisible Children*.

96. See Carmen and Moody, *Working Women*.

97. Ibid. See Shaver, Critique of the Feminist Charges, pp. 82–89.

98. See Campagna and Poffenberger, *Sexual Trafficking*.

99. See Carmen and Moody, *Working Women*; Romenesko and Miller, Female Street Hustlers, pp. 109–35.

100. See Barry, *Sexual Slavery*; Sereny, *Invisible Children*.

101. See Romenesko and Miller, Female Street Hustlers, pp. 109–35.

102. See Jenness, *Making It Work*.

103. See Bascow and Campanile, Attitudes Toward Prostitution, pp. 135–41.

104. See Alexander, Prostitution, pp. 184–214.

105. See Barry, *Sexual Slavery*.

106. See Giobbe, Liberal Lies About Prostitution, pp. 67–81; Wynter, Whisper, pp. 266–70.

107. See Shrage, Oppose Prostitution?, pp. 347–61.

108. See Barry, *Sexual Slavery*.

109. See Arrington, Under the Gun, pp. 173–78.

110. See Bell, Introduction, pp. 11–21; Bullough and Bullough, *Women and Prostitution*; Canadian Organization for the Rights of Prostitutes, Realistic Feminists, pp. 204–17; Carmen and Moody, *Working Women*; Pheterson, *Rights of Whores*.

111. See Cooper, Prostitution, pp. 98–119.

112. See Pheterson, *Rights of Whores*.

113. See Barry, *Sexual Slavery*; Cooper, Prostitution, pp. 98–119; Musheno and Seeley, Prostitution Policy, pp. 237–55.

114. See Pheterson, *Rights of Whores*.

115. Ibid. See Jenness, *Making It Work*; West, U.S. PROStitutes, pp. 279–89.

116. See Canadian Organization for the Rights of Prostitutes, Realistic Feminists, pp. 204–17; Cooke, Sex Trade Workers and Feminists, pp. 190–203; Pheterson, *Rights of Whores*; Scott, Working Girls, pp. 179–80; St. James, Reclamation of Whores, pp. 81–91.

117. See Pheterson, *Rights of Whores*.

118. St. James, Reclamation of Whores, p. 82.

119. See Jenness, *Making It Work*.

# ⋙ 6 ⋘

# Sexual Victimization and Pornography

We live in a violent world where men are more likely than women to be the victims of most forms of physical aggression, including murder.[1] But, there is one important exception, sexual aggression and exploitation. On a daily basis, almost every woman lives with some fear of the men around her.

> Tobie returns to her car in the isolated parking lot. The place seems deserted, but she could never be sure. She scans the area, watching and listening. It is too silent. She forms a fist around her car keys, wondering if they would make an effective weapon should a man jump out.

> June has a headache and nausea in anticipation of going to work. The men at the factory leer, call her obscene and insulting names, and leave cruel "gifts" at her work station. Last week, it was a box of used condoms; the week before, it was a calendar which depicted female bondage. The men don't hesitate to show their resentment; she is the first woman to secure such a highly paid, technical job at the plant.

> Arzelia feels the sweat pouring; her heart pounds. The same man has been following her for eight blocks. When she picks up speed, he does too. The incident brings back nightmare memories of child sexual abuse and rape.

Whether or not they have ever experienced sexual assault or exploitation, most women live with a fear that is likely to make them guarded, anxious, and afraid to go out alone.[2] Fear of sexual violence forces them into lives that are considerably more restricted than those of men. Black women, widowed and divorced women, and older women are especially likely to be worried. Public places such as parking lots, laundromats, parks, deserted business districts, and public transit facilities fill women with apprehension. Sensationalistic news stories encourage women to fear the strangers who may lurk in such places. But, the truth of female sexual victimization is even more disturbing. Most sexually abusive behavior is initiated by known and trusted boys and men, not perfect strangers. Sexual abuse and exploitation are rarely reported or prosecuted but commonly experienced. Economic dependence makes it difficult for many women to defend themselves.[3]

Radical and Liberal Feminists agree on one issue. "Power inequality is seen as the root of all forms of discrimination and violence directed at women."[4] Beyond this point, there is complete disagreement. Radical Feminists think that sex is considerably more dangerous for women than do Liberal Feminists; they define a greater variety of heterosexual experiences as potentially coercive and exploitative. More importantly, Radical Feminists view pornography, especially the violent variety, as causing male sexual violence. According to Radical Feminists, pornography must be criticized at the very least and possibly curbed or eliminated altogether to decrease sexual abuse directed at girls and women. Liberal Feminists aren't so sure. Some Liberal Feminists dislike pornography but oppose restricting it to safeguard free speech. Others argue that a woman-affirming pornography is possible.

As explained in the first chapter, I do not wish to intensify the counterproductive, feminist, pornography debates. Here again, I assume my role as an Empirical Feminist, examining the merits of both Liberal and Radical Feminist ideas in the light of the voluminous scientific literature on sexual victimization and pornography. Chapter 6 begins with a thorough discussion of research and clinical information on child sexual abuse, the sexual coercion and rape of women, and sexual harassment. Whenever possible, feminist theory is used to cast light on scientific findings. The second half of the chapter attempts to answer the question—"Does pornography cause sexual victimization?"—by comparing studies supporting Radical Feminist teachings with those upholding the Liberal Feminist position.

## FEMINISTS EXPOSE HIDDEN EPIDEMICS

Sexual coercion may be motivated by many factors including need for power, anger, psychopathology, allegiance to a criminal subculture, peer pressure to engage in sexual conquests, poor communication skills, a lack of empathy, and an inclination to associate sexual arousal with the infliction of pain or humiliation.[5] To some extent, each coercive act is unique. But, the politics and cultural construction of sexual abuse and exploitation cannot be ignored.[6] Sexual coercion prevails wherever the penis is viewed as a weapon and sex-calloused, brutal men are regarded as heroes. Rare in nonaggressive woman-affirming societies, sexual coercion is most common in those cultures and subcultures in which rigid sex roles are enforced, interpersonal violence is expected, and women are regarded as male property.

Children and women who are physically or mentally disabled and those who are multiply oppressed by racism, religious and cultural prejudice, and poverty are especially likely to experience sexual abuse and exploitation. In a recent survey, almost half of the women with disabilities who responded indicated that they had been raped, sexually abused, or physically assaulted. Canadian and American Indian and Inuit feminists report that epidemic amounts of child sexual abuse, rape, and domestic violence in their home communities are largely the result of the violent conquest of North America by Europeans, resulting in an almost complete destruction of the aboriginal peoples' spiritual values, pride, economic resources, political power, and way of life. Millions of refugee girls and women throughout the world have been abducted, sexually abused, and tortured. Liberal and Radical Feminists alike understand rape and other forms of sexual coercion and exploitation as being driven more by hostility toward women, prejudice, and aggressive inclinations than by sexual desire. During the final three decades of the twentieth century, feminist analysis of sexual victimization has initiated a social revolution, the course of which is documented below.

In 1896, Sigmund Freud presented the controversial theory that neurosis may be caused by childhood sexual trauma.[7] The medical community of his day reacted with furor. To please influential male critics, Freud recanted. No longer would he and his followers believe what women said. Instead, patients' memories of incest and childhood sexual coercion were dismissed as evidence of early sexual fantasies and precocious, seductive behavior. Female victims were blamed for their own experiences with sexual abuse. Until feminists influenced psychotherapists, the psychiatric literature linked sexual abuse to a collusion between a sexually provocative girl and a willing, but somewhat naive, adult male. Feminists, especially Radical Feminists, brought the traditionally private issue of child sexual abuse into the public forum.[8] They challenged the way we think about child sexual abuse while organizing survivors, advancing scientific knowledge, and improving clinical treatment. Until feminists taught them otherwise, most people believed that incest was extremely rare and that the bulk of childhood sexual abuse consisted of isolated incidents between unsupervised youngsters and "perverted" strangers. Girls who had been violated by fathers, stepfathers, un-cles, older brothers, and male cousins were often labeled and treated as sexual delinquents, not child abuse survivors. Today, feminists challenge therapists who believe that mothers are somewhat to blame for father-daughter incest. According to feminists, the responsibility for child sexual abuse should be placed squarely on the shoulders of perpetrators, not women.

Drawing attention to the patriarchal context of sexual abuse, feminists note that the overwhelming majority of incest and other child sexual abuse cases involve a male perpetrator and a female victim.[9] Citing empirical stud-ies and clinical case histories, feminists have conceptualized several reasons why the sex offenders who prey upon girls and boys are so likely to be men.[10] Fathers, they point out, generally have much more power over their families than mothers. Sexual exploitation helps disturbed men maintain a dominant social position over women and children. Because women usually assume a larger role in childcare, the incest taboo may have a stronger impact on women than on men. Socialized to dismiss the potential dangers of erotic contact, men may be less likely than women to believe that chil-dren are always harmed by sexual experiences with older persons. Children may be viewed in erotic ways by some boys and men; men more than women are socialized to expect sexual partners to be smaller, younger, and weaker than themselves. Studies suggest that men are more likely than women to have difficulty discriminating between appropriate, nonsexual physical contact and inappropriate sexual displays of affection with young-sters and other subordinates. This is exacerbated by the fact that the con-ventional male sexual script encourages men to view sex as an overwhelming and uncontrollable drive requiring immediate gratification. Worse still, some pornography eroticizes men's sexual abuse of children and adoles-cents.

When women first compared their life histories in the 1960s and 1970s, it became clear that many had been sexually abused or raped but few felt that there was anyone they could turn to for help.[11] Silenced by racism and negative experiences with the police and social service officials, African-American and Native American and Canadian women continue to be less likely than white women to disclose sexual assault experiences until years after they occurred.[12] Before feminists challenged the medical and criminal justice systems, the courageous women who told others about their rapes were likely to be doubted, treated with insensitivity, and interrogated as if they, not the rapist, had committed a crime. Shared pain contributed to activism. In Canada and the United States, feminists began a grassroots movement to combat rape.[13] The first rape crisis centers were established, often staffed by survivors of sexual assault who volunteered their services after taking a crash course in counseling. Today's feminist treatment programs build on existing cultural traditions. In both Canada and the United States, native women have returned to holistic spiritual curative practices, including pipe ceremonies, sweat lodges, and healing circles employing the sacred Medicine Wheel (which symbolizes the equality of all peoples, the continuity of life, and the principles of honesty, sharing, strength, and kindness), in their efforts to heal survivors of childhood sexual abuse and rape, extended families, and the community as a whole. Women's groups fought to reform rape laws and modify courtroom procedures which permitted defense attorneys to discredit and humiliate victims by questioning them about any and all past sexual experiences. They lobbied to create rape-prevention programs and provide special training for law enforcement and medical personnel who handle sexual assault cases.

Feminists demanded and carried out the first large-scale studies of sexual coercion and abuse. Before this research was undertaken, rape was widely believed to be a rare crime. Unless the accused was a bizarre psychopath, those who accused men of rape were frequently regarded as vindictive women making false charges. Study after study discredited these erroneous beliefs.[14] Evidently, few rapes were reported to police and fewer still went to trial. The typical rapist was not a crazed stranger, ugly misfit, or thug but a physically attractive, somewhat likeable, "normal," and intensely masculine, young man.[15] Not only were many rapists acquaintances, an alarming number were husbands and live-in boyfriends.[16]

Both Liberal and Radical Feminists believe that patriarchal beliefs and institutions create a rape culture.[17] They agree that rape is most likely to take place wherever masculinity is equated with aggression and women are seen as men's sexual and reproductive property. A few, outspoken Radical Feminists have taken this ideology to the extreme, suggesting that all heterosexual intercourse is a form of rape.[18] Arguing that compulsory heterosexuality is at the root of women's oppression, fanatics in the feminist movement maintain that because men as a class have greater physical, economic, and political power, women are never truly free to refuse men sexually. Concluding that fulfilling, consensual heterosexual relationships cannot exist in a patriarchy, extremist Radical Feminists like Andrea Dworkin argue,

> Intercourse is . . . an act of possession in which, during which, because of which, a man inhabits a woman, physically covering her and overwhelming her at the same time penetrating her; . . . He has her, or when he is done, he has had her. By thrusting into her, he takes

her over. His thrusting . . . is taken to be her capitulation to him as a conquerer; . . . he occupies and rules her, expresses his elemental dominance over her, by his possession of her in the fuck.[19]

Feminist attorney Catharine MacKinnon agrees with Dworkin, stating, "Rape and intercourse are not separated by any difference between the physical acts or amount of force involved but, legally, by a standard that revolves around the man's interpretation of the encounter."[20] Like me, most readers will probably reject the notion that there is no difference between intercourse and rape. The majority of heterosexuals have had positive and pleasurable sexual experiences. Tempting as it might seem, however, it would be wrong to discard the ideas of anti-intercourse feminists without first giving them serious thought. Consistent with the statistics on domestic violence, one in ten women report that their present or former husband used force or threats to obtain sexual intercourse and many more women acknowledge that they often have had sex out of duty, not desire. There is some merit to the argument that sex is not always freely given by heterosexual women. However, sharp distinctions should be drawn between sexual coercion and sexual intercourse. There is a great difference between having sex out of a sense of social obligation and rape. Research indicates that men, not just women, comply with sexual requests before being sufficiently aroused to please a partner.[21] A good many women, Radical and Liberal Feminists alike, enjoy sexually satisfying, emotionally rich, and affirming relationships with men. The equation of all heterosexual sex with rape is foolish and misleading. Rather than advancing the cause of women's rights, anti-intercourse Radical Feminists turn away potential supporters.

Sexual harassment is not a new problem. Wherever and whenever women have worked or attended school, they have been subjected to deliberate, repeated, and unwanted sexual attention from male supervisors, co-workers, and clientele. Feminists have neither fabricated nor exaggerated the occurrence of sexual harassment. Instead, they have educated the public about the nature of the problem and suggested constructive solutions. Before feminists became involved in research and legal work during the 1980s, most women regarded sexual harassment as an unalterable and uncomfortable result of having to work for and with men. A personal experience from my undergraduate days comes to mind.

I sought the assistance of my statistics professor during his office hours. We were alone. As he explained the equation that troubled me, I saw his arm reach under the table and felt his hand move up my leg to my upper thigh. I was alarmed and embarrassed. He was an older man, an authority figure. I was afraid to say anything, afraid he might lower my grade or say bad things about me. Escape, escape, that's all I could think about! I shot out of my chair, ran for the door, and abruptly announced that I understood the equation perfectly and required no additional help. It was a lie, of course. For the rest of the semester, it was hard to concentrate in class. Obviously, seeking the instructor's help during office hours was no longer an option. To this day, I believe that my dislike of data analysis began with this unpleasant encounter.

My example is a good introduction to the central issues. What is sexual harassment? It is the abuse of power or authority in an educational institution or workplace to coerce another person into engaging in or tolerating unwanted sexual activity.[22] Alternatively, it is the creation or acceptance of an intimidating, hostile, or sexually offensive work environment which interferes with an employee's ability to perform a job effectively or a student's ability to learn. In the United States and Canada, sexual harassment is defined as a civil rights issue, a form of sex discrimination directed at women more than men.[23] Litigation is based on two situations: quid pro quo harassment and environmental harassment.[24] *Quid pro quo harassment* takes place when an employer or teacher communicates that employment status or academic progress depends upon compliance with certain sexual requests. For example, a woman may get the impression that she is expected to date or sleep with her boss if she wishes to keep her job or get a promotion. *Environmental harassment* is encountered more frequently. It is defined as any offensive sexual conduct or sexist behavior which is allowed to continue by an unresponsive management. My experience with my statistics teacher is an example of environmental harassment. Another example was described in the beginning of this chapter. Remember June who didn't want to go to work because her co-workers were cruel and insulting? Evidently, June worked in a "poisoned environment" for women workers. Even if supervisors failed to engage in the offensive behavior personally, they and the company could be held liable for accepting the abusive situation.

Typically, we think of sexual harassment as involving a perpetrator who has superior status or power within an organization. There are exceptions, however. In environmental harassment, a worker may be harassed by other workers or clients whose offensive actions are tolerated by authorities. Some feminists claim that where women are concerned, *contrapower harassment* is also possible. That is, women in authority may be susceptible to harassment from male subordinates who challenge their right to have higher status or institutional power.[25] For example, many women professors complain that they have been sexually harassed by the men they teach. In some cases, these professors have been the recipients of unwelcome sexual invitations or flirtation. More frequently, they have been made the butt of sexist or obscene remarks, gestures, or rumors. Given women's generally smaller stature and historical lack of power, unwanted sexual behavior from male subordinates is especially threatening. Unfortunately, relating to a female authority figure in a sexual way may be viewed by some as the ultimate test of manhood.

Sexual victimization takes many forms: child abuse and exploitation; individual rape by a stranger, acquaintance, or spouse; group or gang rape; nonviolent sexual coercion or intimidation occurring with or without penetration; sexual harassment in educational institutions and the workplace. To understand the impact of sexual victimization best, it is necessary to collect information from survivors and perpetrators alike. In addition to studying the prevalence of sexual abuse, counting the numbers and types of victims and offenders, feminist researchers investigate qualitative aspects of sexual victimization.

## CHILD SEXUAL ABUSE

When Karen was eight, a man exposed his penis on the bus seat next to her own. She was shocked at first, but her mother put her at ease soon after the incident.

Julie's sole, unwanted, childhood sexual experience took place in the girl's locker room at the community swimming pool. Some of the older boys from the neighboring locker room had drilled a hole in the wall to peek at the undressed girls.

Denise and her brother, Howard, used to play "doctor" when she was four and he was five years old. At his suggestion, they pulled down their underpants to compare genitals visually, pointing and giggling for several minutes.

Bernice will never forgive her cousin, Jack. She was only seven years old; he was sixteen. After taking her for a walk in the woods, he slapped her face and said: "Do what I say or you'll be very sorry." Next, he unzipped his jeans and pulled out his penis. He told Bernice to "suck on it like an ice cream cone."

Which girl is a survivor of child sexual abuse? According to some researchers, all girls are; according to others, only Bernice is. Different defi-

nitions of child sexual abuse produce wildly different estimates of prevalence.[26] Sexual abuse rates are very high (25 percent for girls and 10 percent
for boys) when sexual abuse is defined as any sexual communication that a
child might experience from an adult or older child. The broadest, most
inclusive definition of sexual abuse includes isolated incidents of exhibition-
ism and voyeurism in which no physical contact took place. Prevalence estimates dip to about 12 percent for girls and 5 percent for boys when sexual
abuse is defined as physical contact of a sexual nature, including inappropriate kissing and genital fondling as well as penetration. When child sexual
abuse is stringently defined as intrusive behavior, for example, oral, anal,
and/or vaginal penetration, approximately 1–2 percent of children are
judged to have been sexually abused by older youth or adults.[27]

However child sexual abuse is defined, ethnic, racial, and social class distinctions are largely absent, and there are four female victims for every male
victim.[28] Almost all perpetrators (97 percent) of child sexual abuse are male.
In contrast with popular opinion and recent governmental concern, very
few Canadian and American children seem to have been exploited by the
commercial pornography industry.[29] However, a study of children supervised by Child Protective Services indicated that guardians sometimes sexually exploit their own children for personal gain.[30] Men more than women
made amateur pornographic photographs of children; women more than
men were involved in child prostitution. Other sex differences also occur
among perpetrators. Men are more likely than women to fondle victims and
attempt penetration; women are more likely than men to ask children to
put on erotic performances.[31] Sexually abused children almost always know
their assailants; incest accounts for between 24 and 43 percent of all cases
entering treatment.[32]

## SEXUAL COERCION AND RAPE

Picture four young women sharing these painful memories. While
hugging and kissing her boyfriend, the first woman had made it perfectly clear that more intimate contact was not desired. The young
man ignored her protests and insisted on stroking her clitoris despite
her angry words and unsuccessful efforts to wriggle away from his
tight grip. Two other women remember attempted rapes, one by a
stranger on a darkened street who was stopped when she had
screamed for assistance, another by a steady boyfriend who tried forcing himself on top of her when he was drunk. The fourth woman
remembers a gang rape by the members of her high-school football

team, completed while she was unconscious from ingesting too much alcohol.

Rape occurs whenever force or threat of force is used to penetrate an individual vaginally, orally, and/or anally. Alternatively, it includes penetration attempts made when the person is in no position to give consent as a result of being incapacitated mentally or psychologically, exemplified by the group rape described above. Sexual coercion has a broader definition; it includes all unwanted sexual contact between adolescents or adults, not just undesired oral sex or intercourse. Sexual coercion, unlike sexual assaultive behavior or rape, does not generally involve the explicit use of force or threat. However, sexually coerced women often feel intimidated into compliance by virtue of men's superior size and strength. Sexual coercion includes unwanted sexual intimacy of any sort, including that initiated after persistent verbal pressure.

The prevalence of rape is greatly underestimated by crime statistics, primarily because the typical rape goes unreported.[33] Given the patriarchal tradition of blaming women for getting raped, especially if they knew their assailant, women are reluctant to report sexual assaults to authorities. Most publicized rapes involve extreme levels of violence and physical injury, but the average rapist relies on moderate force. Women who experienced little or no enduring physical injury are especially unwilling to come forward when they fear others will judge them as being insufficiently brutalized to be credible rape victims. Finally, official statistics are misleadingly low because of idiosyncrasies as to how rape is defined and managed by law enforcement personnel. However forcible rape is defined legally, police are free to "unfound" or dismiss charges if they mistrust the woman or don't believe her case will hold up in court.

A recent, large-scale study of U.S. women by the National Victim Center suggested that five times as many women were rape survivors as indicated by Justice Department statistics.[34] Specifically, at least one in eight women experienced one or more forcible rapes, most likely before reaching her eighteenth birthday. In a Canadian study, almost all women who telephoned a rape crisis hotline had been sexually assaulted by someone they knew, often in their own homes.[35] Major studies of community samples and college students reveal that 20 to 40 percent of all women have experienced at least one attempted or completed rape.[36] Although Hispanic women sometimes report lower rates of sexual assault, there are no significant quantitative differences between the rape experiences of black and white women.[37] Female sexual victimization is widespread. In addition to epidemic numbers of attempted and completed rapes, large numbers of women have been verbally coerced into having sexual intercourse and many more have been kissed or fondled against their will. A high proportion of sexual coercion and assault occurs while women are still young adolescents.[38] Domestic violence, like sexual assault, is also commonplace throughout girls' and women's lives. In studies of college students, women are more likely than men to report being physically abused by a romantic partner in a heterosexual relationship.[39] Between 8 and 27 percent of female college students have been pushed, slapped, or punched by a man with whom they had been romantically involved.

Until now, a man could not be prosecuted for raping his wife in some states.[40] Exclusionary language in the criminal code for rape was based on thousands of years of legal tradition. By patriarchal observance, married women sacrificed their sexual autonomy. Wherever women are legally regarded as sexual property of their husbands, they have no right to refuse sex. Tragically, about one in ten married or cohabiting women have been sexually assaulted by a husband or lover.[41] Battered women run the highest risk of being raped by the men they live with, often repeatedly and brutally.[42] The more violent men are, the more inclined they are to rape their wives.[43] Husbands who rape their battered wives stand out as more domineering and brutal than their nonraping, physically abusive counterparts. Why do men rape wives sexually when consensual sex is possible? The answer is simple and bloodcurdling: such men believe that rape is proof of their masculinity and superiority.

About 16 percent of the men who commit and 10 percent of those who attempt sexual assault on women are involved with other assailants.[44] Group or gang rapes, variously called "pulling train," "party rape," and "gang banging," are frequently more brutal and humiliating than individual rapes. Gang rapes are likely to include insults hurled at the victim, forced fellatio, demands for manual masturbation, incidents in which the men masturbate in the woman's presence or ejaculate on her body, pulling, biting, and burning a woman's breasts, urinating on the woman, writing on the woman's body especially if she is unconscious, and publicizing the grim sexual conquest to peers. In gang rapes, the members of hypermasculine, exclusively male groups such as fraternities, military units, street gangs, and athletic teams prove their manly devotion to each other at the expense of the despised class, women.[45] In the minds of those men who manipulate vulnerable and often highly intoxicated women into a gang rape situation, what takes place is not really a sexual assault but consensual group sex with a promiscuous girl. In their own words, fraternity men describe their sexual aggression innocuously as "drunken stupidity, woman chasing, and all around silliness."[46] Although group rapists are very vocal regarding their contempt for homosexual men, there is an unacknowledged homoerotic component to their assaultive behavior. By sharing a woman's body, the men also share an intimacy with each other that would not otherwise be permitted. The individuals they aim to please and impress sexually are other men, not the women they abuse and discard. Stripping their female prey of both clothing and human dignity, group rape participants refer to their victims by such abusive names as "red meat," "fish," "gashes," "hosebags," "heifers," "scum buckets," "life-support systems," "beasts," "bitches," "swatches," and "cracks."[47] Their status in the group is increased by showing contempt for such dehumanized victims and sticking together to deny any wrongdoing afterwards.

## SEXUAL HARASSMENT

Child sexual abuse and rape are not the only forms of sexual victimization. Between 40 and 50 percent of all working women have had one or more experiences at work that met their personal definition of sexual harassment[48] Between 9 and 29 percent of women college students in the United States and Canada have experienced an incident with a faculty member that might be construed as sexual harassment.[49] Men who engage in sexual harassment are often known to behave inappropriately with several women, not just one.

Men and women are equally likely to say they have been the recipients of a variety of friendly and sexual behaviors at work and school, relatively little of which is homosexual.[50] While most men feel flattered by workplace heterosexual attention, women generally feel threatened. Research clarifies why. Women are more likely than men to regard themselves as being sexually harassed.[51] Compared to men, women are less likely to receive sexual attention from an attractive peer or subordinate but are more likely to be approached sexually by a repulsive, powerful member of their organization. Despite their differential susceptibilities, women and men characterize sexual harassment in much the same way. Most agree that expecting a student or worker to date or have sex as a condition of employment or academic progress is definitely sexual harassment. The majority also label negative sexual comments and nonverbal behaviors, like telling a woman her "tits sag" or leaving insulting, sexually explicit paraphernalia at her work station as harassing. There is less certainty as to whether or not compliments or sexually positive nonverbal gestures are forms of sexual harassment. Although almost everyone agrees that sexual touching is inappropriate at work or school, most college students and workers are comfortable with nonsexual touching, for example, a handshake or pat on the back, from either peers or individuals in authority.

## PSYCHOLOGICAL AND SOCIAL FACTORS

However common, sexual victimization is not entirely random. Researchers have identified specific types of individuals who face the greatest risk of becoming either perpetrators or victims of child sexual abuse, sexual assault, and sexual harassment. Understanding risk factors is essential for creating effective prevention and intervention programs. Standardized male sex-role socialization alone does not make a man sexually coercive; female sex-role socialization alone does not turn a woman or girl into a victim. The best predictor of child sexual abuse is family psychopathology.[52] Frequently, those who engage in child sexual abuse have themselves been so abused earlier in their lives. Sexual abuse and incest in particular are directed mostly at youngsters who come from violent homes in which children are punished in an aggressive and physical manner or adults assault each other. Two of the primary risk factors for sexual assault or rape are youth and frequent sexual activity.[53] The more sexual or dating partners a woman has, the younger she is when she first becomes sexually active, the greater her chances are of meeting up with one or more men who will treat her badly. Crime statistics tabulated by law enforcement agencies suggest that poor women and women of color are more likely to be raped than affluent, white women. However, the situation changes when acquaintance rapes, which are unlikely to be reported to the police, are also considered. Educated, upper middle-class, white women are just as likely as women from less privileged groups to report that they have experienced acquaintance rapes.

A number of women have survived repeated sexual assaults.[54] Women who have been sexually abused as children or adolescents, those who have especially liberal attitudes towards sex, women who are aroused by sexually aggressive, exaggeratedly masculine men, and those who have had higher than average levels of sexual activity seem to be more vulnerable to repeated rapes than other women. As explained earlier, battered women are more likely to be raped by their husbands than are women who live with nonviolent men.[55] Particular subcultures and regional communities have higher rates of rape than others.[56] Regions which encourage males to be rugged, individualistic, and aggressive "he-men," such as the southeastern states of the United States, have the highest reported rates of sexual victimization. Fraternity and sorority members are more likely than independent students to believe that it is legitimate for a man to use force in an intimate relationship with a woman. Compared with independent students, fraternity men appear to run a greater risk for engaging in sexual aggression whereas sorority women and the "little sisters" of fraternity men seem more susceptible to sexual victimization. Among college students, sexual aggression occurs most often when a man has proven that he is in charge of the relationship by initiating the date, paying all expenses, and doing all of the driving.[57] Because it interferes with impulse control and good judgment, excessive use of alcohol or street drugs by either or both partners greatly increases the probability of acquaintance rape.[58]

Self-reported sexually aggressive men are more likely than nonviolent men to have had multiple childhood sexual experiences, both forced and voluntary, and come from violent homes.[59] As a group, sexually aggressive men are more hostile toward women and accepting of interpersonal violence than other men. They have had a high number of sexual partners beginning at a very young age, participate in sex for recreational (not affectionate) reasons, and are very dissatisfied with their sex lives despite multiple sexual experiences. Self-reported sexually aggressive men blame women for getting raped. Characteristically, they often have a serious drinking problem and rigid ideas about masculinity. According to some but not all studies, they are heavy users of pornography and have coercive sexual fantasies. So-called "feminine" men, those who value emotional expressiveness and empathy for others over the traditional masculine traits of instrumentality and dominance, rarely or never rape or grab women against their will.[60]

Women from all income, occupational, and educational groups are susceptible to sexual harassment, especially if they are young and unmarried.[61] Several organizational characteristics increase women's likelihood of experiencing sexual harassment. First, women who work predominantly with men or in female-dominated jobs with male supervisors and clientele are more likely to experience sexual harassment than those who have only female supervisors or those who work with equal numbers of men and women. Second, sexual harassment is most likely if women are expected to perform traditional female tasks, like making coffee or purchasing gifts for a manager's family, that are irrelevant to their jobs. Third, women who work in settings where swearing, disrespectful speech, and cruel practical jokes are tolerated are more likely to be sexually harassed than those employed in more professional work environments. Finally, those who have jobs that require physical attractiveness, such as cocktail waitresses and flight attendants, are extremely susceptible to harassment, particularly if flirtation with co-workers and clients is expected.

Sex-role spillover, the inappropriate carryover into work of gender-based expectations for behavior, is responsible for much of the sexual harassment that takes place. Sex-role spillover and concomitantly sexual harassment prevail wherever women are hired to work for men based on their good looks or nurturing and friendly personalities or alternatively, wherever women break into nontraditional, male-dominated careers. Even when no women are present, traditionally masculine work environments tend to be highly charged sexually and are frequently characterized by rough language and aggressive interactions. Starting off as hostile environments for women to enter, male-dominated workplaces are made all the worse if the men present are unwilling to treat women colleagues as equals. A vivid example of this problem is given in the *Hall v. Gus Construction* (1988) case, which appeared before the 8th Circuit Court of Appeals.[62] In this case, a male co-worker called a female worker "Herpes," urinated in the gas tank of her automobile, and failed to make the necessary repairs on her truck until it was needed by a male worker.

College campuses can also be hostile to women. Although women now outnumber men students in many schools, most campus authorities, for example, tenured, high-ranking faculty and upper-level administrators, are men. Male faculty and staff are much more likely than their female counterparts to engage in behaviors with students that others might construe as sexually harassing, such as expecting socializing or dates.[63] Sex-role spillover appears to be taking place here too, with some male faculty and staff attempting to shift their formal academic obligations to students to more informal, romantic relationships. In my own research, the typical faculty initiator of sexual harassment was married, and those who described themselves as relatively unattractive were more likely to expect to have sex with the women they taught than more attractive men.

## RAPE MYTHS AND SEXUAL MISUNDERSTANDINGS

Rape myths, erroneous beliefs about sexual coercion, have enormous impact on adolescents and adults.[64] Rape myths stereotype heterosexual sex as a man's conquest of a woman and assume that sexual aggression is justified when a woman violates the sexual double standard. Capitalizing on the virgin/whore dichotomy, rape myths categorize only a few women as virtuous and most as bad, targeting all sexually active women as fair game for male sexual exploitation. Rape myths deny women the right to say No after initially appearing interested in romance. They promote the idea that women owe men sex. Grounded in patriarchal ideology, rape myths excuse men for sexually aggressive behavior and make women insensitive to the sexual victimization experienced by others. When a girl or woman is sexually abused or exploited, rape myths make her feel guilty or responsible. According to feminist, scientific research, widespread acceptance of the fifteen rape myths described below makes ours a rape-supportive culture. As you read each rape myth, dispute it in your mind. Why is the myth wrong? What are the consequences if a man believes this about the woman he is with? What happens if a woman is raped but believes this about herself? What are the consequences if a rape victim's friends or family believe this myth? What is the rational, woman-affirming alternative to each destructive myth?

*Rape Myth #1:* A man should expect to have sex if the woman has a reputation for promiscuity.

*Rape Myth #2:* A woman who flirts a lot or wears sexy clothing is just asking to have sex or get raped.

*Rape Myth #3:* A man knows that a woman wants sex if she was drinking alcohol or using drugs when they met.

*Rape Myth #4:* Any woman who is willing to go with a man to a private place where they are unlikely to be disturbed by others expects to have genital contact.

*Rape Myth #5:* If a woman allowed a man to kiss and touch her body, he is justified in insisting that they have intercourse too.

*Rape Myth #6:* If a couple has been together a long time but has never slept together, it is reasonable for the man to demand that they have sex.

*Rape Myth #7:* "Prick teasers," women who get men highly excited but refuse to have sexual intercourse, deserve to be raped.

*Rape Myth #8:* No means Yes. All women refuse to have sex with men at first. However, they don't really mean it; women love to be taken by force.

*Rape Myth #9:* Rape is a very rare crime, usually involving a stranger in a dark alley. Men don't rape the women they know.

*Rape Myth #10:* It is impossible to rape an unwilling woman. A lot of women falsely accuse men of rape because they feel guilty about having had sex.

*Rape Myth #11:* Once a woman has agreed to have sexual intercourse or oral sex with a man, she has no right to refuse in the future.

*Rape Myth #12:* Women who have poor judgment in men or who go out at night alone are just asking to get raped. Respectable, sensible women don't get raped.

*Rape Myth #13:* If a woman asked a man out or allowed him to pay all their expenses, he is entitled to sex.

*Rape Myth #14:* Most rape accusations are made by vindictive, jealous, or angry women who are trying to get even with an innocent man.

*Rape Myth #15:* Rapes are always very brutal. If the woman has had little or no enduring physical injury, she couldn't have been raped.

Now that you have read and identified the logical flaws for each rape myth, it is appropriate to consider the scientific research again. Men are significantly more likely than women to agree with rape myths.[65] Membership in fraternities and sororities and exposure to aggressive pornography increases acceptance of these misogynistic beliefs.[66] The more men agree with rape myths, the more willing they are to consider forcing a woman to have sex against her will if they think they can get away with it.[67] Rape myths make up the great cognitive shield of a culture which tolerates sexual violence against women. Disputation of rape myths is a core feature of feminist rape education, psychotherapy, and legal activism. Until the public takes women's sexual victimization seriously, police and courts will be overly lenient with accused perpetrators and many rape victims will be too ashamed or afraid to seek medical, legal, and psychological help. Unless people dispute rape myths, family members and friends may fail to support one another emotionally after sexual victimization has occurred. Every unchallenged rape myth is an excuse or justification for sexual exploitation.

Rape myths contribute to sexual aggression and conflict but other, more subtle belief systems play a role too. Psychologists Antonia Abbey and Mary Koss have done extensive research on sexual miscommunication. According to their findings, men have learned to perceive the world in a much more sexualized way than women. As a consequence, men are more likely than women to misconstrue friendliness as sexual interest.[68] Esther's experience illustrates this problem. She was shocked to be propositioned by a man she had just met at a party. Esther thought she was just being friendly; the man was certain she was coming on to him. Sexual miscommunication, fueled by gender differences in interpreting nonverbal behavior, does not necessarily lead to sexual assault. However, it does contribute to frequent sexual disagreements. In one study, Canadian college students reported that 10 percent of the time that they had engaged in sexual activity with a romantic partner, there was a sexual disagreement during which the man expected greater intimacy than the woman desired.[69] More often than not, the sexual dispute was resolved successfully. Whether or not a couple had engaged in the disputed activity before, the vast majority of men stopped trying to increase physical intimacy once they realized how the woman felt, many apologizing for their brashness. The problem was that a great deal of time and energy had to be expended before some men were convinced that the women's sexual refusals were earnest and should be taken seriously.

Unfortunately, the same men who misread friendly nonverbal behaviors as sexy are unlikely to take women's subtle nonverbal signals of sexual rejection seriously. To convince this type of man that she doesn't want to have sex, a woman must pull out all the stops, using a variety of escalating verbal and nonverbal rejection strategies before the man finally gets the message, if indeed he does at all. The situation is worse among sexually predatory men who will do or say anything to "work a yes out" of a reluctant woman.[70] Unfortunately, many young men feel pressured to have sex with women to prove their masculinity or adult status.[71] If these men accept the rape myth that "No means Yes," they will be unlikely to take a woman's sexual refusal seriously unless she is highly aggressive. But, traditional sex-role socialization discourages women from learning how to defend themselves physically, and women have good cause to be afraid that coercive men, who are often much larger and stronger than they are, might hurt them more if they became involved in a physical struggle to avoid having sex. Sexual miscommunication is complicated further by the existence of a minority of women who admit that they have said No to a new partner on occasion when they meant Yes, largely because they didn't want to appear sexually easy or loose.[72] Masculine sexual scripts that equate self-worth with sexual activity and the sexual double standard that prohibits women from looking too interested in sex contribute considerably to the dynamics of coercive sexual interactions.

## MALE DOMINANCE AND FEMALE SUBJUGATION

Historically, men have always had the potential to dominate women by the threat of rape.[73] Rapes are fostered wherever there is sexual inequality and whenever masculinity is equated with physical aggression. Sociologically speaking, rape and the degradation of women is part of a larger process by which dominant groups control subordinate groups through violence and the threat of violence. Rape and the fear of rape keeps women down in the same way that lynching and the fear of lynching kept black people down earlier in U.S. history and fear of police brutality and excessive incarceration keeps low-income people of color oppressed today. The rape of the women of a conquered people during wartime and civil unrest is not unpredictable; it is a means by which the dominant group of men prove their status to the colonized men who can no longer protect their mothers, daughters, and spouses. Sexually aggressive men are almost always hypermasculine. They are the modern descendants of conquering warriors.[74] To maintain their master status, hypermasculine men use violence and daring against the men they compete with and callous sex against the women they wish to dominate. Any boy or man who displays "inferior" female characteristics, like warmth, empathy, and collaboration, is seen as a legitimate target of humiliation and physical aggression. As pointed out later, the brutal anal rape of another man is not so much a homosexual act as the ultimate act of dominance by a hypermasculine, heterosexual man.

Macho or hypermasculine men are the successful products of a socialization process that teaches "Big boys don't cry," and that shows of anger and violence are preferable to displays of fear, anxiety, and sadness. As boys, they were taught to take pride in acts of daring and be disgusted with anyone (girls and sensitive boys) who lacked their warrior traits. As Donald Mosher and Silvan Tomkins explain, there are three rites of passage into hypermasculinity, three tests that a boy must pass to rise to the top of his male peer group: the fight scene, the danger scene, and the callous sex scene. In the fight scene, a boy must prove that he is tough enough to keep punching and kicking, even when he is badly hurt; he is allowed to show anger and excitement but never distress and fear. In the danger scene, the boy must complete an act of bravado or be willing to risk life or limb to gain peer acceptance. Again, any show of fear or distress would disqualify him. In the callous sex scene, the boy must show other adolescent males that he is capable of having sex with a girl, not for enjoyment or intimacy, but to prove his dominant status. Sex is equated with conquest; its major purpose is to enable the youth to boast to his comrades of his sexual prowess, to ridicule inferior beings (girls) who allowed their bodies to be colonized so easily.

Committed and loving sex is against the rules; the boy must prove that he is not influenced by the girl's needs or desires, that he hasn't the vaguest desire to take responsibility for his sexual behavior. He has memorized the sexual ideology of daring machismo: "You're not a 'real man' until you've scored ten times," or "You're not a real man unless you take what you need."[75] He has become the primary exponent of the "4-F" philosophy: find them, fool them, fuck them, and forget them.[76] For the hypermasculine man, women are inferiors to be conquered or assaulted, not respected and loved.[77] It is not coincidental that the most hypermasculine, misogynistic, and physically abusive husbands are also those most likely to rape their wives, that sexually assaultive behavior, including gang rape, prevails among exclusively male, hypermasculine groups, and that men who are least likely to rape are sensitive, nontraditional men who lack exaggeratedly masculine characteristics.[78] It is not coincidental that convicted rapists hold more negative attitudes towards women's rights than either law-abiding men or incarcerated men who limited their physical aggression to male targets.[79] It may not be coincidental that rape rates peak where sales of macho, outdoors magazines like *Field and Stream* and *American Rifleman* are high.[80]

## A CLOSE LOOK AT THE SEXUALLY COERCIVE MALE

Consistent with feminist theory, there is considerable scientific support for a positive association between hypermasculinity and a predilection for sexual aggression. A composite of recent studies suggests that the following profile is characteristic of males who engage in sexually assaultive and exploitative behavior.[81]

1. Misogyny—Sexually aggressive males accept sex-role stereotypes as truths and view females as adversaries. Opponents of women's rights, they are strong proponents of rape myths.

2. Antisocial Behavior—Sexually aggressive males frequently present a long history of engaging in impulsive, antisocial, and physically violent behavior, including property damage. They have little empathy, anger quickly, and blame others for their problems. Inclined to abuse alcohol and street drugs, they are especially likely to be impulsive and violent when intoxicated.

3. Hypermasculine Ideals—Sexually aggressive males view the ideal man as tough, unfeeling, and violent. Frequently, they belong to exclusively male groups which regard females as sex objects; they are likely to label their own sexually assaultive behavior as simple "seduction."

4. Quantity of Sexual Experience is More Important Than Quality— Sexually aggressive males have had much more sexual experience than other males, beginning at a younger age, but are also more sexually dissatisfied. They judge themselves and other men according to how many different partners they have had, not by the quality of their sexual relationships.

5. Sexual Motivation is Hostile and Power Oriented—The concepts of sex and violence are fused; aggressive, violent, sexual imagery is arousing. Sexually aggressive males use sex to control girls or women; they love to brag about their sexual conquests. Often be-

lieving that they have been hurt, deceived, betrayed, manipulated, belittled, ridiculed, or emotionally smothered by females in the past, they are eager to get even.

Sexually aggressive boys and men are more likely than their nonviolent counterparts to have grown up in violent homes, including those where they too had been victims of sexual coercion.[82] Anger, confusion, and hurt from prior victimization is only a catalyst for becoming a sexually abusive individual, however; not all sexual aggressors are former victims. Hypermasculine socialization provides the script for sexual exploitation. The sexually aggressive man is often just an average "he-man" who has had an opportunity to act on his misogynistic convictions.

## UNCONVENTIONAL PERPETRATORS; UNEXPECTED VICTIMS

Seven-year-old Lillian was sent to a group home for emotionally disturbed youngsters after she was found sexually abusing Bobby, her two-year-old cousin. To her aunt's horror, Lillian was seen inserting a pencil inside Bobby's rectum; the little boy required immediate medical attention.

Cynthia was fifteen but twelve-year-old Carlos appealed to her. Cornering the boy in a deserted spot, she pulled up her short, tight skirt and unzipped his jeans. She said, "Let's fuck!" He was scared and embarrassed. He did what she asked because she suggested that he might be "queer" and didn't want the word to get out on the street that he was still a virgin.

Barbara's story came out in spurts. She really loved her partner but recognized that the relationship was not a good one. Until recently, arguments had been limited to shouting matches but in the past four months, they had escalated to physical violence. With all the fighting, all the hostile epitaphs "bitch," "slut," "whore," that had been directed her way, Barbara hadn't wanted to have sex for quite some time. But then, to her consternation, her lover took her by force two days ago. Barbara had been shoved against the wall and smacked hard with a metal pole. When she came to after fainting from pain and the sight of her own blood, she found her partner performing oral sex on her. It was this sexual violation that convinced her that she needed therapy. When the social worker asked for more information, she was shocked to learn that Barbara's violent lover was another woman.

A little girl who sexually abuses little boys, a young adolescent boy who is coerced into sexual intercourse by an older adolescent girl, a lesbian, battered woman who was sexually assaulted by the woman she loved—such unconventional perpetrators and unexpected victims. Feminists don't often bring up such examples when they write about sexual abuse. But, a truly scientific and scholarly feminist theory must account for discrepancies, for exceptions to the rule that perpetrators of sexual exploitation are male and victims are female.[83] Feminist theory is not any the less powerful for considering exceptions.

Male dominance shapes the rape culture but psychopathology does too. If male dominance was the only factor responsible for sexual aggression, then every male would be an abuser and the experience of sexual coercion would be universal for all females. True too, girls and women may internalize some of the aggressive messages meant for male sex-role socialization. If men and boys are seen as superior and dominant, then members of the subordinate class, girls and women, can gain higher status by imitation. Psychoanalysts have called this process identifying with the aggressor. It occurs whenever an oppressed person attempts to join the ascendant group by rejecting his or her community of origin to behave like the "top dogs." It is a term that applies to black people who have tried to "act white," Jewish concentration camp inmates who identified with the Nazi guards, and Asians who undergo eye surgery to look more European. It is also a term that applies to girls and women who commit sexually aggressive acts. Like their male counterparts, women who batter and girls and women who sexually abuse and intimidate others are often themselves the survivors of severe and chronic childhood sexual abuse and physical assaults.[84] By lashing out at others, they symbolically regain sexual autonomy while expressing rage which heretofore was buried deep inside. Girls who sexually abuse other children present similar histories to those of sexually abusive boys. Most have serious academic problems and deficient peer relationships. They are often seen as oppositional by adults and have engaged in a wide variety of antisocial acts such as stealing and setting fires. Sometimes, their abusive behavior is a cry for help made after their own complaints of victimization went unacknowledged by their families. Alcohol and drug abuse were characteristic in their highly unstable families. Jealous and angry, many girls selected younger relatives for sexual abuse who were resented because they seemed to have been spared the parental brutality that they themselves had suffered.

Sexual abuse of boys by mothers is considered extremely rare, but psychotherapists have seen adult men who report that as boys, they had been expected to sleep with, touch and be touched in a sexual way, and even have sexual intercourse with their mothers.[85] Although mother-son sex was not generally aggressive, the sons often felt ashamed and suffered the same depression and difficulties with intimacy faced by many female incest survivors. In contrast with mother-son incest, female-initiated, heterosexual, sexual coercion is not very unusual. In one study of U.S. college students, most of the men surveyed admitted that they had at least one experience with unwanted heterosexual sex.[86] As feminists would expect, men were more likely than women to say that their unwanted sexual encounters occurred as the result of social pressure from friends to prove that they were sexually active and heterosexual. And, as expected, women were more likely than men to say that they had been physically coerced into sexual activity. However, there were a number of men who had sex out of a sense of obligation to their partner or because they were so intoxicated they could neither stop their partner nor control their own behavior. A recent study of Canadian college students yielded equally intriguing results.[87] Men were more likely than women to say they had been in a situation in which a woman had wanted a higher level of sexual activity than the man. Although women were viewed as using seductive strategies more than coercive ones to get their way, pouting and sulking as well as verbal and physical coercion were also used on sexually reluctant men. Men acknowledged that in some situations, women had tried to sexually influence them through insults, threats, even physical attempts to hold them down, all findings which are inconsistent with the belief that sexual victimization is an exclusively female experience.

Given men's generally greater physical size and strength, sexually coercive women appear to be much less threatening to their partners than sexually coercive men. Since the overwhelming majority of men who have unwanted sex seem to be responding to women's demands largely to protect their masculine self-image and not because they fear for their lives, they should not be labeled as rape victims. However, it also would be wrong to ignore research findings on such men simply because they contradict classical feminist theory. Extremist Radical Feminists are misguided in characterizing all men as sexual beasts and all women as predictable victims of male lust and brutality. Sometimes, the tables are turned and women want sex more or behave more aggressively than their male partners. More importantly, feminists should not ignore the fact that men too get brutally raped by men. As many as 7 percent of adult men in the general population and at least 8 percent of those who have been incarcerated have been raped by one or more men.[88] As described earlier, men who rape other men are generally heterosexually oriented, dominant men who validate their "he-man" status by violating others.[89] Through the violent rape of a man, often conducted by a group, the victim (regardless of his actual sexual orientation) is transformed symbolically from a member of society's dominant group into a despised female, labeled thereafter as a "punk" or "queer." Male rape victims are even more reluctant to come forward than their female counterparts and are often more physically brutalized during the assault. A fully feminist analysis of rape would account for patriarchal reasons for male on male rape as well as those contributing to the more common rape of females.

Police statistics document a few instances (less than 1 percent of all arrests for forcible rape) of female rapists. Typically, female rapists have been involved with helping one man or a group of men sexually assault another woman. Only 0.7 percent of the women surveyed in one U.S. community study indicated that they had been forced into anal or oral sex by another woman who had threatened them physically or exploited them when they were unconscious, drugged, or otherwise incapable of giving consent. Lest this tiny number lull us into complacency, a recent pioneering study of a small sample of U.S. gay and lesbian college students suggested that nearly one in three women felt that she had been coerced into having sex by a lesbian partner at least once in her lifetime.[90] The lesbians in this study may have had an exaggeratedly broad definition of sexual coercion, including, for example, psychological pressure as well as verbal threat and physical force in their conceptualization of aggressive sex. Nonetheless, the realities of sexual aggression in some lesbian relationships should not be overlooked.[91]

Ignored by both the therapeutic and lesbian communities until the recent past, the terror and pain wrought by lesbian battering has gone unacknowledged because of stereotypes about women in general and lesbians in particular. Because lesbians expect other woman-identified women to be independent and self-confident, they find it difficult to accept that other lesbians would remain in an abusive relationship. Because everyone, including psychotherapists, expects women to be sensitive and gentle, it is difficult to imagine a woman physically assaulting anyone, least of all her lover. Thanks to lesbian activists in the battered women's movement, lesbian battery is "out of the closet" at last. Socialized as women, lesbians are substantially less likely than heterosexual men to physically abuse their lovers. However, anecdotal evidence suggests that female-initiated domestic brutality, when it does occur, is similar to the male-initiated variety. Lesbian abuse is mostly verbal, mostly a series of emotionally charged efforts to belittle and control a partner. Like the male batterer, the female one is prone to jealous rages and is likely to accuse her lover of "sleeping around." Typically from a dysfunctional family where alcoholism or drug abuse prevailed, often physically and/or sexually abused by parent figures as a child, the battering lesbian keeps her lover in a perpetual state of vigilance while undermining her sense of autonomy and self-worth. Attempts by the abused partner to end the relationship are likely to be met by physical violence. Coercive sex may follow the physical violence. Superficially, the sex is meant to "heal" the conflict. But, in reality, it is largely an attempt by the battering partner to clarify her complete control over the relationship just as surely as a violent husband conveys dominance through marital rape. Women remain in abusive lesbian relationships for the same reasons they remain in violent heterosexual ones. They may be economically dependent. They may be afraid and feel helpless. They may have such a bad image of themselves that they think they deserve the abuse. Socially isolated, they don't know where to find help.

Although men are significantly more physically aggressive than women, women are perfectly capable of being verbally and physically abusive with intimate partners. A truly inclusive feminist theory of sexual coercion must account for girls and women who identify with the aggressor and men's sexual victimization of other men. Feminism is not served by bashing men or recommending that women live in isolation. Feminism is about moving all of humanity towards peace, equality, prosperity, health, and affirmation.

## THE CONSEQUENCES OF SEXUAL ABUSE, RAPE, AND SEXUAL HARASSMENT

Danielle's performance in high school is much poorer than expected. According to her teachers, she is depressed and withdrawn. For the past year, she has been truant on several occasions. Danielle ran away from home three times during the past six months.

Jodie has difficulty concentrating and is often hyperactive and aggressive at her nursery school. Frequently, she is engaged in a frantic form of masturbation; the youngster just can't seem to keep her hands out of her pants. Although her vocabulary is quite limited, she knows all the street words for sexual activities and the genitalia.

Child sexual abuse, especially incest, may be associated with serious short- and long-term consequences. The problematic behaviors exhibited by Danielle and Jodie are consistent with some of the earliest symptoms presented by sexual abuse victims. Because children and adolescents are often afraid to disclose their abuse to others,[92] their victim status may be communicated indirectly to concerned adults through signs of emotional distress. Younger children may have problems with age-inappropriate bed wetting, excessive sexual play or sexually precocious behavior, hyperactivity, aggressive behavior, sleep disturbances, and somatic symptoms of emotional distress.[93] Older children and adolescents may show signs of lowered self-esteem, difficulty trusting others—especially adults, depression, anxiety, panic attacks, phobias, obsessive-compulsive behaviors, rebellious behaviors like running away, being accident prone, self-injurious behavior, poor school performance, concentration problems, somatic complaints, and promiscuity or pseudomaturity. The short- and long-term impact of child sexual abuse varies according to the nature of the abuse and the extent to which it was repeated. An isolated, very mild, nonpenetrative childhood sexual experience may have no discernible impact. The worst psychological consequences are associated with highly traumatic experiences such as sexual penetration with a sharp object. Post-traumatic hyperarousal is common in highly traumatized victims who for some time afterwards will startle easily and be prone to distractibility and nightmares.

Adult survivors of child sexual abuse are especially susceptible to a variety of psychological problems.[94] For women, these may include relationship and sexual difficulties related to mistrust and poor self-image, depression, fear and anxiety, chronic anger, and antisocial behaviors such as child abuse. Some adult survivors of sexual abuse are predisposed to revictimization. In other words, they may be raped repeatedly throughout their youth or end up in long-term relationships with physically abusive partners. A number of adult survivors of childhood sexual abuse have been diagnosed to have post-traumatic stress disorder, a form of "battle fatigue" in which they continue to re-experience childhood traumas through flashbacks and nightmares. Others block out the pain with dissociation disorders. Memories may be repressed while negative feelings are denied. Parts of the body may feel numb, especially when current life experiences threaten to conjure up lost memories. Extreme abuse leads to dissociation. Psychotherapists now believe that one out of four patients who suffer from multiple personality disorders had been sexually abused as children. Their debilitating disorder helps them deny or avoid memories of the severe sexual abuse that they had been forced to endure.

There is no uniform adult reaction to rape or sexual assault.[95] Some women sob uncontrollably afterwards; others are calm, almost overly subdued. Community surveys suggest that between 20 and 50 percent of all sexually assaulted women have been revictimized, prior sexual assault experiences exacerbating any new trauma.[96] Like some child sexual abuse survivors, rape victims are susceptible to post-traumatic stress disorder.[97] In addition to somatic symptoms from physical injuries, the psychological trauma they endured can lead to a variety of health complaints including skeletal muscle tension, headaches, fatigue, disturbed sleep, jumpiness, and gastrointestinal irritability. The symptoms such women present are similar to those of combat veterans. Weeks or months after the rape, there may be nightmares, flashbacks, and a great fear of being trapped in a setting similar to that in which the rape took place. Many women change their telephone number and residence during this period. Excessive alertness, anxiety attacks, and extensive requests for social support are characteristic. Without appropriate therapeutic intervention, some rape victims continue to suffer from impaired social adjustment, anxiety, and depression long after the rape occurred.

Sexual dysfunctions are the longest lasting problems associated with rape or a history of child sexual abuse. Immediately after they were assaulted, almost all adult rape victims either stop having sex with their regular partners temporarily or greatly reduce their sexual frequency. Years later, one in three rape victims and numerous adult survivors of child sexual abuse continue to complain of sexual difficulties. Typically, such women have little difficulty achieving orgasm once sufficiently aroused. However, they are more likely than nonvictims to feel sexually inhibited, have difficulty with arousal, experience pain during sexual intercourse, and be diagnosed with vaginismus (involuntary, vulvar, muscle contractions which prevent penetration). Sexual harassment does not generally have the devastating effects of child sexual abuse and rape. However, the impact is far from innocuous.[98] As a result of sexual harassment, some women have had their careers interrupted because they were forced to quit or were dismissed. Other victims of harassment have experienced diminished job satisfaction. Self-confidence may be impaired, and harassment victims may find themselves understandably angry and resentful about their mistreatment. Somatic complaints and anxiety symptoms are not uncommon. Sexual harassment hurts organizations, not just individuals. Diminished productivity, poor employee morale, absenteeism, excessive job turnover, and expensive court cases all have been associated with sexual harassment.

Any objective consideration of the long-term effects of child sexual abuse, rape, and sexual harassment should acknowledge human strength and resilience. Sexual abuse and exploitation do not inevitably lead to emotional disturbance. Many women go on to lead happy, productive, sexually fulfilled lives despite experiences with abuse. Too much research on problems associated with sexual abuse is based on women who require lengthy psychological treatment; this is not a representative population. Studying a community sample of African-American and European-American women, Gail Wyatt and her colleagues learned that most adult survivors of child sexual abuse who came from close and loving families were well-adjusted women with high self-esteem, a positive outlook, and good skills in protecting themselves from future sexual exploitation.[99] Similarly, rape survivors who came from close families did not shut off their sexual desires with consensual partners the way that women from rejecting families often did.

## FEMINIST REFORM EFFORTS

Radical and Liberal Feminists have been united in the battle against female sexual victimization on three fronts: helping survivors, providing education, and lobbying for legal change.[100] Service agencies for rape and sexual abuse victims and advocacy groups for preventing sexual assault were nonexistent in both Canada and the United States until the 1970s.[101] Thanks to the grassroots organizational work of feminists, there are twenty-four-hour rape crisis hotlines, treatment facilities and shelters for sexual assault victims and battered women, victim advocacy programs, and sexual assault educational services in hundreds of communities throughout North America. Unfortunately, neither the United States nor the Canadian government has provided sufficient funding or organizational support for rape crisis and education centers. Without feminists' private fund-raising efforts and volunteer labor, victims of sexual assault would have nowhere to turn. Feminists have not limited themselves to rallying against rape and childhood sexual abuse; they have also tackled sexual harassment. Until feminists came into the picture, sexual harassment was a bad experience with no name and no remedy. Today, it is illegal and is considered a form of sex discrimination.[102] Sexual harassment cases are now routinely handled by personnel managers, administrators, corporate and university grievance boards, the court system, and government agencies such as the Equal Employment Opportunity Commission in the United States.

Feminists have become increasingly concerned about the co-option of some rape and sexual abuse prevention programs by antifeminists. Educators who urge women to dress conservatively, avoid nonmarital sex, live in fear, and never go out alone are part of the problem, not part of the solution. Effective programs for preventing rape, child sexual abuse, and sexual harassment empower girls and women; challenge misogynistic beliefs, and enable men and women to reject rigid sexual scripts; improve their communication skills; and feel better about themselves. Communication skills assume a key role in feminist educational programs. Feminist educators clarify that good sex requires respecting a partner's feelings, talking openly about one's own sexual desires and intentions throughout the sexual encounter, and securing verbal consent before expecting a partner to progress from cuddling to genital contact. Good rape prevention programs also teach women and men how to handle a partner's rejection without feeling devastated or getting angry. Programs aimed at preventing sexual abuse and exploitation should be realistic. Not all men respond well to a woman's verbal assertiveness; some heterosexual interactions are risky and explosive. It is necessary to teach girls and women self-defense, how they might escape from a dangerous situation by yelling, running, and fighting back physically. Such training shouldn't be theoretical; these skills should be practiced, rehearsed, and reinforced repeatedly. Finally, educators should explain the legal ramifications of sexually inappropriate and abusive behavior and how and where victims can obtain assistance.

Until feminists protested, rape laws were biased against women.[103] When outside witnesses were unavailable, assessment as to whether or not a rape took place was based solely on testimony, the woman's word versus the man's, with male police officers and attorneys tempted to regard the woman as a less credible witness. Since only women who were severely bruised and bloodied were likely to be believed, the criminal justice system discriminated against the overwhelming majority of sexual assault victims who had been raped by moderate force. Before feminists challenged rape laws, women had to prove that penetration (typically vaginal penetration) had taken place and was against their will. This legal requirement made it next to impossible to prosecute sex crimes that did not involve penetration, like urinating and ejaculating on a victim or demanding that a victim perform fellatio. The requirement also ignored the fact that some sexually traumatized women may be so upset, they wash away physical evidence before seeking a gynecological examination to establish evidence that a rape occured. Rape laws, as originally written, discriminated against male victims too. By definition, men couldn't be raped since it was physiologically impossible for them to experience forced vaginal intercourse. Finally, the law regarded married women as the sexual and reproductive property of their husbands. Marital rape was not a crime until feminists disputed the patriarchal idea that husbands had a legal right to force themselves on their own wives.

U.S. feminists have had some mixed success changing various state rape laws and serving as victims' advocates in court. In most jurisdictions, women are no longer routinely asked embarrassing questions about their sexual histories by defense attorneys representing men accused of sexual assault. Although some states were more reluctant than others to drop the marital rape exemption, a man can be prosecuted for raping his wife in all fifty states.[104] Canadian feminists have been more successful than their American counterparts in making needed legal reforms, exemplified by the Canadian Parliament's passage of bill C-127 in January 1983.[105] An excellent model for feminist legal reform, there is no exemption for marital rape in bill C-127. Gender bias in wording has been eliminated in this bill to permit prosecuting female perpetrators and providing justice for male victims of sexual assault. Rather than limiting the law to one particular act or deeming involuntary vaginal intercourse as the most serious sexual offense by definition, C-127 considers a variety of coercive sexual behaviors. In Canada but not the United States, the seriousness of a sexual crime is equated with the extent to which force was involved instead of the nature of genital juxtapositions. Three levels of sexual assault are stipulated in Canada's rape law: sexual assault; sexual assault with a weapon, and aggravated (life threatening) sexual assault. Although the Canadian Supreme Court struck down the "rape shield" provision of C-127 in 1991 because attorneys argued that blanket restrictions on questions related to a victim's past sexual history violated defendants' rights to a free trial, additional feminist reforms have been approved. Under Canadian law, a rape case can be successfully prosecuted based largely on the woman's testimony, without either corroborating testimony or physical evidence presented in court. In 1992, the Canadian Parliament passed the "No means No" law which requires defendants in rape trials to prove how they confirmed that the woman actively demonstrated her willingness to have sex; a lack of definiteness in her refusal could not in itself be evidence for consent.

Is Canada a feminist utopia? Not quite yet. Male victims of sexual assault and women who were raped by acquaintances and husbands remain reluctant to test the law. Antiwoman prejudices have not been eliminated from police departments and the criminal justice system. As pointed out aptly by Canadian psychologist Sandra Byers: "Attitudes are harder to change than the law and many Canadian women may be unaware of their legal rights."[106]

## SEXUAL VICTIMIZATION AND PORNOGRAPHY

However united feminists are in their analysis of the patriarchal roots of female sexual victimization, they are deeply divided in their opinions about pornography. As pointed out earlier, Radical Feminists generally believe that pornography, especially violent pornography, should be closely regulated or suppressed because it may inspire men to sexually abuse women. Liberal Feminists, in contrast, maintain that the danger of infringing on free speech by censoring or restricting sexually explicit material far outweighs any possible benefits. To understand the feminist debates and pornography research, we must employ a broad historical and cultural perspective. Nearly every society has produced art work or literature that has had the objective of either informing the user about sexual matters or increasing arousal.[107] Generally, such materials have been produced by and for men and until recently were available only to the wealthy and privileged. During the late nineteenth and twentieth centuries, sexually explicit material was made inexpensive for the first time through mass production. The first social debates about pornography were ignited, not by the emergence of a new phenomenon, but by the reality of an ordinary citizen's access to materials regarded as socially dangerous by the self-appointed moral guardians of the time.

Before feminists take a stand on pornography, they should come to terms with the historical role of pro-censorship political leaders in using obscenity laws to suppress woman-affirming information and artistic creations. Religious zealot Anthony Comstock, as Special Agent for the Postmaster General, responsible for censoring obscene or morally dangerous materials sent through the U.S. mail between 1873 and 1915, succeeded in burning numerous books as well as hounding and imprisoning several individuals who were concerned with women's sexual and reproductive rights. George Bernard Shaw was nearly prevented by Comstock from showing his play, *Mrs. Warren's Profession*, in the United States because it portrayed a woman prostitute sympathetically. A special target of Comstock, Margaret Sanger, the mother of the American birth control movement, was indicted on nine counts for violating federal statutes for her role in distributing *The Woman Rebel*, a tract on birth control information. Had Sanger not fled to England, she might have had to serve a lengthy prison term for "obscenity." Fortunately, the case was eventually dropped, and Sanger was able to return to the United States but not before her husband served thirty days in jail for distributing the pamphlet *Family Limitation*. Attacks on women's freedom of expression and right to information by guardians of the patriarchy were not limited to the United States. In 1928, a British judge ordered the destruction of Radclyffe Hall's pioneering novel about lesbian life, *The Well of Loneliness*.

Pro-choice, feminist readers, no doubt, might see an uncanny resemblance between historical efforts by patriarchal spokesmen to protect women from "obscenity" and current efforts by American ultraconservatives to decrease women's access to information about abortion, birth control, and anything contradicting "traditional family values." The issue of limiting women's choices is not irrelevant to the current pornography debates between Radical and Liberal Feminists. After all the theories are presented, after all scientific evidence is taken into account, after all the women have testified about pornography, it still boils down to one central question: Who should speak for the rest of us? Who can say for sure whether or not sexually explicit material should be banned for being socially harmful or permitted as generally harmless or beneficial? Whatever the reader concludes, it is certain that pornography, especially "soft" or less explicit pornography, is widely distributed.[108] Each month, eleven million copies of the top thirteen men's magazines, including *Forum*, *Penthouse*, and *Playboy*, are circulated in the United States. About 13 percent of all videotapes currently sold contain "adult" or sexually explicit content. Adult videos have a bigger market share than comedy, drama, children's programs, music videos, and horror films. By the mid 1980s, cable TV channels carrying R-rated programming reached over 14.5 million U.S. homes with access to X-rated programming available but more restricted. About 9 percent of Americans rent an X-rated videotape each year. Men remain the primary market for sexually explicit material. However, among young adults, women are nearly as likely as men to rent or purchase an "adult" video in the United States, and adolescent Canadians report watching sexually explicit videos more frequently than their elders.

Pornography has changed in recent years. The old "hard core" focus on a "meat shot . . . a close-up of penetration" which proves that "real sex," as defined by men, has taken place has given way to some extent to more women's and couple-oriented materials.[109] The bulk of sexually explicit materials produced, however, continue to depict an unequal battle of the sexes in which women are seen accommodating their sexuality and desire to that of men. Feminist film critic, Linda Williams, argues that some men may use pornography to compensate for their threatened masculinity, escaping to a fantasy world where penises are always hard, women are always willing, and men are firmly, pun intended, in charge of everything. Phallocentric or not, only 10 percent of X-rated films contain sadistic or sexually violent content.[110] Radical Feminist criticism to the contrary, there is far less murder, general violence, and rape in X-rated films than in many R-rated films and TV dramas.

## BITTER ARGUMENTS AMONG FEMINISTS OVER PORNOGRAPHY

Since the 1980s, pornography has bitterly divided the women's rights movement with extremists from both sides declaring that their opponents couldn't possibly be real feminists.[111] The conflict between procensorship and anticensorship activists has had the unhappy effect of distracting everyone from the issues that originally united the second wave of feminism, such as reproductive rights, domestic violence, education, jobs, women's health, and childcare. True, Radical Feminists are more likely than Liberal

Feminists to be antagonistic to pornography and stress the dangers of sex for women. However, divisions in the women's movement should not be oversimplified; a diversity of opinions exists within the two major camps.

Among Radical Feminists, extremists wish to ban all pornography, regardless of content or whether or not the producers and majority of consumers are women. In contrast, moderate Radical Feminists distinguish between "pornography" and "erotica," defining the former as depictions of sexual violence and female subordination, which they hate, and the latter as depictions of sexual activity between affectionate equals, which they like. Some Radical Feminists just want to educate the public about misogynistic messages in pornography, hoping to change public opinion without infringing upon either personal autonomy or the freedom of the marketplace. Others urge consumer boycotts of material that they find offensive. Still others advocate litigation against specific producers and distributors of pornography for "damages" suffered by women at the hands of sexually aggressive men who consumed this material. Yet another group lobbies for censorship. Even the procensorship Radical Feminists are divided into those who wish to censor only depictions of interpersonal violence and the extremists who think all erotic material should be censored.

Liberal Feminists are no more unanimous than their Radical counterparts. There are extremists who embrace all forms of pornography with revolutionary fervor as tools for liberating oppressed sexual minorities. In contrast, moderates have neutral feelings about sexually explicit materials but think that consumers and women in particular should be free to purchase what they desire. The Liberal Feminist camp even includes women who, despite their vehement opposition to censorship as an infringement of free speech, agree with their Radical counterparts that pornography probably plays a role in sexual violence directed at women.

## RADICAL FEMINISTS EXAMINE PORNOGRAPHY

Whether they oppose all sexually explicit material or only that which portrays sexual violence, Radical Feminists argue that pornography is a tool of the patriarchy. According to Radical Feminist theory, men's control over women's sexuality is central to all institutionalized male domination and pornography provides the scripts for that domination.[112] To support their premise, Radical Feminists have encouraged sexually victimized women to speak out against pornography. Most of the stories told by such women are tragic and shocking. Former pornographic star Linda Marchiano, for example, testified that she had been repeatedly raped and sexually abused, both on and off screen, during the filming of *Deep Throat*, a male sexual fantasy about a woman who achieves orgasm only through fellatio. Victims of domestic violence have talked about their husbands and boyfriends sexually assaulting and torturing them as they were forced to act out the scenes from particular violent pornographic films or literature. Bloodthirsty, misogynistic imagery certainly exists in some pornography. There are films that show a man achieving orgasm by injuring or killing a woman; there are eroticized portrayals of gang rapes; there are magazines that depict weapons of torture, such as hot irons and knives, next to a nude, bound woman's breasts or vulva. It is not difficult to find examples of pornography that sanitize or romanticize sexual violence, that present sexualized and dehumanized caricatures of women. If much of pornography is a "hate literature" against women, as Radical Feminists plead, then it is especially dangerous because it can so readily be mistaken for "sexual facts" by young men who have been denied an adequate sex education.

To those Liberal Feminists and civil libertarians who protest that any restriction on pornography is also a restriction of "free speech," Radical Feminists reply that only privileged persons (read in affluent, white men) enjoy the full rights of citizens. Women, they argue, are denied free speech, silenced by the misogynistic messages of pornography. As lawyer Catharine MacKinnon explains, "Where feminism criticizes the ways in which women have been socially determined . . . , liberalism is voluntaristic, meaning it acts like we have choices, that we do not have."[113] Rather than being a form of free speech, pornography is equated with the systematic practice of exploiting and subordinating women.[114] Pornography, Radical Feminists reason, presents women as sexually insatiable "things," not people. Pornography, they go on to say, shows women enjoying pain, humiliation, rape, and penetration by objects or animals, in postures or positions of sexual submission, tied up, cut up, or hurt, reduced to various body parts—vaginas, breasts, buttocks, and nothing more. Pornography, they continue, is a hate literature with real victims: the sex workers who must perform repulsive acts to make a living, women who are sexually coerced by misogynistic men who might in part have been inspired by violent pornography, and all women whose access to a decent job or education is impaired by men whose minds have been poisoned by pornography.

Radical Feminists resent being compared to the orthodox religious groups that have always opposed pornography.[115] As they point out, strictly religious people oppose pornography for its sexual content; Radical Feminists do so for its themes of male dominance, female subordination, and sexual violence. Indeed, the one scientific study comparing feminists' and Christian fundamentalists' attitudes toward pornography provides some confirmation for this distinction.[116] Feminists as a group have had more experience examining pornography than fundamentalists. Fundamentalists define pornography as any material that shows explicit nudity or sexual acts; antipornography feminists define it as any exploitative or degrading depiction of women. But protest as they might, antipornography feminists have more in common with the religious foes of pornography than they might think. Both groups believe that individual rights and freedom should be sacrificed for what they perceive to be the welfare of the general population. Both groups regard pornography as a "moral issue," not a political one, and have coordinated efforts testifying against commercial sex to various governmental commissions.

Since the 1980s, extreme Radical Feminists have proposed several pieces of legislation in the United States that would enable individuals who see themselves as "victims" of pornography to sue those who publish and distribute it.[117] After unsuccessful attempts to adopt antipornography ordinances in Indianapolis, Indiana; Minneapolis, Minnesota; Suffolk County, New York; and Bellingham, Washington, they have submitted proposed bills that would enable victims of sexual assaults to recover "damages" from pornographers to both the Commonwealth of Massachusetts and the U.S. Congress. The Pornography Victim's Compensation Act, currently under congressional consideration, would make commercial producers, distributors, exhibitors, and sellers of obscene material liable for any sexual offense determined by a court to have been a major cause (or motivating factor) for a sex offender's actions. Disturbing to proponents of judicial rights, the proposed Pornography Victim's Compensation Act holds pornographers responsible for forcible sex crimes, whether or not these crimes had been prosecuted or proven in a separate criminal proceeding, and stipulates that any evidence is admissible "except the testimony of the offender."[118]

On February 27, 1992, the Supreme Court of Canada upheld the obscenity portion of its criminal code, which ruled that suppression of materials that harmed women took precedence over freedom of expression, making it legitimate to outlaw pornography that was perceived as harmful to women.[119] In *Butler v. Her Majesty the Queen*, the Court unanimously redefined obscenity along Radical Feminist lines as sexually explicit material that involves violence or degradation. The Canadian decision applies to materials judged to degrade men, not just those involving women and children. Lawyer Kathleen Mahoney argued the case on behalf of the Women's Legal Education and Action Fund of Toronto; Catharine MacKinnon, an American law professor and Radical Feminist who supports restricting pornography in the United States, helped write the legal brief. The Canadian decision still gives individual prosecutors considerable autonomy in interpreting community standards regarding the acceptability of pornographic materials. Historically, Canadian regulation of obscenity has varied greatly across provinces with Quebec, for example, having very liberal laws and Ontario being highly restrictive. Nonetheless, by concluding that violent and degrading pornography harms women, the decision establishes a major legal precedent. According to the Canadian Court, exposure to violent and degrading pornography humiliates and exploits the women who are depicted, belittles and dehumanizes all women, and interferes with progress towards sexual equality. To date, Canada remains the only nation that has redefined obscenity in terms of harm to women rather than as material that offends moral values. Two years after the *Butler* decision, Liberal Feminist fears that Canadian obscenity law would be directed at materials produced by and for gay individuals and women have been confirmed. Canadian Customs officials continue to ban the importation of all representations of anal intercourse. To date, the three key obscenity cases following the Canadian Supreme Court decision concern gay erotic materials including the lesbian magazine *Bad Attitude*. Canadian legal scholar Lise Gotell points out that lower Canadian courts applied *Butler* case language, "degrading and dehumanizing," to determine that the gay pornography was obscene.

Radical Feminists are a hardworking, committed group. One study suggests that their fervor may have come in part from life in the trenches. Feminists who want to control pornography are more likely than anticontrol feminists to have worked with female victims of violence as counselors, health care providers, and law enforcement officers and to have had personal experiences as survivors of sexual abuse and battery.[120] It would be wrong to conclude that antipornography feminists necessarily dislike all erotic materials. Most Radical Feminists have no objection to sexually explicit depictions of naked adults engaged in conventional and consensual heterosexual and homosexual activity. Nor do most Radical Feminists oppose serious artistic and scientific treatments of human sexuality. Instead, the majority of Radical Feminists wish to eliminate sexually explicit material which they believe exploits children, shows sexual violence as acceptable, or depicts women in a degrading fashion.

## LIBERAL FEMINISTS EXAMINE PORNOGRAPHY

In the interest of expedience, some Radical Feminists have been willing to form a coalition with various right-wing political groups that also oppose pornography.[121] Critics of the 1986 "Meese Report," for instance, note that the 2,000-page report by the U.S. Attorney General's Pornography Commission omitted any discussion of women who have had positive or liberating experiences with erotica as well as feminist arguments against censorship.[122] According to legal scholar Robin West, the Meese Report blended "feminist antipornography rhetoric with conservative ideology. The result is a feminist-conservative argument against pornography that is neither feminist nor conservative but a peculiar blend of both."[123] Liberal Feminists and some moderate Radical Feminists are disturbed by the actions of those Radical Feminists who have joined forces with the politically ultra-conservative foes of pornography.[124] Since most opponents of pornography also object to the goals of the women's rights movement, Liberal Feminists fear a blanket condemnation of erotica in the future, including feminist work with sexual content and not just sexist or violent pornography. As pointed out in the last chapter, nineteenth and early twentieth century feminists who opposed prostitution joined forces with right-wing groups of their day, but the coalition bore bitter fruit for feminists. Eventually, the movement to end the commercial sexual exploitation of girls and women was co-opted by powerful men who were unsympathetic to the lower socio-economic status women who so often ended up in prostitution. As a consequence, the sex workers whom feminists hoped to protect were trampled down further still by the patriarchal establishment. Only time will tell if history repeats itself with the current antipornography movement.

Liberal Feminists do not dispute everything that Radical Feminists say about pornography. Few would dispute, for instance, that most pornography today is produced to please men, not women, or that some contains content that is, at best, insensitive to women and, at worst, blatantly sexist and demeaning. Fewer still would deny that eroticized portrayals of violence against women are offensive. No matter how personally disturbing some examples of pornography might be, however, all Liberal Feminists and some moderate Radical Feminists argue that censorship is worse. How, then, do Liberal Feminists differ from their extremist Radical Feminist counterparts? They start with five different assumptions about pornography:[125] (1) Pornography does not cause women's inequality or sexual victimization; (2) Any suppression of free speech is dangerous; (3) When it comes to the depiction of violence against women, pornography is neither the only nor the worst culprit; (4) Imagery is not violence—the artistic depiction of antisocial behavior (such as rape) is not the same thing as the behavior in question; (5) Women can enjoy pornography too.

According to Liberal Feminists, sexist and violent pornography is the window-dressing of the patriarchy, a symptom of misogynistic views but not the central cause of women's oppression. The elimination of pornography, Liberal Feminists argue, would not guarantee the success of the women's movement. Some of the most male-dominated societies which have ever existed, for example, the Puritan society in colonial Massachusetts and contemporary Islamic fundamentalist regimes, have oppressed women in the extreme while banning pornography entirely. Moreover, research suggests that the typical viewer of an X-rated film is more likely to support women's equality than someone who never saw a pornographic film. Why? Because viewing pornographic films is more commonplace among college graduates than among those who have had little education. One of the best predictors of liberal attitudes towards women is exposure to higher education. Liberal Feminists do not believe that men sexually abuse women simply because they have been exposed to pornography. For them, sexual violence cannot be explained so simply. Not every man feels aroused by violent depictions of sex; many are repulsed. Even those who find depictions of sexual aggression titillating will not necessarily engage in rape. Psychology is more sophisticated than "monkey see—monkey do." Behavior is influenced, not only by the immediate situation, but by a variety of factors including past learning, personality, social values, and current thoughts and expectations.

Liberal Feminists and anticensorship Radical Feminists worry that suppression of pornography, even blatantly sexist and violent material, is wrong because free speech includes the liberty to distort reality or say distasteful things. Any exceptions to free speech, they argue, can be used by the defenders of the status quo to suppress freedom of speech in general. Some of the groups who have been most active in the antipornography movement are as deeply opposed to the equality of women as they are to sexually explicit materials. Citizens and women in particular, censorship opponents say, are politically empowered when given the opportunity to read and say what they choose, not when they must submit to further restrictions. If pornography is subject to censorship or possible litigation, Liberal Feminists conclude, there is no evading the problem of deciding who has the right or ability to know what is best for women. Women vary tremendously in their political perspectives, ethical beliefs, and sexual attitudes. Even feminists disagree about what is arousing and what is demeaning to women. It is dubious that there is any single, correct, feminist perspective on pornography and unlikely that the current antipornography feminist ideologists represent women who differ from themselves in ethnicity, race, religion, politics, education, socioeconomic status, and age.

According to Liberal Feminists, there is a moralistic and intolerant theme in the procensorship arguments made by their Radical counterparts. By damning pornography in its entirety or making a distinction between "good" (woman-affirming) and "bad" (sexist) material, there is an inclination to divide women along paternalistic lines into the "good" and the "bad." Good women either reject pornography or prefer gentle, egalitarian, sensuous erotica; bad women like the crude, male-oriented, "hard core" variety. Pornography, like other human creations, has the potential to transcend gendered dichotomies. Not all women like sanitized sex; not all women share the prevailing, "politically correct," definition of pornography. Whether or not they approve of pornography, Liberal Feminists argue that suppressing it will do women no good. First, they note that substantially more sexual violence is portrayed in general audience and R-rated films, books, and television programs than in hard-core pornography.[126] Moreover, the use of sexual imagery and nude or partially clothed women in advertising is widespread and increasingly common.[127] Daytime soap operas, any episode of which reaches between three and ten million viewers, have become extraordinarily explicit, dramatizing topics like childhood sexual abuse, rape, homosexuality, sadomasochistic sex, sexually transmitted diseases, sexual dysfunctions, fetishes, and extramarital sex.[128] Nonetheless, well over half the audience for soaps are children and teenagers. If pornography was eliminated overnight, only a tiny fraction of the mass-media depictions of women as either sex objects or the targets of violence would disappear.

One of the strongest arguments made by antipornography Radical Feminists is that there is no difference between showing a woman being sexually abused on film and sexual abuse itself. Liberal Feminists think that this is fallacious reasoning. Images, however plausible or offensive, are not the same thing as reality. Although some sex workers may have been abused by the men who produce pornographic films, most are probably just "acting." Whether or not we approve of their roles or like the plot, it is wrong to think that all the women who model or star in pornography are obvious victims of sexual exploitation. Finally, Liberal Feminists argue that pornography can play a positive role in women's lives. Although men purchase more pornography than women, women are equally aroused by it—providing there is no violent content.[129] Generally, women don't require romantic imagery or a reference to committed relationships to be "turned on"; sensual depictions of recreational sex with a stranger excite women as well as men. And, as I point out at the end of this chapter, increasing numbers of feminist women are producing, starring in, and marketing pornography. Ultimately, feminism should validate women's rights to be sexual, not further constrict it.[130] Well-executed feminist pornography can raise questions about women's traditional roles while attacking joylessness and oppression.

## DOES PORNOGRAPHY HARM WOMEN?

Does pornography harm women? Most Radical Feminists answer Yes whereas most Liberal Feminists say No or are neutral. Adding to the debate, numerous scientific studies have examined this issue. Can we draw any firm conclusions from this research? Not yet. Almost an equal number of studies suggest that pornography might contribute to sexual violence as those which suggest that it is probably harmless. Another ticklish problem is that most research linking pornography with sexual aggression is correlational, but correlation, the extent to which two independent variables are associated statistically, does not necessarily imply causation. Suppose, for instance, a sociologist found that men who recently rented an X-rated video were more likely than men who had not done so to agree with rape myths and report that when their wife or girlfriend said No, they tried to have sex anyway. Scientifically speaking, we could not conclude that viewing pornography caused men to have sexually aggressive attitudes and behaviors. The men may have been attracted to pornography because they were already sexually aggressive and misogynistic. On the other hand, both pornography and sexual aggression might be especially appealing to particular groups of men such as very young men, hypermasculine men, or those employed in particular occupations. All of this would be highly speculative. Questionnaire, interview, and field studies cannot account for all the factors that might contribute to sexual aggression. Only rigorous scientific experiments control conditions sufficiently for researchers to infer causation. However, there is a big difference between laboratory research on pornography and men's use of pornography in their homes. The majority of experimental studies investigating pornography are too artificial to generalize to the real world. Even the best executed studies are beset with methodological problems which limit their meaningfulness.

Scientists disagree about whether or not pornography causes sexual aggression. A number of Canadian and U.S. studies of incarcerated rapists fail to find a preference for violent pornography among known sex offenders.[131] On the other hand, several other studies suggest that sexually coercive men use pornography, and violent pornography in particular, more than other men.[132] Sexually aggressive college men admit to being heavier users of pornography, including "soft-core" publications like *Playboy* and *Penthouse*, than nonaggressive men. Homemade and purchased images of "brothers" with stiff erections, paired with a scantily clad, semiconscious woman, are popular among fraternity members who have a reputation for participating in gang or "party" rapes. In two studies of female rape victims living in San Francisco, California, one in ten community residents and one out of four street prostitutes spontaneously described experiences with sexually coercive men who had used specific material from pornography as a script for attempting forced sex. No less vicious than the men who rape prostitutes, obsessive marital rapists are known to assault their wives with weapons and objects, just as they had seen done in violent pornographic films. Adding to

the horror, some of these marital rapists photograph or keep written records of their acts of brutality, to either relive violent sexual conquests or
share memories of their rapes with other men. Finally, some clinicians who
treat sadistic sex offenders believe that these men are more drawn to violent
pornography than are other men.

Radical Feminists are right to point out that some sexually aggressive
men appear to use pornography, especially sexist and violent pornography,
more than other men. But, they are unjustified in concluding that a statisti-
cal association between heavy pornography use and sexual aggression in certain studies is scientific proof that pornography causes male sexual aggression for three reasons.[133] First, only studies using aggressive pornography
suggest an association between sexually explicit material and antisocial behavior. Aggressive tendencies actually decrease immediately after men have
been exposed to pornography depicting consensual sex. And, when men are
exposed to pornography for several weeks, the sexually explicit material becomes so boring that even sexual arousal declines. Second, correlation
doesn't imply causation. There are many other factors such as culture,
learning, peer group influence, psychopathology, and hypermasculine personality which might better account for sexual aggression. The key is not
the content of pornography but how an individual interprets that content.
Third, not all studies confirm the expectation that pornography use is extensive among convicted sex offenders. Sex offenders do not necessarily
have greater exposure to pornography than law-abiding men. Many therapists who specialize in the treatment of sex offenders believe that violent
pornography plays little or no role in the men's abusive behavior.

Numerous laboratory studies with male college students in both the
United States and Canada provide empirical support for the Radical Feminist claim that violent pornography might harm women.[134] In such studies,
men are exposed to one of three types of stimuli: nonerotic and nonviolent
material (in which neither sexual activity nor physical aggression occurs),
nonviolent pornographic material (which depicts a couple engaging in mutually consenting sex), and violent pornographic material (which typically
romanticizes the rape of a woman). After exposure to violent pornography
and in none of the other two conditions, college men, especially those predisposed to sexual aggression, become more accepting of rape myths, which
blame women for their own sexual victimization, and are more likely to
think that it is okay for a man to use physical aggression against a woman
in an intimate relationship. Exposure to violent pornography, but not the
nonviolent variety, has caused some college men to develop more calloused
attitudes towards real life rape victims and give a higher level of electrical
shock to a woman, but not a man, after they have been angered and the

experimenter has instructed them to punish another student for errors on a learning task. There is absolutely no evidence that exposure to nonviolent pornography causes an angered young man to administer higher intensity electrical shocks to a young woman. Consistent with Liberal Feminist beliefs, experimental evidence suggests that male laboratory aggression is directed more by the violent content of a film, illustration, or a story than by its erotic content.

Men behave almost as aggressively towards women in the laboratory after being exposed to a nonpornographic film that showed a man using physical aggression on a woman as when they had seen sex and violence combined. This has an important implication for Radical Feminists. "Slasher films," which combine a mild erotic component with graphic brutality towards women, are more widely distributed and available to young people than are X-rated films. In the typical slasher film, women are routinely "stabbed, beaten, tortured, raped, decapitated, burned, drilled with electric drills, cut with saws, scalped, and shot in the head with nail guns."[135] By pairing pleasant scenes of attractive, semiclad, young women enjoying themselves with violent atrocities that occur shortly afterwards, the producers of slasher films condition viewers to be more comfortable with and less fearful of depictions of women being tortured and murdered. After undergraduate men were exposed to a steady diet of slasher films, they developed more callous attitudes towards rape victims than men who had been spared the opportunity of watching one slasher film daily for five consecutive days. Women students, too, became desensitized to antiwoman violence and less sympathetic to victims of sexual aggression after prolonged exposure to films like *Texas Chainsaw Massacre*, *I Spit On Your Grave*, and *Toolbox Murders*. Although they are usually overlooked by Radical Feminists, slasher films and the TV programs that imitate them appear to be more harmful to women than nonviolent pornography.

The well-known Canadian and U.S. scientists who have found an association between exposure to violent pornography and male aggression in their laboratories believe that their work lends some support to the Radical Feminist claim that pornography is the theory and rape is the practice. But, do these tightly designed experiments prove, without doubt, that violent pornography causes sexual aggression in the real world? Definitely not.[136] Psychology experiments conducted with undergraduate volunteers cannot help but be artificial or contrived. The young college students who participate in such studies are not laboratory rats; they know that they are being looked at and often do their best to please the scientists. Let's take another look at the experimental design of the classic study that purports to show a link between exposure to violent pornography and male aggression. As in so many social psychology experiments, a young man is asked to interact with a stranger who is actually a trained confederate of the experimenter. It is improbable that he would respond to someone he knows in quite the same way that he will treat a stranger. There are other problems. To appeal to the authority figure who is in charge, the typical young man is willing to do whatever he is asked. Most likely, he assumes that he won't be forced to do anything bad or dangerous since the experiment was approved by a campus committee devoted to the protection of human subjects. So, when an experimenter asks him to give electrical shocks (usually bogus) to another student for mistakes on a learning task, he has little reason to either question his instructions or think that he might really hurt someone. Besides, the typical study gives him no alternatives; he is supposed to shock another student and the only thing left to his judgment is how much shock to deliver.

Does laboratory aggression predict what a young man will do in a darkened room with his date? Doubtfully. Guy Grenier and William Fisher, two Canadian researchers, designed an ingenious variation of the classic pornography and aggression experiment.[137] First, each young man was angered by receiving criticism and electrical shocks in the laboratory as in the typical experiment. Next, the young man was asked to watch a violent pornographic film depicting a woman enjoying her rape, again as in the typical study. After this, however, came the creative ending. In addition to having an opportunity to deliver electrical shocks of varying intensity to a young woman for errors on a learning task, the experimental subject was given other options. He was told that if he preferred, he could just talk to the woman on an intercom or leave the experiment early. Guess what? Almost all the young men who participated selected the nonaggressive alternatives.

It is unclear as to whether or not aggressive pornography plays a role in motivating men to engage in rape. But, whether or not it does, the male-oriented variety can have a negative impact on women. In a small study of Canadian undergraduate women, women had positive emotional reactions to feminist erotica, a slide show illustrating mutually pleasurable sex between partners who were equal in status, but negative emotional reactions to both sexist and violent pornographic slides.[138] The greater her past experiences had been with forced sex, the more negatively a woman felt after viewing violent pornography. Even nonaggressive men are occasionally aroused by romanticized depictions of rape.[139] Therefore, it is reasonable to inquire if there are consistent differences between men and women in their reactions to sexually aggressive imagery. Do depictions of coercive sex always upset women? The answer, surprisingly enough, is Not Always. A small but vocal minority of women produce and consume sexually aggressive erotica for their own use. For this sexual avant garde, enjoying scenes of mild bondage, including those involving female couples, is not inconsistent with feminist values. Why? Because these women believe that neither Radical Feminists nor right-wing moralists have the right to impose their sexual standards on everybody else. More importantly, sexually aggressive imagery is commonplace in material marketed to women in mainstream culture. For example, romanticized rapes are a common theme in today's increasingly explicit romance novels.[140] In a typical plot, a beautiful and innocent adolescent is violated by a sensual, but psychologically calloused, older man. There is a struggle for dominance, but the couple eventually falls in love and marries. Between rape and domesticity, there are numerous explicit erotic scenes involving the "rake" whom the woman comes to love. Some novels are just sensual; others involve rape or bondage. At least twenty million women are loyal readers of these books in the United States alone. It would be wrong to conclude that there is something psychologically wrong with these women or that consumption of such novels is harmful. The typical avid reader of romance novels has sex more often and finds sex more gratifying than does the average nonreader. Inspired by the novels, such readers cultivate sexual fantasies more than other women. Fantasies of being taken by a handsome, seductive, powerful hero seem to enhance women's sexual pleasure with regular partners. Romance novels are popular among women of all ages and occupations. In contrast with the expectations of some feminists, women who read romances feel just as good about themselves and are just as assertive and free of relationship problems as nonreaders.

By now, it is clear that a large body of research casts doubt on the Radical Feminist assumption that pornography always harms women. Some scholarly work, such as the analysis of romance novels presented above, also suggests that sexually explicit material can have positive effects. The most reliable effect of exposure to pornography for women or men is a temporary increase in sexual arousal.[141] Enhanced arousal can be a good thing. Instead of causing social upheaval, it usually makes people more interested in having sex with their regular partners. Sex therapists, for example, have found that exposure to sexually explicit materials can help their clients become less anxious about and more interested in sex.[142] A total ban on sexually explicit material would present major barriers to sex therapists and inhibit sex education efforts.

If Radical Feminists are right, rape rates should be higher wherever men are most exposed to pornography. Although the occasional study supports this claim, most others do not.[143] In one study, rape rates were unrelated to the sale of "soft-core" pornography. In another, rape rates were actually lower in regions of the United States which had the highest circulation of men's magazines such as *Playboy* or *Penthouse*. It is important to keep in mind that correlation doesn't prove causation. Young men, for example, are more likely to engage in violent behavior (including sexual violence) and read pornography than older men. If a particular study finds rape rates highest where men's magazines have the highest sales, it is difficult to know whether to attribute such a finding to men's exposure to pornography or more likely, the youthfulness of the male population purchasing most such magazines. Finally, published rape rates greatly underestimate the actual occurrence of sexual assault; relatively few rapes are brought to the attention of the criminal justice system.

To the delight of some Liberal Feminists and the dismay of most Radical ones, one study reported that X-rated films were more likely to show a woman and man interacting as equals than R-rated films (in which the typical plot involved male domination and female subordination). Another study actually found a positive association between the circulation of sexually explicit men's magazines and gender equality, measured by indexes of women's economic and political power in a given state. It would be naive, of course, to conclude that pornography made men more egalitarian; pornography sales were lowest in politically conservative states which have a high proportion of fundamentalist Christians. It may be conservative politics and hypermasculinity, not pornography, that best predicts how women are treated. Sales of "macho" outdoors magazines like *Field and Stream* and the *American Rifleman* are more positively related to the number of reported rapes in a region than is the sale of sexually oriented men's magazines.[144]

## WOMEN WHO EMBRACE PORNOGRAPHY

Traditionally, men have been the major consumers of pornography, and most sexually explicit material has been created to satisfy men, not women. Today, a few pioneering women challenge male domination of the pornography industry. With the advent of VCRs and subsequently the home rental and purchase of X-rated videos, women could experiment without encumbrance. No longer was the sexually adventurous woman obliged to do business with a run-down, male-dominated, adult bookstore or theater, located in a dangerous neighborhood. Now, there was a market for a uniquely feminine erotica. Blush Entertainment, which produces Fatale films for lesbians, and Femme Distribution, which produces heterosexual erotica for women and couples, are among the new companies reaching out to a growing women's market. Both firms are managed or owned by women. Both give women creative and economic opportunities denied by the male-dominated industry. For the first time, women can write, produce, and direct an erotic film—not just star in one. For the first time, pornography looks at sex through women's eyes. In one film produced by Femme Distribution, for example, the equation of heterosexual sex with the vigorous, rod-and-piston action of intercourse is taken as high comedy whereas sex as the leisurely meeting of eyes and souls is extolled. In films distributed by Blush, strip-teasing is transformed into a uniquely lesbian art form in which women of all sizes, shapes, and colors perform for an all-woman audience while poking fun at conventional sexual scripts.

In the same way that the VCR increased women's access to X-rated films, woman-owned businesses make it easier and more appealing to purchase sex toys, massage oils, and books. In addition to trendy, new retail stores selling a variety of condoms, massage oils, and sex toys to a sophisticated clientele concerned understandably with "safer-sex," there are woman-owned mail-order businesses. These include two distinctively feminist operations, San Francisco's Good Vibrations and New York's Eve's Garden, both of which provide consumers with well-written catalogues filled with intelligent advice about vibrators and other products. For homemakers and working women alike, pleasure parties have replaced some of the Tupperware parties.[145] Playfully, in the warm and encouraging company of their sisters, women can handle, talk about, and purchase a variety of sexy clothing and sexual products. New erotic periodicals have emerged such as the humorously raunchy *On Our Backs* and *Bad Attitude* for lesbian readers, sexually explicit magazines which forge new ground despite exceptionally low budgets.

Some of the material in the new pornographic publications and videos appear to be variations of the best and worst of mainstream pornography. Dominant sexual attitudes and fantasies, like any aspect of culture, will take a long time to change. As Radical Feminists are quick to point out, aggressive themes have not been eliminated from the new pornography.[146] Indeed, some pornography, created by and for women, includes themes of highly coercive and exploitative sexuality, the same content that disturbs so many women who have criticized the male-dominated pornography establishment. What should feminists who oppose pornographic depictions of sexual violence do? I recommend tolerance. Sexual fantasies are not deeds; the artistic depiction of one woman who is sexually overpowering another is not a rape and will not necessarily cause a rape. Women have the right to be aroused by imagery that might seem distasteful or antifeminist to others. Freedom of thought and speech are fundamental in a democracy. Sensuality, self-acceptance, even love, cannot thrive in the presence of a sexual thought police.

There is much that is highly innovative about the new women's erotica. Not all imitates the mainstream of heterosexual, male, erotic sensibilities. In lesbian sex magazines, for example, a richer and more varied view of female beauty is promoted than is found either in men's entertainment magazines or in widely circulated women's and teenage girls' magazines. Older women, heavier women, highly athletic women, women who have short, cropped hair or delightfully bizarre hairstyles, and women with little or no makeup are featured as centerfolds. The twenty-something, slim but curvaceous woman with the predictable face of Miss Universe is not the sole model of female beauty. Erotic costumes include work boots, leather jackets, and flannel shirts—sensible clothes for women who take care of themselves. The sensual is not necessarily equated with spike heels, scratchy lingerie, and corsets—accessories that seem to symbolize female helplessness in male pornography since they so impede comfort and movement. Women's pornography generally contains more positive images of women of color and interracial love-making than pornography created by and for heterosexual men. In erotic stories, women are seen as being in charge of orchestrating sex, not just as the object of a partner's desires. The language used to arouse readers is a language that comes from a woman's understanding of sexual responsiveness and sensitivity.

Women know best what arouses them. What excites most women is not just sexual intercourse; it is not even orgasm alone. For many women, the entire process of bodies touching, uniting, and responding is exciting. A lover's eyes may arouse women just as much as his or her genitals; the complete relationship between sexual partners, including the emotional bond which heightens physical communication, make up the erotic.[147] It is this uniquely female conceptualization of sex which explains why romance novels are consumed by 28 percent of American women, often with the same passion with which men read pornography. Far more than conventional, male-produced pornography, romance novels titillate the reader with an intimate and detailed description of the unfolding of intimacy, the spirituality behind passion. Feminist pornography presents women with an opportunity to rewrite romance novels in more woman-affirming and sexually explicit ways. In addition to giving women permission to have sexual interests, as does current romance fiction, feminist pornography also has the potential of presenting women as strong and sexually autonomous. It might demonstrate an even more revolutionary spirit by depicting men, not as studs as in much of the pornography produced by men, but as partners who are warm, intelligent, creative, and sensitive.

Unlike men, women don't just want to see bodies in motion, portrayed from a spectator's distance like a sexual version of a track and field event. Women don't want to see themselves divided into parts—buttocks, vulva, clitoris, thighs, and breasts. Nor do women want to see a man divided into parts, the rest of his body serving mainly as the life-support system for his penis. Women don't need to see magnifications of the genitals, so detailed they rival medical illustrations. Nor are they overly impressed by the beads of artificial sweat which miraculously appear on the faces and bodies of X-rated film actresses without ever spoiling elaborate coiffures or makeup. Many women are aroused by witty, flirtatious conversation, and subtleties of nonverbal behavior, activities rarely depicted in conventional male pornography but characteristic of romantic novels and soaps. Many women would prefer to see bodies like their own in pornographic films and magazines, real bodies, not just airbrushed and filtered examples of youthful physical perfection.

A truly feminist movement should validate all women's right to be sexual.[148] When feminists say that the sex industry hurts all women or exploits sex workers, our middle-class and moralistic biases are showing. As I explained in the last chapter, sex work remains the highest paying alternative for many women. Rather than telling sex workers that they are wrong, rather than insisting that they are the ultimate, tragic victims of the patriarchy, we can show them our respect and appreciation. Why can't we help sex workers organize unions to improve their working conditions or better still, help them raise capital to start or support their own woman-owned and affirming erotic businesses?[149] With more women in charge, the pornography business could take the patriarchy by surprise, becoming one of the best proselytizers for feminism. After all, more people are exposed to pornography than to feminist books, periodicals, and films. With humor and artistry, pornography could show women in a new light. A woman-affirming pornography could switch the focus of sex from satisfying men to women's pleasure or mutual pleasure.[150] By depicting women who love women and showing women taking the sexual initiative with men, there is a shift in power relationships, a change in outlook. A feminist-inspired pornography could be a place where women artists, writers, photographers, and filmmakers help the rest of us dream about new directions, explore uncharted and nonexploitative possibilities. Feminist pornography could be a laboratory for testing the politics of equality. Perhaps a woman-affirming pornography would help people become more self-accepting and tolerant of social and sexual diversity.

## NOTES

1. See Harris, Aggression.
2. See Gordon and Riger, *Female Fear*.
3. See Gottfried, Feminist Agenda for Economic Change, pp. 173–83.

4. Stock, Male Power, Hostility, and Sexual Coercion, p. 62.

5. See Ross and Allgeier, Meanings and Motivations of Sexual Coercion.

6. See Canadian Panel, *Violence Against Women*; Cole, Rothblum, and Espin, Refugee Women; Russell, *Sexual Exploitation*; Sanday, *Fraternity Gang Rape*; Stock, Male Power, Hostility, and Sexual Coercion, pp. 61–74.

7. See Young, Cloak of Innocence, pp. 189–95.

8. See Adams, Trachtenberg, and Fisher, Feminist Views of Child Sexual Abuse, pp. 359–96.

9. See Canadian Panel, *Violence Against Women*; Knudsem, Child Sexual Coercion, pp. 17–28; Lystad, Sexual Abuse in the Home, pp. 3–31; Russell, *Sexual Exploitation*.

10. See Adams, Trachtenberg, and Fisher, Feminist Views of Child Sexual Abuse, pp. 359–96; Russell, *Sexual Exploitation*.

11. See Largen, History of Women's Movement, pp. 69–73.

12. See Canadian Panel, *Violence Against Women*; Wyatt, Newcomb, and Riederle, *Sexual Abuse and Consensual Sex*.

13. See Canadian Panel, *Violence Against Women*; Ellis, Re-Defining Rape, pp. 96–99; Harney and Muehlenhard, pp. 3–15; Wyatt, Newcomb, and Riederle, *Sexual Abuse and Consensual Sex*.

14. See Wyatt, Newcomb, and Riederle, *Sexual Abuse and Consensual Sex*.

15. See Warshaw, *I Never Called It Rape*.

16. See Russell, *Sexual Exploitation*; Scheyett, Marriage Is the Best Defense, pp. 8–23.

17. See Brownmiller, *Against Our Will*; Finkelhor and Yllo, *License to Rape*; Russell, *Sexual Exploitation*.

18. See Dworkin, *Intercourse*; Jeffreys, Sexology and Antifeminism, pp. 14–27; MacKinnon, Pleasure Under Patriarchy, pp. 65–90.

19. Dworkin, *Intercourse*, p. 63.

20. MacKinnon, Pleasure Under Patriarchy, p. 88.

21. See Muehlenhard and Cook, Men's Self-Reports, pp. 58–72; O'Sullivan and Byers, Women's Strategies, pp. 30–34; O'Sullivan and Byers, Female Use of Sexual Influence.

22. See Byers and Price, Guidelines, p. 371; Koen, Defining Hostile Environment, pp. 289–301; McKinney and Maroules, Sexual Harassment, pp. 29–44.

23. See Gutek and Dunwoody, Understanding Sex in the Workplace, pp. 249–69.

24. See McKinney and Maroules, Sexual Harassment, pp. 29–44.

25. See Grauerholz, Sexual Harassment of Women Professors, pp. 789–801.

26. See Salter, Epidemiology of Child Sexual Abuse, pp. 108–38.

27. See Knudsem, Child Sexual Coercion, pp. 17–28.

28. See ibid. and Alter-Reid et al., Sexual Abuse of Children, pp. 249–66; Kercher and McShane, Characterizing Child Sexual Abuse, pp. 364–82; Salter, Epidemiology of Child Sexual Abuse, pp. 108–38.

29. See Jarvie, Child Pornography and Prostitution, pp. 307–28.

30. See Kercher and McShane, Characterizing Child Sexual Abuse, pp. 364–82.

31. See ibid. and Johnson, Female Child Perpetuators, pp. 571–85.

32. See Alter-Reid et al., Sexual Abuse of Children, pp. 249–66.

33. See Canadian Panel, *Violence Against Women;* Harney and Muehlenhard, Rape, pp. 3–15; Koss and Harvey, *Rape Victim;* Renner and Wackett, Social and Stranger Rape, pp. 49–56; Russell, *Sexual Exploitation;* Warshaw, *I Never Called It Rape;* Williams, Rape in America, pp. 3–4.

34. See Williams, Rape in America, pp. 3–4.

35. See Renner and Wackett, Social and Stranger Rape, pp. 49–56.

36. See Canadian Panel, *Violence Against Women;* Koss, Gidyez and Wisniewski, Scope of Rape, pp. 162–70; Koss and Harvey, *Rape Victim;* O'Brien, Date Rape, pp. 6–10; Wyatt, Newcomb, and Riederle, *Sexual Abuse and Consensual Sex.*

37. See Wyatt, Newcomb, and Riederle, *Sexual Abuse and Consensual Sex.*

38. See Canadian Panel, *Violence Against Women;* White, Prospective Analysis of Sexual Assault.

39. See Alzenman and Kelley, Violence and Acquaintance Rape, pp. 305–11; Sandberg, Jackson, and Petretic-Jackson, Attitudes Regarding Sexual Coercion and Aggression, pp. 302–11; Stets and Pirog-Good, Physical and Sexual Abuse, pp. 63–76.

40. See Finkelhor and Yllo, *License to Rape;* Muehlenhard, Conversation; Scheyett, Marriage Is the Best Defense, pp. 8–23.

41. See Hanneke, Shields, and McCall, Prevalence of Marital Rape, pp. 350–62; Finkelhor and Yllo, *License to Rape.*

42. See Bowker, Marital Rape, pp. 347–52; Finkelhor and Yllo, *License to Rape;* Frieze, Causes and Consequences of Marital Rape, pp. 532–53; Hanneke, Shields, and McCall, Prevalence of Marital Rape, pp. 350–62.

43. See Frieze, Causes and Consequences of Marital Rape, pp. 532–53.

44. See Warshaw, *I Never Called It Rape;* Sanday, *Fraternity Gang Rape.*

45. See Brownmiller, *Against Our Will;* Sanday, *Fraternity Gang Rape.*

46. Sanday, *Fraternity Gang Rape,* p. 11.

47. Ibid., pp. 11, 32–33.

48. See Gutek, *Sex and the Workplace;* Gutek and Dunwoody, Understanding Sex in the Workplace, pp. 249–69; Riger, Sexual Harassment Policies and Procedures, pp. 497–505.

49. See Mazer and Percival, Students' Experiences of Sexual Harassment, pp. 1–19; McCormack, Sexual Harassment of Students, pp. 21–32; McCormick et al., Sexual Harassment of Students, pp. 15–23.

50. See Gutek, *Sex and the Workplace;* Gutek et al., Sexuality and the Workplace, pp. 255–65; McCormick et al., Sexual Harassment of Students, pp. 15–23.

51. See Gutek, *Sex and the Workplace;* Gutek et al., Sexuality and the Workplace, pp. 255–65; Mazer and Percival, Ideology or Experience?, pp. 135–47; McCormick et al., Sexual Harassment of Students, pp. 15–23; McKinney and Maroules, Sexual Harassment, pp. 29–44; Powell, Definitions of Sexual Harassment, pp. 9–19.

52. See Adams, Trachtenberg, and Fisher, Feminist Views of Child Sexual Abuse, pp. 359–96; Alter-Reid et al., Sexual Abuse of Children, pp. 249–66; Henderson, English, and MacKenzie, Sexually Aggressive Children, pp. 89–108; Johnson, Female

Child Perpetuators, pp. 571–85; Knudsem, Child Sexual Coercion, pp. 17–28; Lystad, Sexual Abuse in the Home, pp. 3–31; Youngstrom, Children Who Abuse, p. 46.

53. See Koss, Gidyez, and Wisniewski, Scope of Rape, pp. 162–70; Russell, *Sexual Exploitation;* White, Prospective Analysis of Sexual Assault; Williams, Rape in America, pp. 3–4;

54. See Allgeier, Reducing Victim Vulnerability, pp. 1–4; Koss and Dinero, Sexual Victimization, pp. 242–50; Ruch et al., Repeated Sexual Victimization, pp. 1–19.

55. See Bowker, Marital Rape, pp. 347–52; Finkelhor and Yllo, *License to Rape;* Frieze, Causes and Consequences of Marital Rape, pp. 532–53; Hanneke, Shields, and McCall, Prevalence of Marital Rape, pp. 350–62; Yegidis, Wife Abuse and Marital Rape, pp. 62–68.

56. See Kalof, Rape-Supportive Attitudes, pp. 1–14; Koss, Gidyez, and Wisniewski, Scope of Rape, pp. 162–70; Martin and Hummer, Fraternities and Rape, pp. 457–73; Sanday, *Fraternity Gang Rape.*

57. See Muehlenhard and Linton, Sexual Aggression in Dating Situations, pp. 186–96.

58. See ibid. and Koss and Harvey, *Rape Victim;* Warshaw, *I Never Called it Rape.*

59. See Greendlinger and Byrne, Coercive Sexual Fantasies pp. 1–11; Koss and Dinero, Predictors of Sexual Aggression, pp. 133–46; Poppen and Segal, Sexual Coercion, pp. 689–701; Sanday, *Fraternity Gang Rape;* Warshaw, *I Never Called it Rape;* Youngstrom, Rapist Studies, pp. 37–38.

60. See Ross and Allgeier, Correlates of Males' Feminine Identification.

61. See Gutek, *Sex and the Workplace;* Gutek and Cohen, Sex Ratios, Sex-Role Spillover, and Sex at Work, pp. 97–115; Gutek and Dunwoody, Understanding Sex and the Workplace, pp. 249–69; Gutek and Morasch, Sex-Ratios, Sex-Role Spillover, and Sexual Harassment, pp. 55–74.

62. See Koen, Defining Hostile Environment, pp. 289–301.

63. See McCormick et al., Sexual Harassment of Students, pp. 15–23.

64. See Check and Malamuth, Empirical Assessment, pp. 414–23; Goodchilds and Zellman, Sexual Signaling, pp. 234–43; Koss and Harvey, *Rape Victim;* Muehlenhard, Misinterpreted Dating Behaviors, pp. 20–37; Muehlenhard, Friedman, and Thomas, Is Date Rape Justifiable?, pp. 297–310; Zellman and Goodchilds, Becoming Sexual in Adolescence, pp. 49–63.

65. Ibid.

66. See Kalof, Rape-Supportive Attitudes, pp. 1–14; Kalof and Cargill, Fraternity and Sorority Membership, pp. 419–25; Malamuth, Aggression Against Women, pp. 19–52; Sanday, *Fraternity Gang Rape;* Warshaw, *I Never Called It Rape.*

67. See Check and Malamuth, Empirical Assessment, pp. 414–23.

68. See Abbey, Misperceptions of Friendly Behavior, pp. 173–94; Abbey, Misperception, Acquaintance Rape, and Alcohol; Abbey et al., Perceptions of Sexual Intent, pp. 108–26; Koss and Harvey, *Rape Victim.*

69. See Byers and Lewis, Dating Couples' Disagreements, pp. 15–29.

70. See Sanday, *Fraternity Gang Rape.*

71. See Muehlenhard, "Nice Women" Don't Say Yes, pp. 95–108.

72. Muehlenhard and Hollabaugh, Token Resistance to Sex, pp. 872–79.

73. See Brownmiller, *Against Our Will*; Reiss, *End to Shame*.

74. See Mosher and Tomkins, Macho Man, pp. 60–84.

75. Ibid., p. 72.

76. Ibid.

77. See Burkhart and Fromuth, Psychological Understandings of Sexual Coercion, pp. 75–90.

78. See Brownmiller, *Against Our Will*; Bowker, Marital Rape, pp. 347–52; Finkelhor and Yllo, *License to Rape*; Frieze, Causes and Consequences of Marital Rape, pp. 532–53; Hanneke, Shields, and McCall, Prevalence of Marital Rape, pp. 350–62; Martin and Hummer, Fraternities and Rape, pp. 457–73; Ross and Allgeier, Correlates of Males' Feminine Identification; Sanday, *Fraternity Gang Rape*; Yegidis, Wife Abuse and Marital Rape, pp. 62–68.

79. See Scott and Tetreault, Attitudes of Rapists and Other Violent Offenders, pp. 375–80.

80. See Donnerstein, Linz, and Penrod, *Question of Pornography*.

81. See Burkhart and Fromuth, Psychological Understandings of Sexual Coercion, pp. 75–90; Burkhart and Stanton, Acquaintance Rape, pp. 43–65; Check and Malamuth, Empirical Assessment, pp. 414–23; Harney and Muehlenhard, Rape, pp. 3–15; Lisak and Roth, Sexually Aggressive Men, pp. 795–802; Koss and Dinero, Predictors of Sexual Aggression, pp. 133–46; Koss and Harvey, *Rape Victim*; Mahoney, Shively, and Traw, Sexual Coercion and Assault, pp. 2–8; Malamuth, Aggression Against Women, pp. 19–52; Peterson and Franzese, Sexual Abuse of Women, pp. 223–28; Pryor, Sexual Harassment; Rapaport and Burkhart, Sexually Coercive College Males, pp. 216–21; Warshaw, *I Never Called It Rape*.

82. See Warshaw, *I Never Called It Rape*; Youngstrom, Children Who Abuse, p. 46.

83. See Stevenson, Feminist Sexual Science.

84. See Henderson, English, and MacKenzie, Sexually Aggressive Children, pp. 89–108; Johnson, Female Child Perpetuators, pp. 571–85.

85. See Krug, Sexual Abuse by Mothers, pp. 111–19.

86. See Muehlenhard and Cook, Men's Self-Reports, pp. 58–72.

87. O'Sullivan and Byers, Women's Strategies, pp. 30–34; O'Sullivan and Byers, Female Use of Sexual Influence.

88. See Koss and Harvey, *Rape Victim*.

89. See Russell, *Sexual Exploitation*.

90. See Waterman et al., Sexual Coercion, pp. 118–23.

91. See Leeder, Lesbian Battering Couple, pp. 81–99; Lobel, *Naming the Violence*.

92. See Wyatt, Aftermath of Child Sexual Abuse, pp. 61–81.

93. See Alter-Reid et al., Sexual Abuse of Children, pp. 249–66; Hoier et al., Impact of Sexual Abuse, pp. 100–42; Knudsem, Child Sexual Coercion, pp. 17–28.

94. See Lipovsky and Kilpatrick, Sexual Abuse Victim, pp. 430–76.

95. See Koss and Harvey, *Rape Victim*.

96. See Ruch et al., Repeated Sexual Victimization, pp. 1–19.

97. See Gordon and Riger, *Female Fear*; Koss and Harvey, *Rape Victim*.

98. See Gutek and Dunwoody, Understanding Sex and the Workplace, pp. 249–69; McKinney and Maroules, Sexual Harassment, pp. 29–44.

99. See Wyatt, Newcomb, and Riederle, *Sexual Abuse and Consensual Sex.*

100. See Largen, History of the Women's Movement, pp. 69–73.

101. See Clark, Violence Against Women and Children, pp. 420–31; Koss and Harvey, *Rape Victim.*

102. See Gutek and Dunwoody, Understanding Sex in the Workplace, pp. 249–69; Koen, Defining Hostile Environment, pp. 289–301.

103. See Clark, Violence Against Women and Children, pp. 420–31; Ellis, Re-Defining Rape, pp. 96–99; Finkelhor and Yllo, *License to Rape;* Gordon and Riger, *Female Fear;* Harney and Muehlenhard, Rape, pp. 3–15; Scheyett, Marriage Is the Best Defense, pp. 8–23.

104. See Finkelhor and Yllo, *License to Rape;* Muehlenhard, Conversation; Scheyett, Marriage Is the Best Defense, pp. 8–23.

105. Byers, Telephone Conversation. See Canadian Panel, *Violence Against Women;* Clark, Violence Against Women and Children, pp. 420–31; Ellis, Re-Defining Rape, pp. 96–99.

106. Byers, Telephone Conversation.

107. See Kendrick, *Secret Museum.*

108. See Hawkins and Zimring, *Pornography in a Free Society.*

109. See Williams, *Hard Core,* especially pp. 72; 161; 234.

110. See Reiss, *End to Shame.*

111. See Baron, *Women Against Censorship,* pp. 94–98; Chancer, Pornography Debates Reconsidered, pp. 74–84; Elson, Passions Over Pornography, pp. 52–53; Killoran, Feminists and the Pornography Debate, pp. 443–56; Philipson, Repression of History and Gender, pp. 113–18; Reiss, *End to Shame;* West, Feminist-Conservative Anti-Pornography Alliance, pp. 681–711.

112. See Ashley and Ashley, Sex as Violence, pp. 352–71; Collins, Pornography and Social Policy, pp. 8–26; Diamond, Pornography and Repression, pp. 129–44; Dworkin, *Pornography;* Leidholdt, When Women Defend Pornography, pp. 125–31; MacKinnon, Pleasure Under Patriarchy, pp. 69–90; MacKinnon, Death of Feminism, pp. 3–13; Stock, Male Power, Hostility, and Sexual Coercion, pp. 61–74.

113. MacKinnon, Death of Feminism, p. 12.

114. See Dworkin and MacKinnon, *Pornography and Civil Rights.*

115. See Killoran, Feminists and the Pornography Debate, pp. 443–56.

116. See Cowan, Chase, and Stahly, Attitudes Toward Pornography Control, pp. 97–112.

117. See Dworkin and MacKinnon, *Pornography and Civil Rights;* Elson, Passions Over Pornography, pp. 52–53; Kendrick, *Secret Museum;* U.S. Congress, Pornography Victims' Compensation Act.

118. U.S. Congress, Pornography Victims' Compensation Act, p. 4.

119. See Byers, Letter to Author; Gotell, Electronic Mail to Women's Studies List; Lewin, Canada Court Says Pornography Harms Women, p. B7(L); Royalle, Kunis, and Delaney, Views from the Trenches; Williams, Canadian Court Bans Pornography, p. 6.

120. See Cowan, Chase, and Stahly, Attitudes Toward Pornography Control, pp. 97–112.

121. See Feldman-Summers, Dangers of Censorship, pp. 179–84; Reiss, *End to Shame*; Royalle, Kunis, and Delaney, Views from the Trenches.

122. See West, Feminist-Conservative Anti-Pornography Alliance, pp. 681–711.

123. Ibid., p. 685.

124. See Feldman-Summers, Dangers of Censorship, pp. 179–84; Reiss, *End to Shame*; Royalle, Kunis, and Delaney, Views from the Trenches; West, Feminist-Conservative Anti-Pornography Alliance, pp. 681–711.

125. See Chancer, Pornography Debates Reconsidered, pp. 74–87; Collins, Pornography and Social Policy, pp. 8–26; Fisher, Response to Erotica, pp. 226–44; Hollibaugh, Desire for the Future, pp. 401–12; Jarvie, Pornography and/as Degradation, pp. 13–27; Reiss, *End to Shame*; West, Feminist-Conservative Anti-Pornography Alliance, pp. 681–711.

126. See Fisher and Barak, Pornography, Erotica, and Behavior, pp. 65–88.

127. See Alexander and Judd, Nudity in Advertising, pp. 26–29.

128. See Greenberg and D'Alessio, Sex in the Soaps, pp. 309–21; Logan, Why Soaps are so Sexy, pp. 4–10, 12, 16, 21.

129. See Fisher, Response to Erotica, pp. 226–44.

130. See Reiss, *End to Shame*; West, Feminist-Conservative Anti-Pornography Alliance, pp. 681–711.

131. See Fisher, Electronic Mail; Fisher and Barak, Pornography, Erotica, and Behavior, pp. 65–83.

132. See Donnerstein, Linz, and Penrod, *Question of Pornography*; Finkelhor and Yllo, *License to Rape*; Russell, *Sexual Exploitation*; Sanday, *Fraternity Gang Rape*; Silbert and Pines, Sexual Abuse, pp. 857–68; Warshaw, *I Never Called It Rape*.

133. See Abramson and Hayashi, Pornography in Japan, pp. 173–83; Donnerstein, Pornography, Its Effect, 53–84; Donnerstein, Linz, and Penrod, *Question of Pornography*; Fisher and Barak, Pornography, Erotica, and Behavior, pp. 65–83.

134. See Check and Malamuth, Empirical Assessment, pp. 414–23; Donnerstein, Pornography, Its Effect, 53–84; Donnerstein, Pornography Commission Report, pp. 185–87; Donnerstein, Linz, and Penrod, *Question of Pornography*; Malamuth, Aggression Against Women, pp. 19–52.

135. Donnerstein, Linz, and Penrod, *Question of Pornography*, p. 113.

136. See Fisher and Barak, Pornography, Erotica, and Behavior, pp. 65–83.

137. Ibid.

138. See Senn and Radtke, Reactions to Mainstream Violent Pornography, Nonviolent Pornography, and Erotica, pp. 143–55.

139. See Donnerstein, Linz, and Penrod, *Question of Pornography*.

140. See Coles and Shamp, Readers of Erotic Romances, pp. 187–209.

141. See Byrne and Kelley, Pornography and Sex Research, pp. 1–15; Pickard, Female Responses to Sexual Material, 91–117.

142. See Yaffe, Therapeutic Uses, pp. 119–50.

143. See Baron, Pornography and Gender Equality, pp. 363–80; Baron and

Straus, Sexual Stratification, Pornography, and Rape, pp. 186–209; Gentry, Pornography and Rape, pp. 277–88; Donnerstein, Linz, and Penrod, *Question of Pornography*.

144. See Donnerstein, Linz, and Penrod, *Question of Pornography*.

145. See Philipson, Repression of History and Gender, pp. 113–18.

146. See Jeffreys, Eroticizing Women's Subordination, pp. 132–35; Jeffreys, Sexology and Antifeminism, pp. 14–27.

147. See Milne, Porn, pp. 18–20; Ogden, *Women Who Love Sex;* Pickard, Female Responses to Sexual Material, pp. 91–117.

148. See Hollibaugh, Desire for the Future, 401–12.

149. See Killoran, Feminists and the Pornography Debate, pp. 443–56.

150. See Milne, Porn, pp. 18–20.

# ✺ 7 ✺

# Woman-Affirming Models
# of Sexual Fulfillment

What is sex?; what is sexual pleasure for women? According to most sexologists, sex is a biologically driven, mechanical, matter of hydraulics. Heated up by the moment and hormones, body parts swell naturally and genitals connect inevitably. Tab A is inserted into slot B. If she is free of guilt and anxiety, all a woman needs to achieve ecstasy, instantly and easily, is the right partner. Ecstasy, of course, boils down to the "Big O," orgasm. Sex is scripted as a linear, goal-oriented activity in which a male protagonist tries to reach first base, second base, and third base with a female target. Home run is sexual intercourse. Sex is orgasm is a touchdown is hitting the jackpot is scoring. Sexual pleasure is quantitative, not qualitative or spiritual. Did you come? Did you come big? How many orgasms did you have? How long did they last? How many times did you do it?

But, is this true? Is human sexual fulfillment simply a matter of looking good, getting it up, and putting out? Absolutely not! Sex and its pleasures or lack of pleasures is no more natural nor purely biological than cuisine, table manners, fashionable clothing, or musical tastes; all, to some extent, are products of history and culture.[1] The limits and possibilities of sex are taught to us during childhood and adolescence. Just as we are taught that girls and women should cook, clean, and take care of babies, we are taught too that it is boys and men who should initiate, control, and dominate the erotic.

When adults speak to girls about sex, it is to frighten them into controlling their sexuality. As Michelle Fine explains, what is missing for girls and women is a discourse of desire.[2] When girls ask women about sexual pleasure, the adults get uncomfortable and change the subject. No wonder, then, women often associate sex with social obligation. Consider this New Zealand woman's description of her sex life:

> Like he always . . . wanted to have sexual intercourse in the morning and that was just . . . how it was. Like, you know, you had a fuck then you got up and . . . had your breakfast. (laughs) And I never really enjoyed sex . . . like I didn't even question it. . . . Because, you know, that person wanted me, and I was in a relationship, we were going out together and isn't this what everybody does?[3]

Feminists disagree on many issues related to women's sexuality save one. Whether they are Radical Feminists who are concerned about sexual danger from hostile and aggressive men or Liberal Feminists committed to increasing women's sexual freedom, they recognize that sex is as much political as it is biological. Sex is socially constructed as something that men do to women, not something that belongs to women. This is why women have more restricted sexual vocabularies than men.[4] This is also why many men define sex as something they do to women and the female orgasm as something men give to women. Women are musical instruments to be tuned and played by men. Consider these comments made by two British undergraduate men describing their sexual experiences with women.

> Yeah, touching certain buttons does play a very big part of it, certain positions play a really big part of it.[5]

> I would put it down to the man and his technique. Yes I think pressing the right buttons is important, but you also have to have the right mental attitude, because I think if a woman has an orgasm you probably feel more of a man. You know the other person has enjoyed it, and it was because of you and your penis, you gave her that, you gave her one.[6]

By taking responsibility for orchestrating sex, men are not necessarily giving women a break. In a recent study of young and middle-aged Italians, men were significantly more likely than women to blame partners for unsatisfactory sexual experiences, even though they were much more likely than women to experience orgasm.[7] It is dehumanizing to equate sexuality with genital juxtapositions and intercourse.[8] We are more than our genitals. In the grim reality of a phallocracy, any man who has erectile problems is no longer a man. As feminist sex therapist and researcher, Wendy Stock, ex-

plains, "it must be painful to equate self-worth with a flap of skin and carti-
lage hanging between one's legs, particularly when this appendage is not
performing according to prescribed standards."[9]

Stereotypically, women are expected to desire sex less than men. But sex
therapists are seeing an increase of husbands who are less interested in sex
than their wives.[10] According to Janet Wolfe, who practices feminist Rational-Emotive Behavior Therapy, male sexuality is burdened with cultural
scripts that equate manhood with toughness and the possession of a magic,
swordlike, "magnificent penis," which should be ready for action at all
times, no matter how a man feels or what health problem he may suffer
from. Male sexual anxiety is fueled by conventional sexual scripts. The real
business end of sex is at the end of his penis; penetration and intercourse
are all that matters. The man is supposed to locate and press the right
buttons on the woman's body. He is in charge of orchestrating at least two
orgasms: his and hers. As for women, traditional sex-role socialization virtually guarantees sexual alienation. Women are prized in the patriarchy for
their purity, for saving their vagina for one special man. In other words,
good women are sexually inhibited. Therefore, women's disinterest in sex
results less from individual psychopathology than from the systematic control of women's sexuality by the dominant culture.[11]

## FEMINISTS DISAGREE ABOUT WHAT SEX IS OR SHOULD BE

Almost all feminists agree that sex is socially constructed and politicized.
They also agree that women are more likely than men to be sexually exploited or unsatisfied. But Radical and Liberal Feminists disagree vehe-
mently as to what women should do. Because women are so often the sexual
victims of violent men, a few Radical Feminists argue that men are the
enemy and heterosexual women are "sleeping with the enemy."[12] According
to such logic, "Lesbians couldn't have bad sex and heterosexuals couldn't
have good sex."[13] But, as explained throughout this book, many Radical
Feminists are satisfied heterosexuals and there are a number of lesbian Radical Feminists who can see the positive possibilities of heterosexual relationships. These politically moderate women argue that woman-affirming sex is
possible with a man if the woman is assertive about her desires and the man
is empathic and feminist. It would be wrong to associate the Radical Feminist movement with a limited sexual ideology.

Radical Feminists have made important contributions to the discourse on
sex therapy. They have denounced conventional sex therapists justifiably for
enforcing what they disparage as compulsory heterosexuality. British psychologist, Jenny Kitzinger, for example, has criticized sex therapists for be-

lieving, without exception, that sexually abused women should resume heterosexual activity.[14] When the survivors of sexual abuse show little interest in sex with men or have difficulty performing heterosexual intercourse, Kitzinger argues that they have rejected men for legitimate reasons. Conventional therapists are chastised for their failure to question basic patriarchal assumptions—that heterosexual sex must be reclaimed, regardless of the sexual violence that took place in a woman's past, and that celibacy or lesbianism cannot be healthy alternatives. Few Liberal Feminists would take issue with Kitzinger's articulate criticism. However, given the Liberal Feminist commitment to expanding female sexual turf, most take issue with more extreme Radical Feminist arguments.

Beginning in the 1970s, extremist Radical Feminists competed with ultraright political ideologues in their obsession with rules for appropriate sexual behavior. In place of the standard prescription for missionary-position intercourse in marriage, orthodox Radical Feminists made up their own rules for politically correct sex.[15] Politically correct sex rejected the heterosexual man's emphasis on erotic goals or orgasms. Hugging and kissing were okay; orgasm seeking and penetration were rejected. Lesbians were urged to take turns in initiating sex; both women were supposed to be equally soft but equally strong. Sex was to be completely "natural"; women weren't supposed to use sex toys, have fantasies about someone else, or view pornography. Sexually explicit language was forbidden as degrading, no matter how personally arousing. Politically correct lesbian and bisexual women "would tolerate nothing that resembled the [so-called] raw sexuality of male eroticism."[16] Heterosexual sex became politically incorrect by definition, even if the man was sensitive or espoused feminist ideology.[17] Lesbian sexuality was no less scrutinized. As lesbian sex therapist, Margaret Nichols joked, politically correct lesbian lovemaking was defined so strictly, few women could fully comply with its dictates:

> Two women lie side by side (tops or bottoms are strictly forbidden—lesbians must be nonhierarchical); they touch each other gently and sweetly all over their bodies for several hours (lesbians are not genitally/orgasm oriented, a patriarchal mode). If the women have orgasms at all—and orgasms are only marginally acceptable because, after all, we must be process-, rather than goal-oriented—both orgasms must occur at exactly the same time in order to foster true equality and egalitarianism.[18]

While it may be true that an unexamined male and heterosexual bias prevails in conventional sex therapy, the dictates of politically correct Radical Feminist sex have been equally harmful.[19] Politically correct sex is bland; it lacks passion. Politically correct feminists may be damaging the very phenomena they so want to nurture, women's sexual autonomy. Margaret Nichols complains that some lesbians "spend more time discussing the political correctness of sex than they spend doing sex."[20] This discourse contributes directly to women's sexual dissatisfaction.

Liberal Feminists argue against stifling women's sexuality with rigid rules for politically correct sex.[21] Muriel Dimen says, "Erotic pleasure mushrooms when there are no musts. . . . Sexual intimacy is too generous an experience to exclude anything."[22] Lillian Faderman holds: "until women are free to explore their own sexuality any way they wish, they will never be truly free."[23] Carol Vance tells us, "feminism must speak to . . . the repression of female desire that comes from ignorance, invisibility, and fear. Feminism must put forward a politics that resists deprivation and supports pleasure."[24] I agree with these Liberal Feminists. The rest of this chapter builds on these feminist insights.

## CONVENTIONAL SEX THERAPY: SCIENCE OR DOGMA?

Psychotherapists and medical professionals including sex therapists are neither neutral nor totally objective. Generally, their assumptions and practices reflect prevailing beliefs about right and wrong and good and bad.[25] Historical developments seem to have played a more important role in defining sexual psychopathology than scientific advances. In modern times alone, experts have switched from damning masturbation as a symptom or cause of mental illness early in the twentieth century to praising it as the key, for women at least, to becoming orgasmic. After several decades of telling the general public that good "normal" women had little interest in sex (or at least less interest than men), health care professionals reversed course. Women's inhibited sexual desire became their major clinical concern. Later, the experts changed direction yet again. Inspired by anxieties about AIDS, sex is now supposed to be dangerous for women. Having lots of sex, especially sex with different casual partners, is again regarded as a major psychiatric problem.

Physicians, psychotherapists, and nurses have transformed sex from a moral issue best addressed by the clergy to a health issue best addressed by the medical establishment. The medicalization of sexuality has been less than enlightening.[26] By equating sex with biology and sexual problems with disease, intimate relationships are trivialized and mystified. Sex, after all, is more than muscular contractions and swelling. Relationship problems, not faulty tissues or hormone imbalances, often play the decisive role in sexual unhappiness.[27] Partners do not always want the same things. So, it is often arbitrary to label one partner as dysfunctional and the other as sexually healthy. How many times a week or month should a person want sex to be "normal"? Just because one partner wants sex less (or more), why is treatment required? Who makes up the rules? Do sex experts dwell too much on physiology? Aren't feelings just as important? Sex therapists, Bernie Zilbergeld and Carol Rinkleib Ellison, explain, "And, as we should know by now but somehow keep forgetting, erections and vaginal lubrication/swelling can and do occur in the absence of any sexual feeling."[28]

Kinsey and Masters and Johnson are regarded as major figures in the history of sexology. However great their contributions have been, we must not think of these pioneers as infallible.[29] Kinsey served women poorly by insisting that all male-female differences in sexual expression reflected biology; he overlooked cultural and historical factors. Masters and Johnson, in contrast, made the opposite mistake. By focusing on male and female similarity in sexual response and ignoring gender differences in their own data, Masters and Johnson made male sexuality the standard of normality. Even if the clitoris and penis have similar functions, men and women do not have equal power in either heterosexual relationships or society in general. Equally important, the classic research on sexual response and traditional sex therapy overlooks the fact that sexual satisfaction is more closely linked with emotional aspects of a relationship than with either the frequency of intercourse or the intensity and timing of orgasm. We must never forget that we are studying and treating people, not sexual engines.

Our best sexological data is tainted by volunteer bias. Sexually conservative people are far less likely to participate in sex research than those who like sex and engage in masturbation and genital relations regularly. We tread on thin ice when we assume that sex research participants represent the general population. Compared to the average woman, women who volunteer for laboratory studies of sexual response are much more likely to masturbate and think about sex frequently.[30] More importantly, sex researchers and therapists customarily ignore poor people and members of minority groups. However miniscule our scientific knowledge of human sexuality might be, it is for the most part relevant mainly to white, middle-class, well-educated, young, and healthy individuals. The conventional sex therapy and sexual response literature has another striking characteristic. In it, lesbians and bisexual women are either invisible or mythologized.[31] There is no serious study on the prevalence of sexual dysfunctions among lesbians. The myth that women intuitively know how to pleasure one another instantly has gained wide acceptance among sex researchers and educators who should know better, even though lesbian psychotherapists report that their clients have much the same sexual problems as heterosexual women.

Heterosexism, the belief that heterosexuality is superior to all other sexual orientations, contributes to the invisibility of women who love women.[32] At most, major sex therapy textbooks have a token chapter addressing gay or lesbian sexuality. More often, only heterosexual couples are discussed. To date, the best and most complete information on lesbians' and bisexual women's sexual functioning is authored by lesbians writing for small, woman-owned publishing houses. Since these books are not widely distributed, I suspect that the vast majority of sex therapists and counselors remain ignorant of lesbian contributions to sexology. Tragically, such ignorance is not benign. Many lesbian and bisexual women initially attempt to make a heterosexual adjustment. In doing so, they may be more likely than other women to experience problems with lubrication, arousal, or orgasm.[33] A heterosexist therapist who overlooks the possibility that a seemingly heterosexual woman has not yet come to terms with an erotic preference for other women will do her a great disservice.

Modern sex therapy is excessively partner-oriented. Although masturbation is no longer condemned as a sign of immaturity or emotional disturbance, neither is it celebrated. Like the general population, many sex therapists view masturbation as a second-rate activity, a good way for a woman to learn about her body but not an end in itself.[34] Ultimately, traditional sex therapists aim to teach women to improve their sexual performance during coitus. Penetration, not woman's autonomous sexual experience, is emphasized. But, for many women, masturbation may be more exciting and a more reliable source of orgasm than partner sex in general and sexual intercourse in particular.[35] Why is masturbation disparaged? Feminist artist and sexual revolutionary, Betty Dodson, shares this witty insight: "[In] a society that doesn't have economic equality between the sexes, I was forced to bargain with my cunt for any hope of financial security. . . . the only available script is . . . the cock in the hole, preceded by some ritualized foreplay that isn't playful."[36] Not only does Dodson advocate masturbation as a legitimate form of sexual expression, she also says, "To become responsible for our own orgasms is a basic statement about independence and establishes us as people with something worth sharing."[37] Confirming Dodson's ideas, psychologists Mary Beth Oliver and Janet Hyde report that male-female differences in masturbation are among the strongest sex differences in the research literature.[38] Until women empower themselves sexually by masturbating, their research suggests, sexual pleasure will continue to elude many women.

Dodson defines self-loving as not just masturbating to orgasm but having a full, sensual love affair with one's own body.[39] Long before sex therapists advocated genital self-examination to help women become more sexually self-affirming, Dodson and her friends experimented with genital portrait sessions. During these, each participant was asked to arrange her vulva and pubic hair as desired before being photographed or illustrated. Dodson believes that her genital show-and-tell groups enabled women to resolve negative feelings about their bodies. Such groups also provided women with a good opportunity to discuss genital hygiene and health. Betty Dodson and lesbian sex therapist Jo Ann Loulan advocate the use of sex toys during masturbation.[40] This point of view contrasts sharply with the beliefs of traditional, heterosexually scripted, sex therapists who continue to regard masturbation as second-rate sex and masturbation with a vibrator as second-rate masturbation. Consistent with the Liberal Feminist tradition for expanding women's sexual boundaries, Dodson and Loulan argue that sex toys are fun and that nobody, famous sex therapists included, has the right to tell women how they may or may not pleasure themselves.

## ENGINEERING PLEASURE: THE SEARCH FOR A MAGIC BUTTON

Ever since Sigmund Freud said there were two types of female orgasm, feminists and sexual scientists have argued about the nature and purpose of women's sexual pleasure.[41] According to Freudians, immature, male-identified women who had unresolved "penis envy" (read in lesbians, bisexual women, and feminist heterosexuals) favored clitoral stimulation, reaching ecstasy only when they or their partner stimulated the magic, highly innervated, blood-engorged little button that sits atop the inner lips of the vagina. Freud thought that the clitoris was a tiny, inferior penis. On the other hand (or should I say thanks to the services of the right phallus), Freud believed that mature women (read in happy homemakers who cheerfully accepted female social inferiority) were believed to achieve orgasm vaginally, during sexual intercourse. Vaginal orgasm was supposed to be the result of penile penetration alone; no hands or tongue were thought to be necessary. And, the emotionally healthy woman was presumably polite enough to come at the same time as her husband. The orthodox Freudians would certainly not approve of a rebellious woman who climaxed first or demanded that her partner bring her to orgasm after he was through! Dual orgasm theory was publicized by women's magazines and popular psychology books. Nobody can estimate how many women spent how many millions of dollars and countless hours on psychiatrists' couches trying, often unsuccessfully, to achieve the talking cure for their neuroses, which they hoped would enable them to achieve the right type of climax, vaginal orgasm during coitus.

In the 1960s, Masters and Johnson did women a great service by suggesting that physiologically speaking, women's orgasms were quite similar regardless of how they were induced and that the clitoris is a great deal more responsive to sexual stimulation than the vagina. Relying on surveys and interview data, other sex researchers liberated women still further by pointing out that a sizeable number of otherwise sexually responsive women required direct clitoral stimulation to achieve orgasm; indirect stimulation from penile thrusting alone was insufficient. Women were grateful that climax during intercourse was no longer regarded as necessary for psychological maturity. Research aside, however, many continued to say that the orgasms they received from masturbation or a partner's direct contact with the clitoris felt different than those experienced during coitus. So, in the 1980s, a group of sex researchers began to re-examine the possibilities of vaginal erotic sensitivity. Working with a small and highly sexually responsive group of women in the laboratory, the researchers were convinced that some women had heightened erotic sensitivity in the anterior wall of the vagina near the neck of the bladder.[42] They called this controversial area the "G spot," in honor of Grafenburg, a physician who first discussed the possibility that this portion of the vagina could be exquisitely sensitive to touch.

At first, the research team thought that they had discovered a new magic button. It appeared that deep vaginal stimulation near the urethra was associated, not only with female orgasm in a few women, but with the "ejaculation" of a fluid that was initially identified as chemically similar to the secretions from a man's prostrate gland but was later identified by other scientists as urine. The work created an enormous amount of publicity, but studies purporting to find evidence for this new female pleasure button have been harshly criticized. Sexologists pointed to methodological problems. The early G-spot work was based on small, nonrepresentative samples of women, and the results were not readily replicated in other laboratories. Mainstream scientists were reluctant to give up Masters and Johnson's laboratory-based conclusion that the clitoris played a central role in triggering sexual response, regardless of how and where women were stimulated to achieve orgasm.[43] Today, it is generally thought that evidence favoring the G spot is inconclusive and that it is uncertain just how many women in the general population may have vaginal, erotic sensitivity. However, research examining the possibilities of vaginal eroticism has not been abandoned. Sex researchers and therapists have long known of women and men who purposefully stimulate tissue adjacent to the urethra to create pleasurable sensations. And, very carefully conducted laboratory studies of small samples of women, all free of urological or gynecological disorders, suggest that anterior wall vaginal stimulation is associated simultaneously with heightened pain tolerance, no reduction of tactile sensitivity, increased heart rate, higher blood pressure, and erotic stimulation sufficient for producing orgasm.[44]

Could it be that women have the potential to possess more than one magic button? Feminist theorists, not just sexual scientists, have strong opinions. Some feminists argue that research on anterior wall vaginal sensitivity is good because it expands women's options for pleasure. Others reject efforts to localize female sexual response because they believe that sex is more than pushing the right buttons.[45] Arguing that sex researchers must stop comparing women with men, feminist critics of the G spot are disturbed because the original studies of erotic sensitivity in the vagina seemed to suggest that women should experience orgasm just like men, climaxing from sexual intercourse alone and spurting out a fluid while they did so. I agree that sex researchers and therapists shouldn't be in the business of telling women the scientifically correct way to enjoy sex. I also agree that male sexuality should not be the standard for understanding or appreciating female sexuality. But, I object strongly to any notion of politically correct sexual response. A clitorally induced orgasm is no more inherently feminist than a vaginally induced one. Sexual scientists' empirical interests do not necessarily symbolize their politics. Beverly Whipple, the single most important investigator of vaginal erotic sensitivity, has long been active in the feminist perspectives special interest group of The Society for the Scientific Study of Sex. Just because someone is interested in vaginal sensitivity hardly proves that she has neglected the women's movement.

It is time for scientists and feminists alike to stop arguing politics over women's genitals. Let us respect and listen to what women have to say about what arouses them and provides them with pleasure. Let us keep in mind that women are diverse and that the ultimate source of sexual pleasure may be the human mind, not some peripheral part of their anatomy.[46] There is more to sex, indeed there is more to emotional experience in general, than transitory changes in peripheral physiology. To truly appreciate sex, we must be aware of the diversity of human experience and the awe-inspiring resilience of the human spirit. We humans are a remarkable species. Laboratory research suggests that a few special women can produce elevated blood pressure, even orgasm, from sexual fantasy alone.[47] Even more remarkable, a few women can still experience weak orgasms after undergoing the ravages of female genital circumcision, an ancient surgical procedure involving the removal of the clitoris and labia. Tragically, many African communities still force young girls to undergo this painful, dangerous mutilation to "safeguard" premarital chastity and remind girls of their subordinate, social status.[48]

Female sexual responsiveness belongs to women, not to men, and is not limited to some compartmentalized, erotic zone. As I will explain later, some paraplegic and quadriplegic women are able to experience sexual feelings and even orgasm in the upper part of their bodies after spinal cord injury has denied them all possibility of genital sensation.[49] Women's sexuality is a whole body and whole mind experience; it is more than a matter of touching certain magic buttons.

## EQUATING SEX WITH GENITAL SWELLINGS AND JUXTAPOSITIONS

Sexual experience in the Masters and Johnson tradition is nothing more than an orderly sequence of changes in heart rate, blood flow, and muscle tension.[50] The body responds mechanically to stimulation. There is no sense of time or place; the source of stimulation or the quality of a relationship with a partner is irrelevant. The genitals swell and pulse in a cultural and historical vacuum. Learning, sex-role socialization, political power, and even thought are irrelevant. In the world according to Masters and Johnson, sexual response boils down to the same four arbitrary stages for every woman and man: *excitement* (the beginning of physiological change); *plateau* (the height of tumescence); *orgasm* (reflexive and generally pleasurable, pelvic spasms that may be accompanied by blurred consciousness); and *resolution* (the body's return to a resting state). "Overall, one is left with an impressive but essentially disjointed description of physiological events."[51] Women and men, despite evidence to the contrary, are supposed to be identical in their sexual response cycle.[52] We are given the misleading impression that the laboratory observation of sex is sex. But, as Leonore Tiefer explains, there is no single "normal, inherent, universal pattern" of sexual response from which any deviation signifies dysfunction or abnormality.[53]

Almost all contemporary laboratory research on sexual response is in the Masters and Johnson tradition. Modern sex therapy, even the diagnostic labels for sexual "dysfunctions" that prevail, is a reification of a medical model that describes sex in terms of a limited and unvarying number of physiological stages, each accounted for largely in terms of the presence or absence of tumescence.[54] Few question the equation of "real sex" with genital swellings and juxtapositions. Instead, most leading sex therapists are satisfied if allowed to make minor theoretical adjustments to Masters and Johnson's ideas. Psychiatrist Helen Singer Kaplan, for example, insists that desire should precede excitement and orgasm.[55] Her new preliminary stage of sexual response, *desire*, is defined, not as mere sexual interest, but as a primitive drive originating from deep inside the emotional center of the brain. By definition, then, people who have sex in the absence of initial desire, whether or not they experience pleasure or orgasm eventually, are sexually dysfunctional. The right way to have sex is to have desire first.[56] Low sexual desire or at least less sexual desire than a partner and taking "too long" to go through all the supposed stages of sexual response, become legitimized as reasons for professional help. From her extensive therapeutic experience with lesbian couples, psychologist Jo Ann Loulan offers two supplementary stages to Masters and Johnson's human sexual response cycle as modified by Helen Singer Kaplan.[57] Refreshingly, Loulan believes that a simple *willingness* to have sex, for whatever reason, is a justifiable reason for hopping into bed and often precedes or takes the place of either desire or physical signs of excitement. In true feminist fashion, Loulan adds a new final stage of sexual response, *pleasure*, arguing that many of us (and women in particular) have sex to feel good or to share good feelings with someone else, not just to experience orgasms.

Women more than men think of sex in relational and spiritual terms.[58] Women are more likely than men to link their sexual satisfaction to having a steady, sensitive bed partner who didn't ask them to engage in sexual activities that they disliked but the partner enjoyed.[59] Cuddling, self-disclosing, even gazing into a partner's eyes are highly valued by women. A feminist vision of sexuality considers whole people, not just their genitals. Intellectual stimulation, the exchange of self-disclosures, and whole body sensuality may feel just as "sexy" as orgasms.[60]

## THE VENERATION OF ORGASMS

Sex-role traditional men and most sexologists look at sex in competitive and quantitative terms; they count and measure orgasms. Standard sex therapy instructs women how to "achieve" orgasm, adjusting to the patterns and preferences of the typically male partner.[61] Nothing matters about sex more than the achievement of "the Big O." Men "score" and sexual scientists keep score. The questions asked, the studies completed, reveal a great deal about which aspects of sex are deemed important. The frequency of female orgasm during marital intercourse, for example, is correlated with self-rated marital happiness.[62] Multiorgasmic women, women who have a series of orgasms in the absence of additional stimulation, are compared with women who experience "only" a single orgasm during sexual activity.[63] Lesbians, bisexual women, and heterosexual women are compared in terms of number of orgasms per week and self-evaluations of how "long" and "strong" their climaxes were.[64] Rhythmic contractions are counted; the strength of pelvic musculature is assessed; orgasmic intensity is estimated.[65] The ability to experience orgasm isn't sufficient. Although at least one in three American women are unable to achieve orgasm through intercourse alone, in the "look Ma-no hands" school of sex therapy, requiring a partner's hands or tongue to climax is a bona fide sexual dysfunction for which expensive and time-consuming sex therapy might be recommended.[66]

It is time for sex therapists and laboratory sexologists to examine their basic assumptions. Is it really true that all good things, including relationship satisfaction and psychological adjustment, are related to the frequency and intensity of orgasms? Several studies with nonclinical samples suggest that orgasm is not always central to women's sexual satisfaction, least of all orgasm during intercourse.[67] To their credit, sex therapists teach clients sensate focus exercises or how to appreciate each other sensually without feeling any pressure to perform sexually or reach orgasm. Yet, as Canadian sex therapist Lee Handy and his colleagues point out, most clinicians continue to assess their therapeutic success by tracking the frequency and reliability of orgasms. I am not trying to devalue orgasms. Nor am I suggesting that sex therapists should be unconcerned about helping women (and men) become orgasmic.[68] What I am doing is questioning the exaggerated importance given to orgasms. Sex is or can be much more.

We live in a culture in which women feel pressured to be frequently orgasmic, easily orgasmic, and multiply orgasmic. By the time heterosexual women reach midlife, many have faked orgasms to avoid upsetting men or prove their sexual adequacy. Sociologist, Lillian Rubin, explains,

> Women's orgasms are now big business—books, films, therapies, and the like, all part of a highly profitable industry devoted to telling us how to make it happen, all selling the notion that good sex must end in orgasm. Anything else is portrayed as not quite good enough, not quite the real thing. That means that women are now under the same performance pressures that men have experienced for so long—pressure that sometimes feels incompatible with internal needs.[69]

Women shouldn't feel pressured to "measure up" to men's sexuality or for that matter to compete with other women. Instead, women should feel free to enjoy sexuality on their own terms. A feminist vision of sexual salvation would redefine lovemaking to include behaviors other than genital contact and orgasm.

## THE TYRANNY OF INTERCOURSE

Since her illness, Martha has grown to dislike sexual intercourse. Penetration is so uncomfortable that she encourages her lover to get it over with as soon as possible. She has no trouble enjoying direct clitoral stimulation; it's just intercourse she hates.

Bill requests sex from his wife twice a week. His approach is mechanical. After about two minutes of what vaguely passes for "foreplay" he gets on top of her to do "the real stuff." He is proud of his "staying power"; he is able to thrust for several minutes before ejaculating. Bill says little before, during, or after sex. He is reluctant to show physical affection unless it is likely to result in intercourse.

Ellen loves it when Janice, her lover, "eats her," but doesn't want to do the same for Janice. Although she is willing, if somewhat reluctant, to bring Janice to orgasm manually on occasion, she thinks it would be "stupid, unnecessary, and boring" for her to perform oral sex.

Which one of these individuals has a sexual dysfunction? According to our present psychiatric diagnostic system, only Martha does (dyspareunia). Influenced by a nonconscious equation of sexual activity with reproductive potential, clinicians equate sexual dysfunction with "physical failures" in the performance of intercourse[70] and frequently overlook the male partner's contributions to a woman's sexual problems.[71] Certainly, good therapists treat individuals and couples for deficiencies in tenderness, poor communication, sexual selfishness, disinterest in oral sex, an unwillingness to cuddle, and many problems unique to lesbian and gay relationships. However, none of these problems are regarded as serious enough to warrant an official psychiatric diagnosis. For a number of heterosexual women, intercourse feels obligatory rather than playful.[72] Yet the experts keep on pushing sexual intercourse as the ultimate sexual experience. Health care providers sometimes go to extremes to enforce this point of view. After surgery or pelvic radiation for gynecological cancer, the standard medical procedure is to return a heterosexual woman to her prior level of coital frequency as soon as possible.[73] This may please her male partner but is hardly best for the woman. Noncoital activities that may bring greater pleasure and less discomfort to the woman are rarely explored.

If "normal" sexuality is equated with the sexual experiences and concerns of the average person, then sex therapists may have excessively high standards for adult sexual functioning. Recent studies with representative samples of heterosexual adults suggest that a large proportion of the general population, most of whom will never seek the assistance of a sex therapist, would be classified as having one or more sexual dysfunctions.[74] More than one in five, heterosexual, middle-aged women describe sexual intercourse as either unappealing or more obligatory than pleasurable. Almost half of all heterosexual women surveyed admit that they find it difficult to get excited or to achieve orgasm; another third say that they find it difficult to maintain sexual excitement after initial arousal. Between 8 and 23 percent of community samples have dyspareunia (or painful intercourse). When asked to describe their sexual difficulties, women list problems that are largely ignored by the sex experts.[75] In one nonclinical study of middle-class, married couples, a fourth or more of the women complained that their partner chose an inconvenient time to initiate sex, that it was difficult to enjoy sex because they couldn't relax, were disinterested, or were "turned off," and that there was too little foreplay before intercourse or too little tenderness afterwards. None of these problems would be classified as a sexual dysfunction in the psychiatric diagnostic manual. However, the presence of such woman-oriented problems predicted female sexual dissatisfaction far better than whether the woman or her partner had an official, psychiatric disorder of intercourse.

Women who have difficulties reaching climax by any means (about one in ten "normal" women) are viewed as suffering from *primary orgasmic dysfunction*.[76] But, even easily orgasmic women may not escape the professional concern of traditional sex therapists. The diagnosis, *secondary orgasmic dysfunction*, is reserved for women who are orgasmic only via masturbation or direct clitoral stimulation; it is also given to women who require specific sexual positions to climax or have orgasms with some (but not all) partners. Yet, most women who are able to achieve orgasm during sexual intercourse use the same (or ask their partner to use the same) manual and tactile vulvar stimulation that they employ during masturbation. Does this make them sexually dysfunctional? I don't think so!

I am inclined to agree with sociologist, Ira Reiss, who would like to do away with the term "sexually dysfunctional" altogether.[77] As Reiss explains, such terminology gives statistically average, heterosexual erotic behavior an inappropriate medical legitimacy. Sex therapists should be in the business of helping people enjoy themselves and their partners in a variety of ways, not assuming the role of a sex police who place stigmatizing labels on people who fail to conform to rigid sexual rules. Like Reiss, I am a harsh critic of the "look-Ma-no hands" approach to female sexual response. Despite the pressure to become increasingly orgasmic from sex therapists and popular writers, only one in five women describes orgasm as her most important source of sexual pleasure.[78] Excessive concern with achieving orgasm from intercourse alone is a waste of therapy dollars and time.

Disinterest in genital sexual activity, diagnosed as *inhibited (hypoactive) sexual desire* by clinicians, has become the major reason lesbian and heterosexual couples seek sex therapy.[79] Yet, it is difficult to pinpoint what this diagnosis means. There is so much variability in the frequency with which individuals desire or have genital interactions that the concepts, normal or abnormal sexual desire, seem virtually meaningless. When couples have sexual disagreements, they generally fall into a pattern in which one partner initiates sex most of the time and the other habitually refuses. It would be wrong to reflexively label the refusing individual as sexually dysfunctional since he or she may desire sex and have sex fairly often even if the partner is dissatisfied. Yet, this is often the case. Usually the partner who wants sex more wins out by getting the therapist to label the less sexually interested partner as having a problem.[80] Sex therapists are all too quick to assume that women should be constantly ready for sex if their partner is attractive, loving, and appropriate (whatever that means).[81] Too often, relationship dynamics are overlooked and the woman is blamed for her sexual disinterest—she is too depressed, her hormones aren't balanced; she has allowed her medical illness to get in the way of sexual feelings; she is showing her anger by denying sex to her partner; she is anxious; she has too many sexual conflicts; she is overinvolved emotionally, and so forth.[82]

Too many clinicians falsely assume that frequent genital sexual activity is always joyous. Women may have sex regularly out of fear, guilt, obligation, a desire to please, and economic need. Although these women may appear sexually "normal" in terms of coital frequency, they may enjoy sex less than those who have sex less often but only when they want it. Believing in absolute rules for how much sex people should have, regardless of life circumstances, is sexual dogma—not sexual science. The diagnosis, inhibited sexual desire, which has become the medical equivalent of "not tonight dear, I have a headache," fails to consider that it is difficult for women to feel sexual desire when they are locked in a power struggle with an intimate partner.[83] Rather than being a symptom of psychopathology, inhibited sexual desire may be the predictable outcome of a culture that diminishes women's power and thwarts female sexual pleasure.[84]

Taught that the only "real sex" is sexual intercourse, heterosexual women are susceptible to two sexual problems that are largely unknown to lesbians, *dyspareunia*, painful coitus, and *vaginismus*, involuntary spasms of the vaginal musculature which prevent penetration.[85] Dyspareunia is sometimes linked to psychological factors such as relationship problems, sexual anxiety or guilt, a history of rape or sexual abuse, and/or sexual initiation by a clumsy or brutal partner.[86] However, dyspareunia is generally caused by medical problems such as endometriosis, recurrent urinary tract infections or inflammation, pelvic inflammatory disease, tumors, tears from delivery, and damage to or malformation of the uterus and vagina.[87]

Sex therapists treating women for dyspareunia often recommend water-soluble lubricating jelly to ease friction during coitus and in some cases, hormonal replacement therapy for postmenopausal women who experience vaginal dryness even when sufficiently aroused. Couples are also encouraged to experiment with various coital positions, especially those that allow the woman to be on top of the man and in charge of how and where her partner thrusts inside her. However, there is a more radical (and feminist) approach for minimizing or eliminating dyspareunia. Couples can simply be encouraged to expand their sexual repertoire beyond coitus, experimenting with any of a number of mutually enjoyable sexual activities including massage, joint masturbation, oral sex, and the dramatic enactment of sexual fantasies.

Vaginismus is an involuntary spasm of the vaginal musculature that occurs in response to attempts to insert an object or penis into the vagina.[88] The spasm is usually limited to muscles around the vaginal opening, but some women experience spasms in their thighs, anus, abdomen, and buttocks. In severe cases, women cannot use tampons or undergo a conventional pelvic examination. Women who have vaginismus are a diverse group. Some women develop vaginismus in response to untreated dyspareunia. But, typically, psychological, not medical, factors contribute to the problem. These psychological or historical factors include but are not limited to sexual trauma, anger at or fear of a partner, general rebellion against male domination, and sexual anxiety related to religious orthodoxy or sex-negative family values. Outwardly, women with vaginismus consent to intercourse; on a core level, however, they say No. These women do not necessarily hate sex; a number are highly orgasmic in response to masturbation or a partner's fingers or tongue. For this reason, vaginismus lends itself to feminist analysis more than any other supposed female, sexual dysfunction. In conventional sex therapy, vaginismus patients are trained to become more relaxed and comfortable with the insertion of fingers, progressively larger objects, and finally partners' penises inside their vaginas. A feminist therapist would also give women the alternative of rejecting sexual intercourse and more radically still, their male partners, as a cure.

Whether a woman presents herself to a therapist with vaginismus, orgasmic dysfunction, or inhibited sexual desire, a feminist practitioner would not assume automatically that a male partner must be pleased or that the problem should be fixed. In a culture that emphasizes compulsory hetero-sexuality, many lesbian and bisexual women get married or live with men when they would be much happier with women. Their subsequent diffi-culties with lubrication, orgasm, or coitus reflect a sense of being trapped in heterosexuality, not an absence of sexual interest or desire.[89]

Our unquestioning acceptance of sexual intercourse as the be-all-and-end-all of sexual expression hurts men, not just women. The rules for male sexuality are rigid, pun intended. Male sexuality is a hard penis that is thrust inside a vagina. Ejaculation shouldn't occur too rapidly or take too long. Any man who fails in this enterprise is less than a man. Modern sex therapy has created the pseudoproblem of *premature ejaculation*, for the man who comes too quickly. Interestingly enough, there is no female parallel of pre-mature orgasm for the woman who achieves climax before her partner.[90] Men are supposed to be in charge of orchestrating sex; they must control themselves and the sexual encounter even when they are supposed to be sexually disinhibited.

*Erectile failure* or impotence is diagnosed when a man cannot achieve an erection that is sufficiently hard for penetration. According to one British study, the best predictor of both wives' and husbands' marital dissatisfaction is erectile failure, not female sexual dysfunction.[91] Why is male sexual per-formance so important that heterosexual women value a hard penis more than their own sexual experience? More often than not, medical problems such as diabetes and vascular disease play a major role in causing erectile failure.[92] But, men aren't allowed to have difficulties with erection, no mat-ter how sick they might be. Instead of exploring alternative ways of en-joying sex and providing a woman with sexual pleasure, the medical and mental health establishment sells men expensive and often uncomfortable assessment procedures, drugs, surgeries, and devices such as penile im-plants—all manufactured with the express purpose of producing a "hard on," however pleasureless. Men are encouraged to measure their manhood, not in terms of life-long achievements or capacity for intimacy, but genital tumescence alone.[93] This is a particularly cruel sexual ideology to market to aging men, a group which is more susceptible to health problems that limit erectile ability than younger counterparts.

At least since their work was popularized during the sexual revolutions of the 1960s and 70s, conventional sex therapists emphasized the diagnosis and treatment of sexual deficiencies, not sexual excesses. That is women and their partners were treated to overcome too little sexual intercourse, hypo-active sexual interest, and weak or absent orgasms. This emphasis began to change at the end of the twentieth century, mostly in response to a resur-gence of moral and religious conservatism as well as sexual hysteria stirred up by the AIDS pandemic. For the first time in many years, experts worried that there could be too much of a good thing, too much sex. Clinicians began to treat women and men for *sexual addiction*, which was defined in terms of a loss of control over sexual impulses and the persistent, compulsive enactment of a particular form of sexual behavior despite harmful consequences.[94]

Like drug and alcohol addiction, sexually addictive behavior is described as producing pleasure while enabling an individual to escape from anxiety and internal discomfort. Sexual addiction remains a highly controversial diagnosis. On the one hand, clinicians point to individuals who have long histories of engaging in self-destructive sexual behavior. For example, a woman might have sexual intercourse with numerous men without using a condom or lose a beloved primary partner, friends, and employment because her obsession with numerous, sexual liaisons prevents her from functioning effectively. But, how do we define sexual addiction? Who should define the politically or medically correct sexual frequency or number of partners? Liberal Feminists emphasize that the concept, sexual addiction, has particular dangers for women who have traditionally been damned as "whores" by the patriarchy for practicing sexual autonomy or engaging in sex for obvious economic benefit. Doubtlessly, there are women as well as men who need help in managing sexual feelings and behavior. But, we must be careful not to use the concept of addiction to promote the belief that some women are sexual sinners who deserve to be punished or that nonmonogamous sex is always "sick." A woman-affirming prescription for female sexuality would embrace sexual diversity.

## FEMINIST SEX THERAPY

Feminist sex therapists and writers emphasize holistic pleasure.[95] Cuddling, touching, and hugging may be prized, not just as a means to an end, but as fulfilling in their own right. Rigid rules for sex are rejected. Sex isn't just two people climaxing around the same time; sex includes holding a partner while she or he masturbates, experimenting with sexual initiation and fantasy, and redefining lovemaking to include any sensual interaction that gives one or both partners pleasure. While orgasms are not rejected, neither are they viewed as essential. Women are not pressured to be frequently orgasmic or multiorgasmic or flexibly orgasmic. Rather, women are encouraged to see themselves as sexual actors (not objects) who have the right to direct when and how they make love. Female orgasms, feminists believe, belong to women, not partners.[96] Women may learn to be orgasmic in all-women support groups. But it is up to them whether or not they explain their sexual circuitry to others.

Realistically, Liberal Feminist therapists point out that sex, especially sex with a long-term partner, isn't spontaneous but often requires effort and creativity.[97] Arguing that the greatest sex organ is the brain, not the genitals, feminist therapists teach women that sex, like any other aspect of intimacy, involves thought, planning, talk, work, and collaboration. Liberal Feminist ideology has played a more important role in feminist sex therapy than the more sexually cautious Radical Feminist variety. Sex with a partner is viewed as playful, not dangerous, and sex for one is celebrated too. Betty Dodson writes, "Masturbation is . . . not just for kids or for those in-between lovers or for old people who end up alone. Masturbation is the ongoing love affair that each of us has with ourselves throughout our lifetime."[98]

Feminist commentators give women permission to enjoy sex instead of seeing it as a service performed for a partner's benefit.[99] As illustrated in these quotes, lesbian sexual rebels use humor to redefine women's sexuality in terms of pleasure, not politics.

Unlike free-basing or biting your nails, using a vibrator is neither physiologically addictive nor a nervous habit.[100]

As helpful as feminism has been . . . , it has not yet developed as a philosophy that explains sexuality, or the erotic. Understanding why you are making fifty-nine cents to every man's dollar is hardly the jumping-off point to determining the source of your lust.[101]

More than most therapists, feminist sex therapists are acutely aware of the dynamics of power.[102] They work hard to avoid reinforcing traditional sex roles and dominance patterns. Feminist therapists encourage women to define sexual problems in their own words, to engage in dissent during treatment, and to learn how to be assertive. Like other well-trained clinicians, feminist sex therapists assume that both partners bear some responsibility for an individual's or the couple's sexual difficulties. However, they also recognize that men are more likely than women to have superior resources and power in a heterosexual relationship and that some lesbian relationships fall short of the egalitarian standard. Feminist therapists deal with the power relationship that exists, not one which is idealized. They reject a step-by-step mechanistic approach to therapy.

Thanks to the efforts of Radical Feminists, feminist therapists realize that childhood sexual abuse, rape, and other forms of sexual assault are so common among the general population that sexual trauma must always be considered as a possible cause of women's sexual problems.[103] As clarified in chapter 6, survivors of sexual assault are predisposed to having both short- and long-term sexual problems. Immediately after sexual assault or exploitation, women are often repulsed by the idea of sexual activity, even with a loving, consensual partner. Whether they are attracted primarily to men or to women, many survivors continue to experience inhibited sexual desire and intense anxiety and fear in reaction to erotic activity years after the sexual trauma took place. Some women have no difficulty achieving orgasm but find the experience disgusting and shameful. Sexual activity may be endured because the women do not think that they have a right to deny their bodies to anyone, especially if they fear a partner will abandon them for refusing to have sex. Sexual abuse and assault survivors may find it difficult to be affectionate and sexual with the same person; sexless relationships may feel safer and more intimate. As this Canadian woman explains, sexual abuse survivors may experience highly negative feelings about their own bodies, not just their sexual interactions with partners:

It's my pubic hair which bothers me—it looks so gross. . . . It serves no purpose, it's unattractive and it blatantly draws attention to something which is private. I just don't like it. I know where the feelings stem from. They stem from (the offender) who started his business as soon as he discovered I had pubic hair. Things were never the same after that.[104]

Feminist sex therapists never push women into sexual activity prematurely. Effective treatment of the sexual abuse or assault survivor empowers women to say No to sex, not just Yes. Feminist therapists avoid oversimplifying women's sexual experiences. They realize that easily orgasmic or multiorgasmic sexual abuse or rape survivors may be just as likely to experience themselves as sexually dysfunctional as those who are unable to get aroused. Such women may feel betrayed by their own bodies every time they climax as does this unfortunate woman.

I was becoming quite aroused. Then I had a flashback. . . . my level of excitement skyrocketed and I had an orgasm and started to cry very hard. I felt totally overwhelmed by the orgasm, like my body was turning in on itself and was being pierced in a million different places. I hate the feeling of orgasm. . . . when I woke up I felt really alone.[105]

Girls and women survive sexual abuse and assault through detachment or emotional distancing. Feminist sex therapists empower women by showing a healthy respect for their detachment. They reject the simplistic idea that speedy and frequent resumption of genital sex is the best and only successful outcome for sex therapy.

## SAFER SEX FOR WOMEN

For women, even the sexual rebels among us, sexual salvation depends on safety: safety from exploitation and sexual violence, safety from unwanted pregnancy, and safety from sexually transmitted disease. Until the development of effective antibiotic treatments at midcentury, sexually active women feared gonorrhea and syphilis, both of which could be passed to their newborn children.[106] The discovery of penicillin is at least partially responsible for the many sexual revolutions of the twentieth century. From the 1940s to the beginning of the 1980s, the citizenry seemed to rejoice in the knowledge that sexual activity, including promiscuous sexual activity, did not appear to be a serious health risk. The sexually transmitted diseases of the day were either curable or, in the case of genital herpes, unlikely to be deadly to adults. Then came the 1980s; then came the deadly retrovirus, AIDS.

No book promoting women's sexual rights and pleasures would be complete without a consideration of Acquired Immunodeficiency Syndrome (AIDS). There is much promising research and increasingly effective treatment for HIV positive people (asymptomatic or healthy individuals who are infected with the AIDS virus) and AIDS patients. But, thus far, there is no cure for this devastating disease. Girls and women are the fastest growing group of people with AIDS worldwide.[107] In New York City, AIDS is the leading cause of death of women aged 24 to 34. No woman can afford to ignore AIDS but women of color have particular cause for alarm; three out of four women with AIDS in the United States are black or Hispanic.[108] As this book goes to press, females comprise 6 percent of all white persons, 26 percent of all black persons, 18 percent of all Hispanic persons, 12 percent of all Asian and Pacific Island persons, and 17 percent of all American Indian and Alaskan Native persons diagnosed with AIDS. Although many women contracted AIDS primarily from IV drug use, heterosexual contact has become an increasingly important risk factor. Many HIV positive women and female AIDS patients are poor.[109] Tragically, low-income women receive less prevention-oriented health care information and poorer medical care than the rest of the population. Because sex between women does not typically involve the exchange of bodily fluids, lesbians appear to be at much lower risk of acquiring HIV positive status or AIDS than heterosexual women. But, lesbians do not enjoy a zero risk status.[110] Many self-identified lesbians have used IV drugs or have had sex with men in recent years. Unprotected cunnilingus, especially vigorous oral sex performed on a menstruating woman, has been implicated in recent years as a potential source of infection.

Right-wing opponents of women's rights have argued that the only way to prevent AIDS is to be celibate or limit sex to a monogamous, long-term, heterosexual relationship, consummated only after both partners test negative for HIV antibodies.[111] Statements of this kind are moralistic, not woman-affirming. We must come to terms with the fact that love isn't the only reason that women have sex, that celibacy isn't always workable, and that a good many of us (or at least our partners) may not be monogamous. More than one sexually faithful woman has acquired AIDS from her long-term partner whom she mistakenly believed did not use IV drugs or had not had unprotected sex with others. Promiscuous people who consistently use condoms and other safer sex techniques are likely to test negative for HIV antibodies. A key to preventing AIDS is safer sex, not avoiding sex.

Latex condoms, especially those used in conjunction with water-based lubricants or the contraceptive spermaticide, Nonoxynol-9, greatly reduce the risk of infection with the virus that causes AIDS. But, few women use condoms every time they have sex, even though they are more positive about "rubbers" than men and are responsible for between 40 and 60 percent of the purchases made.[112] Traditional sex-role socialization, the belief that women aren't supposed to be sexually interested or assertive, is responsible for unreliable condom use. Women are less likely than men to carry condoms with them in anticipation of a possible sexual encounter.[113] Women look at condoms as something to use with a new partner; they are reluctant to insist on their use by a long-term partner.[114] Women place themselves at risk with the comforting fairy tale that they won't get infected by good men. Some women don't ask partners to use condoms because they don't want men to reject them or get angry. If women have been battered or sexually victimized, they are reluctant to discuss condoms because they are justifiably afraid for their lives.

Safer sex education involves helping women become assertive, teaching them to pick partners who will listen, and empowering them with the idea that they have a right to insist on protection during sexual activity. Safer sex requires more than the use of a condom during intercourse or fellatio (oral stimulation of the penis). Field testing reveals that although very few condoms break during use, about 6 percent slip off during intercourse and another 6 percent slip off during withdrawal.[115] Couples need adequate instruction in the proper use of condoms. Safer sex education recognizes that sexual intercourse is not the only form of heterosexual activity and that female, as well as male couples, require instruction on the prevention of sexually transmitted disease. We need to teach women that their needs are just as important as men's and that simply limiting their number of sexual partners does not automatically protect them from AIDS.[116] Sexual scripts must be enriched; couples need instruction in how to flirt and engage in passionate talk as they negotiate to reduce their risk of acquiring AIDS from consensual sexual activity. As Mara Adelman explains, too many health educators have discouraged people from practicing safer sex by sanitizing and impoverishing the erotic, suggesting that the ideal way of contracting for sex is

> a doctor-patient relationship, where sexual partners take diagnostic histories of each other's sexual pasts. The model is revealed in pre-scriptions on how to quiz one's partner on sexual histories, select compliance-gaining strategies, and engage in preventative sex. Discussion of passion, eroticism, lust, or the subjective experience of desire is ignored in the emergent medical imagery for sexual interaction.[117]

An exhaustive description of safer sex is beyond the scope of this chapter.[118] However, here are some general guidelines. AIDS is spread by contact with an infected person's bodily fluids. Therefore, women should minimize their contact with a partner's ejaculate, vaginal fluids, and blood. Sexually active women should prepare themselves for the possibility of having sex by stocking up on condoms, other rubber products (such as latex squares and gloves which offer protection during oral sex and manual stimulation of the genitals), Nonoxynol-9 (a spermicide jelly which kills the AIDS virus), and/or water-based, sexual lubricants. Safer sex involves staying away from street drugs and either abstaining from alcohol or using it in moderation. Drugs and alcohol suppress the immune system and good judgment; IV drugs are a major risk factor in contracting AIDS. Sex toys, such as vibrators, should not be shared with partners and require thorough cleaning after use. "Outercourse" is recommended. There are no safer sexual behaviors than masturbating in a partner's presence, superficial kissing, sharing sexual fantasies, massaging, cuddling, and experimenting with erotic dress and striptease.

## CELEBRATING CULTURAL AND SEXUAL DIVERSITY

Much of what we know or think we know about women's sexuality is based on research with middle-class, young, able-bodied, heterosexual white women. Feminist sexologists, in contrast, study the diversity of sexual values and experiences among women who vary in age, health status, sexual orientation, socioeconomic status, and cultural group or ethnicity.[119] In this section of the chapter, I criticize traditional sex researchers for their insensitivity to women's cultural and physical diversity and explore how poor women, women of color, lesbians, older women, and physically disabled women write about their own lives.

Affluent individuals often regard poor women with contempt, expecting lower socioeconomic status women to be promiscuous and sexually irresponsible. Since slavery, African-American women have been stereotyped as heavy-set, asexual "mammies" whose sole purpose is to nurture children and serve the white master; man-hating "Sapphires" who emasculate black men; and as hypersexual and immoral "Jezebels" just asking to be sexually exploited by black and white men alike.[120] Hispanic and Asian American women, in contrast, are stereotyped as either long-suffering martyrs who have sex largely out of duty to their husbands or as exotic and passive sexual playthings ready to do anything white men desire. And, what about the first Americans and Canadians? Like their male counterparts, North American Indian and Inuit (Arctic) women are, for the most part, invisible in the dominant culture. Lesbian and bisexual women are stereotyped as either wayward heterosexuals just waiting for the right man to set them straight or as social rejects who are too unattractive to find or hold on to a man. Women of color in the lesbian and bisexual community face the possibility of triple discrimination based on gender, ethnicity, and sexual orientation. This triple whammy is only slightly mitigated by the fact that compared to heterosexuals, white gay men and lesbians are less prejudiced toward members of racial and religious minority groups and more likely to be advocates of women's rights and civil rights.[121] In a society in which youth and physical perfection are worshipped, mature women and women who are disabled or ill face unique forms of sexual discrimination. Typically, they are seen as disinterested in sex and unattractive. Sometimes, they are regarded as too old or too handicapped to have "real sex." A major purpose of this chapter is to refute mistaken and pejorative beliefs about women from nondominant groups.

## Low-Income, Urban Women

Contemporary research contradicts the image of poor women and women of color as either sexually insatiable or sexually deficient. A recent study of inner-city, low-income women indicated that heterosexual black and white women did not differ in sexual frequency, behaviors leading to orgasm, level of sexual satisfaction, and concerns about an intimate relationship.[122] Most were able to experience orgasm and the majority indicated having at least moderate sexual satisfaction. Not unlike their more affluent counterparts, low-income women said that they wished that their partners would engage in more foreplay and verbal communication about sex. Poor heterosexual women have intercourse and orgasms about as frequently as middle-class women but are less inclined to masturbate. Contemporary inner-city women are no less likely than affluent women to experience cunnilingus (oral stimulation of the vulva) or manual stimulation of their genitals. Recent research challenges the popular idea that the sexual experiences of the poor somehow don't measure up to those who have more money. Many low-income women have satisfying sex with men; their bedroom experiences are hardly limited to abbreviated, brutish intercourse. One-third of the time, poor, inner-city women initiated sex with their heterosexual partners.

### African-American Women

The classic "scientific" description of African-American sexuality differs little from the stereotypes propagated by prejudiced people in the white majority. According to mainstream sociologists, black people are more involved with sex than white people; early and frequent sexual intercourse as well as sex outside a primary, committed relationship are considered characteristic.[123] Sometimes, these ideas are presented in positive terms. That is, black people are supposed to be less puritanical than white people. More often than not, however, the patriarchal scientific model of female black sexuality is quite negative. Black women's supposed "promiscuity" is sometimes presented as the historical result of slavery during which time women were obliged to have multiple partners to produce slave babies. Alternatively, black women's allegedly excessive sexual activity is linked to current oppression. Alienated by racism and economic discrimination, black women are presumed to readily engage in sex with multiple men to escape from the painful reality of their lives. Supposedly too, there is an absence of reliable men to choose from because poverty, racism, frequent incarceration and high death rates for African-American males, and the welfare system have destabilized the black family. The "scientific" portrait of black women as sexually permissive is not entirely the product of racist imagination. Some sociological studies suggest that African-American women are (or at least have been) more likely than white women to hold liberal attitudes towards heterosexual sex and practice sexual intercourse outside marriage.[124] But, data isn't dogma, and there is something seriously wrong with much of the research on black women's sexuality. Often, social scientists frame their questions and interpretations in terms of male, white, middle-class assumptions. Frequently, studies confound group differences based on social class with those based on race.[125]

Regardless of ethnicity or race, poor people may be more sexually permissive outside of marriage than middle-class people. Yet, sexual scientists have typically tested theories of racial differences by comparing poor black women with more affluent white women. In studies in which groups are similar in socioeconomic and educational status, black women turn out to be no different than white women or more conservative sexually.[126] Just as in the dominant population, there is a tremendous sexual variation among black Americans, with distinct differences between people whose families immigrated from the Caribbean and those whose African ancestors were taken directly to the United States as slaves long ago.[127] Many black women, especially those from middle-class families, view themselves as more sexually conservative than comparable white women. Typically, parents had not discussed sex while they grew up except to issue warnings about the dangers of premarital sex; these teachings were strongly reinforced by black church groups. In glaring contrast with the stereotype of the black Jezebel, many African-American women report a higher level of sexual guilt and less varied heterosexual behavior than comparable white women. Cautiously, many such women require a lengthy courtship period and some promise of commitment before consenting to sexual intercourse.

How, if at all, do black and white Americans differ sexually? It is difficult to say. Supposedly, black people are less likely than white people to engage in masturbation and are more likely to confine heterosexual activity to limited foreplay plus intercourse. However, recent studies suggest that this is no longer true. Masturbation, oral sex, and manual stimulation of a partner's genitals have gained wider acceptance in the black community, especially among young people.[128] Fewer and fewer black men have internalized the racist myth of the African-American "super stud" whose all-powerful penis should be a woman's sole source of sexual pleasure.[129] Seeking to affirm women's sexuality, black feminists have criticized men who limit lovemaking to penetration and penile thrusting, noting that sexual satisfaction is greatest for those black women who take the initiative and engage in a variety of sexual activities with partners.[130] According to sexologist Herb Samuels, who has asked large numbers of minority college students to describe their sexual experiences during the past two decades, most young black men have responded to women's desires; sexual variety has become a stable part of African-Americans' sexual scripts.[131]

African-American lesbian feminists have been active, combating heterosexism and male dominance in the black community.[132] Pointing out that they have assumed a major role in the larger black liberation movement from the beginning, lesbian feminists of color argue that it is time for heterosexual brothers and sisters to accept them and join the political struggle for gay and lesbian rights. Finally, African-American feminists have criticized the mass media and cosmetics industry for promoting white standards of beauty.[133] Since the nineteenth century, black women have been urged to buy products that will straighten their hair and lighten their skin. Beauty images distorted by racism make it difficult for African-American women to feel good about themselves and for African American men to appreciate their sexual attractiveness.

### North American Indians and Inuits

Traditionally, North American Indians and Inuits (Arctic peoples) have honored women for their nurturance and strength.[134] Whether they are girls, mothers, or grandmothers, women are viewed as men's equals in a number of communities and, in some cases, women are the most significant members of their society. Traditional attitudes towards menstruation and women's aging bodies vary among the indigenous peoples of Canada and the United States but are often more woman-affirming than those held in the dominant culture. Commonly, menstruation is considered to be not a "curse," but a time of spiritual awakening and enhanced feminine power. Menopause is associated not with the loss of beauty and purpose, but with liberation from reproductive responsibilities accompanied by increased opportunities for leadership and enhanced status as a wise community elder. Before contact with Europeans, cultural beliefs about sex education, nudity, masturbation, and appropriate sexual behavior differed greatly among North American Indian nations and Inuit peoples. Some cultures restricted women's sexuality considerably, but most were permissive by European standards. In particular aboriginal communities, women were encouraged to take the sexual initiative and premarital and extramarital sex were tolerated. In some cultures, homosexuality was regarded as disgraceful. In others, lesbians and gay men were looked upon as two-spirited people, a distinction that earned them high spiritual status, love, and respect.

The sexual beliefs and experiences of contemporary North American Indian and Inuit women are influenced by many factors: traditional cultural beliefs and practices, the dominant culture, and all too often—extreme poverty and a history of oppression. Today as in the past, North American Indian and Inuit women are taught to love their bodies and especially to honor their capacity to have children. For many, procreation is the major purpose of sex. Children are seen as a great gift in traditional societies. Moreover, cultural survival depends on replenishing a way of life that was nearly destroyed by genocide, land-grabbing, and economic upheaval; 80 percent of all adults are unemployed in some reservations. Having large families is also important because until recently, the Canadian and U.S. governments forcibly removed Indian children to large government-controlled residential schools, denying women their cherished role of nurturing and guiding future generations. Of course, an exaggerated emphasis on reproduction has some sexual costs. Traditional women aren't supposed to have sex just for enjoyment and are frowned upon for using contraception or having abortions, regardless of how they personally feel about the possibility of repeated, unplanned pregnancies. Given the emphasis on procreation, lesbians may be rejected for turning away from their obligation to bear children. On the other hand, homohatred is uncharacteristic of native North American societies. Those who honor their traditions respect sexual diversity and support gay women and men, often giving them leadership roles in their communities.

Poverty takes its toll on sexual pleasure. Housing on reservations and in urban slums is often limited and crowded. In some Canadian Inuit communities, three large families are obliged to share the same small house. It may be impossible for a couple to have sexual relations privately. To minimize children's opportunities to witness their most intimate interactions, some aboriginal couples are obliged to limit their sexual activity to hurried intercourse. But, as I have pointed out throughout this book, procreative sex without the sensual trimmings is not conducive to female sexual pleasure. Be this as it may, it would be misleading to draw any absolute conclusions about the sexuality of North American Indian and Inuit women. Like other women of color, their sexual experiences and values vary greatly as a function of cultural nuances, education, intermarriage, socioeconomic status, and the extent to which they feel integrated into mainstream American or Canadian society.

## Latinas

Latinas are Hispanic women whose families originated in Central America, South America, and the Caribbean. In the United States, a large proportion of Latinas trace their roots to Mexico, Puerto Rico, and Cuba.[135] Varying considerably in ancestry, Hispanic women may be European, Indian, African-Caribbean, or combinations thereof. They may speak Spanish all of the time, some of the time, or not at all. Sexual attitudes and behaviors vary in this diverse population. As Herb Samuels explains, sharing the same skin color or cultural heritage does not imply that people also have uniform sexual attitudes and experiences.[136]

Despite their rich cultural variability, Latinas share a few common characteristics that may have a profound impact on their sexuality.[137] Many Latinas have been exposed to the strict, sexual dictates of the Catholic Church. Whether they eventually reject church dogma or not, women from devout families often have been raised to believe that menstruation is shameful because it is God's punishment for Eve's original sin, and women face dire consequences for losing their virginity before marriage. Traditional Latinas grow up with the belief that nonprocreative sex, including masturbation and oral sex, is sinful and socially destructive. At the same time, many grow up in the shadow of a rigid sexual double standard. Men's sexual conquests of women are equated with heightened masculinity. Sexually active heterosexual women and lesbians, in contrast, are disparaged as "whores" or "mannish" women who are unfit for motherhood, the most exalted role available to them. Lest their virtue come under suspicion, traditional Latinas are taught that "good" women shouldn't act like they enjoy sex, even with their husbands. Sexual role playing is so strongly emphasized in traditional culture that Latina lesbians are more likely than their Anglo counterparts to adhere to butche and femme roles. Cultural values aside, the "macha," or more masculine-appearing Latina lesbian, does not generally dominate her romantic relationship.

On the positive side, Latin culture emphasizes the desirability of warm and close family ties and legitimizes the expression of tender emotions more than Anglo culture. Traditional Hispanic couples are touch-oriented, exchanging multiple caresses and love pats daily. Equally positive for women, standards for female beauty are flexible. Full-figured women, not just thin ones, are considered highly attractive; young women with all kinds of figures show pride in their bodies by wearing colorful, tight, and slinky clothes. Among lesbian and bisexual couples in particular, there is a special appreciation for the beauty of older and darker skinned women. Notwithstanding the affirming emphasis on sensuality, traditional Hispanic culture also promotes sex-negative messages. Because the asexual Virgin Mary symbolizes the ideal woman, some Latinas are afraid to become sexually aroused. For devout Catholics, sex may be a duty to a husband, not a pleasure, and is expected to take place clothed and in total darkness. Telling a man how to be a better lover is generally forbidden in traditional Latin culture as is complaining about his extramarital liaisons or irrational jealousy. Cultural messages to be passive and avoid contraception make traditional Hispanic women especially susceptible to unwanted pregnancies and sexually transmitted diseases.[138]

It would be wrong to paint an overly gloomy picture of Latina sexuality.[139] Traditional Hispanic men are often devoted husbands because of the strong cultural emphasis on carrying out family responsibilities and having a loyal wife. The sexual scripts of young Hispanics, like those of contemporary black couples, place increasing emphasis on sexual variety and women's pleasure. Acculturated women, those who speak English frequently and are influenced by the dominant culture, have broken away from the sexual double standard. Compared to traditional Latinas, acculturated teenage girls are more likely to be sexually active before marriage, and acculturated women are more likely to carry condoms with them and have had more than one sexual partner. In sharp contrast, acculturated Hispanic men have for the most part rejected male sexual privilege, having sex with fewer women than traditional men from their culture. According to one recent survey, Mexican-American women are generally more sexually liberal than women whose families originated in Puerto Rico. A testament to the creative, indomitable human spirit, a number of traditional Hispanic women have learned how to be sexually adventurous without explicitly compromising their "virtue" as defined by the patriarchy. Anal intercourse, for example, is popular among some unmarried couples from the Dominican Republic as a means of enjoying sex while preserving the woman's technical virginity. Unfortunately, it is unclear whether these young Dominican couples use condoms during anal sex to prevent transmission of HIV and other sexually transmitted diseases.

### Asian Americans

Asian-American women are even more culturally diverse than Latinas. They come from multiple linguistic and religious traditions, originating from numerous countries throughout Asia and the Pacific islands. A large proportion of North American Asians trace their roots to China, the Philippines, Japan, Vietnam, Korea, and India.[140] Given their cultural diversity, therefore, any generalizations about Asian-American sexuality should be viewed as tentative. This is particularly true given an interracial marriage rate as high as 50 percent.

The traditional Asian family emphasizes harmonious relationships. This means that women and men alike expect to sacrifice autonomy for the sake of the extended family. Shame and the fear of dishonoring family members exert a powerful influence on individual behavior. Generally, couples aren't supposed to discuss sexuality openly although there may be a strong cultural emphasis on sexual pleasure in some Asian cultures.[141] Among some Asian groups, such as Japanese Americans, both women and men are expected to be self-disciplined, expressing emotions in a very controlled fashion.[142] In no way does this imply a desire for emotional distance. Traditional Japanese-American women feel affection and sexual interest deeply. Instead of being demonstrative, however, love is communicated indirectly, through thoughtful actions more than words. Springing from an agrarian tradition in which human sexual pleasure is equated with a fruitful harvest, many Asian cultures place a positive emphasis on sensuality, nudity, masturbation, and sexual pleasure. These good qualities may be negated by less woman-affirming traditions. Generally, women are expected to be sexually submissive, tolerating insensitivity and men's sexual indiscretions for the sake of family honor. Lesbianism is looked down upon as inconsistent with the woman's maternal role and the traditions of the patriarchal, extended family. Again, as for many other groups, it would be inappropriate to view Asian women in stereotypical ways. There is tremendous diversity in the extent to which they accept or reject the sexual values of mainstream culture and those of their culture of origin. Highly educated, economically affluent, acculturated Asian women are likely to look at sex much the same way as white Canadian and American women from the same social class.

### Lesbians and Bisexual Women

For lesbian and bisexual couples, friendship and emotional sharing are generally more highly valued than is genital sexual contact.[143] Although some women view this as a deficit, complaining that "sex" with other women lacks variety and occurs far too rarely, others are perfectly satisfied. Sex therapists who promote the idea that good sexual relationships require frequent genital contact fail to recognize the masculine origin of our obsession with counting shared orgasms. Often lesbian relationships are not consummated until women feel strong emotional attachment. In the lesbian community, friendships with ex-lovers are resilient; the threads of shared experiences and confidences bind women together.

Although some women are satisfied with relatively low rates of genital sex in their long-term relationships, it should not be assumed that lesbian and bisexual women limit themselves to hugging and kissing.[144] Mutual masturbation and cunnilingus are very popular, younger women being more sexually adventurous than older ones.[145] Body rubbing is also highly valued, especially by African-American couples. Even by male, heterosexual, quantitative standards, many lesbians enjoy a vigorous and enviable sexuality. Generally, bisexual women and lesbians complain of fewer sexual problems than do gay men and indicate that they are readily and highly aroused by partners. Women who love women characterize their orgasms as more regular, stronger, and longer lasting than those described by heterosexual women. Heterosexual women often feel insecure about their physical appearance because no one can live up to the impossible standards of advertising and the mass media. Lesbians, in contrast, have broader definitions of beauty. As a group, women who love women are more self-accepting than are heterosexual women. "In relating sexually to another woman's body, a lesbian has the opportunity to come to love her own body."[146]

Obviously dyspareunia (painful intercourse) is not a problem for lesbians. And, lesbians are less likely than heterosexual women to experience vaginismus (involuntary pelvic contractions) or an inability to achieve orgasm.[147] But, women who love women are not immune from sexual problems. Growing up in a culture in which women's genitals are viewed as smelly, unattractive, and unpalatable, some lesbians and bisexual women have a phobia about performing oral sex. Their most frequent sexual complaint, however, is low sexual frequency. The primary reasons that female couples seek sex therapy is that one or both partners are reluctant to initiate genital sexual activity. Lesbian sex therapist Margaret Nichols explains these difficulties in terms of female, sex-role socialization: "Our relationships represent the pairing of two relatively sexually inhibited individuals" neither of whom has been encouraged to pay attention to her own desires or seduce a partner.[148] Lesbians, like heterosexual women, are products of a sexual double standard according to which "good girls" don't get hot or initiate sex. Even butche lesbians, women who delight in wearing mannish dress and demonstrating physical strength and emotional independence, are unlikely to describe themselves as masculine in their sexual interactions with other women.[149]

At the risk of being labeled politically incorrect by Radical Feminists, lesbian sex therapists and popular authors encourage women to speak up when they want more sex.[150] According to Margaret Nichols, "We might reflect on the fact that, contrary to our feminist beliefs, perhaps a little pressure is good for a relationship; pressure can simply reflect the desires of one partner rather than be evidence of assaultive behavior."[151] Pat Califia rejects the myth that women automatically know how to please each other. She believes that the shortage of lesbian-oriented pornography, an absence of sex manuals for women who love women, and Radical Feminist rhetoric contribute to women's sexual difficulties.[152] Defining lesbians in Liberal Feminist terms, she states, "We are not simply arch-feminists. We are women who think about touching each other, who undress each other, and explore the sensual possibilities of our own and our lovers' bodies."[153] Susan Hamadock asks lesbian therapists to provide sex education for the female couples they treat and make inquiries into women's erotic interactions even if sexual concerns are not brought up as the presenting problem.[154] Marny Hall argues that therapists can help women describe what the decline in sexual frequency has meant to them without buying into the androcentric assumption that more genital sex is necessarily better.[155] Woman-affirming treatment for lesbian couples addresses power imbalances and techniques for increasing sensuality and emotional sharing. With this goal in mind, Jo Ann Loulan gives women permission to be more sexually creative and playful in both masturbation and partnered sex.[156] Both Jo Ann Loulan and Laura Brown believe that internalized, antigay prejudice is a source of many sexual problems faced by female couples, whether or not they publicly proclaim their lesbian pride.[157]

## Middle-Aged and Older Women

Rosa is a pleasantly chubby woman in her late fifties. She no longer menstruates and has noticed some increased vaginal dryness when she masturbates or has sex with her husband. Other than this change, which is readily corrected by the use of a nonprescription, feminine lubricant, sex is satisfying. In fact, Rosa thinks that she and Sam are better in bed than when they were younger. They have finally learned to take their time, combining pleasant conversation with sensual lovemaking and "just joking around," as they call it.

At 85, Betty (Rosa's mother) is a remarkably healthy and vigorous woman. A widow, she lives alone and does charitable volunteer work. Betty enjoys going to concerts, restaurants, and movies with several women friends. She does regret, however, the absence of a man in her life. But, Betty is not sexually inactive. She feels good about her body and masturbates regularly to orgasm. Neither Rosa, her friends, nor her primary physician know about her secret sexual life; she is afraid to "embarrass" them.

In a patriarchal society, women are valued according to their youthful beauty and procreative abilities. But, as Rosa and Betty prove, sexual interest and pleasure play a central role in the lives of older women. As women age, they may feel more in charge of their sexuality than when they were younger; heightened sexual autonomy and self-confidence yield qualitatively better sexual experiences for heterosexual and lesbian women alike.[158] Unfortunately, sex researchers and health care providers don't always appreciate this. Frequently, older women are compared with younger ones and found deficient according to arbitrary, quantitative, sexual standards. Immediately before, during, and especially after menopause, when menstruation ceases, the ovaries decrease their production of estrogens and androgens. Supposedly, this depletion of hormones is associated with decreased sexual interest, increased vaginal dryness, reduced vaginal elasticity, and diminished clitoral sensation.[159] Supposedly too, orgasms take more time and become less intense in the aging woman, and sex requires more effort.

Menopause typically occurs when women are in their early fifties. Certainly, many women do experience sexual difficulties during or after the onset of menopause. Estrogens facilitate vaginal lubrication; androgens are associated with heightened sexual interest in both women and men. It stands to reason that decreased production of these hormones may be problematic (especially for heterosexual women who rely on intercourse as their primary sexual outlet). However, women live one-third of their lives after their reproductive capacity has ended. Too much supposedly "scientific" literature falsely attributes all age-related changes in women's sexual behavior and psychological adjustment to endocrine changes. True too, all too many studies that associate aging with diminished sexual capacity are based on women who have sought medical help for menopausal and postmenopausal distress. This is hardly a random sample of older women! Women who aren't having sexual problems are unlikely to seek medical attention. Hormone replacement therapy (HRT) may be very helpful for many women and can reduce the risk of osteoporosis (brittle bones) and other illnesses. However, HRT is not necessary for every woman and has health risks for some. Even after natural menopause, the adrenal glands (and to a lesser extent, the ovaries) continue to produce androgens which help maintain women's sexual interest.[160] Postmenopausal women may still produce an adequate quantity of these hormones. The main hormonal deficiency for postmenopausal women, then, is in estrogens, not androgens. Estrogens are responsible for the lubrication and strengthening of vaginal tissues which makes intercourse comfortable; they play absolutely no role in creating sexual arousal or ensuring orgasmic intensity.

Equating sex with intercourse, some American physicians limit HRT to oral estrogens cycled with nonandrogenic progesterone. True, this treatment makes a woman better able to tolerate penetration but what about her sexual pleasure? As pointed out repeatedly in this book, penetration is not necessarily women's favorite erotic activity. Whether or not they receive HRT, many older women enjoy sexual activities other than intercourse. Moreover, treatment with estrogens and progesterone alone binds up free androgens in the woman's body and may actually make her less interested in sex than if she wasn't receiving HRT. Any woman who is considering HRT should tell her physician or nurse that she is interested in receiving androgens too, not just estrogens. Studies of postmenopausal women reveal that androgen treatment is associated with heightened sexual interest and activity which in turn is related to reduced vaginal atrophy. HRT is not a magic answer to every sexual difficulty an aging woman might face. Before they prescribe hormones, health care providers need to examine other variables that could influence sexual enjoyment.[161] Perhaps the woman's partner is no longer interested in sex. Maybe she is depressed or is grieving the loss of her partner through death or divorce. Cultural forces may have shaped this woman's beliefs about sex and aging too. Poor, uneducated, and sex-role traditional women are more likely to fear the impact of aging on their sexuality than middle-class, highly educated, and feminist women.

Generally, women outlive the men in their lives. But, the death of a loving sexual partner is a major issue for women regardless of sexual orientation. Through no choice of their own, many elderly lesbians, like most widows their age, are celibate.[162] Yet, older women may retain sexual pleasure and the joy of living even when faced with the absence of a partner or with serious physical disabilities.[163] Sexual fantasies, erotic dreams, and clitoral sensation continue long after menopause. Many women will masturbate their whole lives or continue to engage in genital sex on a regular basis providing a partner is available. Emotional exchanges and the expression of physical affection are possible even for women who are no longer able to enjoy genital activity. There is no age or health limit on sexual humor, flirting, touching, and stroking. Remembrance, reliving the past in the mind's eye, includes the joy of recalling the best aspects of an elderly woman's past sexual relationships. More vivid than youthful, sexual fantasies, sexual remembrance is a celebration of a life well lived, not just a sign of continued sexual interest.

## Women Who Are Physically Disabled and Chronically Ill

In our culture, sex is viewed as belonging to healthy people who have perfect bodies.[164] Too frequently, the sexual concerns of the medical patient or disabled person are seen as irrelevant or beyond remedy. In some cases, able-bodied persons distance themselves from individuals who are disabled or ill. "Disability is often associated with sin, stigma, and a kind of 'untouchability.' Anxiety, as well as a sense of vulnerability and dread, may cause others to respond to the 'imperfections' of a disabled woman's body with terror, avoidance, pity, and/or guilt."[165] People who live with a disability aren't expected to be sexual. They are either ignored, pitied, or stereotyped as "super crips" or "super invalids" whose remarkable courage and achievements in the face of pain, disfigurement, sensory loss, and poor mobility are presumed to compensate for their imagined asexuality. Here too, sexist practices occur. In a patriarchal society, women, especially those who are disabled and ill, are regarded as the passive receptacles for male sexual advances more than as sexual actors in their own right. Yet, sex is a core feature of the human experience.

Learning how to be sexual or to remain sexual may be necessary for effective coping with disabilities and illnesses. As Pamela Walker, a 38-year-old woman with polio who uses a power wheelchair explains, "one of the hardest things disabled people face is being seen as sexless by a society that places a high value on sexuality."[166] Most women, including those who are seriously disabled or ill, hope to continue experiencing sexual intimacy for the rest of their lives. No one has ever explained this better than Barbara Rosenblum. Before being diagnosed with terminal breast cancer, this courageous and articulate woman found sex to be free and untroubled. She understood her body and its cycles of sexual interest. Weakened and sickened by cancer and chemotherapy, however, she had to find new ways to be sexual. Doing this was a necessary part of holding on to life and giving something back to Sandra Butler, her loving partner and devoted care giver.

> Now it is clear that I will never have a full head of hair again. . . . Losing my pubic hair, I felt naked and embarrassed, inadvertently returned to pre-pubescence. I was too exposed and didn't want to be touched. . . . The vaginal tissue was thinning and becoming more sensitive to pressure and friction. It began to hurt when . . . I had sex. . . . We stopped making love. Instead we found new ways of being intimate. . . . Our hands found new ways to console each other. . . . I would touch Sandy's throat in a spot I knew contained all her tears: she would sob. And right in the midst of chemotherapy infusions . . . Sandy helped me relax by touching my back and neck lightly.[167]

Maintaining sexual activity in the face of illness or disability is no easy task.[168] It requires creativity and hard work on the part of patients, loved ones, nursing staff, and physicians. Since some medications interfere with sexual functioning, dosage changes and alternative drugs may need to be considered. Patients who require bladder and bowel care as a result of spinal cord injury, neurological disease, or ostomy must learn how to engage in preventative management to preclude accidental leakage and have a sense of humor when accidents inevitably occur. Those who lack genital sensation may want to use self-hypnosis or sensate focus and massage to enhance sexual pleasure in nongenital areas. Relaxation training and self-employed sexual imagery may be helpful to other patients. For medical patients more than anyone else, the sex act itself needs to be redefined in feminist terms. Sexual intercourse, especially intercourse with the man on top of the woman, may no longer be possible if the patient or her partner experience mobility problems or coital pain. Couples may benefit from experimenting with various forms of oral sex, shared fantasies, and whole body sexual touching. Pain cannot be overlooked. Some injuries and illnesses cause constant and severe pain experienced throughout the patient's body. In other cases, pain is not generalized but is specific to the genitals. Although research suggests that sexual imagery and genital stimulation can reduce women's awareness of pain,[169] this is not true for everybody. An individual who has arthritis may require an analgesic or anti-inflammatory drug before engaging in any form of sexual activity to minimize pain, stiffness, or fatigue.[170] Women with chronic interstitial cystitis, an incurable bladder disorder, and other diseases associated with genital pain and dyspareunia may benefit both from pain-alleviating medication and from exploring which time periods for sexual activity, sexual positions, and sexual techniques are least likely to exacerbate symptoms.[171] Orgasm itself may be abandoned for alternative forms of sexual pleasure. Some urologic and gynecological patients have no difficulty achieving orgasm but are afraid to do so because their pain increases substantially afterwards.

Disability and chronic illness can inspire us to redefine sexuality, rewriting scripts for interacting with loving partners.[172] Sexual interest is related to general health and psychological adjustment. Heart patients and their health care providers must sort out the extent to which declining sexual interest is the product of a weakened heart versus the result of depression or anxiety about illness.[173] For these women, learning how to resume sexual activity safely is just as important as resuming physical exercise. Women with chronic obstructive pulmonary diseases such as bronchitis, emphysema, and asthma are challenged to maintain sexual arousal in the face of fears regarding breathlessness.[174] A woman who has diabetes must face the possibility of impaired vaginal lubrication, vulval tumescence, and orgasm.[175] More disturbing, her sensations of sexual excitement may bear a frightening resemblance to the symptoms of low blood sugar. To stop blaming themselves, women need to understand that illness, injury, and medication can sometimes alter or even destroy sexual response. End-state renal disease, treated via dialysis or kidney transplants, for example, can reduce sexual desire and arousal as well as interfere with a woman's ability to achieve orgasm.[176] Both multiple sclerosis and diabetes can decrease vaginal lubrication and response.

The medical establishment needs to overcome its own sexism in health care practice. Following surgery and pelvic radiation for gynecological cancer, the standard medical practice is to preserve the woman's sexual availability (or capacity for intercourse) with a male partner.[177] Too little attention is given to the woman's feelings about scarring and other bodily changes or the pain that she might experience from resuming conventional heterosexual activity. Even less attention is given to the possibility that the woman may not personally like intercourse; alternative forms of sexual expression are equally important to women regardless of sexual orientation. Physicians and nurses must also come to terms with their historic dismissal of the sexual concerns of women with spinal cord injury (SCI).[178] There is substantially more information available on the sexual adjustment of men with SCI than on women with SCI, not only because most patients are men, but also because the sexual pleasure of paralyzed women is viewed as being of little consequence in a male-dominated culture. Why? The answer is that women with SCI remain fertile and can continue to give birth (painlessly) after injury. Since women's reproductive capabilities and ability to give pleasure to men remain intact despite spinal cord injury, their sexual desires and experiences are ignored. Yet, women with spinal cord injuries report experiencing sexual pleasure from tactile stimulation where sensation remains, especially around their breasts. Evidence of human adaptability, some women with SCI even experience orgasm (muscle tension and rapid respiration followed by pleasurable sensations of spasticity and decreased tension) in the area of their bodies above the injury to the cord. Given the derogatory label, "phantom orgasm," the sensations of this nongenitally based orgasm are no less real to the patient with SCI than is conventional orgasm to the physically intact individual. The feminist reconstruction of sexual discourse is not only valuable for women in general; it is essential for affirming the sexual rights and pleasures of both men and women who are chronically ill and physically disabled!

## SEXUAL SATISFACTION AND SEXUAL EQUALITY

The most sexually satisfied women are those who have a rewarding, equitable relationship with an emotionally giving partner.[179] Women like sex just as much as men but for somewhat different reasons. For men, the best things about sex are having fun, feeling good about their performance, and experiencing orgasm. For women, having a sensitive, considerate lover who touches, caresses, and cuddles them as much as they want is of utmost importance. Fortunately, even though they were told that respectable women never let themselves go, many women have learned to love sex anyway. Who are these women? Let me tell you a little about them.[180] They are courageous and innovative. Recognizing that sexual learning continues after they are no longer young, they regard sex as a life-long adventure. Comfortable with their bodies, these women have examined their genitals with their eyes and hands, refuting the idea that they should be ashamed of their sexuality.

Sexually satisfied women refuse to believe that there is one right skin color or one right hair texture. They dispute the media myths which suggest that sexy women must be perfectly beautiful and can't have any body fat. They pick sensitive partners who don't feel threatened by their sexual assertiveness. Rejecting conventional sex roles, they allow themselves to develop the so-called "masculine" and "androgynous" traits, independence, assertiveness, and self-confidence, along with the so-called "feminine" characteristics, empathy, warmth, and nurturance. They aren't afraid to ask for what they want. They don't think women should be innocuous, sexual innocents and reject the popular idea that life is only meaningful if a woman is in a "relationship." They feel empowered sexually because they have empowered themselves in the rest of their lives. Taking responsibility for their sexual pleasure and orgasms, they are sexual actors, not sex objects.

Consistent with Liberal Feminist thinking, rejection of traditional sexual scripts and advocacy of profeminist goals are strongly and positively associated with sexual autonomy and pleasure for both women and men. True, the personal is political. But, even more importantly, the political can shape the personal for the better. The struggle for women's sexual rights and pleasures may not be easy. However, it is not impossible either. Women have the right to change the sexual rules. Heterosexual sex doesn't have to be two and one-half minutes of thrusting after penetration with the man on top and the woman on the bottom.[181] Female sexuality need no longer be characterized primarily in terms of its relationship to male sexuality.[182] Celibacy can be redefined as self-loving instead of personal failure.[183]

It is all right to stop counting orgasms. It is all right for women to look at their bodies, to know what their vulvas look like, to know what feels good. It is all right for women to say what they like and don't like and expect a partner to listen. It is all right to have sex for love, and it is equally acceptable to have sex just for pleasure. It is all right to make the first move; it is also all right to decide against making any moves. It is all right to say Yes, and it is also all right to say No. The only rule is not to hurt someone else, not to exploit or coerce another person sexually. Women's sexuality belongs to all women. There is no politically correct way of being sexual. There is no scientifically proven, "normal" way of being sensual.

# NOTES

1. See Gagnon, Scripts, pp. 27–59; Jemail and Geer, Sexual Scripts, pp. 513–22; McCormick, Sexual Scripts, 3–27; Tiefer, Social Constructionism, pp. 70–94.

2. See Fine, Missing Discourse of Desire, pp. 31–59.

3. Gavey, Heterosexual Coercion, p. 334.

4. See Simkins and Rinck, Male and Female Sexual Vocabulary, pp. 160–72.

5. Gilfoyle, Wilson, and Brown, Sex, Organs, and Audiotape, p. 222.

6. Ibid., p. 223.

7. See Maass and Volpato, Self-Serving Attributions About Sexual Experiences, pp. 517–42.

8. See Valverde, *Sex, Power, and Pleasure.*

9. Stock, Propping Up the Phallocracy, p. 28.

10. See Wolfe, *When He Has a Headache.*

11. See Richgels, Hypoactive Sexual Desire, pp. 123–35; Loulan, Sex Practices of 1566 Lesbians, pp. 221–34.

12. Webster, Eroticism and Taboo, p. 387.

13. Ibid.

14. Kitzinger, Compulsory Heterosexuality, pp. 399–418.

15. See Faderman, *Odd Girls and Twilight Lovers.*

16. Ibid., p. 232.

17. See Campbell, Feminist Sexual Politics, pp. 19–39; Echols, Taming of the Id, pp. 50–72.

18. Nichols, Lesbian Sexuality, pp. 97–98.

19. See Hamadock; Lesbian Sexuality, pp. 207–19; Nichols, Lesbian Sexuality, pp. 97–98; Loulan, *Lesbian Passion.*

20. Nichols, Lesbian Sexuality, p. 100.

21. See Dimen, Politically Correct?, pp. 138–48; Newton and Walton, More Precise Sexual Vocabulary, pp. 242–50; Vance, Pleasure and Danger, pp. 1–27.

22. Dimen, Politically Correct?, p. 142.

23. Faderman, *Odd Girls and Twilight Lovers*, p. 250.

24. Vance, Pleasure and Danger, p. 23.

25. See Leiblum and Pervin, Sex Therapy from a Sociocultural Perspective, pp. 1–24; Leiblum and Rosen, Changing Perspectives on Sexual Desire, pp. 1–17.

26. See Tiefer, Social Constructionism, pp. 70–94.

27. See Zilbergeld and Ellison, Desire Discrepancies, pp. 65–101.

28. Ibid., p. 69.

29. See Irvine, *Disorders of Desire;* Leiblum and Pervin, Sex Therapy from a Sociocultural Perspective, pp. 1–24; Tiefer, A Feminist Critique, pp. 5–22; Tiefer, Feminist Perspectives on Sexology, pp. 16–26.

30. See Riley, Women Who Volunteer for Sexual Response Studies, pp. 131–40.

31. See Brown, Internalized Oppression, pp. 99–107; Califia, *Sapphistry.*

32. See Lorde, *I Am Your Sister;* Valverde, *Sex, Power, and Pleasure.*

33. See Coleman, Bisexual Women in Marriages, pp. 87–99.

34. See Barbach, Anorgasmic Women, pp. 107–46; Barbach, *Women Discover Orgasm;* Tiefer, Criticisms of "The Human Sexual Response Cycle," pp. 1–23.

35. See Handy et al., Feminist Issues in Sex Therapy, pp. 69–80; Rosen and Beck, *Patterns of Sexual Arousal;* Valverde, *Sex, Power, and Pleasure.*

36. Dodson, *Liberating Masturbation,* pp. 2–3.

37. Ibid., p. 9.

38. Oliver and Hyde, Gender Differences in Sexuality, pp. 29–51.

39. Dodson, *Liberating Masturbation;* Dodson, *Sex for One.*

40. Ibid. and Loulan, *Lesbian Passion.*

41. See Aletsky, Sexism and Sexuality; Bancroft, *Human Sexuality;* Hyde, *Half the Human Experience.*

42. See Bancroft, *Human Sexuality;* Ladas, Whipple, and Perry, *G Spot;* Perry and Whipple, Pelvic Muscle Strength, pp. 22–39; Whipple and Komisaruk, The G Spot, Orgasm, and Female Ejaculation, pp. 227–37.

43. See Alzate and Hoch, The "G Spot"; Bancroft, *Human Sexuality;* Schover and Jensen, *Sexuality and Chronic Illness.*

44. See Komisaruk and Whipple, Physiological and Perceptual Correlates of Orgasm, pp. 69–73; Whipple and Komisaruk, Analgesia Produced in Women, pp. 130–40; Whipple and Komisaruk, The G Spot, Orgasm, and Female Ejaculation, pp. 227–37; Whipple, Ogden, and Komisaruk, Imagery-Induced Orgasm, pp. 121–33.

45. See Tavris, *Mismeasure of Woman.*

46. See Rosen and Beck, *Patterns of Sexual Arousal.*

47. See Komisaruk and Whipple, Physiological and Perceptual Correlates of Orgasm, pp. 69–73; Ogden, *Women Who Love Sex;* Whipple, Ogden, and Komisaruk, Imagery-Induced Orgasm, pp. 121–33.

48. See Lightfoot-Klein, Genitally Circumcised and Infibulated Females, pp. 375–92; Walker and Parmar, *Warrior Marks.*

49. See Zwerner, Sexuality Counseling for Women with Spinal Cord Injuries, pp. 91–100.

50. See Rosen and Beck, *Patterns of Sexual Arousal;* Tiefer, Criticism of "The Human Sexual Response Cycle," pp. 1–23; Tiefer, Feminist Perspective on Sexology, pp. 16–26.

51. Rosen and Beck, *Patterns of Sexual Arousal,* p. 41.

52. See Irvine, *Disorders of Desire.*

53. Tiefer, Feminist Perspective on Sexology, p. 22.

54. See Ellison, Sex Therapy with Women, pp. 327–33; Irvine, *Disorders of Desire;* Tiefer, Criticisms of "The Human Sexual Response Cycle," pp. 1–23.

55. See Kaplan, *Disorders of Sexual Desire;* Rosen and Beck, *Patterns of Sexual Arousal.*

56. See Tiefer, Criticisms of "The Human Sexual Response Cycle," pp. 1–23.

57. See Loulan, *Lesbian Sex.*

58. See Baily, Hendrick, and Hendrick, Love, Sexual Attitudes, and Self Esteem, pp. 637–48; Duffy and Rusbult, Satisfaction and Commitment, pp. 1–23; Hatfield et al., What is Desired in the Sexual Relationship, pp. 39–52; Hendrick, Hendrick,

and Slapion-Foote, Sexual Attitudes, pp. 1630–42; Stock, Sex Roles and Sexual Dysfunction, pp. 249–75.

59. See Lawrance, Sexual Satisfaction.

60. See Ogden, Women and Sexual Ecstasy, pp. 43–56; Ogden, *Women Who Love Sex.*

61. Ibid.

62. See Gebhard, Marital Orgasm, pp. 70–78.

63. See Darling, Davidson, and Jennings, Multiorgasmic Experience in Women, pp. 527–40.

64. See Bressler and Lavender, Sexual Fulfillment, pp. 109–22.

65. See Morokoff, Female Orgasm, pp. 147–65; Perry and Whipple, Pelvic Muscle Strength, pp. 22–39.

66. See Reiss, *End to Shame;* Schover and Jensen, *Sexuality and Chronic Illness.*

67. Handy et al., Feminist Issues in Sex Therapy, pp. 69–80.

68. See Barbach, Anorgasmic Women, pp. 107–46; Barbach, *Women Discover Orgasm.*

69. Rubin, Women at Midlife, p. 74.

70. See Tiefer, A Feminist Critique, p. 9.

71. See Rosen and Beck, *Patterns of Sexual Arousal.*

72. See Gavey, Heterosexual Coercion, pp. 325–51; Mancini and Orthner, Recreational Sexuality Preferences, pp. 96–106.

73. See Bos, Sexuality of Gynecological Cancer Patients, pp. 217–24; Darty and Potter, Social Work with Challenged Women, pp. 83–100.

74. See Bancroft, *Human Sexuality;* Frank, Anderson, and Rubinstein, Sexual Dysfunction in "Normal" Couples, pp. 111–15; Spector and Carey, Incidence and Prevalence of the Sexual Dysfunctions, pp. 389–408.

75. See Frank, Anderson, and Rubinstein, Sexual Dysfunction in "Normal" Couples, pp. 111–15.

76. See LoPiccolo, Direct Treatment of Sexual Dysfunction, pp. 1–17; LoPiccolo and Stock, Sexual Dysfunction, pp. 158–67; Rosen and Beck, *Patterns of Sexual Arousal.*

77. See Reiss, *End to Shame.*

78. See Rosen and Beck, *Patterns of Sexual Arousal.*

79. See Kaplan, *Disorders of Sexual Desire;* LoPiccolo, Low Sex Desire, pp. 29–64; Nichols, Low Sexual Desire in Lesbian Couples, pp. 387–412; Nichols, Inhibited Sexual Desire, pp. 49–66; Richgels, Hypoactive Sexual Desire, pp. 123–35; Spector and Carey, Incidence and Prevalence of Sexual Dysfunctions, pp. 389–408.

80. See Leiblum and Rosen, Changing Perspectives on Sexual Desire, pp. 1–17.

81. See Kaplan, *Disorders of Sexual Desire.*

82. See Nichols, Inhibited Sexual Desire, pp. 49–66; Richgels, Hypoactive Sexual Desire, pp. 123–35.

83. Irvine, *Disorders of Desire*, pp. 210–11.

84. See Nichols, Low Sexual Desire in Lesbian Couples, pp. 387–412.

85. See Rosen and Beck, *Patterns of Sexual Arousal.*

86. Lazarus, Dyspareunia, pp. 147–66.

87. See Abarbanel, Coital Discomfort, pp. 241–59; Rosen and Beck, *Patterns of Sexual Arousal.*

88. See Leiblum, Pervin, and Campbell, Treatment of Vaginismus, pp. 113–38; LoPiccolo, Direct Treatment of Sexual Dysfunction, pp. 1–17; LoPiccolo and Stock, Sexual Dysfunction, pp. 158–67; Rosen and Beck, *Patterns of Sexual Arousal;* Valins, *When a Woman's Body Says No.*

89. See Coleman, Bisexual Women in Marriages, pp. 87–99.

90. See Reiss, *End to Shame.*

91. See Rust and Golombok, Stress and Marital Discord, pp. 25–27.

92. See LoPiccolo, Direct Treatment of Sexual Dysfunction, pp. 1–17.

93. See Stock, Propping Up the Phallocracy, pp. 23–42.

94. See Goodman, Sexual Addiction, pp. 303–14; Reiss, *End to Shame.*

95. See Aletsky, Sexism and Sexuality; Blumstein and Schwartz, *American Couples;* Brown, Internalized Oppression, pp. 99–107.

96. See Barbach, *Women Discover Orgasm.*

97. See Loulan, *Lesbian Passion;* Wolfe, *When He Has a Headache.*

98. Dodson, *Sex for One,* p. 3.

99. See Ogden, *Women Who Love Sex;* Valverde, *Sex, Power, and Pleasure.*

100. Bright, *Lesbian Sex World,* p. 25.

101. Ibid., p. 30.

102. See Ellison, Sex Therapy with Women, pp. 327–33; Handy et al., Feminist Issues in Sex Therapy, pp. 69–80; Stock, Sex Roles and Sexual Dysfunction, pp. 249–75; Stock, Power Dynamics in Relationships, pp. 62–99; Valentich and Gripton, Gender-Sensitive Practice, pp. 11–18.

103. See Becker, Impact of Sexual Abuse, pp. 298–318; Jehu, Sexual Dysfunctions Among Women Clients, pp. 53–70; McCabe, Adult Sexual Dysfunction, pp. 133–41; Rosen and Beck, *Patterns of Sexual Arousal;* Weiner, Sex Therapy with Survivors, pp. 253–64.

104. Jehu, Sexual Dysfunctions Among Women Clients, p. 61.

105. Ibid., p. 64.

106. See Allgeier and Allgeier, *Sexual Interactions.*

107. See Richardson, *Women and AIDS;* Shayne and Kaplan, Poor Women and AIDS, pp. 21–37.

108. See Centers for Disease Control, *HIV/AIDS Surveillance Report.*

109. See Richardson, *Women and AIDS;* Shayne and Kaplan, Poor Women and AIDS, pp. 21–37.

110. See Einhorn, Lesbians and AIDS, p. 10; Falco, *Lesbian Clients.*

111. See Reiss, *End to Shame.*

112. See ibid. and Adelman, Sustaining Passion, pp. 481–94; Campbell, Peplau, and DeBro, Women, Men, and Condoms, pp. 273–88; Ehrhardt et al., Prevention of Heterosexual Transmission of HIV, pp. 37–67.

113. See Juran, Heterosexual Sexual Changes.

114. See Ehrhardt et al., Prevention of Heterosexual Transmission of HIV, pp. 33–67; Fullilove et al., Black Women and AIDS Prevention, pp. 47–64.

115. See Trussell, Warner, and Hatcher, Condom Slippage and Breakage Rates, pp. 20–23.

116. See Campbell, Peplau, and DeBro, Women, Men, and Condoms, pp. 273–88; Fullilove et al., Black Women and AIDS Prevention, pp. 47–64.

117. Adelman, Sustaining Passion, p. 488.

118. See Ogden, *Everywoman's Guide;* Richardson, *Women and AIDS;* and Whipple and Ogden, *Safe Encounters.*

119. See Christensen, Sex Therapy with Ethnic and Racial Minority Women, pp. 187–206; Vance, Pleasure and Danger, pp. 1–27.

120. See Christensen, Sex Therapy with Ethnic and Racial Minority Women, pp. 187–206; hooks, *Ain't I a Woman;* hooks, *Black Looks;* Jewell, *From Mammy to Miss America;* West, Developing an "Oppositional Gaze."

121. See Beran et al., Attitudes Toward Minorities, pp. 65–83.

122. See House, Faulk, and Kubovchik, Sexual Behavior of Inner-City Women, pp. 172–84.

123. See Weinberg and Williams, Black Sexuality, pp. 197–218.

124. Ibid.

125. See Wyatt, Sexual Experience of Afro-American Women, pp. 17–39.

126. See Butts, Group Discussion by Black Women, pp. 41–43; Weinberg and Williams, Black Sexuality, pp. 197–218; Wyatt, Sexual Experience of Afro-American Women, pp. 17–39; Wyatt, Newcomb, and Riederle, *Sexual Abuse and Consensual Sex.*

127. See Fullilove et al., Black Women and AIDS Prevention, pp. 47–64; Samuels, Realm of the Other; Wilson, Black Culture and Sexuality, pp. 29–46; Wyatt, Sexual Experience of Afro-American Women, pp. 17–39; Wyatt and Dunn, Sex Guilt in Multiethnic Samples, pp 471–85; Wyatt and Lyons-Rowe, African American Women's Sexual Satisfaction, pp. 509–24; Wyatt, Newcomb, and Riederle, *Sexual Abuse and Consensual Sex.*

128. See ibid. and Weinberg and Williams, Black Sexuality, pp. 197–218.

129. See Samuels, Realm of the Other; Wilson, Black Culture and Sexuality, pp. 29–46.

130. See Wyatt and Lyons-Rowe, African American Women's Sexual Satisfaction, pp. 509–24.

131. See Samuels, Realm of the Other.

132. See Gomez and Smith, Black Lesbian Health, pp. 40–57; Lorde, *I Am Your Sister.*

133. See hooks, *Black Looks;* Jewell, *From Mammy to Miss America;* West, Developing an "Oppositional Gaze."

134. See Canadian Panel, *Violence Against Women;* Echohawk, Acculturation of American Indian Women, pp. 45–55; Locke, Re-Affirmation of Self; Medicine-Eagle, *Buffalo Woman Comes Singing;* Niethammer, *Daughters of the Earth;* Williams, Berdache, pp. 57–60.

135. See Hyde, *Half the Human Experience.*

136. See Samuels, Realm of the Other.

137. See Burgos and Perez, Sexuality in the Puerto Rican Culture, pp. 135–50;

Castillo, La Macha, pp. 24–48; Espin, Sexuality in Hispanic/Latin Women, pp. 149–64; Pavich, Mexican Culture and Sexuality, pp. 47–65; Trujillo, Chicana Lesbians, pp. 186–94.

138. See Ehrhardt et al., Prevention of Heterosexual Transmission of HIV, pp. 37–67.

139. See Dolcini et al., Demographic Characteristics of Heterosexuals with Multiple Partners, pp. 208–14; Marin et al., Partners and Condom Use Among Hispanics, pp. 170–74; Samuels, Realm of the Other.

140. See Hyde, *Half the Human Experience*.

141. See Christensen, Sex Therapy with Ethnic and Racial Minority Women, pp. 187–206.

142. See Hirayama and Hirayama, Sexuality of Japanese Americans, pp. 81–98.

143. See Becker, *Unbroken Ties*; Bell and Weinberg, *Homosexualities*; Johnson, *Staying Power*; Nichols, Low Sexual Desire in Lesbian Couples, pp. 387–412; Rothblum and Brehony, *Boston Marriages*.

144. See Blumstein and Schwartz, *American Couples*.

145. See Bell and Weinberg, *Homosexualities*; Bressler and Lavender, Sexual Fulfillment, pp. 109–22; Coleman, Hoon, and Hoon, Arousability and Sexual Satisfaction, pp. 58–73.

146. Rothblum and Cole, Lesbianism: Affirming Nontraditional Roles, p. 32.

147. See Falco, *Lesbian Clients*.

148. Nichols, Lesbian Sexuality, p. 100.

149. See Rosenzweig and Lebow, Femme on the Streets? Butch in the Sheets?, pp. 1–20.

150. See Nichols, Lesbian Sexuality, pp. 97–125.

151. Ibid., p. 104.

152. See Califia, *Sapphistry*.

153. Ibid., p. xiii.

154. See Hamadock, Lesbian Sexuality, pp. 207–19.

155. See Hall, Sex Therapy, pp. 137–56.

156. See Loulan, *Lesbian Passion*; Loulan, Sex Practices of 1566 Lesbians, pp. 221–34; Loulan, *Lesbian Erotic Dance*.

157. See ibid. and Brown, Internalized Oppression, pp. 99–107.

158. See Cole and Rothblum, Lesbian Sex at Menopause, pp. 184–93; Rubin, Women at Midlife, pp. 61–82.

159. See Cole, Sex at Menopause, pp. 159–68; Mansfield, Voda, and Koch, Heterosexual Midlife Women; McCoy, Menopause and Sexuality, pp. 73–100; Sherwin, Psychoendocrinology of Aging, pp. 181–98.

160. See McCoy, Menopause and Sexuality, pp. 73–100.

161. See Sherwin, Psychoendocrinology of Aging, pp. 181–98.

162. See Kehoe, Lesbians Over 65, pp. 139–52.

163. See Genevay, Older Women, pp. 87–101; Renshaw, Sex, Intimacy, and the Older Woman, pp. 43–54.

164. See Bullard, Desire Disorders in the Medically Ill and Physically Disabled, pp. 348–84; Cole, Women, Sexuality, and Disabilities, pp. 277–94; Galler,

Myth of the Perfect Body, pp. 165–72; Schover and Jensen, *Sexuality and Chronic Illness*.

165. Galler, Myth of the Perfect Body, p. 167.

166. Walker, Disability and (Bi)sexuality, p. 23.

167. Butler and Rosenblum, *Cancer in Two Voices*, pp. 130–32.

168. See Bancroft, *Human Sexuality*; Bullard, Desire Disorders in the Medically Ill and Physically Disabled, pp. 348–84; Schover and Jensen, *Sexuality and Chronic Illness*.

169. See Whipple, Ogden, and Komisaruk, Imagery-Induced Orgasm, pp. 121–33.

170. See Bullard, Desire Disorders in the Medically Ill and Physically Disabled, pp. 348–84.

171. See McCormick and Vinson, Women with Interstitial Cystitis, pp. 109–19.

172. See McCormick, Sexual Scripts, pp. 3–27.

173. See Bancroft, *Human Sexuality*.

174. See Schover and Jensen, *Sexuality and Chronic Illness*.

175. See ibid. and Bancroft, *Human Sexuality*; Loulan, *Lesbian Sex*.

176. See Schover and Jensen, *Sexuality and Chronic Illness*.

177. See Bos, Sexuality of Gynecological Cancer Patients, pp. 217–24; Darty and Potter, Social Work with Challenged Women, pp. 83–100.

178. See Higgins, Sexual Response in Adults with Spinal-Cord Injury, pp. 387–410; Schover and Jensen, *Sexuality and Chronic Illness*; Zwerner, Sexuality Counseling for Women with Spinal Cord Injuries, pp. 91–100.

179. See Lawrance, Sexual Satisfaction.

180. See Darling, Davidson, and Jennings, Multiorgasmic Experience in Women, pp. 527–40; Dixon, Sexuality and Relationship Changes, pp. 115–33; Kimlicka, Cross, and Tamai, Self-Esteem, Body Satisfaction, and Sexual Satisfaction, pp. 291–95; Kirkpatrick, Sex Roles and Sexual Satisfaction, pp. 444–59; Koblinsky and Palmeter, Attitudes Toward Sexual Behaviors, pp. 32–43; Meshorer and Meshorer, *Ultimate Pleasure*; Obstfeld, Lupfer, and Lupfer, Gender Identity and Sexual Functioning, pp. 248–58; Ogden, *Women Who Love Sex*; Radlove, Sexual Response and Gender Roles, pp. 87–105; Rosenzweig and Daily, Dyadic Adjustment/Sexual Satisfaction, pp. 42–55; Safir et al., Psychological Androgyny and Sexual Adequacy, pp. 228–40; Spencer and Zeiss, Sex Roles and Sexual Dysfunction, pp. 338–47; Stock, Sex Roles and Sexual Dysfunction, pp. 249–75.

181. See Allgeier and Fogel, Coital Position, pp. 588–89; See Dodson, *Liberating Masturbation*.

182. See Hamadock, Lesbian Sexuality, pp. 207–19.

183. See Dodson, Betty, *Sex for One*; Loulan, *Lesbian Passion*.

# ❧ 8 ❧

# Sexual Rights and Pleasures in the Next Century

The nineteenth century saw the emergence of the first wave of feminism. This political movement was concerned in part with women's sexual salvation, defined at the time as freedom from commercial sexual slavery, freedom to remain unmarried, and the recognition of wives' rights within marriage. The twentieth century gave birth to scientific interest in sexology, sexual revolutions, modern psychotherapy including sex therapy, and new waves of feminist activity. Twentieth-century feminists, like their nineteenth century counterparts, were deeply concerned about women's sexual rights and pleasures. Liberal Feminists sought to expand women's sexual pleasure and autonomy; Radical Feminists sought to protect girls and women from sexual abuse and exploitation. Lesbian and bisexual activists showed us that sexual and political salvation meant recognizing the rights of women who loved women.

Although their contributions are not widely known, women played a major role in the early history of sex research.[1] According to distinguished historian Vern Bullough, Katharine Bement Davis (1860–1935), a sociologist and prominent feminist, was instrumental in securing funding for most sex research conducted in the United States between 1912 and 1930. In 1929, Davis published an exhaustive study of the sex lives of 2,200 middle-class women, ages twenty-one to eighty-three; her sample included large numbers of lesbians as well as heterosexual women. Davis was not the only first-wave feminist to make a significant contribution to the fledgling field of sexology. After decades of research, physician Clelia Duel Mosher (1863–1940) provided scientific evidence that the women of her day were especially susceptible to menstrual distress, not because they belonged to "the weaker sex," but because they were obliged to wear bone-crushing corsets that destroyed abdominal muscles and damaged internal organs. Well ahead of her times, Mosher also suggested that menopausal anxiety was greatest for those women who led the most restricted, sex-role traditional lives.

No discussion of women's contributions to sexology, however brief, would be complete without acknowledging birth control advocate Margaret Sanger (1879–1966) and her English counterpart, Marie Stopes (1880–1958). Both Sanger and Stopes were instrumental in providing women from all walks of life with sex and contraceptive information during the first quarter of the twentieth century. Sanger was particularly courageous because the dissemination of birth control information was illegal in the United States when she began her important work. Sanger fled to Europe in 1914, after being indicted for mailing family planning literature, which was deemed obscene in the United States at the time, only to be arrested when she returned in 1916, for opening the first American birth control clinic.

Despite the important contributions of the foremothers of modern sex research, women and feminists lost ground at mid-century. From the 1940s through the late 1970s, sex research, sex education, and sex therapy were largely male-dominated institutions. Feminists would not remain silent, however. Throughout the 1980s and 1990s, second-wave feminists from both within and outside the discipline challenged sexologists to be more sensitive to the concerns of women and minorities.

What will the twenty-first century bring? I interviewed thirteen prominent feminist sex researchers and therapists, many of them cherished friends, to find out. In this chapter, I share insights from their collective scholarly, clinical, and personal experience.

## PROFILES OF THIRTEEN FEMINIST SEX RESEARCHERS AND THERAPISTS

I wish I could have talked with everyone who has made an important contribution to feminist sexology. Regrettably such a project would require a book in itself. So, I concentrated instead on the professional contributions and thoughts of eleven women and two men. Before summarizing this highly published group's opinions, let me tell you something about each individual.

### E. Sandra Byers

A clinical psychologist who teaches at the Department of Psychology, University of New Brunswick at Fredericton in Eastern Canada, Dr. Sandra

Byers specializes in sex therapy and women's problems in her private practice.[2] She is acting director of Muriel McQueen Fergusson Centre for Family Violence Research and president of the Canadian Sex Research Forum. A fellow of The Society for the Scientific Study of Sex, Byers received the Merit Award from her university in 1993 in appreciation of her outstanding research and teaching. Byers has devoted her scientific career to the study and prevention of sexual aggression in dating relationships, predictors of sexual satisfaction, and women's and men's strategies for influencing a sexual partner. Often, her work challenges prevailing sexual scripts. She points out,

> We have many stereotypes about male and female sexual behavior and nobody bothers to find out whether the stereotypes are accurate. . . . We have a stereotype that men initiate sex more often and women refuse sex more often. It turns out . . . it is true that men initiate [more] but it is not true that women refuse more. . . . I love research that debunks or identifies the myths.[3]

### Ellen Cole

A counseling psychologist, Dr. Ellen Cole is director of the Masters of Arts program at Prescott College in Arizona where she teaches courses on women and sexuality.[4] In addition, she maintains a private practice in sex therapy. Co-editor of the journal, *Women & Therapy*, she and Esther Rothblum, who was also interviewed for this chapter, received a Distinguished Publication Award from the Association for Women in Psychology for a jointly edited book. Ellen Cole is an expert on menopause, sibling abuse, and feminist therapy. Overseeing the book series, "Innovations in Feminist Studies," she holds national office in the Feminist Therapy Institute. As editor of the 1988 book *Women and Sex Therapy: Closing the Circle of Sexual Knowledge*, Cole recalls with pride,

> Feminists and sex therapists were . . . not talking to one another. And, at that point, I don't think that feminism had really in any major way effected mainstream or even progressive sex therapy. I really think that . . . my most important contribution was pulling that collection of articles together.[5]

### Irene Frieze

A social psychologist and the previous director of women's studies at the University of Pittsburgh, Dr. Irene Frieze is a fellow of the American Psychological Association (APA) which she has served twice as council representative.[6] She is a recipient of the Association for Women in Psychology's Distinguished Career Award. In 1992, Frieze, a past president of the Psychology of Women division of the APA, was named one of the 100 Most Eminent Women Psychologists of All Time by that group. As a scientist, Frieze has published numerous articles on love and intimacy in long-term relationships, scripts or sex-role stereotyped expectations for heterosexual dates, and sexual exploitation and violence. Supported by a 1994 Fulbright grant, she has begun studying changing sex roles in Eastern Europe. An expert on sexual harassment and marital rape, she has used her scientific findings to fight for women's rights. After learning that one-third of all women in violent marriages have been victims of brutal marital rapes, she testified to the Pennsylvania legislature, asking to modify laws which at the time excluded marital rape from prosecution.

### Janet Hyde

Trained as a mathematical psychologist, Dr. Janet Hyde teaches psychology and women's studies courses at the University of Wisconsin at Madison.[7] Past editor of *Psychology of Women Quarterly*, she is presently an associate editor of *The Journal of Sex Research* and serves on the editorial boards of two feminist, scholarly journals. Author or editor of five books, Janet Hyde has written two popular textbooks, *Half the Human Experience: The Psychology of Women* and *Understanding Human Sexuality*. President-elect of the Psychology of Women division of the American Psychological Association, she is a past board member of The Society for the Scientific Study of Sex. Hyde thinks that her biggest contribution to feminist sexology is her college sexuality textbook. She says, "I tried always to highlight the contributions of women from the very first edition. . . . And I also did some subtle things that I don't know if people noticed . . . I . . . put [the] female anatomy [illustration] first which no other book had ever done. Everybody always put male anatomy first, . . . assum[ing] that female anatomy is . . . [much too] complicated [to do otherwise]."[8] Janet Hyde identified her research on sex differences in sexual experience as constituting her second major feminist contribution to sexual science. According to Hyde, almost all studies show that compared to females, males masturbate significantly more often and are much more likely to approve of casual sex.[9] These findings, she asserts, have enormous implications.

### Clint Jesser

A sociologist and anthropologist, Dr. Clint Jesser has taught sociology for nearly three decades at Northern Illinois University.[10] Building on his personal experiences in men's awakening groups, he has recently completed a feminist book on men, *Oh My Loving Brother: Some Personalized Steps Towards a Men's Movement*. Jesser defines his feminist awakening during the 1960s in this way:

> Like my first feminist [feeling] was not really a reaction but sort of like a jolt. . . . My wife started to embark on some big changes in her life, got herself some advanced degrees, got herself a better paying job . . . got a whole new self-image which really frightened me at the time. . . . So, in the mix of the flux and change of all that, I began to look more at what the feminists were all writing.[11]

Inspired by his wife and women students, Jesser helped found the Women's Studies program at his university. His personal growth as a man shaped his research as well. First, he examined college students' attitudes towards the feminist movement. Next, following up his advocacy of female sexual empowerment, he studied young peoples' strategies for sexually influencing partners and heterosexual sexual miscommunication. As a man, teacher, and researcher, Jesser has struggled to "bridge this dual worldism," as he calls it, "between men and women in the area[s] of sexual signalling and . . . [social] training in wants and desires."[12]

## Charlene Muehlenhard

Clinical psychologist Dr. Charlene Muehlenhard teaches psychology and women's studies courses at the University of Kansas.[13] In 1993, she was inducted into her university's Commission on the Status of Women Hall of Fame. She has served The Society for the Scientific Study of Sex as mid-continent president and co-chair of the Feminist Perspectives Special Interest Group. Muehlenhard is well known for her systematic research on sexual coercion and aggression, especially acquaintance rape among college students. Like many I interviewed, Charlene Muehlenhard's feminist research challenges traditional sexual scripts. One of the first scientists to study how women initiate dates with men, she has also broken new ground by asking men about unwanted sexual experiences with dating partners.

## Gina Ogden

A certified sex therapist, Dr. Gina Ogden is a marriage and family therapist with a private practice in Cambridge, Massachusetts.[14] She is the author of three popular books: *Safe Encounters: How Women Can Say Yes to Pleasure and No to Unsafe Sex*, written with her friend, Beverly Whipple, who was also interviewed for this chapter; *Everywoman's Guide to Understanding Sexual Style and Creating Intimacy;* and most recently, *Women Who Love Sex.* Ogden views herself as a pioneer in the study of extra-genital stimulation and spontaneous orgasms (which she calls "thinking off"), two areas of women's sexuality that have been ignored by others. She believes that sexual response is holistic, mobile, and spiritual, beginning "long before you enter the bedroom and . . . last[ing] long afterwards because it affects your whole life."[15]

### Letitia Anne Peplau

A social psychologist specializing in the interdisciplinary study of close relationships, Dr. Peplau teaches psychology and women's studies courses at the University of California, Los Angeles.[16] President of The International Society for the Study of Personal Relationships, she is a fellow of the American Psychological Association and a member of the editorial board of *The Journal of Social Issues.* When asked to describe her major contribution to sexual scholarship, Peplau points to the work she and her colleagues published on the close relationships of lesbians and gay men.

> Part of the point that we wanted to make in that research was that the stereotypes that have tried to define lesbians and gay men in terms of their sexuality are too narrow. I wanted to argue that loving a same-sex partner has a lot to do with love and caring and companionship and things you don't do in bed and the lives you build together. And, in fact as we thought about where to publish that research, we deliberately avoided "sex journals" because we wanted to make a political statement about the lesbian experience having to do with a lot more than sexuality.[17]

Another research contribution to feminist sexology has been Peplau's long-term study of heterosexual romantic relationships. She was one of the first scientists to systematically study sexual scripts, the idea that we are guided by a variety of motives and goals for pursuing sexual intimacy, many of which are not necessarily erotic.

### Esther Rothblum

A clinical psychologist who has a faculty appointment in psychology at the University of Vermont, Dr. Esther Rothblum co-edits the journal, *Women & Therapy.*[18] Past chair of the Committee on Lesbian and Gay Concerns of the American Psychological Association, she edited *Loving Boldly: Issues Facing Lesbians* and wrote *Boston Marriages: Romantic but Asexual Relationships Among Contemporary Lesbians.* Rothblum has also written extensively on weight and female body fat as a feminist issue. In recognition of lifetime achievement in research, she has been named a university scholar at the University of Vermont. Rothblum's research for *Boston Marriages* has yielded rich information about alternative (and nongenital) definitions of intimacy. Speaking of the women she interviewed, she remarks,

> The women are really indistinguishable from other [lesbian] couples with the exception that they don't have sex. . . . But, they keep that a secret because . . . [otherwise] people will no longer see them as a couple [and] . . . will approach one or the other and say, "Well, if you're celibate, why don't you have sex with me?". . . . It really raises a lot of interesting issues about what is a couple and how often do you need to have sex to be considered a couple?[19]

## Michael Stevenson

A developmental psychologist and former director of women and gender studies at Ball State University in Indiana, Dr. Michael Stevenson is book review editor for *The Journal of Sex Research* and a member of the editorial advisory board of the *Journal of Psychology & Human Sexuality.*[20] Active in men's studies organizations and in the development of curriculum and research which examines men's lives in feminist terms, he recently visited Indonesia on a Fulbright fellowship, consulting with women's studies colleagues at two different universities. Stevenson believes that feminism has "important consequences for not just the way we do science but the way we teach which are tremendously beneficial."[21] A lot of Stevenson's empirical work has been on antigay prejudice. He has also published extensively on feminist pedagogy, the influence of divorce on children, and the impact of women on male-dominated institutions such as the military. He has recently completed an edited book on sex roles throughout the lifespan.

## Wendy Stock

Dr. Wendy Stock is a feminist clinical psychologist and sex therapist.[22] Before joining the faculty at Pacific Graduate School of Psychology in Palo Alto, California in 1993, Stock taught at Texas A & M University. In 1992, the Texas branch of the National Organization of Women honored her as Feminist Activist of the Year. Stock is a member of the editorial board of

*Psychology & Human Sexuality* and has served The Society for the Scientific Study of Sex as western regional representative and co-chair of the Feminist Perspectives Special Interest Group. In her professional writing, Stock is especially noted for her analysis of the linkage between traditional sex roles, power inequality, and sexual dysfunctions. She has written a great deal on the contributions of pornography to a rape culture.

### Leonore Tiefer

Trained in physiological and comparative psychology as well as sexology, Dr. Leonore Tiefer is employed by the departments of urology and psychiatry at Montefiore Medical Center in Bronx, New York.[23] Past president of the International Academy of Sex Research, Tiefer edits a newsletter for the World Research Network on the Sexuality of Women and Girls. A fellow of the American Psychological Association, she is an associate editor of *The Journal of Sex Research* and a consulting editor for both the *Journal of Psychology & Human Sexuality* and *Archives of Sexual Behavior*. Tiefer notes, "I had the advantage and disadvantage of getting into sexology before feminism came along as an intellectual point of view. And so, I had already established a reputation as a kind of orthodox sex researcher when my eyes were opened to the importance of gender as a dimension in sexual scholarship."[24]

As a feminist philosopher of science, Tiefer points out,

> Men and women really haven't been studied in a neutral fashion . . . They've been studied more with male behavior and values taken as the norm and this has infiltrated to concepts and theories in a markedly pervasive [and subtle] way . . . I think that that's primarily what I've been trying to do: to show how all the terminology . . . , methods of sex therapy, [and] . . . names of the disorders and problems that you can have with regard to sexuality are not really neutral and that this lack of neutrality has really done women a serious disservice.[25]

### Beverly Whipple

Dr. Beverly Whipple is a nurse-scientist at the College of Nursing, Center for Molecular and Behavioral Neuroscience, and Institute of Animal Behavior at Rutgers, the State University of New Jersey.[26] Widely known for her work on vaginal eroticism, she is a fellow of both the American Academy of Nursing and The Society for the Scientific Study of Sex. The 1991 recipient of the New Jersey State Nurses Association's Nursing Excellence Award for Research, Whipple has served several terms as a national officer and board member of The Society for the Scientific Study of Sex and the American Association of Sex Educators, Counselors, and Therapists.

Whipple began her sex research career identifying the G spot as a potential source of sexual pleasure and examining women who ejaculated fluids during sexual activity. More recently, she has studied how direct stimulation of the vagina can produce a strong pain-blocking or analgesic effect which can make childbirth more tolerable. Both Beverly Whipple and Gina Ogden have begun studying women who experience orgasm without touching themselves or being touched. Recently, Whipple has begun studying the sexual responsiveness of women with spinal cord injury. Until now, most medical literature concentrated exclusively on the fact that "women with spinal cord injury can conceive and give birth."[27] Whipple hopes to give women with spinal cord injury a more personally empowering, pleasure-oriented understanding of their sexuality.

## FEMINIST SEX RESEARCH

Feminism and Science: Don't the two words contradict each other? Not according to the sexologists I interviewed. Unanimously, the group agreed that feminists could be and often were serious sexual scientists; a few seemed irritated that I would even question such a possibility. But, how could this be true? Aren't scientists supposed to be completely objective? How can a person who has strong political convictions also be a scientist? According to feminists, there is no such thing as scientific objectivity. The questions scientists ask, their methodology, even the way they interpret results are inevitably shaped by some kind of ideology, usually the one held by dominant groups. What makes feminist scientists unique then, is not that they have strong opinions, Clint Jesser and Janet Hyde explain, but that feminists are likely to "state up front" exactly what their opinions are.[28] Esther Rothblum puts it this way: "You can do feminist science and you can do science that is absolutely sexist or racist or inconsiderate or biased."[29] Wendy Stock points out,

I think that if you're a good scientist you are aware of the extent to which paradigms shape what questions get asked and who asks them and what answers we're looking for. At least, . . . [feminists have] an awareness . . . that science as well as everything else that we do is socially constructed.[30]

What makes feminists or anybody for that matter scientists is not an absence of values but the use of systematic methods to make observations, collect information, and make interpretations. Sandra Byers says, "To me [being] scientists means that our beliefs are open to validation. We put our beliefs to the test, whatever methodology we use."[31] Recognizing science "as only one way to describe people's experience," Michael Stevenson goes on to say that feminist sex researchers do "not necessarily cling to the very narrow definition of what science is."[32] Janet Hyde agrees.[33] Even if science isn't the only way to study sexuality, Charlene Muehlenhard adds, it is probably best suited for testing and promoting feminist ideas because ours is a culture in which science enjoys enormous prestige and legitimacy.[34] Anne Peplau and Janet Hyde concur:

> Science has historically had some very stupid things to say about women's lives, some things that have probably been extremely harmful. . . . But I don't think that was inherent in the commitment to empirical and systematic work. . . . I think that if women were to abandon science, to say that we are going to leave that thing to the boys, [it] would be a big mistake.[35]

> You know if we abandon . . . [science and quantitative analysis], they're just going to be used against us. So what we [feminist scholars] need to do is to get better at them than the other people. . . . so we can produce some powerful results.[36]

Feminists don't just apply scientific principles, they try to humanize the face of science. Anne Peplau tells students, "Before you go and do that questionnaire, why don't you go and talk to some women?"[37] Whenever Irene Frieze does research, she recruits a large and diverse group of women to work with her.[38] Esther Rothblum advises sexologists,

> You have to realize your own role as being incredibly powerful. . . . You do not have an equal footing with your so called subjects, participants, or clients. . . . You're the one whose asking the questions and they're the ones who are answering. . . . You sort of know what you're going to do with the data and all they can do is just answer. . . . The feminist [contribution to sex research] . . . is the analysis of power and also the realization that certain groups have less power, including women, and that those groups are particularly vulnerable to misinterpretations as to how the data are presented.[39]

Feminist sexual science clearly is not an oxymoron. How then do feminist sex researchers define themselves and their work? First, they all acknowledge that gender plays a major role in our lives and our sexualities. Second, they believe that sound research can support women in their battle for equal rights.[40] In addition, the best feminist scientists don't just lump women or men together. Increasingly, their work accounts for the way that gender interacts with other important variables—income, age, race, culture, ethnicity, region, religion, sexual orientation, and health or physical difference.[41]

Sensitive to group and individual differences in sexual discourse, feminists argue that sexology has too long ignored or distorted the female experience.[42] For example, Wendy Stock provides a Radical Feminist critique of a widely cited 1984 study by Abramson and Hayashi that described almost no reported rape in Japan despite men's extensive use of violent pornography.[43]

Japan at least at the time [of this study] . . . didn't have any rape crisis centers for women. . . . In Japan, . . . women who have been raped are viewed as dishonored, . . . [un]marriageable, and . . . at fault. And, they had nowhere to go! Only recently have they established [rape] crisis centers in [Japan] . . . and, they were flooded with calls. And so, it's only been since then that they've started collecting [accurate] statistics. . . . Even before I knew these statistics, I was questioning . . . whether . . . there was virtually no rape or extremely little rape in Japan.[44]

In criticizing this study, Stock wanted to demonstrate how and why a feminist perspective is needed. A feminist sexologist, she explains, would not assume automatically that crime statistics reflected an oppressed group's reality. Realizing that women in most of the world are afraid to report rape to authorities, a feminist would ask questions like "Why do so few women report rape in Japan?"

Feminist sexology is not the same as nonsexist research![45] The nonsexist scientist is neutral; sex-role stereotypes are avoided; equal numbers of men and women are examined. The feminist scientist, in contrast, might focus on women (or men) exclusively. More importantly, she or he is guided by feminist political theory and involves the individuals studied in the research process as much as possible.[46] According to Anne Peplau, feminist sexual scientists are "trying to put women center stage rather than to bring them in as an afterthought and trying to take women's personal experiences seriously."[47]

## FEMINIST SEX THERAPY

Feminist therapists don't treat malfunctioning genitals; they treat clients as whole persons who have come by their sexual problems honestly in a culture which expects women to look after others but not themselves.[48] Their major goal is to empower women, not necessarily to instruct clients to be more pleasing or knowledgeable sexual partners. Wendy Stock shares an example of this feminist treatment philosophy from her practice:

> A female client . . . came in just saying that she did not want to have sex, that she was too angry at her husband. . . . Rather than having her start doing sensate focus exercises, we looked at the past. I mean, this is just good therapy; we looked at her anger and what made her turn off in the first place. . . . A fundamental assumption that I shared with her was that she probably didn't want to have sex for good reason and that my goal was not to get her to have sex [but] . . . to help her to address issues that were making her uncomfortable in the relationship. . . . If she never had sex again with her husband or anyone else, that was her choice. So I didn't define sex, having sex, as a therapeutic goal. And, I think most conventional sex therapists would have. . . . My own training would have.[49]

Effective feminist therapists treat their clients as equals, avoiding the temptation to come across as dispassionate experts or authority figures. Sandra Byers explains,

> Part of being a feminist sex therapist . . . is modeling in my own life, modeling in my relationships with my clients . . . a different way of relating to people than has been their experience. . . . For example, in therapy, giving women the power to make their own decisions . . . control the course of therapy. . . . Feminist therapy is having a different kind of relationship with the client. . . . If you have that kind of relationship, then there is something very powerful in that regardless of what you say.[50]

So long as women have fewer options and greater economic dependence than men, it is difficult for them to be assertive with male partners or experiment with new ways of being sexual. Not only should feminists understand this, Leonore Tiefer advises, they should also recognize how female subordination interferes with sex therapy.

A woman might not express her distress about sex . . . because she would be afraid of losing the marriage and this would be a socioeconomic loss to her. . . . Likewise, she might not express her honest opinions about her partner, her husband, because . . . she doesn't want to rock the boat.[51]

Of course, clients often do have the goal of enjoying sex more or becoming a more sensitive partner. Feminist therapists help clients feel more positive about their bodies and sexuality. But, unlike conventional therapists, they also clarify how sex-role stereotypes and power inequalities contribute to sexual problems and can be modified. This approach is affirming for both women and men, Ellen Cole explains,

If I were to pick out any particular issue heterosexual couples [face], the men seem to have high anxiety about performance and the women have a difficult time asking for what they want . . . I think that without a feminist analysis, it would really not be possible to treat those issues. . . , Men are socialized to orchestrate sex and women are socialized to . . . give pleasure and not to know how to ask for it.[52]

When asked to apply feminist analysis to the sex therapy problems brought in by female couples, Cole agreed that the problem was treating two nurturers in a close relationship, neither of whom was able to ask for what she wanted sexually. Unfortunately, the feminist approach is rather unique in the sex therapy community. Apolitical and conventional in social values, most sex therapists view sexual difficulties as the result of individual psychopathology or faulty relationship dynamics.

## SINGLE MOST IMPORTANT ISSUE

What is the single most important issue associated with women's sexual salvation? Half the feminist sexologists focused on research issues and the other half addressed political ones. But this is an oversimplification. Those primarily concerned with sex research recognized science as inherently political, and those primarily concerned with the political believed feminist sexology could inspire meaningful social change.

Here is what those who focused on research had to say.[53] Sex researchers in general have a credibility problem because they study a taboo topic which falls outside traditional disciplines. When the feminist framework is added, sex research becomes even less respectable. The little grant money available has strings attached; there is no money to study pleasure or sexual satisfaction. To get funded, a research project must be couched in terms of medical diagnoses, disease processes, sexual violence, or dysfunction. But how can we promote a sex-positive world if we are only allowed to study sex-negative phenomena?

According to the scientists I interviewed, many feminist sexual scholars have been just as insensitive to diversity as their mainstream counterparts, for the most part studying healthy, white, middle-class, heterosexual women. Replacing a sexology of affluent white men with a sexology of affluent white women was not regarded as an improvement. It is essential, they explained, that feminist scientists examine the sexual attitudes and experiences of women who vary in race, ethnicity, religious group, occupation, region, health and ability status, social class, sexual orientation, and age without manufacturing new stereotypes. A feminist sexology of diversity would recognize individual differences among women belonging to the same demographic group. There is no such thing as the typical rural woman, typical woman of color, typical Jewish woman, typical lesbian, typical poor woman, typical older woman, or typical disabled woman!

Most of the feminist scientists I spoke with concluded that research methods would be improved if sexologists were more sensitive to the people they studied. Complaining about sexism and heterosexism in sexology is insufficient, they argued. It is time for feminists to redefine sex and see that our questionnaires and instruments reflect changing definitions. Surely sex is not limited to penetration and orgasm; don't kisses, touches, and loving glances count? We should be challenging conventional assumptions about sexuality in our studies. Why do we ask women only if they are married, single, divorced, or widowed? What about the woman who lives with a lover, perhaps another woman, perhaps a man she hasn't married? Let's take a cue from other feminist researchers and really talk to people when we do sex research; let's ask women and men to tell us their stories in their own words. And, let's stop measuring orgasms and calling that science! Woman-affirming research, Sandra Byers maintains, would consider sexual experience qualitatively, not just quantitatively.

> When you read the literature, they always draw conclusions from studies that find that men masturbate more, or men have more sexual thoughts, or men have more sexual fantasies, that men are more sexual or enjoy sex more or are more interested in sex [than women]. There's a value judgment always at the end of those studies [that more is better]. . . . It's always a male more![54]

The next step in feminist sex research is delineating what women view as sexual experience instead of continuing to quiz them only about sexual experiences previously identified as important by men. This kind of work would expand our understanding of not just women's sexuality, but men's as well.

Seven of the thirteen sexologists I interviewed believed that political action was of primary importance.[55] A number of issues were raised. Criticizing both the pornography industry and antiabortion movement, Ellen Cole argued that the patriarchal culture's objectification of women as vessels only for men's pleasure or sperm struck her as the most important feminist issue of our time. Following up complaints from students and junior colleagues, Wendy Stock identified sexual harassment within the sexology community as the single most important issue for feminist sexual scholars and therapists. Acknowledging the many women who are unhappy with their sexuality, Janet Hyde advocated considering sexual well-being as one of a number of health rights for women. Both she and Michael Stevenson thought that feminists should try to attract more men to the movement. Stevenson argues,

> Given the changes that have occurred in women's lives over the past thirty years, we haven't seen the corresponding changes [in men] partly because . . . feminist scholars and the women's movement have focused pretty exclusively on women's experience without looking at what kind of impact that has on men or the kind of educational experiences or whatever that men need in order to understand what's happening to the women in their lives. . . . We are now at a point where that has to happen.[56]

Anne Peplau objects to feminist therapists who, oddly enough, have lost sight of political factors in women's lives.[57] Clinicians specializing in treating women who have survived sexual assault or domestic violence, for instance, often psychologize clients' problems and work exclusively on individual change. How can sexologists consider themselves feminists if they ignore the need for fundamental political, social, and economic changes in women's lives? Gina Ogden and Leonore Tiefer agree.

> What was pulling my wires out was that I was seeing . . . [defects] in feminist sex therapy. . . . Therapy by its definition . . . is a patriarchal [institution in which] there's one person who knows more than the other person [and] . . . a whole lot of money changes hands. . . . So, who does it leave out? It leaves out many, many people, particularly if they're not white, middle-class, heterosexual. . . . Whether or not these women can pay is maybe a moot point because my sense is

that the very focus of therapy, I mean just the very notion of therapy, leaves them out.[58]

I'm not at all convinced that the world would be better with twice as many sexologists. . . . I think the world would definitely be better with twice as much sex education. . . . But, I don't see that most sex researchers or sex therapists have done anything to change the laws or change the school boards or fight censorship or do anything that needs to be done to get more sex education going. . . . We should be doing political work, not just professional work. . . . Censorship is not even on the horizon, it's right here. . . . Well I want to see the sex therapists out there handing out literature to get progressive people elected to the school board. Now, I don't see them out there.[59]

## WOMEN'S SEXUALITY IN THE TWENTY-FIRST CENTURY

Is sexual salvation just around the corner? Esther Rothblum thought that any such speculation was premature: "The issues that are going to be important in the next century, [she concluded], are currently things we don't even have a language for."[60] More pessimistically, Leonore Tiefer argued, "I think that we have had an impact on our colleagues to chastise them about politically incorrect language and certainly socially unwanted behavior. Have we gotten them to look at their concepts and theories yet? Have we gotten them to change their methods? Not that I can see."[61] Tiefer went on to credit extremist Radical Feminists with being quite successful in getting the public's attention. But, she worried aloud, rather than affirming women's right to sexual pleasure, antipornography feminists have helped create a sex-negative culture in which the erotic is linked to sexual violence and shame.

Eleven of the thirteen feminist sexologists were optimistic about the future. Beverly Whipple exclaimed, "We will have equality! It may take us longer than we hoped but . . . women will have more choices."[62] Ellen Cole agreed.[63] Irene Frieze reminded us how much women's sexual rights and pleasures have improved in the past 100 years, especially during the last two decades.[64] Ideas that were initially revolutionary such as sexual pleasure for women as a right, and not a luxury, have gained wider acceptance. Sandra Byers brought this home:

I certainly have women clients coming in right now . . . who had sexual experiences with a man and did not feel satisfied after he had his orgasm and the man's ready to turn over. And they basically said,

"Hey, wait a minute. There's another person here! Now here's what I want you to do." You know, I don't think these women would have done that a generation ago.[65]

Anne Peplau talked about the positive impact gay-affirming research has had on the everyday lives of lesbian couples. When Peplau was growing up, she had no idea that lesbians existed; nobody ever talked about them. Yet the day we talked, she was planning a baby shower for a lesbian couple.[66] Wendy Stock and Clint Jesser suggested that feminist sexologists have put us on the correct path by asking the kinds of questions that need to be asked.[67] Charlene Muehlenhard credits feminist activists with alerting scientists, therapists, and the general public to issues of great importance to women, such as marital and date rape, which erstwhile had been ignored.[68] Gina Ogden and Michael Stevenson concluded that it is time for feminist sexologists to take the show on the road.[69] Woman-affirming sex education, they agreed, should be aimed at everyone, not just a few sexual scholars, economically privileged psychotherapy clients, or fortunate college students. Since so many people rely on the mass media for information, they surmised, it was time for serious feminist sexologists to write popular books and articles and become guests on talk shows. Hopefully, this book takes a step in the right direction.

## NOTES

1. Bullough, Letter to Author; Bullough, In *Human Sexuality: An Encyclopedia*, pp. 570–71; Sternberg, In *Human Sexuality: An Encyclopedia*, pp. 167; 403; 528–29.

2. Byers, Telephone Interview.

3. Ibid.

4. Cole, Telephone Interview.

5. Ibid.

6. Frieze, Telephone Interview.

7. Hyde, Telephone Interview.

8. Ibid.

9. Ibid.; See Oliver and Hyde, Gender Differences in Sexuality, pp. 29–51.

10. Jesser, Telephone Interview.

11. Ibid.

12. Ibid.

13. Muehlenhard, Telephone Interview.

14. Ogden, Telephone Interview.

15. Ibid.

16. Peplau, Telephone Interview.

17. Ibid.

18. Rothblum, Telephone Interview.

19. See ibid. and Rothblum and Brehony, *Boston Marriages*.

20. Stevenson, Telephone Interview.

21. Ibid.

22. Stock, Telephone Interview.

23. Tiefer, Telephone Interview.

24. Ibid.

25. Ibid.

26. Whipple, Telephone Interview.

27. Ibid.

28. Hyde, Telephone Interview; Jesser, Telephone Interview.

29. Rothblum, Telephone Interview.

30. Stock, Telephone Interview.

31. Byers, Telephone Interview.

32. Stevenson, Telephone Interview.

33. Hyde, Telephone Interview.

34. Muehlenhard, Telephone Interview.

35. Peplau, Telephone Interview.

36. Hyde, Telephone Interview.

37. Peplau, Telephone Interview.

38. Frieze, Telephone Interview.

39. Rothblum, Telephone Interview.

40. Hyde, Telephone Interview; Tiefer, Telephone Interview.

41. Muehlenhard, Telephone Interview; Rothblum, Telephone Interview; Stevenson, Telephone Interview.

42. Stock, Telephone Interview.

43. See Abramson and Hayashi, Pornography in Japan, pp. 173–83.

44. Stock, Telephone Interview.

45. Frieze, Telephone Interview; Hyde, Telephone Interview.

46. Frieze, Telephone Interview; Muehlenhard, Telephone Interview; Rothblum, Telephone Interview.

47. Peplau, Telephone Interview.

48. Byers, Telephone Interview; Cole, Telephone Interview; Ogden, Telephone Interview; Stock, Telephone Interview; Tiefer, Telephone Interview.

49. Stock, Telephone Interview.

50. Byers, Telephone Interview.

51. Tiefer, Telephone Interview.

52. Cole, Telephone Interview.

53. Byers, Telephone Interview; Frieze, Telephone Interview; Jesser, Telephone Interview; Muehlenhard, Telephone Interview; Peplau, Telephone Interview; Rothblum, Telephone Interview; Whipple, Telephone Interview.

54. Byers, Telephone Interview.

55. Cole, Telephone Interview; Hyde, Telephone Interview; Ogden, Telephone Interview; Peplau, Telephone Interview; Stevenson, Telephone Interview; Stock, Telephone Interview; Tiefer, Telephone Interview.

56. Stevenson, Telephone Interview.
57. Peplau, Telephone Interview.
58. Ogden, Telephone Interview.
59. Tiefer, Telephone Interview.
60. Rothblum, Telephone Interview.
61. Tiefer, Telephone Interview.
62. Whipple, Telephone Interview.
63. Cole, Telephone Interview.
64. Frieze, Telephone Interview.
65. Byers, Telephone Interview.
66. Peplau, Telephone Interview.
67. Jesser, Telephone Interview: Stock, Telephone Interview.
68. Muehlenhard, Telephone Interview.
69. Ogden, Telephone Interview; Stevenson, Telephone Interview.

# Bibliography

Abarbanel, A. R. 1978. Diagnosis and Treatment of Coital Discomfort. In *Handbook of Sex Therapy*, ed. J. LoPiccolo and L. LoPiccolo, 241–59. New York: Plenum.

Abbey, Antonia. 1987. Misperceptions of Friendly Behavior as Sexual Interest: A Survey of Naturally Occurring Incidents. *Psychology of Women Quarterly* 11:173–94.

Abbey, Antonia D. 1991. Misperception, Acquaintance Rape, and Alcohol: What Are the Links? Paper presented at the Conference on Gender Research and Theory, Nags Head Conference Center, 26–31 May, Highland Beach, FL.

Abbey, Antonia; Cozzarelli, Catherine; McLaughlin, Kimberly; and Harnish, Richard J. 1987. The Effects of Clothing and Dyad Sex Composition on Perceptions of Sexual Intent: Do Women and Men Evaluate These Cues Differently? *Journal of Applied Social Psychology* 17(2):108–26.

Abramson, Paul R. 1990. Sexual Science: Emerging Discipline or Oxymoron? *The Journal of Sex Research* 27:147–65.

Abramson, Paul R., and Hayashi, Haruo. 1984. Pornography in Japan: Cross-Cultural and Theoretical Considerations. In *Pornography and Sexual Aggression*, ed. N. M. Malamuth and E. Donnerstein, 173–83. Orlando, FL: Academic Press.

Adams, Jann H.; Trachtenberg, Susan; and Fisher, Jane E. 1992. Feminist Views of Child Sexual Abuse. In *The Sexual Abuse of Children*. Vol. 1, *Theory and Research*, ed. W. O'Donohue and J. H. Geer, 359–96. Hillsdale, NJ: Lawrence Erlbaum Associates.

Adelman, Mara A. 1992. Sustaining Passion: Eroticism and Safe-Sex Talk. *Archives of Sexual Behavior* 21:481–94.

Aletsky, Patricia J. 1982. Sexism and Sexuality: Implications for Sex Therapy and

Research. Paper presented at the annual meeting of the American Psychological Association, August, Washington, D.C.

Alexander, M. Wayne, and Judd, Ben B. 1986. Differences in Attitudes Toward Nudity in Advertising. *Psychology* 23:26–29.

Alexander, Priscilla. 1987a. Interview with Nell. In *Sex Work: Writings by Women in the Sex Industry*, ed. F. Delacoste and P. Alexander, 53–55. Pittsburgh: Cleis Press.

Alexander, Priscilla. 1987b. Prostitution: A Difficult Issue for Feminists. In *Sex Work: Writings by Women in the Sex Industry*, ed. F. Delacoste and P. Alexander, 184–214. Pittsburgh: Cleis Press.

Alexander, Priscilla. 1987c. Prostitutes Are Being Scapegoated for Heterosexual AIDS. In *Sex Work: Writings by Women in the Sex Industry*, ed. F. Delacoste and P. Alexander, 248–63. Pittsburgh: Cleis Press.

Alexander, Priscilla. 1987d. Why this Book? In *Sex Work: Writings by Women in the Sex Industry*, ed. F. Delacoste and P. Alexander, 14–18. Pittsburgh: Cleis Press.

Aline. 1987. Good Girls Go to Heaven: Bad Girls Go Everywhere. In *Sex Work: Writings by Women in the Sex Industry*, ed. F. Delacoste and P. Alexander, 131–34. Pittsburgh: Cleis Press.

Allgeier, Elizabeth Rice. 1987. Sexual Coercion: Reducing Victim Vulnerability. *Sexual Coercion and Assault* 2(3):1–4.

Allgeier, Elizabeth R., and Allgeier, Albert R. 1991. *Sexual Interactions*. 3d ed. Lexington, MA: D. C. Heath.

Allgeier, Elizabeth R., and Fogel, Arthur F. 1978. Coital Position and Sex Roles: Responses to Cross-Sex Position in Bed. *Journal of Consulting and Clinical Psychology* 46:588–89.

Alter-Reid, Karen; Gibbs, Margaret S.; Lachenmeyer, Juliana Rasic; Sigal, Janet; and Massoth, Neil A. 1986. Sexual Abuse of Children: A Review of the Empirical Findings. *Clinical Psychology Review* 6:249–66.

Alzate, Heli, and Hoch, Zwi. 1986. The "G Spot" and "Female Ejaculation": A Current Appraisal. *Journal of Sex & Marital Therapy* 12:211–20.

Alzenman, Marta, and Kelley, Georgette. 1988. The Incidence of Violence and Acquaintance Rape in Dating Relationships Among College Men and Women. *Journal of College Student Development* 29:305–11.

Ambert, Anne-Marie. 1983. Separated Women and Remarriage Behavior: A Comparison of Financially Secure Women and Financially Insecure Women. *Journal of Divorce* 6:43–54.

Arrington, Marie. 1987. Under the Gun. In *Good Girls/Bad Girls: Feminists and Sex Trade Workers Face to Face*, ed. L. Bell, 173–78. Seattle: Seal Press.

Ashley, Barbara Renchkovsky, and Ashley, David. 1984. Sex as Violence: The Body Against Intimacy. *International Journal of Women's Studies* 7:352–71.

Averill, James R., and Boothroyd, Phyllis. 1977. On Falling in Love in Conformance with the Romantic Ideal. *Motivation and Emotion* 1:235–47.

Bailey, William C.; Hendrick, Clyde; and Hendrick, Susan S. 1987. Relation of Sex and Gender Role to Love, Sexual Attitudes, and Self-Esteem. *Sex Roles* 16:637–48.

Bancroft, John. 1989. *Human Sexuality and Its Problems.* 2d ed. London: Churchill Livingston.

Barbach, Lonnie. 1980a. Group Treatment of Anorgasmic Women. In *Principles and Practice of Sex Therapy*, ed. S. R. Leiblum and L. A. Pervin, 107–46. New York: Guilford Press.

Barbach, Lonnie. 1980b. *Women Discover Orgasm: A Therapist's Guide to a New Treatment Approach.* New York: Free Press.

Baron, L. 1986. Review of *Women Against Censorship*, ed. by V. Burstyn. *Sexual Coercion and Assault* 1:94–98.

Baron, Larry. 1990. Pornography and Gender Equality: An Empirical Analysis. *The Journal of Sex Research* 27:363–80.

Baron, Larry, and Straus, Murray A. 1984. Sexual Stratification, Pornography, and Rape in the United States. In *Pornography and Sexual Aggression*, ed. N. M. Malamuth and E. Donnerstein, 186–209. Orlando, FL: Academic Press.

Barry, Kathleen. 1984. *Female Sexual Slavery.* New York: New York University Press.

Bascow, Susan A., and Campanile, Florence. 1990. Attitudes Toward Prostitution as a Function of Attitudes Toward Feminism in College Students. *Psychology of Women Quarterly* 14:135–41.

Becker, Carol S. 1988. *Unbroken Ties: Lesbian Ex-Lovers.* Boston: Alyson Publications.

Becker, Judith V. 1989. Impact of Sexual Abuse on Sexual Functioning. In *Principles and Practice of Sex Therapy*, 2d ed., *Update for the 1990s*, ed. S. R. Leiblum and R. C. Rosen, 298–318. New York: Guilford Press.

Bell, Alan P., and Weinberg, Martin S. 1978. *Homosexualities: A Study of Diversity Among Men and Women.* New York: Simon and Schuster.

Bell, Alan P.; Weinberg, Martin S.; and Hammersmith, Sue Kiefer. 1981. *Sexual Preference: Its Development in Men and Women.* Bloomington: Indiana University Press.

Bell, Laurie. 1987. Introduction. In *Good Girls/Bad Girls: Feminists and Sex Trade Workers Face to Face*, ed. L. Bell, 11–21. Seattle: Seal Press.

Benjamin, Harry, and Masters, R. E. L. 1964. *Prostitution and Morality.* New York: Julian Press.

Beran, Nancy J.; Claybaker, Connie; Dillon, Cory; and Haverkamp, Robert J. 1992. Attitudes Toward Minorities: A Comparison of Homosexuals and the General Population. *Journal of Homosexuality* 23(3):65–83.

Berger, Raymond M. 1984. Realities of Gay and Lesbian Aging. *Social Work* 29:57–62.

Blumenfeld, Warren J., and Raymond, Diane. 1988. *Looking at Gay and Lesbian Life.* Boston: Beacon Press.

Blumstein, Philip, and Schwartz, Pepper. 1985. *American Couples.* New York: Pocket Books.

Bos, Gerjanne. 1986. Sexuality of Gynecological Cancer Patients: Quantity and Quality. *Journal of Psychosomatic Obstetrics and Gynaecology 5*:217–24.

Bowker, Lee H. 1983. Marital Rape: A Distinct Syndrome? *Social Casework* 64:347–52.

Bracey, Dorothy H. 1979. The Juvenile Prostitute: Victim and Offender. *Victimology 8*:151–60.

Brannock, Jo Ann C., and Chapman, Beata E. 1990. Negative Sexual Experiences with Men Among Heterosexual Women and Lesbians. *Journal of Homosexuality 19*:105–09.

Bressler, Lauren C., and Lavender, Abraham D. 1986. Sexual Fulfillment of Heterosexual, Bisexual, and Homosexual Women. *Journal of Homosexuality 12*:109–22.

Bright, Susie. 1990. *Susie Sexpert's Lesbian Sex World.* Pittsburgh: Cleis Press.

Brock, Debi. 1989. Prostitutes as Scapegoats in the AIDS Panic. *Resources for Feminist Research/Documentation sur la Recherche Feministe (RFR/DRF) 18*(2):13–17.

Brown, Laura S. 1986. Confronting Internalized Oppression in Sex Therapy with Lesbians. *Journal of Homosexuality 12*:99–107.

Browning, Christine. 1987. Therapeutic Issues and Intervention Strategies with Young Adult Lesbian Clients: A Developmental Approach. *Journal of Homosexuality 14*:45–52.

Brownmiller, Susan. 1975. *Against Our Will: Men, Women, and Rape.* New York: Bantam Books.

Buhrke, Robin A., and Fuqua, Dale R. 1987. Sex Differences in Same- and Cross-Sex Supportive Relationships. *Sex Roles 17*:339–52.

Bullard, David G. 1988. The Treatment of Desire Disorders in the Medically Ill and Physically Disabled. In *Sexual Desire Disorders*, ed. S. R. Leiblum and R. C. Rosen, 348–84. New York: Guilford Press.

Bullough, Vern L. 1994. Letter to Author, 5 March.

Bullough, Vern L. 1994. Stopes, Marie Charlotte, Carmichael. In *Human Sexuality: An Encyclopedia*, ed. V. L. Bullough and B. Bullough, 570–71. New York: Garland Publishing Company.

Bullough, Vern, and Bullough, Bonnie. 1987. *Women and Prostitution: A Social History.* Buffalo, NY: Prometheus Books.

Bullough, Vern L., and Bullough, Bonnie. 1993. *Cross Dressing, Sex, and Gender.* Philadelphia: University of Pennsylvania Press.

Burgos, Nilsa M., and Perez, Yolanda I. Diaz. 1986. An Exploration of Human Sexuality in the Puerto Rican Culture. In *Human Sexuality, Ethno-Culture, and Social Work*, ed. L. Lister, 135–50. New York: Haworth.

Burkhart, Barry, and Fromuth, Mary Ellen. 1991. Individual Psychological and Social Psychological Understandings of Sexual Coercion. In *Sexual Coercion: A Sourcebook on Its Nature, Causes, and Prevention*, ed. E. Grauerholz and M. A. Koralewski, 75–90. Lexington, MA: Lexington Books.

Burkhart, Barry R., and Stanton, Annette L. 1988. Acquaintance Rape. In *Violence in Intimate Relationships*, ed. G. W. Russell, 43–65. New York: PMA Press.

Buss, David M. 1988. From Vigilance to Violence: Tactics of Mate Retention in American Undergraduates. *Ethology and Sociobiology* 9:291–317.

Butler, Sandra, and Rosenblum, Barbara. 1991. *Cancer in Two Voices*. San Francisco: Spinsters Book Company.

Butts, June Dobbs. 1982. Further Thoughts on a Group Discussion by Black Women About Sexuality. In *Women's Sexual Experience: Explorations of the Dark Continent*, ed. M. Kirkpatrick, 41–43. New York: Plenum.

Buunk, Bram. 1982. Anticipated Sexual Jealousy: Its Relationship to Self-Esteem, Dependency, and Reciprocity. *Personality and Social Psychology Bulletin* 8:310–16.

Buunk, Bram, and Hupka, Ralph B. 1987. Cross-Cultural Differences in the Elicitation of Sexual Jealousy. *Journal of Sex Research* 23:12–22.

Byers, E. Sandra. 1988. Effects of Sexual Arousal on Men's and Women's Behavior in Sexual Disagreement Situations. *The Journal of Sex Research* 25:235–54.

Byers, E. Sandra. 1992a. Letter to Author, 6 October.

Byers, E. Sandra. 1992b. Telephone Conversation with Author, 2 July.

Byers, E. Sandra. 1993. Telephone Interview with Author, 28 April. Tape Recording.

Byers, E. Sandra, and Heinlein, Larry. 1989. Predicting Initiations and Refusals of Sexual Activities in Married and Cohabiting Heterosexual Couples. *The Journal of Sex Research* 26:210–31.

Byers, E. Sandra, and Lewis, Kim. 1988. Dating Couples' Disagreements Over the Desired Level of Sexual Intimacy. *The Journal of Sex Research* 24:15–29.

Byers, E. Sandra, and Price, Dorothy. 1986. Guidelines for the Elimination of Sexual Harassment. *Canadian Psychology* 27:371.

Byrne, Donn, and Kelley, Kathryn. 1984. Introduction: Pornography and Sex Research. In *Pornography and Sexual Aggression*, ed. N. M. Malamuth and E. Donnerstein, 1–15. Orlando, FL: Academic Press.

Caldwell, Mayta A., and Peplau, Letitia Anne. 1984. The Balance of Power in Lesbian Relationships. *Sex Roles* 10:587–99.

Califia, Pat. 1988. *Sapphistry: The Book of Lesbian Sexuality*. 3d ed, revised. Tallahassee, FL: Naiad Press.

Campagna, Daniel S., and Poffenberger, Donald L. 1988. *The Sexual Trafficking in Children: An Investigation of the Child Sex Trade*. Dover, MA: Auburn House.

Campbell, Beatrix. 1987. A Feminist Sexual Politics: Now You See It, Now You Don't. In *Sexuality: A Reader*, ed. Feminist Review, 19–39. London: Virago.

Campbell, Susan Miller; Peplau, Letitia Anne; and DeBro, Sherrine Chapman. 1992. Women, Men, and Condoms: Attitudes and Experiences of Heterosexual College Students. *Psychology of Women Quarterly* 16:273–88.

Canadian Organization for the Rights of Prostitutes (CORP). 1987. Realistic Feminists. In *Good Girls/Bad Girls: Feminists and Sex Trade Workers Face to Face*, ed. L. Bell, 204–17. Seattle: Seal Press.

Canadian Panel on Violence Against Women. 1993. *Final Report of the Canadian*

*Panel on Violence Against Women.* Ottawa: Minister of Supplies and Services Canada.

Carmen, Arlene, and Moody, Howard. 1985. *Working Women: The Subterranean World of Street Prostitution.* New York: Harper and Row.

Carole. 1987. Interview with Barbara. In *Sex Work: Writings by Women in the Sex Industry,* ed. F. Delacoste and P. Alexander, 166–74. Pittsburgh: Cleis Press.

Carroll, Janell L.; Volk, Kari D.; and Hyde, Janet S. 1985. Differences Between Males and Females in Motives for Engaging in Sexual Intercourse. *Archives of Sexual Behavior 14*:131–39.

Carter, Sunny. 1987. A Most Useful Tool. In *Sex Work: Writings by Women in the Sex Industry,* ed. F. Delacoste and P. Alexander, 159–65. Pittsburgh: Cleis Press.

Castillo, Ana. 1991. La Macha: Toward a Beautiful Whole Self. In *Chicana Lesbians—The Girls Our Mothers Warned Us About,* ed. C. Trujillo, 24–48. Berkeley, CA: Third Woman Press.

Centers for Disease Control (CDC). 1993. *HIV/AIDS Surveillance Report, November 1.* Rockville, MD: CDC National AIDS Clearinghouse.

Chancer, Lynn. 1988. Pornography Debates Reconsidered. *New Politics 2*:74–84.

Check, James V. P., and Malamuth, Neil. 1985. An Empirical Assessment Of Some Feminist Hypotheses About Rape. *International Journal of Women's Studies 8*:414–23.

Christensen, Carole Pigler. 1988. Issues in Sex Therapy with Ethnic and Racial Minority Women. *Women & Therapy* 7(2/3):187–206.

Christopher, F. Scott, and Frandsen, Michela M. 1990. Strategies of Influence in Sex and Dating. *Journal of Social and Personal Relationships* 7:89–105.

Clark, Lorenne M. G. 1989–90. Feminist Perspectives on Violence Against Women and Children: Psychological, Social Service, and Criminal Justice Concerns. *Canadian Journal of Women and the Law 3*:420–31.

Clark, Russell D., and Hatfield, Elaine. 1989. Gender Differences in Receptivity to Sexual Offers. *Journal of Psychology & Human Sexuality 2*:39–55.

Cochran, Susan D., and Peplau, Letitia Anne. 1985. Value Orientations in Heterosexual Relationships. *Psychology of Women Quarterly 9*:477–88.

Cole, Ellen. 1988. Sex at Menopause: Each in Her Own Way. *Women & Therapy* 7(2/3):159–68.

Cole, Ellen. 1993. Telephone Interview with Author, 3 May. Tape Recording.

Cole, Ellen, and Rothblum, Esther D. 1991. Lesbian Sex at Menopause: As Good as or Better than Ever. In *Lesbians at Midlife: The Creative Transition,* ed. B. Sang, J. Warshow, and A. J. Smith, 184–93. San Francisco: Spinsters Book Company.

Cole, Ellen; Rothblum, Esther D.; and Espin, Oliva M., eds. 1992. Refugee Women and Their Mental Health: Shattered Societies, Shattered Lives. [Special Issue]. *Women & Therapy 13*:1–3.

Cole, Sandra S. 1988. Women, Sexuality, and Disabilities. *Women & Therapy* 7 (2/3):277–94.

Coleman, Eli. 1982a. Changing Approaches to the Treatment of Homosexuality. In *Homosexuality: Social, Psychological, and Biological Issues*, ed. W. Paul et al., 81–85. Beverly Hills, CA: Sage.

Coleman, Eli. 1982b. Developmental Stages of the Coming Out Process. In *Homosexuality: Social, Psychological, and Biological Issues*, ed. W. Paul et al., 149–58. Beverly Hills, CA: Sage.

Coleman, Eli. 1985. Bisexual Women in Marriages. In *Bisexualities: Theory and Research*, ed. F. Klein and T. J. Wolf, 87–99. New York: Haworth.

Coleman, Emily M.; Hoon, Peter W.; and Hoon, Emily F. 1983. Arousability and Sexual Satisfaction in Lesbian and Heterosexual Women. *The Journal of Sex Research* 19:58–73.

Coleman, Marilyn, and Ganong, Lawrence H. 1985. Love and Sex-Role Stereotypes: Do Macho Men and Feminine Women Make Better Lovers? *Journal of Personality and Social Psychology* 49:170–76.

Coles, Claire, and Shamp, M. Johnna. 1984. Some Sexual, Personality, and Demographic Characteristics of Women Readers of Erotic Romances. *Archives of Sexual Behavior* 13:187–209.

Collins, Barbara A. 1990. Pornography and Social Policy: Three Feminist Approaches. *Affilia* 5(4):8–26.

Cooke, Amber. 1987a. Sex Trade Workers and Feminists: Myths and Illusions. In *Good Girls/Bad Girls: Feminists and Sex Trade Workers Face to Face*, ed. L. Bell, 190–203. Seattle: Seal Press.

Cooke, Amber. 1987b. Stripping: Who Calls the Tune? In *Good Girls/Bad Girls: Feminists and Sex Trade Workers Face to Face*, ed. L. Bell, 92–99. Seattle: Seal Press.

Cooper, Belinda. 1989. Prostitution: A Feminist Analysis. *Women's Rights Law Reporter* 11:98–119.

Cooper, Marc. 1992. Queer Baiting in the Culture War. *Village Voice*, October 13, 29–35.

Cowan, Gloria; Chase, Cheryl J.; and Stahly, Geraldine B. 1989. Feminist and Fundamentalist Attitudes Toward Pornography Control. *Psychology of Women Quarterly* 13:97–112.

Critelli, Joseph W.; Myers, Emilie J.; and Loos, Victor E. 1986. The Components of Love: Romantic Attraction and Sex-Role Orientation. *Journal of Personality* 54:354–68.

Daly, Martin; Wilson, Margo; and Weghorst, Suzanne J. 1982. Male Sexual Jealousy. *Ethology and Sociobiology* 3:11–27.

Darling, Carol Anderson; Davidson, J. Kenneth; and Jennings, Donna A. 1991. The Female Sexual Response Revisited: Understanding the Multiorgasmic Experience in Women. *Archives of Sexual Behavior* 20:527–40.

Darty, Trudy E., and Potter, Sandra J. 1983. Social Work with Challenged Women: Sexism, Sexuality, and the Female Cancer Experience. *Journal of Social Work & Human Sexuality* 2(1):83–100.

De Cecco, John P., and Elia, John P. 1993. A Critique and Synthesis of Biological

Essentialism and Social Constructionist Views of Sexuality and Gender. *Journal of Homosexuality* 24(3/4):1–26.

DeLamater, John. 1987. Gender Differences in Sexual Scenarios. In *Females, Males, and Sexuality: Theories and Research*, ed. K. Kelley, 127–39. Albany: State University of New York Press.

D'Emilio, John, and Freedman, Estelle B. 1988. *Intimate Matters: A History of Sexuality in America*. New York: Harper and Row.

Desai, Sampada R.; McCormick, Naomi B.; and Gaeddert, William P. 1990. Malay and American Undergraduates' Beliefs About Love. *Journal of Psychology & Human Sexuality* 2:93–116.

De Schampheleire, Dirk. 1990. MMPI Characteristics of Professional Prostitutes: A Cross-Cultural Replication. *Journal of Personality Assessment* 54:343–50.

Diamond, Irene. 1980. Pornography and Repression. In *Women: Sex and Sexuality*, ed. C. R. Stimpson and E. S. Person, 129–44. Chicago: University of Chicago Press.

Dimen, Muriel. 1984. Politically Correct? Politically Incorrect? In *Pleasure and Danger: Exploring Female Sexuality*, ed. C. S. Vance, 138–48. Boston: Routledge and Kegan Paul.

Dixon, Joan K. 1984. The Commencement of Bisexual Activity in Swinging Married Women Over Age Thirty. *The Journal of Sex Research* 20:71–90.

Dixon, Joan K. 1985. Sexuality and Relationship Changes in Married Females Following the Commencement of Bisexual Activity. In *Bisexualities: Theory and Research*, ed. F. Klein and T. J. Wolf, 115–33. New York: Haworth.

Dodson, Betty. 1974. *Liberating Masturbation: A Meditation on Self Love*. New York: Published and Distributed by Betty Dobson, Box 1933, New York, NY 10001.

Dodson, Betty. 1987. *Sex for One: The Joy of Selfloving*. New York: Harmony Books.

Dolcini, M. Margaret, et al., 1993. Demographic Characteristics of Heterosexuals with Multiple Partners: The National AIDS Behavioral Surveys. *Family Planning Perspectives* 25:208–14.

Donnerstein, Edward. 1984. Pornography: Its Effect on Violence Against Women. In *Pornography and Sexual Aggression*, ed. N. M. Malamuth and E. Donnerstein, 53–84. Orlando, FL: Academic Press.

Donnerstein, Edward. 1986. The Pornography Commission Report: Do Findings Fit Conclusions? *Sexual Coercion and Assault* 1:185–87.

Donnerstein, Edward; Linz, Daniel; and Penrod, Steven. 1987. *The Question of Pornography: Research Findings and Policy Implications*. New York: Free Press.

Dosser, David A.; Balswick, Jack O.; and Halverson, Charles F. 1986. Male Inexpressiveness and Relationships. *Journal of Social and Personal Relationships* 3:241–58.

Duberman, Martin. 1991. *Cures: A Gay Man's Odyssey*. New York: Plume.

DuBois, Ellen C., and Gordon, Linda. 1984. Seeking Ecstasy on the Battlefield: Danger and Pleasure in Nineteenth-Century Feminist Sexual Thought. In

*Pleasure and Danger: Exploring Female Sexuality*, ed. C. S. Vance, 31–49. Boston: Routledge and Kegan Paul.

Duffy, Sally M., and Rusbult, Caryl E. 1985/86. Satisfaction and Commitment in Homosexual and Heterosexual Relationships. *Journal of Homosexuality 12*:1–23.

Dworkin, Andrea. 1987. *Intercourse*. New York: Free Press.

Dworkin, Andrea. 1989. *Pornography: Men Possessing Women*. New York: E. P. Dutton.

Dworkin, Andrea, and MacKinnon, Catharine A. 1988. *Pornography and Civil Rights: A New Day for Women's Equality*. Minneapolis: Organizing Against Pornography, A Resource Center for Education and Action.

Echohawk, Marlene. 1982. Sexual Consequences of Acculturation of American Indian Women. In *Women's Sexual Experience: Explorations of the Dark Continent*, ed. M. Kirkpatrick, 45–55. New York: Plenum.

Echols, Alice. 1984. The Taming of the Id: Feminist Sexual Politics, 1968–83. In *Pleasure and Danger: Exploring Female Sexuality*, ed. C. S. Vance, 50–72. Boston: Routledge and Kegan Paul.

Echols, Alice. 1989. The New Feminism of Yin and Yang. In *Gender in Intimate Relationships: A Microstructural Approach*, ed. B. J. Risman and P. Schwartz, 48–57. Belmont, CA: Wadsworth.

Edelstein, Judy. 1987. In the Massage Parlor. In *Sex Work: Writings by Women in the Sex Industry*, ed. F. Delacoste and P. Alexander, 62–69. Pittsburgh: Cleis Press.

Ehrenreich, Barbara; Hess, Elizabeth; and Jacobs, Gloria. 1987. *Re-making Love: The Feminization of Sex*. Garden City, NY: Anchor Press/Doubleday.

Ehrhardt, Anke A.; Yingling, Sandra; Zawadzi, Rezi; and Martinez-Ramirez, Maria. 1992. Prevention of Heterosexual Transmission of HIV: Barriers for Women. *Journal of Psychology & Human Sexuality 5*:37–67.

Einhorn, Lena. 1989. New Data on Lesbians and AIDS. *Off Our Backs*, April, 10.

Eldridge, Natalie S., and Gilbert, Lucia. A. 1990. Correlates of Relationship Satisfaction in Lesbian Couples. *Psychology of Women Quarterly 14*:43–62.

Elise, Dianne. 1986. Lesbian Couples: The Implications of Sex Differences in Separation-Individuation. *Psychotherapy 23*:305–10.

Ellis, Megan. 1988. Re-Defining Rape: Re-Victimizing Women. *Resources for Feminist Research/Documentation sur la Recherche Feministe RFR/DRF 17*(3):96–99.

Ellison, Carol Rinkleib. 1984. Harmful Beliefs Affecting the Practice of Sex Therapy with Women. *Psychotherapy 21*:327–33.

Elson, John. 1992. Passions Over Pornography. *Time*, March 30, 52–53.

Enck, Graves E., and Preston, James D. 1988. Counterfeit Intimacy: A Dramaturgical Analysis of an Erotic Performance. *Deviant Behavior 9*:369–81.

Engel, John W., and Saracino, Marie. 1986. Love Preferences and Ideals: A Comparison of Homosexual, Bisexual, and Heterosexual Groups. *Contemporary Family Therapy 8*:241–50.

Espin, Oliva M. 1984. Cultural and Historical Influences on Sexuality in Hispanic/ Latina Women: Implications for Psychotherapy. In *Pleasure and Danger: Exploring Female Sexuality*, ed. C. S. Vance, 149–64. Boston: Routledge and Kegan Paul.

Evans, Hilary. 1979. *Harlots, Whores, and Hookers: A History of Prostitution*. New York: Dorset Press.

Everts, Rev. Kellie. 1987. Triple Treat. In *Sex Work: Writings by Women in the Sex Industry*, ed. F. Delacoste and P. Alexander, 37–38. Pittsburgh: Cleis Press.

Faderman, Lillian. 1981. *Surpassing the Love of Men: Romantic Friendship and Love Between Women from the Renaissance to the Present*. New York: William Morrow and Company.

Faderman, Lillian. 1986. Love Between Women in 1928: Why Progressivism is Not Always Progress. *Journal of Homosexuality* 12:23–42.

Faderman, Lillian. 1989. A History of Romantic Friendship and Lesbian Love. In *Gender in Intimate Relationships: A Microstructural Approach*, ed. B. J. Risman and P. Schwartz, 26–31. Belmont, CA: Wadsworth.

Faderman, Lillian. 1991. *Odd Girls and Twilight Lovers: A History of Lesbian Life in Twentieth-Century America*. New York: Columbia University Press.

Falco, Kristine. L. 1991. *Psychotherapy with Lesbian Clients: Theory into Practice*. New York: Brunner/Mazel.

Faludi, Susan. 1991. *Backlash: The Undeclared War Against American Women*. New York: Crown.

Feldman-Summers, Shirley. 1986. A Comment on the Meese Commission Report and the Dangers of Censorship. *Sexual Coercion and Assault* 1:179–84.

Ferguson, Ann; Philipson, Ilene; Diamond, Irene; Quinby, Lee; Vance, Carole S.; and Snitow, Anne B. 1984. Forum: The Feminist Sexuality Debates. *Signs: Journal of Women in Culture and Society* 10:106–35.

Fine, Michelle. 1992. Sexuality, Schooling, and Adolescent Females: The Missing Discourse of Desire. In *Disruptive Voices: The Possibilities of Feminist Research*, ed. M. Fine, 31–59. Ann Arbor: University of Michigan Press.

Finkelhor, David, and Yllo, Kersti. 1985. *License to Rape: Sexual Abuse of Wives*. New York: Free Press.

Fisher, William A. 1983. Gender, Gender-Role Identification, and Response to Erotica. In *Changing Boundaries: Gender Roles and Sexual Behavior*, ed. E. R. Allgeier and N. B. McCormick, 226–44. Palo Alto, CA: Mayfield.

Fisher, William A. 1992. Electronic Mail to Author, 15 September.

Fisher, William A., and Barak, Azy. 1991. Pornography, Erotica, and Behavior: More Questions than Answers. *International Journal of Law and Psychiatry* 14:65–83.

Foa, Uriel G., et al. 1987. Gender-Related Sexual Attitudes: Some Crosscultural Similarities and Differences. *Sex Roles* 16:511–19.

Foucault, Michel. 1978. *The History of Sexuality*. Vol. 1, *An Introduction*. Translated by Robert Hurley. New York: Vintage Books. Originally published as *La Volente de Savior* (Paris: Editions Gallimard, 1976).

Frank, Ellen; Anderson, Carol; and Rubinstein, Debra. 1978. Frequency of Sexual Dysfunction in "Normal" Couples. *New England Journal of Medicine 299*:111–15.

Freund, Matthew; Lee, Nancy; and Leonard, Terri. 1991. Sexual Behavior of Clients with Street Prostitutes in Camden, NJ. *The Journal of Sex Research 28*:579–91.

Freund, Matthew; Leonard, Terri L.; and Lee, Nancy. 1989. Sexual Behavior of Resident Street Prostitutes with Their Clients in Camden, NJ. *The Journal of Sex Research 26*:460–78.

Frieze, Irene Hanson. 1983. Investigating the Causes and Consequences of Marital Rape. *Signs 8*:532–53.

Frieze, Irene. 1993. Telephone Interview with Author, 10 May. Tape Recording.

Fullilove, Mindy Thompson; Fullilove, Robert E.; Haynes, Katherine; and Gross, Shirley. 1990. Black Women and AIDS Prevention: A View Towards Understanding the Gender Rules. *The Journal of Sex Research 27*:47–64.

Gagnon, John H. 1974. Scripts and the Coordination of Sexual Conduct. In *Nebraska Symposium on Motivation, 1973.* Vol. 21, ed. J. K. Cole and R. Dienstbier, 27–59. Lincoln: University of Nebraska Press.

Gagnon, John H. 1990. The Explicit and Implicit Use of the Scripting Perspective in Sex Research. *Annual Review of Sex Research 1*:1–43.

Galler, Roberta. 1984. The Myth of the Perfect Body. In *Pleasure and Danger: Exploring Female Sexuality*, ed. C. S. Vance, 165–72. Boston: Routledge and Kegan Paul.

Garnets, Linda; Hancock, Kristin A.; Cochran, Susan D.; Goodchilds, Jacqueline; and Peplau, Letitia Anne. 1991. Issues in Psychotherapy with Lesbians and Gay Men: A Survey of Psychologists. *American Psychologist 46*:964–72.

Gavey, Nicola. 1992. Technologies and Effects of Heterosexual Coercion. *Feminism & Psychology 2*:325–51.

Gebhard, Paul H. 1972. Factors in Marital Orgasm. In *The Social Dimensions of Human Sexuality*, ed. R. R. Bell and M. Gordon, 70–78. Boston: Little Brown.

Gemme, Robert. 1993. Prostitution: A Legal, Criminological and Sexological Perspective. *The Canadian Journal of Human Sexuality 2*(4):227–37.

Genevay, B. 1982. In Praise of Older Women. In *Women's Sexual Experience: Explorations of the Dark Continent*, ed. M. Kirkpatrick, 87–101. New York: Plenum.

Gentry, Cynthia S. 1991. Pornography and Rape: An Empirical Analysis. *Deviant Behavior 12*:277–88.

Gibson-Ainyette, Ivan; Templer, Donald I.; Brown, Ric; and Veaco, Lelia. 1988. Adolescent Female Prostitutes. *Archives of Sexual Behavior 17*:431–38.

Gilfoyle, Jackie; Wilson, Jonathan; and Brown. 1992. Sex, Organs and Audiotape: A Discourse Analytic Approach to Talking About Heterosexual Sex and Relationships. *Feminism & Psychology 2*:209–30.

Giobbe, Evelina. 1990. Confronting the Liberal Lies About Prostitution. In *The*

*Sexual Liberals and the Attack on Feminism*, ed. D. Leidholdt and J. G. Raymond, 67–81. New York: Pergamon Press.

Gomez, Jewelle L., and Smith, Barbara. 1991. Taking the Home Out of Homophobia: Black Lesbian Health. In *Piece of My Heart: A Lesbian of Colour Anthology*, ed. M. Silvera, 40–57. Toronto: Sister Vision Press.

Gonsiorek, John C. 1982. Results of Psychological Testing on Homosexual Populations. In *Homosexuality: Social, Psychological, and Biological Issues*, ed. W. Paul, et al., 71–79. Beverly Hills, CA: Sage.

Goodchilds, Jacqueline D., and Zellman, Gail L. 1984. Sexual Signaling and Sexual Aggression in Adolescent Relationships. In *Pornography and Sexual Aggression*, ed. N. M. Malamuth and E. Donnerstein, 234–43. Orlando, FL: Academic Press.

Goodman, Aviel. 1992. Sexual Addiction: Designation and Treatment. *Journal of Sex & Marital Therapy 18*:303–14.

Gordon, Margaret T., and Riger, Stephanie. 1989. *The Female Fear*. New York: Free Press.

Gotell, Lise. 1993. Electronic Mail to Women's Studies List on Canadian Pornography Laws, 30 March.

Gottfried, Heidi. 1991. Preventing Sexual Coercion: A Feminist Agenda for Economic Change. In *Sexual Coercion: A Sourcebook on Its Nature, Causes, and Prevention*, ed. E. Grauerholz and M. A. Koralewski, 173–83. Lexington, MA: Lexington Books.

Granik, Lisa, and Shields, Eileen. 1989. The First U.S. Conference on Trafficking in Women Internationally. *Off Our Backs*, January, 1–3.

Grauerholz, Elizabeth. 1989. Sexual Harassment of Women Professors by Students: Exploring the Dynamics of Power, Authority, and Gender in a University Setting. *Sex Roles 21*:789–801.

Grauerholz, Elizabeth, and Serpe, Richard T. 1985. Initiation and Response: The Dynamics of Sexual Interaction. *Sex Roles 12*:1041–59.

Green, Susan K., and Sandos, Philip. 1983. Perceptions of Male and Female Initiators of Relationships. *Sex Roles 9*:849–52.

Greenberg, Bradley S., and D'Alessio, Dave. 1985. Quantity and Quality of Sex in the Soaps. *Journal of Broadcasting and Electronic Media 29*:309–21.

Greenberg, Jeff, and Pyszczynski, Tom. 1985. Proneness to Romantic Jealousy and Responses to Jealousy in Others. *Journal of Personality 53*:468–79.

Greendlinger, Virginia, and Byrne, Donn. 1987. Coercive Sexual Fantasies of College Men as Predictors of Self-Reported Likelihood to Rape and Overt Sexual Aggression. *The Journal of Sex Research 23*:1–11.

Gutek, Barbara A. 1985. *Sex and the Workplace*. San Francisco: Jossey-Bass.

Gutek, Barbara A., and Cohen, Aaron Groff. 1987. Sex Ratios, Sex-Role Spillover, and Sex at Work: A Comparison of Men's and Women's Experiences. *Human Relations 40*:97–115.

Gutek, Barbara A., and Dunwoody, Vera. 1987. Understanding Sex in the Workplace. In *Women and Work*. Vol. 2, *An Annual Review*, ed. A. H. Stromberg, L. Larwood, and B. A. Gutek, 249–69. Newbury Park, CA: Sage.

Gutek, Barbara A., and Morasch, Bruce. 1982. Sex-Ratios, Sex-Role Spillover, and Sexual Harassment of Women at Work. *Journal of Social Issues 38(4)*:55–74.

Gutek, Barbara A.; Nakamura, Charles Y.; Gahart, Martin; Handschumacher, Inger; and Russell, Dan. 1980. Sexuality and the Workplace. *Basic and Applied Social Psychology 1(3)*:255–65.

Haeberle, Erwin J. 1981. Swastika, Pink Triangle, and Yellow Star—The Destruction of Sexology and the Persecution of Homosexuals in Nazi Germany. *The Journal of Sex Research 17*:270–87.

Hall, Marny. 1987. Sex Therapy with Lesbian Couples: A Four-Stage Approach. *Journal of Homosexuality 14*:137–56.

Hamadock, Susan. 1988. Lesbian Sexuality in the Framework of Psychotherapy: A Practical Model for the Lesbian Therapist. *Women & Therapy 7(2/3)*:207–19.

Handy, Lee C.; Valentich, Mary; Cammaert, Lorna P.; and Gripton, James. 1984/85. Feminist Issues in Sex Therapy. *Journal of Social Work & Human Sexuality 3(2/3)*:69–80.

Hanneke, Christine R.; Shields, Nancy M.; and McCall, George J. 1986. Assessing the Prevalence of Marital Rape. *Journal of Interpersonal Violence 1*:350–62.

Hansen, Gary L. 1985a. Dating Jealousy Among College Students. *Sex Roles 12*:713–21.

Hansen, Gary L. 1985b. Perceived Threats and Marital Jealousy. *Social Psychology Quarterly 48*:262–68.

Harney, Patricia A., and Muehlenhard, Charlene L. 1991. Rape. In *Sexual Coercion: A Sourcebook on Its Nature, Causes, and Prevention*, ed. E. Grauerholz and M. A. Koralewski, 3–15. Lexington, MA: Lexington Books.

Harris, Mary B. 1991. Gender Differences in Experiences of Aggression. Paper presented at the Conference on Gender Research and Theory, Nags Head Conference Center, 26–31 May, Highland Beach, FL.

Hartley, Nina. 1987. Confessions of a Feminist Porno Star. In *Sex Work: Writings by Women in the Sex Industry*, ed. F. Delacoste and P. Alexander, 142–44. Pittsburgh: Cleis Press.

Hatfield, Elaine. 1983. What Do Women and Men Want from Love and Sex? In *Changing Boundaries: Gender Roles and Sexual Behavior*, ed. E. R. Allgeier and N. B. McCormick, 106–34. Palo Alto, CA: Mayfield.

Hatfield, Elaine, and Rapson, Richard L. 1987. Gender Differences in Love and Intimacy: The Fantasy v. the Reality. *Journal of Social Work & Human Sexuality 5*:15–26.

Hatfield, Elaine, et al. 1988. Passionate Love: How Early Does It Begin? *Journal of Psychology & Human Sexuality 1*:35–51.

Hatfield, Elaine, et al. 1989. Gender Differences in What Is Desired in the Sexual Relationship. *Journal of Psychology & Human Sexuality 1*:39–52.

Hawkins, Gordon, and Zimring, Franklin E. 1988. *Pornography in a Free Society*. Cambridge: Cambridge University Press.

Hellwege, Dennis R.; Perry, Katye; and Dobson, Judith. 1988. Perceptual Differences in Gender Ideals Among Heterosexual and Homosexual Males and Females. *Sex Roles 19*:735–46.

Henderson, Ann Fleck. 1984. Homosexuality in the College Years: Developmental Differences Between Men and Women. *Journal of American College Health* *32*:216–19.

Henderson, John E.; English, Diana J.; and MacKenzie, Ward R. 1988. Family Centered Casework Practice with Sexually Aggressive Children. *Journal of Social Work & Human Sexuality* 7:89–108.

Hendrick, Clyde, et al. 1984. Do Men and Women Love Differently? *Journal of Social and Personal Relationships* 1:177–95.

Hendrick, Clyde, and Hendrick, Susan. 1986. A Theory and Method of Love. *Journal of Personality and Social Psychology* 50:392–402.

Hendrick, Clyde, and Hendrick, Susan S., 1988. Lovers Wear Rose Colored Glasses. *Journal of Social and Personal Relationships* 5:161–83.

Hendrick, Susan S., and Hendrick, Clyde. 1987a. Love and Sexual Attitudes, Self-Disclosure and Sensation Seeking. *Journal of Social and Personal Relationships* 4:281–97.

Hendrick, Susan, and Hendrick, Clyde. 1987b. Multidimensionality of Sexual Attitudes. *The Journal of Sex Research* 23:502–26.

Hendrick, Susan S.; Hendrick, Clyde; and Adler, Nancy L. 1988. Romantic Relationships: Love, Satisfaction, and Staying Together. *Journal of Personality and Social Psychology* 54:980–88.

Hendrick, Susan; Hendrick, Clyde; and Slapion-Foote, Michelle J. 1985. Gender Differences in Sexual Attitudes. *Journal of Personality and Social Psychology* 48:1630–42.

Herek, Gregory M. 1986. American Psychological Association Testimony on Violence Against Lesbians and Gay Men. Statement before the United States House of Representatives Committee on the Judiciary Subcommittee on Criminal Justice, 9 October, Washington, D.C.

Herek, Gregory M. 1989. Hate Crimes Against Lesbians and Gay Men: Issues for Research and Policy. *American Psychologist* 44:948–55.

Herek, Gregory M.; Kimmel, Douglas C.; Amaro, Hortensia; and Melton, Gary B. 1991. Avoiding Heterosexist Bias in Psychological Research. *American Psychologist* 46:957–63.

Higgins, Glenn E., Jr. 1978. Aspects of Sexual Response in Adults with Spinal-Cord Injury: A Review of the Literature. In *Handbook of Sex Therapy*, ed. J. LoPiccolo and L. LoPiccolo, 387–410. New York: Plenum.

Hirayama, Hisashi, and Hirayama, Kasumi. 1986. The Sexuality of Japanese Americans. In *Human Sexuality, Ethnoculture, and Social Work*, ed. L. Lister, 81–98. New York: Haworth.

Hirschman, Elizabeth C. 1987. People as Products: Analysis of a Complex Marketing Exchange. *Journal of Marketing* 51:98–108.

Hoier, Tamara S.; Shawchuck, Carita R.; Pallotta, Gina M.; Freeman, Tim; Inderbitzen-Pisaruk, Heidi; MacMillan, Virginia M.; Malinosky-Rummell, Robin; and Green, A. L. 1992. The Impact of Sexual Abuse: A Cognitive-Behavioral Model. In *The Sexual Abuse of Children*. Vol. 2, *Clinical Issues*, ed. W.

O'Donohue and J. H. Geer, 100–42. Hillsdale, NJ: Lawrence Erlbaum Associates.

Hollibaugh, Amber. 1984. Desire for the Future: Radical Hope in Passion and Pleasure. In *Pleasure and Danger: Exploring Female Sexuality*, ed. C. S. Vance, 401–12. Boston: Routledge and Kegan Paul.

Hong, Sung-Mook. 1986. Romantic Love, Idealistic or Pragmatic: Sex Differences Among Australian Young Adults. *Psychological Reports* 58:922.

hooks, bell. 1981. *Ain't I a Woman: Black Women and Feminism.* Boston, MA: South End Press.

hooks, bell. 1992. *Black Looks: Race and Representation.* Boston, MA: South End Press.

House, William C.; Faulk, Alberta; and Kubovchik, Margaret. 1990. Sexual Behavior of Inner-City Women. *Journal of Sex Education & Therapy* 16:172–84.

Howard, Judith A.; Blumstein, Philip; and Schwartz, Pepper. 1986. Sex, Power, and Influence Tactics in Intimate Relationships. *Journal of Personality and Social Psychology* 51:102–09.

Hutchins, Loraine, and Kaahumanu, Lani. (Eds.). 1991. *BI Any Other Name: Bisexual People Speak Out.* Boston: Alyson Publications.

Hyde, Janet Shibley. 1991. *Half the Human Experience: The Psychology of Women*, 4th ed. Lexington, MA: D. C. Heath.

Hyde, Janet Shibley. 1993. Telephone Interview with Author, 26 April. Tape Recording.

Irvine, Janice M. 1990. *Disorders of Desire: Sex and Gender in Modern American Sexology.* Philadelphia: Temple University Press.

James, Jennifer, and Davis, Nanette J. 1982. Contingencies in Female Sexual Role Deviance: The Case of Prostitution. *Human Organization* 41:345–50.

Jarvie, Ian. 1991. Pornography and/as Degradation. *International Journal of Law and Psychiatry* 14:13–27.

Jarvie, I. C. 1992. Child Pornography and Prostitution. In *The Sexual Abuse of Children.* Vol. 1, *Theory and Research*, ed. W. O'Donohue and J. H. Geer, 307–28. Hillsdale, NJ: Lawrence Erlbaum Associates.

Jeffreys, Sheila. 1990a. Eroticizing Women's Subordination. In *The Sexual Liberals and the Attack on Feminism*, ed. D. Leidholdt and J. G. Raymond, 132–35. New York: Pergamon Press.

Jeffreys, Sheila. 1990b. Sexology and Antifeminism. In *The Sexual Liberals and the Attack on Feminism*, ed. D. Leidholdt and J. G. Raymond, 14–27. New York: Pergamon Press.

Jehu, Derek. 1989. Sexual Dysfunctions Among Women Clients Who Were Sexually Abused in Childhood. *Behavioural Psychotherapy* 17:53–70.

Jemail, Jay Ann, and Geer, James. 1977. Sexual Scripts. In *Progress in Sexology: Selected Papers from the Proceedings of the 1976 International Congress of Sexology*, ed. R. Gemme and C. C. Wheeler, 513–22. New York: Plenum.

Jenness, Valerie. 1993. *Making It Work: The Prostitutes' Rights Movement in Perspective.* New York: Aldine De Gruyter.

Jesser, Clinton J. 1978. Male Responses to Direct Verbal Sexual Initiatives of Females. *The Journal of Sex Research 14*:118–28.

Jesser, Clinton. 1993. Telephone Interview with Author, 18 April. Tape Recording.

Jewell, K. Sue. 1993. *From Mammy to Miss America and Beyond: Cultural Images and the Shaping of U.S. Social Policy.* New York: Routledge.

Johnson, Mary. 1987. CABE and Strippers: A Delicate Union. In *Good Girls/Bad Girls: Feminists and Sex Trade Workers Face to Face,* ed. L. Bell, 109–13. Seattle: Seal Press.

Johnson, Susan E. 1990. *Staying Power: Long-Term Lesbian Couples.* Tallahassee, FL: Naiad Press.

Johnson, Toni Cavanagh. 1989. Female Child Perpetuators: Children Who Molest Other Children. *Child Abuse and Neglect 13*:571–85.

Juran, Shelley. 1992. Heterosexual Sexual Changes, Condom Use and Experience, (and Male/Female Comparisons) as a Response to a Concern About AIDS. Paper presented at the 35th annual meeting of The Society for the Scientific Study of Sex, 12–15 November, San Diego.

Kalof, Linda. 1993. Rape-Supportive Attitudes and Sexual Victimization Experiences of Sorority and Nonsorority Women. *Sex Roles 29*:1–14.

Kalof, Linda, and Cargill, Timothy. 1991. Fraternity and Sorority Membership and Gender Dominance Attitudes. *Sex Roles 25*:419–25.

Kantrowitz, Melanie Kaye. 1986. To Be a Radical Jew in the Late 20th Century. In *The Tribe of Dina: A Jewish Women's Anthology.* ed. M. K. Kantrowitz and I. Klepfisz, 264–87. Montpelier, VT: Sinister Wisdom.

Kaplan, Helen Singer. 1979. *Disorders of Sexual Desire.* New York: Simon and Schuster.

Karen. 1987. The Right to Protection from Rape. In *Sex Work: Writings by Women in the Sex Industry,* ed. F. Delacoste and P. Alexander, 145–46. Pittsburgh: Cleis Press.

Kassoff, Elizabeth. 1989. Nonmonogamy in the Lesbian Community. *Women & Therapy 8*:167–82.

Kehoe, Monika. 1986. Lesbians Over 65: A Triply Invisible Minority. *Journal of Homosexuality 12*(3/4):139–52.

Kelley, Harold H., et al. 1983. Analyzing Close Relationships. In *Close Relationships,* ed. H. H. Kelley, et al., 20–67. New York: W. H. Freeman and Company.

Kelley, Kathryn; Pilchowicz, Elaine; and Byrne, Donn. 1981. Response of Males to Female-Initiated Dates. *Bulletin of the Psychonomic Society 17*:195–96.

Kendrick, Walter. 1988. *The Secret Museum: Pornography in Modern Culture.* New York: Penguin.

Kennedy, Elizabeth Lapovsky, and Davis, Madeline D. 1993. *Boots of Leather, Slippers of Gold: The History of a Lesbian Community.* New York: Routledge.

Kercher, Glen, and McShane, Marilyn. 1984. Characterizing Child Sexual Abuse on the Basis of a Multi-Agency Sample. *Victimiology 9*:364–82.

Killoran, M. Maureen. 1983. Sticks and Stones Can Break My Bones and Images

Can Hurt Me: Feminists and the Pornography Debate. *International Journal of Women's Studies* 6:443–56.

Kimlicka, Thomas; Cross, Herbert; and Tarnai, John. 1983. A Comparison of Androgynous Feminine, Masculine, and Undifferentiated Women on Self-Esteem, Body Satisfaction, and Sexual Satisfaction. *Psychology of Women Quarterly* 7:291–95.

King, Donna. 1990. "Prostitutes as Pariah in the Age of AIDS": A Content Analysis of Coverage of Women Prostitutes in the *New York Times* and the *Washington Post* September 1985–April 1988. *Women and Health* 16:155–76.

Kirkpatrick, Carole Schmidt. 1980. Sex Roles and Sexual Satisfaction in Women. *Psychology of Women Quarterly* 4:444–59.

Kitzinger, Celia. 1987. *The Social Construction of Lesbianism*. London: Sage.

Kitzinger, Jenny. 1992. Sexual Violence and Compulsory Heterosexuality. *Feminism & Psychology* 2:399–418.

Kleinke, Chris L.; Meeker, Frederick B.; and Staneski, Richard A. 1986. Preference for Opening Lines: Comparing Ratings by Men and Women. *Sex Roles* 15:585–600.

Knudsem, Dean D. 1991. Child Sexual Coercion. In *Sexual Coercion: A Sourcebook on Its Nature, Causes, and Prevention*, ed. E. Grauerholz and M. A. Koralewski, 17–28. Lexington, MA: Lexington Books.

Koblinsky, Sally A., and Palmeter, Jill G. 1984. Sex-Role Orientation, Mothers' Expression of Affection Toward Spouse, and College Women's Attitudes Toward Sexual Behaviors. *The Journal of Sex Research* 20:32–43.

Koen, Clifford M., Jr. 1989. Sexual Harassment: Criteria for Defining Hostile Environment. *Employee Responsibilities and Rights Journal* 2:289–301.

Komisaruk, Barry R., and Whipple, Beverly. in press. Physiological and Perceptual Correlates of Orgasm Produced by Genital or Non-Genital Stimulation. In *The Proceedings of the First International Conference on Orgasm*, ed. P. Kothari, 69–73. New Delhi, India.

Koss, Mary P., and Dinero, Thomas E. 1988. Predictors of Sexual Aggression Among a National Sample of Male College Students. *Annals of the New York Academy of Sciences*, vol. 528, 133–46.

Koss, Mary P., and Dinero, Thomas E. 1989. Discriminant Analysis of Risk Factors for Sexual Victimization Among a National Sample of College Women. *Journal of Consulting and Clinical Psychology* 57:242–50.

Koss, Mary; Gidyez, Christine; and Wisniewski, Nadine. 1987. The Scope of Rape: Incidence and Prevalence of Sexual Aggression and Victimization in a National Sample of Higher Education Students. *Journal of Consulting and Clinical Psychology* 55:162–70.

Koss, Mary P., and Harvey, Mary R. 1991. *The Rape Victim: Clinical and Community Interventions*, 2nd Ed. Newbury Park, CA: Sage.

Krug, Ronald S. 1989. Adult Male Report of Childhood Sexual Abuse by Mothers: Case Descriptions, Motivations and Long-Term Consequences. *Child Abuse and Neglect* 13:111–19.

Kurdek, Lawrence A. 1987. Sex Role Self Schema and Psychological Adjustment in Coupled Homosexual and Heterosexual Men and Women. *Sex Roles 17*:549–62.

Kurdek, Lawrence A. 1988. Relationship Quality of Gay and Lesbian Cohabiting Couples. *Journal of Homosexuality 15*:93–118.

Kurdek, Lawrence A. 1989. Relationship Quality in Gay and Lesbian Cohabiting Couples: A 1–Year Follow-Up Study. *Journal of Social and Personal Relationships 6*:39–59.

Kurdek, Lawrence A., and Schmitt, J. Patrick. 1986. Interaction of Sex Role Self-Concept with Relationship Quality and Relationship Beliefs in Married, Heterosexual Cohabiting, Gay, and Lesbian Couples. *Journal of Personality and Social Psychology 51*:365–70.

Kurdek, Lawrence A., and Schmitt, J. Patrick. 1987. Partner Homogamy in Married, Heterosexual Cohabiting, Gay, and Lesbian Couples. *The Journal of Sex Research 23*:212–32.

Ladas, Alice Kahn; Whipple, Beverly; and Perry, John D. 1982. *The G Spot and Other Recent Discoveries About Human Sexuality.* New York: Holt, Rinehart and Winston.

LaFrance, Marianne. 1991. Gender and the Expression of Emotional Intensity for Valued Personal Possessions. Paper presented at the Conference on Gender Research and Theory. Nags Head Conference Center, 26–31 May, Highland Beach, FL.

LaPlante, Marcia N.; McCormick, Naomi; and Brannigan, Gary G. 1980. Living the Sexual Script: College Students' Views of Influence in Sexual Encounters. *The Journal of Sex Research 16*:338–55.

Largen, Mary Ann. 1976. History of Women's Movement in Changing Attitudes, Laws, and Treatment Toward Rape Victims. In *Sexual Assault: The Victim and the Rapist*, ed. M. J. Walker and S. L. Brodsky, 69–73. Lexington, MA: D. C. Heath.

LaTorre, Ronald A., and Wendenburg, Kristina. 1983. Psychological Characteristics of Bisexual, Heterosexual and Homosexual Women. *Journal of Homosexuality 9*:87–97.

Lawrance, Kelli-an G. 1993. Development and Validation of the Interpersonal Exchange Model of Sexual Satisfaction in Long-Term Heterosexual Sexual Relationships. Ph.D. diss., Department of Psychology, University of New Brunswick, Fredericton N.B. Canada.

Lazarus, Arnold A. 1980. Psychological Treatment of Dyspareunia. In *Principles and Practice of Sex Therapy*, ed. S. R. Leiblum and L. A. Perrin, 147–66. New York: Guilford Press.

Leary, Mark R., and Snell, William E. 1988. The Relationship of Instrumentality and Expressiveness to Sexual Behavior in Males and Females. *Sex Roles 18*:509–22.

Lee, John A. 1976. *The Colors of Love.* Englewood Cliffs, NJ: Prentice Hall.

Leeder, Elaine. 1988. Enmeshed in Pain: Counseling the Lesbian Battering Couple. *Women & Therapy* 7:81–99.

Leiblum, Sandra R., and Pervin, Lawrence A. 1980. Introduction: The Development of Sex Therapy from a Sociocultural Perspective. In *Principles and Practice of Sex Therapy*, ed. S. R. Leiblum and L. A. Pervin, 1–24. New York: Guilford Press.

Leiblum, Sandra R.; Pervin, Lawrence A.; and Campbell, Enid H. 1989. The Treatment of Vaginismus: Success and Failure. In *Principles and Practice of Sex Therapy*, 2d. ed., *Update for the 1990s*, ed. S. R. Leiblum and R. C. Rosen, 113–38. New York: Guilford Press.

Leiblum, Sandra R., and Rosen, Raymond C. 1988. Introduction: Changing Perspectives on Sexual Desire. In *Sexual Desire Disorders*, ed. S. R. Leiblum and R. C. Rosen, 1–17. New York: Guilford Press.

Leidholdt, Dorchen. 1990. When Women Defend Pornography. In *The Sexual Liberals and the Attack on Feminism*, ed. D. Leidholdt and J. G. Raymond, 125–31. New York: Pergamon Press.

Leidholdt, Dorchen, and Raymond, Janice G., eds. 1990. *The Sexual Liberals and the Attack on Feminism*. New York: Pergamon Press.

Leigh, Barbara Critchlow. 1989. Reasons for Having and Avoiding Sex: Gender, Sexual Orientation, and Relationship to Sexual Behavior. *The Journal of Sex Research* 26:199–209.

Lester, David. 1985. Romantic Attitudes Toward Love in Men and Women. *Psychological Reports* 56:662.

Lewin, Tamar. 1992. Canada Court Says Pornography Harms Women and Can Be Banned. *The New York Times*, 28 February, B7(L).

Lightfoot-Klein, Hanny. 1989. The Sexual Experience and Marital Adjustment of Genitally Circumcised and Infibulated Females in the Sudan. *The Journal of Sex Research* 26:375–92.

Linedecker, Clifford L. 1981. *Children in Chains*. New York: Everest House.

Lipovsky, Julie A., and Kilpatrick, Dean G. 1992. The Child Sexual Abuse Victim as an Adult. In *The Sexual Abuse of Children*, Vol. 2, *Clinical Issues*, ed. W. O'Donohue and J. H. Geer, 430–76. Hillsdale, NY: Lawrence Erlbaum Associates.

Lisak, David, and Roth, Susan. 1988. Motivational Factors in Nonincarcerated Sexually Aggressive Men. *Journal of Personality and Social Psychology* 55:795–802.

Lobel, Kerry, ed. 1986. *Naming the Violence: Speaking Out About Lesbian Battering*. Seattle: Seal Press.

Locke, Patricia. 1993. Re-Affirmation of Self: A Multicultural Approach to Empowerment. Plenary session presented at the 18th annual conference of the Association For Women In Psychology, 11–14, March, Atlanta.

Lockett, Gloria. 1987a. Destroying Condoms. In *Sex Work: Writings by Women in the Sex Industry*, ed. F. Delacoste and P. Alexander, p. 158. Pittsburgh: Cleis Press.

Lockett, Gloria. 1987b. What Happens When You are Arrested. In *Sex Work: Writings by Women in the Sex Industry*, ed. F. Delacoste and P. Alexander, 39–40. Pittsburgh: Cleis Press.

Loewenstein, Sophie Freud. 1985. On the Diversity of Love Object Orientations Among Women. *Journal of Social Work & Human Sexuality* 3:7–23.

Logan, Michael. 1992. Why Soaps are so Sexy. *TV Guide*, April 4–10, 12, 16, 21.

Lopez-Jones, Nina. 1987. Workers: Introducing the English Collective of Prostitutes. In *Sex Work: Writings by Women in the Sex Industry*, ed. F. Delacoste and P. Alexander, 271–78. Pittsburgh: Cleis Press.

LoPiccolo, Joseph. 1978. Direct Treatment of Sexual Dysfunction. In *Handbook of Sex Therapy*, ed. J. LoPiccolo and L. LoPiccolo, 1–17. New York: Plenum.

LoPiccolo, Joseph, and Stock, Wendy E. 1986. Treatment of Sexual Dysfunction. *Journal of Counseling and Clinical Psychology* 54:158–67.

LoPiccolo, Leslie. 1980. Low Sexual Desire. In *Principles and Practice of Sex Therapy*, ed. S. R. Leiblum and L. A. Pervin, 29–64. New York: Guilford Press.

Lorde, Audre. 1985. *I Am Your Sister: Black Women Organizing Across Sexualities*. New York: Kitchen Table: Women of Color Press.

Louie, Miriam Ching. 1989. Third World Prostitutes. *Off Our Backs*, November, 14–15.

Loulan, Jo Ann. 1984. *Lesbian Sex*. San Francisco: Spinsters Ink.

Loulan, Jo Ann. 1987. *Lesbian Passion: Loving Ourselves and Each Other*. San Francisco: Spinsters Ink.

Loulan, Jo Ann. 1988. Research on the Sex Practices of 1566 Lesbians and the Clinical Applications. In *Women and Sex Therapy*, ed. E. Cole and E. D. Rothblum, 221–34. New York: Haworth.

Loulan, Jo Ann. 1990. *The Lesbian Erotic Dance: Butche, Femme, Androgyny, and Other Rhythms*. San Francisco: Spinsters Book Company.

Lystad, Mary H. 1982. Sexual Abuse in the Home: A Review of the Literature. *International Journal of Family Psychiatry* 3:3–31.

Maass, Anne, and Volpato, Chiara. 1989. Gender Differences in Self-Serving Attributions About Sexual Experiences. *Journal of Applied Social Psychology* 19:517–42.

MacDonald, A. P., Jr. 1983. A Little Bit of Lavender Goes a Long Way: A Critique of Research on Sexual Orientation. *The Journal of Sex Research* 19:94–100.

MacKinnon, Catharine A. 1987. A Feminist/Political Approach: Pleasure Under the Patriarchy. In *Theories of Human Sexuality*, ed. J. H. Geer and W. T. O'Donohue, 65–90. New York: Plenum.

MacKinnon, Catharine A. 1990. Liberalism and the Death of Feminism. In *The Sexual Liberals and the Attack on Feminism*, ed. D. Leidholdt and J. G. Raymond, 3–13. New York: Pergamon Press.

Mahoney, E. R.; Shively, Michael D.; and Traw, Marsha. 1986. Sexual Coercion and Assault: Male Socialization and Female Risk. *Sexual Coercion and Assault* 1:2–8.

Malamuth, Neil M. 1984. Aggression Against Women: Cultural and Individual

Causes. In *Pornography and Sexual Aggression*, ed. N. M. Malamuth and E. Donnerstein, 19–52. Orlando, FL: Academic Press.

Mancini, Jay A., and Orthner, Dennis K. 1978. Recreational Sexuality Preferences Among Middle-Class Husbands and Wives. *The Journal of Sex Research* 14:96–106.

Mansfield, Phyllis Kernoff; Voda, Ann; and Koch, Patricia Barthalow. In press. Predictors of Sexual Response Change in Heterosexual Midlife Women. *Health Values*.

Marcus, Eric. 1992. *Making History: The Struggle for Gay and Lesbian Equal Rights, 1945–1990, An Oral History*. New York: Harper Collins.

Margolin, Leslie. 1989. Gender and the Prerogatives of Dating and Marriage: An Experimental Assessment of a Sample of College Students. *Sex Roles* 20:91–102.

Marin, Barbara Van Oss; Gomez, Cynthia A.; and Hearst, Norman. 1993. Multiple Heterosexual Partners and Condom Use Among Hispanics and Non-Hispanic Whites. *Family Planning Perspectives* 25:170–74.

Mark, Elizabeth Wyner, and Alper, Thelma G. 1985. Women, Men, and Intimacy Motivation. *Psychology of Women Quarterly* 9:81–88.

Martin, Patricia Yancey, and Hummer, Robert A. 1989. Fraternities and Rape on Campus. *Gender and Society* 3:457–73.

Mazer, Donald B., and Percival, Elizabeth F. 1989a. Ideology or Experience? The Relationships Among Perceptions, Attitudes, and Experiences of Sexual Harassment in University Students. *Sex Roles* 20:135–47.

Mazer, Donald B., and Percival, Elizabeth. 1989b. Students' Experiences of Sexual Harassment at a Small University. *Sex Roles* 20:1–19.

McAdams, Dan P., et al. 1988. Sex and the TAT: Are Women More Intimate Than Men? Do Men Fear Intimacy? *Journal of Personality Assessment* 52:397–409.

McCabe, Marita P. 1989. The Contribution of Sexual Attitudes and Experiences During Childhood and Adolescence to Adult Sexual Dysfunction. *Sexual and Marital Therapy* 4(2):133–41.

McCormack, Arlene. 1985. The Sexual Harassment of Students by Teachers: The Case of Students in Science. *Sex Roles* 13:21–32.

McCormick, Naomi B. 1979. Come-ons and Put-offs: Unmarried Students' Strategies for Having and Avoiding Sexual Intercourse. *Psychology of Women Quarterly* 4:194–211.

McCormick, Naomi B. 1987. Sexual Scripts: Social and Therapeutic Implications. *Sexual and Marital Therapy* 2:3–27.

McCormick, Naomi; Adams-Bohley, Susan; Peterson, Susan; and Gaeddert, William. 1989. Sexual Harassment of Students at a Small College. *Initiatives: Journal of the National Association for Women Deans, Administrators, and Counselors* 52(3):15–23.

McCormick, Naomi B.; Brannigan, Gary G.; and LaPlante, Marcia N. 1984. Social Desirability in the Bedroom: Role of Approval Motivation in Sexual Relationships. *Sex Roles* 11:303–14.

McCormick, Naomi B., and Jesser, Clinton J. 1983. The Courtship Game: Power in the Sexual Encounter. In *Changing Boundaries: Gender Roles and Sexual Behavior*, ed. E. R. Allgeier and N. B. McCormick, 64–86. Palo Alto, CA: Mayfield.

McCormick, Naomi B., and Jones, Andrew J. 1989. Gender Differences in Nonverbal Flirtation. *Journal of Sex Education & Therapy* 15:271–82.

McCormick, Naomi, and Solomon, Dena. 1989. Gender Differences in College Students' Anticipated Experiences with Sexual Jealousy. *SIECCAN Journal (Journal of the Sex Information and Education Council of Canada) 4* (no. 4, Winter):25–29.

McCormick, Naomi, and Vinson, Robert K. 1988. Sexual Difficulties Experienced by Women with Interstitial Cystitis. *Women & Therapy* 7(2/3): 109–19.

McCoy, Norma L. 1991. The Menopause and Sexuality. In *The Menopause and Hormonal Replacement Therapy: Facts and Controversies*, ed. R. Sitruk-Ware and W. H. Utian, 73–100. New York: Marcel Dekker, Inc.

McKinney, Kathleen, and Maroules, Nick. 1991. Sexual Harassment. In *Sexual Coercion: A Sourcebook on its Nature, Causes, and Prevention*, ed. E. Grauerholz and M. A. Koralewski, 29–44. Lexington, MA: Lexington Books.

Medicine-Eagle, Brooke. 1991. *Buffalo Woman Comes Singing: The Spirit Song of a Rainbow Medicine Woman*. New York: Ballantine.

Meichenbaum, Donald; Price, Richard; Phares, E. Jerry; McCormick, Naomi; and Hyde, Janet. 1989. *Exploring Choices: The Psychology of Adjustment*. Glenview, IL: Scott, Foresman and Company.

Meshorer, Marc, and Meshorer, Judith. 1986. *Ultimate Pleasure: The Secrets of Easily Orgasmic Women*. New York: St. Martin's Press.

Miller, Eleanor M. 1986. *Street Women*. Philadelphia: Temple University Press.

Milne, Kirsty. 1987. Porn: What Do Women Want? *New Society*, October 23, 18–20.

Monteflores, Carmen de, and Schultz, Stephen J. 1978. Coming Out: Similarities and Differences for Lesbians and Gay Men. *Journal of Social Issues 34:* 59–72.

Moore, Monica M. 1985. Nonverbal Courtship Patterns in Women: Context and Consequences. *Ethology and Sociobiology 6*:237–47.

Moore, Monica M., and Butler, Diana L. 1989. Predictive Aspects of Nonverbal Courtship Behavior in Women. *Semiotica 76*:205–15.

Moraga, Cherrie, and Anzaldua, Gloria, eds. 1983. *This Bridge Called My Back: Writings by Radical Women of Color*. New York: Kitchen Table: Women of Color Press.

Morgan, Peggy. 1987. Living on the Edge. In *Sex Work: Writings by Women in the Sex Industry*, ed. F. Delacoste and P. Alexander, 21–28. Pittsburgh: Cleis Press.

Morin, Stephen F., and Rothblum, Esther D. 1991. Removing the Stigma: Fifteen Years of Progress. *American Psychologist 46*:947–49.

Morokoff, Patricia. 1978. Determinants of Female Orgasm. In *Handbook of Sex Therapy*, ed. J. LoPiccolo and L. LoPiccolo, 147–65. New York: Plenum.

Mosher, Donald L., and Tomkins, Silvan S. 1988. Scripting the Macho Man: Hypermasculine Socialization and Enculturation. *The Journal of Sex Research* 25:60–84.

Muehlenhard, Charlene L. 1988a. Misinterpreted Dating Behaviors and the Risk of Date Rape. *Journal of Social and Clinical Psychology* 6:20–37.

Muehlenhard, Charlene L. 1988b. "Nice Women" Don't Say Yes and "Real Men" Don't Say No: How Miscommunication and the Double Standard Can Cause Sexual Problems. *Women & Therapy* 7(2/3):95–108.

Muehlenhard, Charlene. 1993. Telephone Interview with Author, 6 May. Tape Recording.

Muehlenhard, Charlene. 1994. Conversation with author, 27 May. Austin, TX.

Muehlenhard, Charlene L., and Cook, Stephen W. 1988. Men's Self-Reports of Unwanted Sexual Activity. *The Journal of Sex Research* 24: 58–72.

Muehlenhard, Charlene L.; Friedman, Debra E.; and Thomas, Celeste M. 1985. Is Date Rape Justifiable? The Effects of Dating Activity, Who Initiated, Who Paid, and Men's Attitudes Toward Women. *Psychology of Women Quarterly* 9:297–310.

Muehlenhard, Charlene L., and Hollabaugh, Lisa C. 1988. Do Women Sometimes Say No When They Mean Yes? The Prevalence and Correlates of Women's Token Resistance to Sex. *Journal of Personality and Social Psychology* 54:872–79.

Muehlenhard, Charlene L.; Koralewski, Mary A.; Andrews, Sandra L.; and Burdick, Cynthia A. 1986. Verbal and Nonverbal Cues that Convey Interest in Dating: Two Studies. *Behavior Therapy* 17:404–19.

Muehlenhard, Charlene L., and Linton, Melaney A. 1987. Date Rape and Sexual Aggression in Dating Situations: Incidence and Risk Factors. *Journal of Counseling Psychology* 34:186–96.

Muehlenhard, Charlene L., and McFall, Richard M. 1981. Dating Initiation from a Woman's Perspective. *Behavior Therapy* 12:682–91.

Muehlenhard, Charlene L., and Scardino, Teresa J. 1985. What Will He Think? Men's Impressions of Women Who Initiate Dates and Achieve Academically. *Journal of Counseling Psychology* 32:560–69.

Murray, Thomas E. 1985. The Language of Singles Bars. *American Speech* 60:17–30.

Murstein, Bernard I. 1991. Dating, Attracting, and Meeting. In *Marriage and Family in Transition*, ed. J. N. Edwards and D. H. Demo, 13–28. Boston: Allyn and Bacon.

Musheno, Michael, and Seeley, Kathryn. 1986. Prostitution Policy and the Women's Movement: Historical Analysis of Feminist Thought and Organization. *Contemporary Crises* 10:237–55.

Nagot, Chrizz Diaz. 1988. Tricked Into Prostitution. *New Directions for Women*, November-December, 10–11.

Naoko, Iyori. 1987. The Traffic in Japayuki-San. *Japan Quarterly* 34:84–88.

Nestle, Joan. 1987. Lesbians and Prostitutes: A Historical Sisterhood. In *Good Girls/ Bad Girls: Feminists and Sex Trade Workers Face to Face*, ed. L. Bell, 131–40. Seattle: Seal Press.

Nevid, Jeffrey S. 1984. Sex Differences in Factors of Romantic Attraction. *Sex Roles* 11:401–11.

Newman, Frances; Cohen, Elizabeth; Tobin, Patricia; and MacPherson, Gail. 1985. Historical Perspectives on the Study of Female Prostitution. *International Journal of Women's Studies* 8:80–86.

Newton, Esther. 1984. The Mythic Mannish Lesbian: Radclyffe Hall and the New Woman. *Signs: Journal of Women in Culture and Society* 9:557–75.

Newton, Esther, and Walton, Shirley. 1984. The Misunderstanding: Toward a More Precise Sexual Vocabulary. In *Pleasure and Danger: Exploring Female Sexuality*, ed. C. S. Vance, 242–50. Boston: Routledge and Kegan Paul.

Nichols, Margaret. 1982. The Treatment of Inhibited Sexual Desire (ISD) in Lesbian Couples. *Women & Therapy* 1:49–66.

Nichols, Margaret. 1987. Lesbian Sexuality: Issues and Developing Theory. In *Lesbian Psychologies: Explorations and Challenges*, ed. Boston Lesbian Psychologies Collective, 97–125. Urbana: University of Illinois Press.

Nichols, Margaret. 1988. Low Sexual Desire in Lesbian Couples. In *Sexual Desire Disorders*, ed. S. R. Leiblum and R. C. Rosen, 387–412. New York: Guilford Press.

Niethammer, Carolyn. 1977. *Daughters of the Earth: The Lives and Legends of American Indian Women*. New York: Collier.

O'Brien, Eileen M. 1989. Date Rape: Hidden Epidemic Makes Campuses Unsafe for Women. *Black Issues in Higher Education*, December 7, 6–10.

Obstfeld, Lisa S.; Lupfer, Michael B.; and Lupfer, Shirley L. 1985. Exploring the Relationship Between Gender Identity and Sexual Functioning. *Journal of Sex & Marital Therapy* 11:248–58.

O'Campo, Martha. 1987. Pornography and Prostitution in the Philippines. In *Good Girls/Bad Girls: Feminists and Sex Trade Workers Face to Face*, ed. L. Bell, 67–76. Seattle: Seal Press.

Ogden, Gina. 1988. Women and Sexual Ecstasy: How Can Therapists Help? *Women & Therapy* 7(2/3):43–56.

Ogden, Gina. 1990. *Everywoman's Guide to Understanding Sexual Style and Creating Intimacy*. Deerfield Beach, FL: Health Communications, Inc.

Ogden, Gina. 1993. Telephone Interview with Author, 19 April. Tape Recording.

Ogden, Gina. 1994. *Women Who Love Sex*. New York: Pocket Books.

Oliver, Mary Beth, and Hyde, Janet Shibley. 1993. Gender Differences in Sexuality: A Meta-Analysis. *Psychological Bulletin 114*, 29–51.

O'Sullivan, Lucia, and Byers, E. Sandra. 1989. Women's Strategies of Influence in Disagreements Over the Desired Level of Sexual Activity. *SIECCAN Journal (Journal of the Sex Information and Education Council of Canada)* 4 (no. 4, Winter):30–34.

O'Sullivan, Lucia, and Byers, E. Sandra. 1990. Female Use of Sexual Influence Strategies in Dating Relationships. Paper presented at symposium, Research on the Traditional Sexual Script. Thirty-third annual meeting of The Society for the Scientific Study of Sex, 1–4 November, Minneapolis.

O'Sullivan, Lucia F., and Byers, E. Sandra. 1993. Eroding Stereotypes: College Women's Attempts to Influence Reluctant Male Sexual Partners. *The Journal of Sex Research 30*:270–82.

Owen, William Foster. 1987. The Verbal Expression of Love by Women and Men as a Critical Communication Event in Personal Relationships. *Women's Studies in Communication 10*:15–24.

Paul, Jay P. 1993. Childhood Cross-Gender Behavior and Adult Homosexuality: The Resurgence of Biological Models of Sexuality. *Journal of Homosexuality 24*(3/4):41–54.

Paul, William. 1982. Minority Status for Gay People: Majority Reaction and Social Context. In *Homosexuality: Social, Psychological, and Biological Issues*, ed. W. Paul, et al., 351–69. Beverly Hills, CA: Sage.

Pavich, Emma Guerrero. 1986. A Chicana Perspective on Mexican Culture and Sexuality. In *Human Sexuality, Ethnoculture, and Social Work*, ed. L. Lister, 47–65. New York: Haworth.

Peplau, Letitia Anne. 1979. Homosexual Love Relationships: A Comparison of Men and Women. Paper presented at the annual meeting of the Pacific Sociological Association, 6 April, Annaheim, CA.

Peplau, Letitia Anne. 1981. What Homosexuals Want. *Psychology Today*, March, 28–38.

Peplau, Letitia Anne. 1982. Research on Homosexual Couples: An Overview. *Journal of Homosexuality 8*:3–7.

Peplau, Letitia Anne. 1983. Roles and Gender. In *Close Relationships*, ed. H. H. Kelley, et al., 220–64. New York: W. H. Freeman and Company.

Peplau, Letitia Anne. 1988. Research on Lesbian and Gay Relationships: A Decade Review. Paper presented at the International Conference on Personal Relationships, University of British Columbia, 3–8 July, Vancouver, British Columbia.

Peplau, Letitia Anne. 1991. Lesbian and Gay Relationships. In *Homosexuality: Research Findings for Public Policy*, ed. J. C. Gonsiorek and J. D. Weinrich, 177–96. Newbury Park, CA: Sage.

Peplau, Letitia Anne. 1993. Telephone Interview with Author, 4 May. Tape Recording.

Peplau, Letitia Anne, and Amarao, Hortensia. 1982. Understanding Lesbian Relationships. In *Homosexuality: Social, Psychological and Biological Issues*, ed. W. Paul, et al., 233–47. Beverly Hills, CA: Sage.

Peplau, Letitia Anne, and Campbell, Susan Miller. 1989. The Balance of Power in Dating and Marriage. In *Women: A Feminist Perspective, 4th Edition*, ed. J. Freeman, 121–37. Mountain View, CA: Mayfield.

Peplau, Letitia Anne, and Cochran, Susan D. 1990. A Relationship Perspective on

Homosexuality. In *Homosexuality/ Heterosexuality: Concepts of Sexual Orientation*, ed. D. P. McWhirter, S. A. Sanders, and J. M. Reinisch, 321–49. New York: Oxford University Press.

Peplau, Letitia Anne; Cochran, Susan D.; and Mays, Vickie. 1986. Satisfaction in the Intimate Relationships of Black Lesbians. Paper presented at the annual meeting of the American Psychological Association, 25 August, Washington, D.C.

Peplau, Letitia Anne; Cochran, Susan; Rooke, Karen; and Padesky, Christine. 1978. Loving Women: Attachment and Autonomy in Lesbian Relationships. *Journal of Social Issues* 34:7–27.

Peplau, Letitia Anne, and Gordon, Steven L. 1985. Women and Men in Love: Gender Differences in Close Heterosexual Relationships. In *Women, Gender, and Social Psychology*, ed. V. E. O'Leary, R. K. Unger, and B. S. Wallston, 257–91. Hillsdale, NJ: Lawrence Erlbaum Associates.

Peplau, Letitia Anne; Padesky, Christine; and Hamilton, Mykol. 1982. Satisfaction in Lesbian Relationships. *Journal of Homosexuality* 8:23–35.

Perper, Timothy. 1985. *Sex Signals: The Biology of Love*. Philadelphia: ISI Press.

Perper, Timothy, and Weis, David L. 1987. Proceptive and Rejective Strategies of U.S. and Canadian College Women. The *Journal of Sex Research* 23:455–80.

Perry, John Delbert, and Whipple, Beverly. 1981. Pelvic Muscle Strength of Female Ejaculators: Evidence in Support of a New Theory of Orgasm. *The Journal of Sex Research* 17:22–39.

Peterson, Steven A., and Franzese, Bettina. 1987. Correlates of College Men's Sexual Abuse of Women. *Journal of College Student Personnel* 28:223–28.

Pheterson, Gail. 1987. The Social Consequences of Unchastity. In *Sex Work: Writings by Women in the Sex Industry*, ed. F. Delacoste and P. Alexander, 215–30. Pittsburgh: Cleis Press.

Pheterson, Gail, ed. 1989. *A Vindication of the Rights of Whores*. Seattle: Seal Press.

Pheterson, Gail. 1990. The Category "Prostitute" in Scientific Inquiry. *The Journal of Sex Research* 27:397–407.

Philipson, Ilene. 1984. The Repression of History and Gender: A Critical Perspective on the Feminist Sexuality Debates. *Signs: Journal of Women in Culture and Society* 10:113–18.

Pickard, Christine. 1982. A Perspective on Female Responses to Sexual Material. In *The Influence of Pornography on Behaviour*, ed. M. Yaffe and E. C. Nelson, 91–117. London: Academic Press.

Pollis, Carol A. 1988. An Assessment of the Impacts of Feminism on Sexual Science. *The Journal of Sex Research* 25:85–105.

Poppen, Paul J., and Segal, Nina J. 1988. The Influence of Sex and Sex-Role Orientation on Sexual Coercion. *Sex Roles* 19:689–701.

Potter, Gary W. 1989. The Retail Pornography Industry and the Organization of Vice. *Deviant Behavior* 10:233–51.

Potterat, John J.; Phillips, Lynanne; Rothenberg, Richard B.; and Darrow, William

W. 1985. On Becoming a Prostitute: An Exploratory Case-Comparison Study. *The Journal of Sex Research* 21:329–35.

Potterat, John J.; Woodhouse, Donald E.; Muth, John B.; and Muth, Stephen Q. 1990. Estimating the Prevalence and Career Longevity of Prostitute Women. *The Journal of Sex Research* 27:233–43.

Powell, Gary N. 1986. Effects of Sex Role Identity and Sex on Definitions of Sexual Harassment. *Sex Roles* 14:9–19.

Pryor, John B. 1991. Sexual Harassment: A Social Psychological Perspective. Paper presented at the conference on Gender Research and Theory, Nags Head Conference Center, 26–31 May, Highland Beach, FL.

Radlove, Shirley. 1983. Sexual Response and Gender Roles. In *Changing Boundaries: Gender Roles and Sexual Behavior*, ed. E. R. Allgeier and N. B. McCormick, 87–105. Palo Alto, CA: Mayfield.

Rapaport, Karen, and Burkhart, Barry R. 1984. Personality and Attitudinal Characteristics of Sexually Coercive College Males. *Journal of Abnormal Psychology* 93:216–21.

Raymond, Janice G. 1989. Putting the Politics Back Into Lesbianism. *Women's Studies International Forum* 12:149–56.

Reiss, Ira L. 1990. *An End to Shame: Shaping Our Next Sexual Revolution*. Buffalo, NY: Prometheus Books.

Remoff, Heather Trexler. 1984. *Sexual Choice: A Woman's Decision*. New York: Dutton/Lewis.

Renner, K. Edward, and Wackett, Carol. 1987. Sexual Assault: Social and Stranger Rape. *Canadian Journal of Community Mental Health* 6:49–56.

Renshaw, Domeena C. 1983. Sex, Intimacy, and the Older Woman. *Women & Health* 8(4):43–54.

Rich, Adrienne. 1980. Compulsory Heterosexuality and Lesbian Existence. In *Women: Sex and Sexuality*, ed. C. R. Stimpson and E. S. Person, 62–91. Chicago: University of Chicago Press.

Richardson, Diane. 1989. *Women and AIDS*. New York: Routledge, Chapman and Hall.

Richgels, Patricia B. 1992. Hypoactive Sexual Desire in Heterosexual Women: A Feminist Analysis. *Women & Therapy* 12(1/2):123–35.

Riger, Stephanie. 1991. Gender Dilemmas in Sexual Harassment Policies and Procedures. *American Psychologist* 46:497–505.

Riley, Alan J. 1990. Are Women Who Volunteer for Sexual Response Studies Representative of Women in General? *Sexual and Marital Therapy* 5:131–40.

Rist, Darrell Yates. 1992. Sex on the Brain: Are Homosexuals Born That Way? *The Nation*, October 19, 424–29.

Rivera, Rhonda. 1982. Homosexuality and the Law. In *Homosexuality: Social, Psychological, and Biological Issues*, ed. W. Paul, et al., 323–36. Beverly Hills, CA: Sage.

Robinson, Paul. 1976. *The Modernization of Sex*. New York: Harper Colophon.

Romenesko, Kim, and Miller, Eleanor M. 1989. The Second Step in Double Jeopardy: Appropriating the Labor of Female Street Hustlers. *Crime and Delinquency 35*:109–35.

Roscoe, Bruce; Kennedy, Donna; and Pope, Tony. 1987. Adolescents' Views of Intimacy: Distinguishing Intimate from Nonintimate Relationships. *Adolescence 22*:511–15.

Rose, Suzanna; Zand, Debra; and Cini, Marie A. 1993. Lesbian Courtship Scripts. In *Boston Marriages: Romantic but Asexual Relationships Among Contemporary Lesbians*, ed. E. D. Rothblum and K. A. Brehony, 70–85. Amherst: The University of Massachusetts Press.

Rosen, Raymond C., and Beck, J. Gayle. 1988. *Patterns of Sexual Arousal: Psychophysiological Processes and Clinical Applications.* New York: Guilford Press.

Rosenzweig, Julie M., and Dailey, Dennis M. 1989. Dyadic Adjustment/Sexual Satisfaction in Women and Men as a Function of Psychological Sex Role Self-Perception. *Journal of Sex & Marital Therapy 15*:42–55.

Rosenzweig, Julie M., and Lebow, Wendy C. 1992. Femme on the Streets, Butch in the Sheets? Lesbian Sex-Roles, Dyadic Adjustment, and Sexual Satisfaction. *Journal of Homosexuality 23*(3):1–20.

Ross, Ronald Richard, and Allgeier, Elizabeth Rice. 1993a. Correlates of Males' Feminine Identification with Sexually Coercive Attitudes and Behaviors. Unpublished manuscript in submission.

Ross, Ronald Richard, and Allgeier, Elizabeth Rice. 1993b. Meanings and Motivations of Sexual Coercion: Sex, Power, and Political Agendas. Unpublished manuscript in submission.

Rothblum, Esther. 1993. Telephone Interview with Author, 20 April. Tape Recording.

Rothblum, Esther D., and Brehony, Kathleen A. 1993. *Boston Marriages: Romantic but Asexual Relationships Among Contemporary Lesbians.* Amherst: The University of Massachusetts Press.

Rothblum, Esther D., and Cole, Ellen. eds. 1988. Lesbianism: Affirming Nontraditional Roles [special issue]. *Women & Therapy 8*(1/2).

Royalle, Candida; Kunis, Richard; and Delaney, Rosemary. 1992. Eroticism and Sexuality: Views from the Trenches. Plenary session presented at the 15th annual meeting of The Society for the Scientific Study of Sex, Eastern Region, 10–12 April, Philadelphia.

Rubin, Gayle. 1984. Thinking Sex: Notes for a Radical Theory of the Politics of Sexuality. In *Pleasure and Danger: Exploring Female Sexuality*, ed. C. S. Vance, 267–319. Boston: Routledge and Kegan Paul.

Rubin, Lillian B. 1982. Sex and Sexuality: Women at Midlife. In *Women's Sexual Experience: Explorations of the Dark Continent*, ed. M. Kirkpatrick, 61–82. New York: Plenum.

Ruch, Libby O.; Amedeo, Stephanie R.; Leon, Joseph J.; and Gartrell, John W. 1991. Repeated Sexual Victimization and Trauma Change During the Acute Phase of the Sexual Assault Trauma Syndrome. *Women and Health 17*:1–19.

Rusbult, Caryl E.; Zembrodt, Isabella M.; and Iwaniszek, John. 1986. The Impact of Gender and Sex-Role Orientation on Responses to Dissatisfaction in Close Relationships. *Sex Roles* 15:1–20.

Russell, Diana E. H. 1984. *Sexual Exploitation: Rape, Child Sexual Abuse, and Workplace Harassment.* Newbury Park, CA: Sage.

Rust, John, and Golombok, Susan. 1990. Stress and Marital Discord: Some Sex Differences. *Stress Medicine* 6:25–27.

Sachiko, Kanematsu. 1988. The Women of Kabukicho. *Japan Quarterly* 35:84–89.

Safir, Marilyn P.; Peres, Yochanan; Lichtenstein, Myrna; Hoch, Zwi; and Shepher, Joseph. 1982. Psychological Androgyny and Sexual Adequacy. *Journal of Sex & Marital Therapy* 8:228–40.

Salovey, Peter, and Rodin, Judith. 1989. Envy and Jealousy in Close Relationships. In *Close Relationships*, ed. C. Hendrick, 221–46. Newbury Park, CA: Sage.

Salter, Anna C. 1992. Epidemiology of Child Sexual Abuse. In *The Sexual Abuse of Children*, Vol. 1, *Theory and Research*, ed. W. O'Donohue and J. H. Geer, 108–38. Hillsdale, NJ: Lawrence Erlbaum Associates.

Samuels, Herbert P. 1993. In the Realm of the Other: Sexual Attitudes and Behavior of Black and Hispanic College Students. Plenary presented at the sixteenth annual meeting of the Eastern Region of The Society for the Scientific Study of Sex, 10–13, June, Penn State, University Park, PA.

Sanday, Peggy Reeves. 1990. *Fraternity Gang Rape: Sex, Brotherhood, and Privilege on Campus.* New York: New York University Press.

Sandberg, Genell; Jackson, Thomas L.; and Petretic-Jackson, Patricia. 1987. College Students' Attitudes Regarding Sexual Coercion and Aggression: Developing Educational and Preventative Strategies. *Journal of College Student Personnel* 28:302–11.

Sanders, Claire. 1990. Tis No Pity She's a Whore. *New Statesman and Society 3*, February 9, pp. 12–14.

Savitz, Leonard, and Rosen, Lawrence. 1988. The Sexuality of Prostitutes: Sexual Enjoyment Reported by "Streetwalkers." *The Journal of Sex Research* 24:200–08.

Schaffer, Bernie, and DeBlassie, Richard R. 1984. Adolescent Prostitution. *Adolescence* 19:689–96.

Scheyett, Anna. 1988. Marriage Is the Best Defense: Policy on Marital Rape. *Affilia* 3(4):8–23.

Schneider, Beth E., and Gould, Meredith. 1987. Female Sexuality: Looking Back into the Future. In *Analyzing Gender: A Handbook of Social Science Research*, ed. B. B. Hess and M. M. Ferree, 120–53. Newbury Park, CA: Sage.

Schneider, Margaret S. 1986. The Relationships of Cohabiting Lesbian and Heterosexual Couples: A Comparison. *Psychology of Women Quarterly* 10:234–39.

Schneider, Margaret. 1989. Sappho Was a Right-On Adolescent: Growing Up Lesbian. *Journal of Homosexuality* 17:111–30.

Schover, Leslie R., and Jensen, Soren Buus. 1988. *Sexuality and Chronic Illness: A Comprehensive Approach.* New York: Guilford Press.

Scott, Ronald L., and Tetreault, Laurie. 1987. Attitudes of Rapists and Other Violent Offenders Toward Women. *Journal of Social Psychology* 127:375–80.

Scott, Valerie. 1987. Working Girls. In *Good Girls/Bad Girls: Feminists and Sex Trade Workers Face to Face*, ed. L. Bell, 179–80. Seattle: Seal Press.

Seng, Magnus J. 1989. Child Sexual Abuse and Adolescent Prostitution: A Comparative Analysis. *Adolescence* 24:665–75.

Senn, Charlene Y., and Radtke, H. Lorraine. 1990. Women's Evaluations of and Affective Reactions to Mainstream Violent Pornography, Nonviolent Pornography, and Erotica. *Violence and Victims* 5:143–55.

Sereny, Gitta. 1985. *The Invisible Children: Child Prostitution in America, West Germany, and Great Britain*. New York: Alfred A. Knopf.

Shaver, Frances M. 1988. A Critique of the Feminist Charges Against Prostitution. *Atlantis* 14:82–89.

Shayne, Vivian T., and Kaplan, Barbara J. 1991. Double Victims: Poor Women and AIDS. *Women and Health* 17:21–37.

Sherwin, Barbara B. 1991. The Psychoendocrinology of Aging and Female Sexuality. In *Annual Review of Sex Research*, vol. 2, ed. J. Bancroft, C. M. Davis, and H. J. Ruppel, 181–98. Lake Mills, IA: The Society for the Scientific Study of Sex.

Shields, Stephanie A. 1991. Questions of Theory in Gender and Emotion. Paper presented at the Conference on Gender Research and Theory, Nags Head Conference Center, 26–31 May, Highland Beach, FL.

Shrage, Laurie. 1989. Should Feminists Oppose Prostitution? *Ethics* 99:347–61.

Shulman, Alix Kates. 1980. Sex and Power: Sexual Bases of Radical Feminism. In *Women, Sex and Sexuality*, ed. C. R. Stimpson and E. S. Person, 21–35. Chicago: University of Chicago Press.

Shumsky, Neil L. 1986. Tacit Acceptance: Respectable Americans and Segregated Prostitution, 1870–1910. *Journal of Social History* 19:665–79.

Silber, Linda. 1990. Negotiating Sexual Identity: Non-Lesbians in a Lesbian Feminist Community. *The Journal of Sex Research* 27:131–40.

Silbert, Mimi H., and Pines, Ayala M. 1983. Early Sexual Exploitation as an Influence in Prostitution. *Social Work* 28:285–89.

Silbert, Mimi H., and Pines, Ayala M. 1984. Pornography and Sexual Abuse of Women. *Sex Roles* 10:857–68.

Simkins, Lawrence, and Rinck, Christine. 1982. Male and Female Sexual Vocabulary in Different Interpersonal Contexts. *The Journal of Sex Research* 18:160–72.

Simmons, Carolyn H.; Vom Kolke, Alexander; and Shimizu, Hideko. 1986. Attitudes Toward Romantic Love Among American, German, and Japanese Students. *Journal of Social Psychology* 126:327–36.

Simon, William, and Gagnon, John H. 1986. Sexual Scripts: Permanence and Change. *Archives of Sexual Behavior* 15:97–120.

Simpson, Jeffrey A.; Campbell, Bruce; and Berscheid, Ellen. 1986. The Association Between Romantic Love and Marriage: Kephart (1967) Twice Revisited. *Personality and Social Psychology Bulletin* 12:363–72.

Smalley, Sondra. 1987. Dependency Issues in Lesbian Relationships. *Journal of Homosexuality* 14:125–35.

Smith, Barbara, ed. 1983. *Home Girls: A Black Feminist Anthology.* New York: Kitchen Table: Women of Color Press.

Spector, Ilana P., and Carey, Michael P. 1990. Incidence and Prevalence of the Sexual Dysfunctions: A Critical Review of the Empirical Literature. *Archives of Sexual Behavior* 19:389–408.

Spencer, S. Lee, and Zeiss, Antonette. 1987. Sex Roles and Sexual Dysfunction in College Students. *The Journal of Sex Research* 23:338–47.

Sprague, Joey, and Quadagno, David. 1989. Gender and Sexual Motivation: An Exploration of Two Assumptions. *Journal of Psychology & Human Sexuality*, 2:57–76.

Sprecher, Susan, and Metts, Sandra. 1989. Development of the Romantic Beliefs Scale and Examination of the Effects on Gender and Gender-Role Orientation. *Journal of Social and Personal Relationships* 6:387–411.

Sternberg, Hilary; Davis, Katharine Bement; Mosher, Clelia Duel; and Sanger, Margaret. 1994. In *Human Sexuality: An Encyclopedia*, ed. V. L. Bullough and B. Bullough, 167; 403; 528–29. New York: Garland Publishing Company.

Sternberg, Robert J. 1986. The Triangular Theory of Love. *Psychological Review* 93:119–35.

Sternberg, Robert J. 1987. *The Triangle of Love: Intimacy, Passion, Commitment.* New York: Basic Books.

Sternberg, Robert J., and Grajek, Susan. 1984. The Nature of Love. *Journal of Personality and Social Psychology* 47:312–29.

Stets, Jan E., and Pirog-Good, Maureen A. 1989. Patterns of Physical and Sexual Abuse for Men and Women in Dating Relationships: A Descriptive Analysis. *Journal of Family Violence* 4:63–76.

Stevenson, Michael R. 1991. Toward a Feminist Sexual Science. Paper presented at symposium, Feminist Forum, at the 7th annual meeting of the Midcontinent Region of The Society for the Scientific Study of Sex, 7–9 June, Kansas City, MO.

Stevenson, Michael. 1993. Telephone Interview with Author, 12 April. Tape Recording.

St. James, Margo. 1987. The Reclamation of Whores. In *Good Girls/Bad Girls: Feminists and Sex Trade Workers Face to Face*, ed. L. Bell, 81–91. Seattle: Seal Press.

Stock, Wendy E. 1984. Sex Roles and Sexual Dysfunction. In *Sex Roles and Psychopathology*, ed. C. Spatz Widom, 249–75. New York: Plenum.

Stock, Wendy. 1985. The Influence of Gender on Power Dynamics in Relationships. In *Contemporary Marriage: Special Issues in Couples Therapy*, ed. D. C. Goldberg, 62–99. Homewood, IL: Dorsey Press.

Stock, Wendy. 1988. Propping Up the Phallocracy: A Feminist Critique of Sex Therapy and Research. *Women & Therapy* 7(2/3)23–42.

Stock, Wendy E. 1991. Feminist Explanations: Male Power, Hostility, and Sexual Coercion. In *Sexual Coercion: A Sourcebook on Its Nature, Causes, and Preven-*

*tion*, ed. E. Grauerholz and M. A. Koralewski, 61–74. Lexington, MA: Lexington Books.

Stock, Wendy. 1993. Telephone Interview with Author, 1 May. Tape Recording.

Storms, Michael D. 1981. A Theory of Erotic Orientation Development. *Psychological Review 88*:340–53.

Sturdevant, Saundra Pollock, and Stoltzfus, Brenda, 1992. *Let the Good Times Roll: Prostitution in the U.S. Military*. New York: The New Press.

Summers, Rosie. 1987. Prostitution. In *Sex Work: Writings by Women in the Sex Industry*, ed. F. Delacoste and P. Alexander, 113–18. Pittsburgh: Cleis Press.

Sundahl, Debi. 1987. Stripper. In *Sex Work: Writings by Women in the Sex Industry*, ed. F. Delacoste and P. Alexander, 175–80. Pittsburgh: Cleis Press.

Swan, Raymond W. 1980. Sex Education in the Home: The U.S. Experience. *Journal of Sex Education & Therapy 6*(2):3–10.

Symanski, Richard. 1981. *The Immoral Landscape: Female Prostitution in Western Societies*. Toronto: Butterworths.

Tavris, Carol. 1992. *The Mismeasure of Woman*. New York: Simon and Schuster.

Testa, Ronald J.; Kinder, Bill N.; and Ironson, Gail. 1987. Heterosexual Bias in the Perception of Loving Relationships of Gay Males and Lesbians. *The Journal of Sex Research 23*:163–72.

Tetzelli, Rick. 1992. Recession-Proof Supermodels. *Fortune*, March 23, 12–13.

Tiefer, Leonore. 1987. Social Constructionism and the Study of Human Sexuality. In *Sex and Gender*, ed. P. Shaver and C. Hendrick, 70–94. Newbury Park, CA: Sage.

Tiefer, Leonore. 1988a. A Feminist Critique of the Sexual Dysfunction Nomenclature. In *Women and Sex Therapy*, ed. E. Cole and E. D. Rothblum, 5–22. New York: Haworth.

Tiefer, Leonore. 1988b. A Feminist Perspective on Sexology and Sexuality. In *Feminist Thought and the Structure of Knowledge*, ed. M. M. Gergen, 16–26. New York: New York University Press.

Tiefer, Leonore. 1991. Historical, Scientific, Clinical, and Feminist Criticisms of "The Human Sexual Response Cycle" Model. In *Annual Review of Sex Research*, vol. 2, ed. J. Bancroft, C. M. Davis, and H. J. Ruppel, 1–23. Lake Mills, IA: The Society for the Scientific Study of Sex.

Tiefer, Leonore. 1993. Telephone Interview with Author, 3 May. Tape Recording.

Tooke, William, and Camire, Lori. 1991. Patterns of Deception in Intersexual and Intrasexual Mating Strategies. *Ethology and Sociobiology 12*:345–64.

Trujillo, Carla. 1991. Chicana Lesbians: Fear and Loathing in the Chicano Community. In *Chicana Lesbians—The Girls Our Mothers Warned Us About*, ed. C. Trujillo, 186–94. Berkeley, CA: Third Woman Press.

Trussell, James; Warner, David Lee; and Hatcher, Robert A. 1992. Condom Slippage and Breakage Rates. *Family Planning Perspectives 24*(1):20–23.

Unger, Rhoda K., and Crawford, Mary. 1992. *Women and Gender: A Feminist Psychology*. New York: McGraw-Hill.

U. S. Congress. Senate Committee on the Judiciary. Pornography Victims' Compensation Act of 1991. 102d Congress, 1st Session, S. 1521.

Valentich, Mary, and Gripton, James. 1992. Gender-Sensitive Practice in Sexual Problems. *The Canadian Journal of Human Sexuality* 1(1):11–18.

Valins, Linda. 1992. *When a Woman's Body Says No to Sex: Understanding and Overcoming Vaginismus*. New York: Penguin.

Valverde, Mariana. 1987. *Sex, Power, and Pleasure*. Philadelphia: New Society Publishers.

Valverde, Mariana. 1989. Beyond Gender Dangers and Private Pleasures: Theory and Ethics in the Sex Debates. *Feminist Studies* 15:237–53.

Vance, Carole S. 1984a. Pleasure and Danger: Toward a Politics of Sexuality. In *Pleasure and Danger: Exploring Female Sexuality*, ed. C. S. Vance, 1–27. Boston: Routledge and Kegan Paul.

Vance, Carole S., ed. 1984b. *Pleasure and Danger: Exploring Female Sexuality*. Boston: Routledge and Kegan Paul.

Vandewiele, Michel, and Philbrick, Joseph L. 1983. Attitudes of Senegalese Students Toward Love. *Psychological Reports* 52:915–18.

Walker, Alice, and Parmar, Pratibha. 1993. *Warrior Marks: Female Genital Mutilation and the Sexual Blinding of Women*. New York: Harcourt Brace & Company.

Walker, Pamela. 1990. Reflecting on Physical Disability and (Bi)sexuality. In *Bisexuality: A Reader and Sourcebook*, ed. T. Geller, 23–25. Ojai, CA: Times Change Press.

Walkowitz, Judith. 1980. The Politics of Prostitution. In *Women: Sex and Sexuality*, ed. C. R. Stimpson and E. S. Person, 145–57. Chicago: University of Chicago Press.

Wardlaw, Cecelia. 1987. Dream Turned Nightmare. In *Sex Work: Writings by Women in the Sex Industry*, ed. F. Delacoste and P. Alexander, 108–12. Pittsburgh: Cleis Press.

Warshaw, Robin. 1988. *I Never Called It Rape: The Ms. Report on Recognizing, Fighting, and Surviving Date and Acquaintance Rape*. New York: Harper and Row.

Waterman, Caroline K.; Dawson, Lori J.; and Bologna, Michael J. 1989. Sexual Coercion in Gay Male and Lesbian Relationships. *The Journal of Sex Research* 26:118–23.

Webster, Paula. 1984. The Forbidden: Eroticism and Taboo. In *Pleasure and Danger: Exploring Female Sexuality*, ed. C. S. Vance, 385–98. Boston: Routledge and Kegan Paul.

Weinberg, Martin S., and Williams, Colin, J. 1988. Black Sexuality: A Test of Two Theories. *The Journal of Sex Research* 25:197–218.

Weiner, Linda J. 1988. Issues in Sex Therapy with Survivors of Intrafamily Sexual Abuse. *Women & Therapy* 7(2/3): 253–64.

Weis, David L., and Slosnerick, Michael. 1981. Attitudes toward Sexual and Nonsexual Extramarital Involvements among a Sample of College Students. *Journal of Marriage and the Family* 43:349–58.

Wekker, Gloria. 1993. Mati-ism and Black Lesbianism: Two Idealtypical Expressions of Female Homosexuality in Black Communities of the Diaspora *Journal of Homosexuality* 24(3/4):145–58.

Wells, Joel W. 1989. Sexual Language Usage in Different Interpersonal Contexts: A Comparison of Gender and Sexual Orientation. *Archives of Sexual Behavior* 18:127–43.

Wells, Joel W. 1990. The Sexual Vocabularies of Heterosexual and Homosexual Males and Females for Communicating Erotically with a Sexual Partner. *Archives of Sexual Behavior* 19:139–47.

West, Carolyn M. 1993. Developing an "Oppositional Gaze"—Black Women and Distorted Beauty Images. Paper presented at the 18th annual conference of the Association For Women In Psychology, 11–14 March, Atlanta.

West, Rachel. 1987. U.S. PROStitutes Collective. In *Sex Work: Writings by Women in the Sex Industry*, ed. F. Delacoste and P. Alexander, 279–89. Pittsburgh: Cleis Press.

West, Robin. 1987. The Feminist-Conservative Anti-Pornography Alliance and the 1986 Attorney General's Commission on Pornography Report. *American Bar Foundation Research Journal* 4:681–711.

Whipple, Beverly. 1993. Telephone Interview with Author, 4 May. Tape Recording.

Whipple, Beverly, and Komisaruk, Barry R. 1988. Analgesia Produced in Women by Genital Self-Stimulation. *The Journal of Sex Research* 24:130–40.

Whipple, Beverly, and Komisaruk, Barry R. 1991. The G Spot, Orgasm, and Female Ejaculation: Are They Related? In *The Proceedings of the First International Conference on Orgasm*, ed. P. Kothari, 227–37. Bombay, India: VRP Publishers.

Whipple, Beverly, and Ogden, Gina. 1989. *Safe Encounters: How Women Can Say Yes to Pleasure and No to Unsafe Sex*. New York: McGraw-Hill.

Whipple, Beverly; Ogden, Gina; and Komisaruk, Barry R. 1992. Physiological Correlates of Imagery-Induced Orgasm in Women. *Archives of Sexual Behavior* 21:121–33.

White, Gregory L. 1981a. Jealousy and Partner's Perceived Motives for Attraction to a Rival. *Social Psychology Quarterly* 44:24–30.

White, Gregory L. 1981b. Some Correlates of Romantic Jealousy. *Journal of Personality* 49:129–47.

White, Gregory L. 1984. Comparison of Four Jealousy Scales. *Journal of Research in Personality* 18:115–30.

White, Gregory L., and Mullen, Paul E. 1989. *Jealousy: Theory, Research, and Clinical Strategies*. New York: Guilford Press.

White, Jacqueline W. 1991. A Prospective Analysis of Sexual Assault: A Preliminary Report. Paper presented at the conference on Gender Research and Theory, Nags Head Conference Center, 26–31 May, Highland Beach, FL.

Williams, Linda. 1989. *Hard Core: Power, Pleasure, and the "Frenzy of the Visible."* Berkeley: University of California Press.

Williams, Mary Ann 1992a. Canadian Court Bans Pornography. *Contemporary Sexuality* 26(4), April, 6.

Williams, Mary Ann 1992b. Rape in America. *Contemporary Sexuality* 26(6), June, 3–4.

Williams, Walter L. 1994. Berdache and Amazon Roles Among American Indians. In *Human Sexuality: An Encyclopedia*, ed. V. L. Bullough and B. Bullough, 57–60. New York: Garland Publishing Company.

Wilson, Pamela M. 1986. Black Culture and Sexuality. In *Human Sexuality, Ethnoculture, and Social Work*, ed. L. Lister, 29–46. New York: Haworth.

Wolfe, Janet L. 1992. *What To Do When He Has a Headache: Creating Renewed Desire in Your Man.* New York: Hyperion.

Wyatt, Gail Elizabeth. 1982. The Sexual Experience of Afro-American Women: A Middle-Income Sample. In *Women's Sexual Experience: Explorations of the Dark Continent*, ed. M. Kirkpatrick, 17–39. New York: Plenum.

Wyatt, Gail Elizabeth. 1990. The Aftermath of Child Sexual Abuse of African American and White American Women: The Victim's Experience. *Journal of Family Violence* 5:61–81.

Wyatt, Gail E., and Dunn, Kristi M. 1991. Examining Predictors of Sex Guilt in Multiethnic Samples of Women. *Archives of Sexual Behavior* 20:471–85.

Wyatt, Gail Elizabeth, and Lyons-Rowe, Sandra. 1990. African American Women's Sexual Satisfaction as a Dimension of their Sex Roles. *Sex Roles* 22:509–24.

Wyatt, Gail Elizabeth; Newcomb, Michael D.; and Riederle, Monika H. 1993. *Sexual Abuse and Consensual Sex: Women's Developmental Patterns and Outcomes.* Newbury Park, CA: Sage.

Wyers, Norman L. 1987. Homosexuality in the Family: Lesbian and Gay Spouses. *Social Work* 32:143–48.

Wynter, Sarah. 1987. Whisper: Women Hurt in Systems of Prostitution Engaged in Revolt. In *Sex Work: Writings by Women in the Sex Industry*, ed. F. Delacoste and P. Alexander, 266–70. Pittsburgh: Cleis Press.

Yaffe, Maurice. 1982. Therapeutic Uses of Sexually Explicit Material. In *The Influence of Pornography on Behaviour*, ed. M. Yaffe and E. C. Nelson, 119–50. London: Academic Press.

Yates, Gary L.; MacKenzie, Richard; Pennbridge, Julia; and Cohen, Eric. 1988. A Risk Profile Comparison of Runaway and Non-Runaway Youth. *American Journal of Public Health* 78:820–21.

Yegidis, Bonnie L. 1988. Wife Abuse and Marital Rape Among Women Who Seek Help. *Affilia* 3(1):62–68.

Yoder, Janice D., and Kahn, Arnold S. 1993. Working Toward an Inclusive Psychology of Women. *American Psychologist* 48:846–50.

Young, Mary de. 1986. "The Cloak of Innocence": The Concept of the Participant Victim in the Child Sexual Abuse Literature. *Sexual Coercion and Assault* 1:189–95.

Youngstrom, Nina. 1992a. Children Who Abuse May Well Abuse Later. *APA Monitor*, June, 1, 46.

Youngstrom, Nina. 1992b. Rapist Studies Reveal Complex Mental Map. *APA Monitor*, July, 37–38.

Zalduondo, Barbara O. De. 1991. Prostitution Viewed Cross-Culturally: Toward Recontextualizing Sex Work in AIDS Intervention Research. *The Journal of Sex Research* 28:223–48.

Zellman, Gail L., and Goodchilds, Jacqueline D. 1983. Becoming Sexual in Adolescence. In *Changing Boundaries: Gender Roles and Sexual Behavior*, ed. E. R. Allgeier and N. B. McCormick, 49–63. Palo Alto, CA: Mayfield.

Zilbergeld, Bernie, and Ellison, Carol Rinkleib. 1980. Desire Discrepancies and Arousal Problems in Sex Therapy. In *Principles and Practice of Sex Therapy*, ed. S. R. Leiblum and L. A. Pervin, 65–101. New York: Guilford Press.

Zwerner, Janna. 1982. A Study of Issues in Sexuality Counseling for Women with Spinal Cord Injuries. *Women & Therapy* 1(3):91–100.

# Index

91, 95, 100, 104; legalization of, 87–88; lesbians and, 100–101; military and, 88, 94–96, 99, 104; minority group status and, 85, 87, 90, 94, 98, 101–2, 107; pimps, 88, 91–92, 100–102, 104, 106–9, 112; sexual slavery, 83, 85, 88–90, 95, 98–100, 108, 110–12, 223; sexually transmitted disease and, 86, 88, 104–6; Social Purity movement, 89–91; stigma of, 83–85, 88, 97; World Whores Congresses, 111–12

Rape. *See* Sexual assault
Raymond, Janice, 77
Reiss, Ira, 189
Relationships: attachment and autonomy needs, 40–42; equality of partners within, 44–45, 76; of lesbians, 69–70; minority group status and, 44, 198–206; personality and, 46; power and influence in, 42–45; satisfying, 51–52, 76; sex differences in emotional expressiveness, 45–46
Romance novels, 4, 162, 165
Rosenblum, Barbara, 211
Rothblum, Esther D., 20, 225, 228–29, 231–32, 238
Rubin, Lillian, 187

Safer sex, 196–98
Samuels, Herb, 201, 203
Sanger, Margaret, 6, 149, 224
Sex: choreography of, 26–29; meaning of, 2, 175–78; politically correct, 75, 178–79, 207
Sex differences, 18–25
Sex therapy, 6, 179–93. *See also* Feminist sex therapy
Sexual addiction, 193
Sexual arousal. *See* Sexual desire
Sexual assault, 127–30; African-American slave women of, 98; African-American women of, 146; blaming

women for, 128; Canadian Law C-127, 147-48; Chinese-American brothel girls of, 98; consequences of, 145–46; defined, 128; disabled women of, 121; female perpetrators and victims, 142; feminist work related to, 8, 10, 122–23, 146–47; gang rape, 129–30; hypermasculinity and, 129–30, 137–39, 163; laws and legal tradition, 129, 147; male dominance and, 136–38; male victims and perpetrators, 141–42; marital rape, 129; military and, 95; minority group status and, 122, 128–29; North American Indian and Inuit women of, 121, 123; perpetrators, 123, 129–30, 132, 137–43; pornography and, 104; prevalence of, 128–29; prostitutes of, 103–4; rape crisis centers, 122, 146; rape myths, 133–36; refugees of, 99; revictimization, 144; risk factors associated with victimization, 131–32, 138. *See also* Feminist: analysis of sexual victimization
Sexual coercion, 26, 77, 120–21, 123–24, 126, 128–29, 133, 139, 143; women and girls as perpetrators, 140–43
Sexual desire, 16, 23, 37, 45–46, 74, 77–79, 90, 121, 124, 145, 149–50, 159, 162, 175, 177, 179, 181, 186, 189, 190–92, 195, 198, 209, 212–13
Sexual disagreements, 25, 26; sexual miscommunication and, 135–36
Sexual dysfunction. *See* Sexual problems
Sexual harassment, 124, 130–33, 146, 237; consequences of, 145; definition of, 125; feminist work related to, 146; sex workers of, 95
Sexual initiation, 22–25
Sexual intercourse, 5, 10, 16–17, 23–28, 85, 165, 175, 181, 184, 189; African-Americans and, 200–201; coercive for males as, 140–41; defined as rape,

## ABOUT THE AUTHOR

NAOMI B. McCORMICK is a Distinguished Teaching Professor in the Department of Psychology at the State University of New York at Plattsburg, where she also teaches Human Sexuality and Women's Studies. A Fellow in Rational-Emotive Therapy, she is also a practicing clinical psychologist who specializes in feminist psychotherapy. Dr. McCormick is the 25th president and a Fellow of The Society for the Scientific Study of Sex, and has been admitted to the International Academy of Sex Research. She is an associate editor of *The Journal of Sex Research*, consulting editor of *Women & Therapy*, and *The Journal of Psychology & Human Sexuality*, and is the editor and co-author of *Exploring Choices: Psychology of Adjustment* (1989), *Changing Boundaries: Gender Roles and Sexual Behavior* (1983), as well as author of over 50 journal articles and book chapters.